LABOR AND EMPLOYMENT

RELATIONS ASSOCIATION SERIES

Contemporary
Issues in
Employment Relations

EDITED BY

David Lewin

First Edition

ISBN 0-913447-92-7

Price: $29.95

LABOR AND EMPLOYMENT RELATIONS ASSOCIATION SERIES

Proceedings of the Annual Meeting
Annual Research Volume
LERA 2006 Membership Directory (published every four years)
LERA Newsletter (published quarterly)
Perspectives on Work (published biannually)

Information regarding membership, subscriptions, meetings, publications, and general affairs of the LERA can be found at the Association website at www.lera.uiuc.edu. Members can make changes to their member records, including address changes, by accessing the online directory at the website or by contacting the LERA National Office.

LABOR AND EMPLOYMENT RELATIONS ASSOCIATION
University of Illinois at Urbana-Champaign
121 Labor & Industrial Relations Bldg.
504 East Armory Ave.
Champaign, IL 61820
Telephone: 217/333-0072   Fax: 217/265-5130
Website: www.lera.uiuc.edu   E-mail: leraoffice@uiuc.edu

CONTENTS

SECTION III: Perspectives on Employment Relations: A Roundtable

CHAPTER 1

Introduction and Integration

DAVID LEWIN
University of California at Los Angeles

The 2006 Labor and Employment Relations Association (LERA) research volume contains eight papers dealing with key issues in contemporary industrial relations. Originally, and following a long-standing tradition of LERA and its predecessor, the Industrial Relations Research Association (IRRA), this volume was conceived intending to provide reviews and summaries of leading industrial relations research that appeared during the last decade or so.[1] While this volume's authors do provide some of this review and summary, they also go further, presenting new empirical evidence in their respective areas of expertise and offering what might be termed "futures forecasting."

Chapter 2, by Joel Cutcher-Gershenfeld, Steve Sleigh, and Frits Pil, assesses the status of collective bargaining as an American institution. The authors combine quantitative analysis of a new, unique survey data set with qualitative analysis of five case studies. Their central thesis is that the institution of collective bargaining is failing to deliver on its potential, in particular its potential for codifying workplace innovation and setting strategic direction for the parties to union–management relationships. There are multiple manifestations of this failure, according to the authors: major restructuring of pension systems for older workers and health benefit plans for younger workers (in plainer language, reduced benefits of both types); labor contract–decimating bankruptcies in such industries as airlines and steel and automobile supply manufacturing; limited redress of worker grievances in nonunion workplaces except through explicitly legally prohibited employment practices or employer "voluntary" adoption of alternative dispute resolution procedures; and increasing income inequality in U.S. society. All of this, they judge, constitutes a (rat) race to the bottom in terms of diminished wages and benefits and work that is increasingly outsourced—a rat race that they say is largely spurred by unilateral employer actions and announcements. From a historical perspective, these developments seemingly constitute a return to "management-determined" wages of the type that Dunlop (1957) wrote about a half-century ago.

In framing their analysis, Cutcher-Gershenfeld, Sleigh, and Pil analogize collective bargaining to another long-standing American institution, Major League Baseball, and argue that collective bargaining is in the bottom of the ninth inning, down by a large number of runs and "at great risk if it cannot spark a rally." But rather than producing such a rally, collective bargaining is, at best, delivering one foul ball after another, the authors conclude from their analysis of survey data drawn from a random sample of matched pairs of chief labor and management negotiators. In particular, the proportion of negotiations in which agreements failed to be reached more than doubled between the mid-1990s and the mid-2000s, as did the proportion of negotiations in which new agreements had yet to be reached more than 30 days after the expiration dates of old agreements. Further, during the same period, the proportion of new collective agreements that contained wage increases declined markedly, as did the proportion of agreements containing benefit increases.

Empirically, Cutcher-Gershenfeld, Sleigh, and Pil make an important contribution to the analysis of collective bargaining by introducing and operationalizing the notion of collective bargaining efficiency. By this, they mean the proportion of cases—negotiations—in which proposed new contract language (and, typically, terms) was actually incorporated into new agreements. Among other findings in this regard, the authors show that in a sample of 2003 negotiations this efficiency rate was significantly higher for "traditional" proposed wage provisions (typically proposed wage increases) than for proposed benefits provisions (typically proposed benefits decreases). Continuing their baseball analogy, the authors regard these outcomes as a series of foul balls rather than, say, base hits (let alone home runs).

More telling is the authors' analysis of collective bargaining institutionalization, or the lack of it, of such "transformational" outcomes as work rule flexibility, new pay systems, work–life balance, employee involvement, and teams. Cutcher-Gershenfeld, Sleigh, and Pil found that only a minority of recently concluded collective bargaining agreements contain specific provisions on any of these subjects, with an overall efficiency rate of about 50% and a range between 70% for work–life balance and 20% for employee involvement. Moreover, the proportion of collective agreements containing provisions on these transformational issues declined notably between the mid-1990s and the mid-2000s. Illustrative or perhaps prototypical of this trend is the American automobile manufacturing industry; the authors show that during a six-year period ending in 2000 there was a marked decline in the use of such supposedly transformational innovations as team-based work, worker involvement in off-line process improvement activities, and organizational practices aimed at enhanced flexibility, skill development, and product quality. It is little wonder, then, that when asked about the direction that the over-all union–management relationship is headed, only about a third of the negotiator pairs studied said that "things were improving," an increasing proportion of management negotiators but a decreasing proportion of union negotiators said that things were improving, and twice as large a proportion of union negotiators as management negotiators said that their collective bargaining relationships were somewhat or very adver-sarial. Based on these unfavorable trends, the authors conclude that the institution of collective bargaining "is not achieving the ninth inning production needed when it comes to the basics or when it comes to innovation."

But this is only part of the story, as the authors make clear in the second half of their chapter, which focuses on variation in and new chal-lenges facing contemporary collective bargaining. For this purpose, Cutcher-Gershenfeld, Sleigh, and Pil provide qualitative analyses of five case examples, two of which represent complete failure—or, in baseball parlance, whiffs (strikeouts)—a third represents a bunt single, a fourth represents a double, and a fifth represents a home run. The first failure occurred in the airline industry, in which, since September 11, 2001, about half the firms in the industry have filed for bankruptcy. Under this circumstance, in which a bankruptcy judge alone in effect determines new terms and conditions of employment, the International Association of Machinists and Aerospace Workers (IAM) and other airline unions "agreed" to draconian pay and benefit reductions and numerous changes in work rules and staffing arrangements. The second failure features a single company, New Piper Aircraft, and the IAM, which in December 2003 won a representation election conducted among the company's 600 production workers. Negotiations for a first contract began almost immediately, continued for nine months, and were about to conclude with an agreement when three hurricanes hit the New Piper manufacturing facility. The company took advantage of this exogenous event by delaying and otherwise putting contract negotiations on hold, believing that the longer it took to get an agreement the less support the union would have. The company turned out to be correct in this regard: about a year and a half later, the IAM was decertified as the representa-tive of New Piper's production workers.

The authors' third case example featured the sale in 2004 of the Boeing Company's largest manufacturing facility to the Canada-based

Onex Corporation, but only under the condition that "successful" negotiations were achieved with the IAM and the International Federation of Professional and Technical Employees (IFPTE), which together represented about 9,000 employees of the aerospace facility. Because Boeing sought aggressive cost savings from its asset sale, Onex proposed significant pay reductions, healthcare cost shifting to employees, elimination of defined-benefit pension arrangements, and other concessions. Unsurprisingly, these proposals were met with stiff opposition from angry and soon-to-be-former Boeing employees. However, IAM and IFPTE representatives met in extended negotiations with Onex management, and a combination of a new, innovative stock option program and the company's commitment to growing the business over the long term convinced union members to vote strongly in favor of—to ratify—a new agreement. The new company, Spirit Aerosystem, is in the authors' words "a work in progress," with the labor–management experience to date representing a "bunt single."

The fourth case example featured DTE, the gas and electric utility enterprise that serves southeast Michigan, and Local 223 of the Utility Workers Union that represented some 4,700 employees. In advance of negotiations over a new collective bargaining agreement, the parties used an interest-based approach to create six new committees, each of which focused on and developed new proposals for dealing with a particular work-related issue. Assisted by an external facilitation team, the employees and management agreed to several mutual gains provisions dealing, as examples, with job security, new technology, work attendance, and bidding on new jobs. However, a similar problem-solving approach was not initially applied to healthcare cost containment, which, as with many companies, was a key issue for DTE. Management's proposals in this regard, which called for numerous adjustments to existing benefit and contribution plans, were met with concern and opposition by bargaining committee members, who feared that union members would not ratify an agreement that incorporated these proposals. Late in the negotiations, however, the union surfaced a new proposal that tied employee healthcare contributions to base pay on a sliding percentage scale, and management responded favorably. A new collective bargaining agreement was reached shortly thereafter, and since then the parties have established new employee–management teams to address particular contractual provisions that have not yet been fully implemented. From the authors' account, it is highly unlikely that the new agreement would have been reached without the early use of interest-based negotiations; hence "the DTE story may count as a double."

The final case example provided by Cutcher-Gershenfeld, Sleigh, and Pil features what they term transformation of negotiations on a massive scale at Kaiser-Permanente, which provides healthcare services to more than 18 million individuals in 18 U.S. states and has well over 100,000 employees who are represented by 10 separate unions. During the mid-1990s and largely in response to increasingly adversarial union–management relations, unions representing about 80% of Kaiser-Permanente's employees formed a coalition and sought a new partnership arrangement with their employer. Though this partnership did not initially focus on collective bargaining, it quickly came to do so and, in 2001, led to the adoption of interest-based negotiations involving the coordination of 31 separate local agreements and creation of a master national agreement. About 200 union representatives, 200 management representatives, and 20 or so external facilitators were involved in this effort, and after initial skepticism on both sides the parties reached agreement not only on existing issues but also on new innovative proposals regarding the tracking of medical errors and near-misses and even the joint design and planning of a new hospital. Despite this success, the implementation of provisions of the 2001 agreement was highly varied. Learning from this experience, in their next interest-based negotiation, which occurred in 2005 and again featured large groups of negotiators and facilitators, the parties paid great attention to implementing contractual provisions regarding performance improvement, service quality, work attendance, and several other aspects of health care delivery. Because this case features the continuity of interest-based bargaining, rather than a short-lived, one-time occurrence, the authors characterize it as a home run.

While obviously mindful of and closely attentive to the overall decline of collective bargaining as a U.S. institution, Cutcher-Gershenfeld, Sleigh, and Pil conclude their chapter by in effect concentrating on the types of recent collective bargaining experiences reflected in the DTE and Kaiser-Permanente case examples: "In these types of agreements, the parties are utilizing the forum of collective bargaining to reach beyond the issues of wages, hours, and working conditions and signal a mutual commitment to broader social concerns. Whether by these means or other methods, the key to seeing collective bargaining come out of this metaphorical ball game a winner will be its again achieving the status . . . of a socially desirable institution." Perhaps so, but the baseball metaphor also raises certain other implications about which proponents of interest-based, mutual-gains, socially desirable bargaining may be not at all sanguine. Consider that in the U.S. private sector, professional baseball and the professional sports industry more broadly employ relatively few, highly skilled workers who are very well organized and represented in both collective bargaining and individual bargaining.

Indeed, professional sports constitute one of the few "industries" in which unionism grew and prospered in recent years and decades. There are (as yet) no good substitutes for the "services" provided by these workers, the demand for their services has become increasingly inelastic, and they represent a large share of the "firms'" labor costs. But this industry and the firms within it are also subject to peculiar if not unique public policies, including exemption from antitrust prosecution, cartel-like revenue sharing, the right to trade worker-players from one firm to another, and accounting rules that let firms amortize and depreciate the costs of their human capital. From this perspective, professional baseball players constitute skilled craft workers who possess considerable bargaining power and have a strong craft union to represent them. It is they who in recent decades have regularly been hitting home runs in terms of their bargaining relationships with employers. But if it is these circumstances and characteristics that are more generally required for U.S. collective bargaining (and, more basically, unionism) to reverse let alone stem its long-term decline, it may be suggested that the wait will be long—indeed, interminable. Another way to put this point about unionism and collective bargaining is that most U.S. private sector workers are waiting and will continue to wait to get an "at bat."

Chapter 3, by Berndt Keller, offers a political economy perspective on the regional integration of employment relationships within the European Union (EU) at three levels of analysis, namely, the company, or micro, level; the sectoral, or meso, level; and the interprofessional, or macro, level. Though this is not an exercise in historical analysis of European employment relations, Keller observes early on that the last half century or so has witnessed several partially overlapping regulatory regimes and stages of development in this regard, including regulatory minimalism during the 1950s and 1960s, rather strict attempted harmonization of national standards from the 1970s to the mid-1980s, a combination of national standards and statutory minimums from the late 1980s to the mid-1990s, and the specification of broad general goals heavily dependent on transnational coordination from the mid-1990s to the present. Today, the governance of European employment relationships is multilevel in nature and operates on the principle of "subsidiarity," which gives strong priority to voluntary agreements over legislative action, emphasizes the prime responsibility of social partners rather than corporate actors for the establishment of regulatory rules, and favors decentralization of competencies at lower levels over centralized decisions at the supranational level. From this perspective, cautions Keller, the ostensibly formidable European directives are subject to flexible or heterogeneous implementation at national, sectoral, regional, and company levels such that substantial variations in practice emerge, and occasionally a directive may even be reversed by particular enterprise-level agreements.

Regarding micro (company) level employment relationships within the EU, worker participation in decision making—management decision making—continues to be a key issue, perhaps especially because of continuing questions about the extent to which the policies and practices of multinational companies (MNCs) fall within the scope of particular corporate governance regulations of EU member states. Early on, which is to say during the 1970s, European regulatory initiatives sought to generalize the German co-determination model of employee participation in decision making to all other European nations under the rubric of "harmonization." These initiatives, including the well-known Vredeling Directives, largely failed because member states did not want to give up (and viewed these initiatives as a challenge to) their sovereignty. Later, beginning in the mid-1980s, employee works councils (EWCs) were established on a purely voluntary basis, with French and German enterprises taking the lead in this respect, but this decentralized approach also met with limited success in terms of the number of EWCs actually established. With enactment of the Maastricht Treaty in 1991, however, EWCs soon became the norm among (large) European enterprises as well as among MNCs, and the growth of such EWCs was further spurred by subsequent extensions of and amendments to the Maastricht Treaty. According to the data presented by Keller, the number of European EWCs (including in MNCs) rose from about 30 during the early 1990s to about 950 in 2004. Lest readers presume that this development represents pervasive European worker participation in decision making, Keller provides two sobering counterweights, one quantitative and one qualitative. Quantitatively, only about one third of all MNCs operating in Europe have complied with the EWC directives of the EU, though the complying MNCs account for roughly two thirds of all European MNC employment. Qualitatively and under the Maastricht Treaty and subsequent directives, procedural requirements for EWCs are emphasized over the scope and content of such involvement. In other words, European regulation of employee involvement in management decision making seemingly represents a triumph of form over substance. Nevertheless, that there is considerable variation in actual employee involvement in the substantive decision making of European enterprises, including MNCs operating in Europe, is attested to by the fourfold typology of such involvement proffered by Keller, namely, the symbolic EWC, the service-oriented EWC, the project-oriented EWC, and the participation-oriented EWC. Empirically determining the distribution of European

EWCs among these four types represents an important research opportunity as well as a research challenge.

Keller next turns his attention to European social dialogues, which are "frequently used instruments of social policy" aimed at "the European peak association of management and labor." These social dialogues can be seen as voluntary guidelines (containing elements of moral suasion) for labor and management, such as "nominal pay increases should be the sum of price increases and productivity growth." Such dialogues were given a considerable boost during the mid-1980s, when Jacques Delors served as president of the European Commission and strongly promoted the concept of a single European market. The number of such dialogues subsequently increased markedly to about 40 and went far beyond employment relations issues. Employer organizations favored the dialogues, mainly because they were nonbinding, whereas more dissatisfied labor unions sought to make the dialogues binding on the parties—and were unsuccessful in doing so. During the early 1990s and under the newly issued Maastricht Social Protocol and Agreement, European social partners who were engaged in contractual relations could reach binding framework agreements. At first, such agreements seemed likely to be reached by major employer and union confederations, but Keller's analysis shows that this did not occur, largely because the employer confederations continued to resist binding agreements. Keller tells a similar story about social dialogues and social partner agreements, or the lack of them, in the wake of the 2000 Lisbon Summit and 2001 Laeken Summit, during which the European Commission took new and more extended steps to transfer responsibility for employment relations policy formulation to labor and management. Nevertheless, a few potentially important European social dialogue labor–management agreements were reached during the early to mid-2000s, including those covering "lifelong development of competencies and qualifications," "telework," and "work-related stress."

For most of its existence, the European Commission has aimed its social dialogues at the national level, but more recently it shifted its attention to the sectoral level. While there is in fact a rather long history of social dialogue agreements having occasionally been reached at the sectoral level in Europe, they were few in number. With more explicit European Commission support, and as Keller shows, the number of agreements rose to about 200 by the end of the 1990s. Some agreements covered specific employment relationship issues, while others covered more wide-ranging sets of issues. This diversity, or heterogeneity, of social dialogue–based labor–management agreements has sparked considerable controversy about the "new" versus the "old" social dialogue guidelines. Proponents of (or adherents to) the old guidelines argue for their superiority on the ground that they were more narrowly limited and attuned to particular employment relationship issues. Proponents of (or adherents to) the new guidelines argue that the employment relationship is but one aspect of a larger social relationship (or contract) and therefore the new guidelines are superior to the old. But Keller convincingly argues that the new is not much if any different from the old in terms of European social dialogues, at least as measured by the incidence of social dialogue–stimulated labor–management agreements, which remains meager.

In light of its experience with social dialogues, meaning quite limited achievement of actual labor–management agreements, one might think that the European Commission would be relatively quiescent in striking out anew. But as Keller shows, beginning in the mid-1990s, the commission attempted to extend its reach to employment policy, which prior to then had been the exclusive province of EU member states. In brief, and following issuance of the European Commission's white paper on growth, competitiveness, and employment, the 1997 Treaty of Amsterdam was adopted, specifying employment policy guidelines—20 of them—for member states. Later expanded beyond employment policy and becoming known as the open method of coordination (OMC), these guidelines called for member states to focus their national policies on the "four pillars" of adaptability, entrepreneurship, equal opportunities, and employability, and to integrate them within their respective social dialogues. From 1997 to 2002, the commission focused its attention on gaining compliance with the guidelines from individual EU member states. More recently, the commission reduced the number of employment policy guidelines from 20 to 10 and replaced the four pillars with three newly dominant objectives, namely, full employment, improving productivity and quality at work, and strengthening social cohesion and inclusion. As with its social dialogues experience, however, the commission has found that its employment policy guidelines have produced relatively little in terms of tangible agreements, largely because its guidelines are voluntary and are not well suited to dealing with core industrial relations issues of particular interest to European labor and management.

Keller concludes his chapter by pointing out that, contrary to the objectives and guidelines issued by various EU authorities, "strict convergence of existing national systems [is] unlikely to happen; instead, tendencies of continuity and path dependency of national employment relations will dominate." This is in rather striking contrast to the prior completion of the European common market and the founding of the

European and Monetary Union (EMU), the latter being best known for the abolishment of national currencies and establishment of the euro as the common European currency (though not, of course, among all European nations). Keller's primary conclusion seems further strengthened by the 2004 expansion from 15 to 25 EU member states, which adds to the diversity of employment relationships among the states that now compose this union. While many lessons may therefore be drawn from Keller's analysis, perhaps the most telling is that a "common market" of otherwise singularly national labor market and employment relationship policies and practices will be far more difficult to achieve, if it can be achieved at all, than a common currency. Stated differently and in retrospect, achievement of a common currency among leading European nations appears to have been an easier challenge than achieving common labor market and employment relationship policies.

Chapter 4, by Alexander J. Colvin, Brian Klaas, and Douglas Mahony, provides a deep and far-ranging analysis of alternative dispute resolution (ADR) policies, procedures, and outcomes, primarily in nonunion U.S. companies. As the authors point out early on, ADR procedures came into being and have become widespread largely as an alternative to unionized grievance procedures and to employment litigation. The well-known decline of unionism in the U.S. private sector means that, over time, fewer and fewer workers are covered by collectively bargained grievance procedures. At the same time, employment legislation covering U.S. private sector workers has grown substantially and, at first blush, implies that more and more workers have legal avenues for resolving employment-related disputes. However, and as Colvin, Klaas, and Mahony make clear, such litigation does not fundamentally overturn the prevailing employment-at-will doctrine, and the effort, procedural steps, and resources required for individual employees or classes of employees to establish the validity of their employment discrimination claims against employers and pursue such claims through the courts are very substantial, if not prohibitive. For their part, though employers typically view employee claims of employment discrimination (or wrongful termination) as lacking merit, they may nevertheless wind up incurring substantial legal expenses in defending themselves against such claims and run the risk of being subject to negative judicial verdicts accompanied by large monetary awards to plaintiffs. Hence, there are incentives for both parties to the employment relationship to favor ADR procedures.

One party's preferred procedure, however, may not be the other's top choice. In this regard, Colvin, Klaas, and Mahony understandably focus attention on arbitration as a particular ADR alternative to the litigation of employment disputes. Such arbitration, which has long been the dominant and widely supported mechanism for resolving disputes under collectively bargained agreements between unionized employees and company management, is, by contrast, especially controversial when it comes to the resolution of employment disputes involving nonunion employees and companies. This is principally because, in the nonunion context, the arbitration process appears to be one-sided, meaning that the employer alone decides whether arbitration will be a condition of employment, determines the rules under which arbitration takes place, specifies the issues that are and are not subject to arbitration, pays for the arbitrator's services, and has a potential repeat-player advantage over a one-time individual employee-player. Despite these reservations, several recent decisions of the U.S. Supreme Court reviewed by Colvin, Klaas, and Mahony have established the enforceability of mandatory employment arbitration agreements. Indeed, these decisions constitute a judicial deferral to arbitration doctrine for the resolution of nonunion employment that appears to be as strong as the same doctrine adopted by the U.S. Supreme Court almost a half-century ago for the resolution of unionized employment disputes.[2]

Lest readers get too caught up in the controversy over the arbitration of nonunion employee disputes, Colvin, Klaas, and Mahony move on to adumbrate the wide variety of extant ADR practices. These include expedited arbitration and grievance mediation in the unionized sector, and open door, management appeal board, peer review, mediation, ombudsperson, and, yes, arbitration in the nonunion sector. As of the mid-2000s, it appears that a majority of nonunion U.S. employers had adopted at least one and typically more than one of these various ADR practices. Although such exogenous forces as unionization threat and employment legislation have been key to some nonunion firms' adoption of ADR practices, Colvin, Klaas, and Mahony analyze the role of endogenous human resource management and organizational conflict management strategies in firms' adoption and use of ADR. From the perspective of human resource management strategy, ADR is considered one component of a high performance work system, while from the perspective of organizational conflict management ADR is structured and shaped to align with a "Contend," a "Settle," or a "Prevent" strategy. Colvin, Klaas, and Mahony next explore the factors associated with employee use of ADR systems and procedures. Here, the authors usefully distinguish between initial stage/step usage and later stage/step usage, with employee perception of mistreatment, trust in management, organizational attachment, and perceived procedural justice "driving" initial stage/step usage (or lack of usage), and employee satisfaction with treatment at initial stage/step usage, dependency on the organizational hierarchy for discretionary rewards, and social support driving later stage/step usage (or lack of usage). These differential drivers or correlates of initial and later stage/step ADR system usage are portrayed as formal models.

The second half of chapter 4 focuses on the consequences to employees and firms of the actual use of ADR systems. Regarding consequences to employees, the authors frame their analysis largely with the exit–voice–loyalty theory of Hirschman (1970) and conclude that there is less support for it from studies of ADR in nonunion settings than from studies of grievance resolution in unionized settings. In particular, the turnover or exit-reducing outcome of grievance procedure usage reported in research on unionized employees is not comparably matched by research on nonunion employees; indeed, exercise of voice by nonunion employees may have no significant effect on turnover or exit or may even be associated with increased turnover or exit. Less equivocal, however, are empirical findings about the correlates of nonunion employees' exercise of voice under ADR systems, which indicate that employee loyalty is significantly negatively associated with their use (that is, the exercise of voice), as is fear of reprisal for using these systems. Hence, nonunion employees who believe that they have been unfairly treated at work are as likely or more likely to engage in withdrawal, neglect, or "suffering in silence" behavior than to exercise voice by invoking ADR procedures.

Regarding the consequences of ADR usage for firms, Colvin, Klaas, and Mahony review a large and wide-ranging body of evidence. Among the highlights of their review are that employers are significantly more likely than employees to win employment arbitration cases brought under ADR procedures and are even more likely to win cases that are decided (outside of ADR) in the federal courts; that employment arbitrators dealing with nonunion employee disputes are significantly more likely than labor arbitrators dealing with unionized employee disputes to rule in favor of the employer; and that peer review panels are not more likely to rule in favor of employees than are managers in general or human resource managers in particular. Going further, other research finds that the attractiveness of a firm to potential job applicants is significantly reduced when the firm has a mandatory employment arbitration procedure in place; that a positive work record or history on the part of disciplined or terminated employees is associated with decision reversal and reinstatement by both labor arbitrators and employment arbitrators; and that employer failure to follow or comply with existing employment dispute resolution procedures when it comes to employee discipline, especially progressive discipline, is associated with the modification or reversal of such discipline by labor and employment arbitrators and even occasionally by the courts.

There is another set of firm or organizational outcomes not taken up by Colvin, Klaas, and Mahony that conceivably can be influenced by ADR systems and procedures; these are such fundamental outcomes as labor costs, productivity, revenue growth, return on capital investment, market share, and even stock price (for publicly traded companies). Interestingly, prior research indicates that the presence of unionized grievance procedures is significantly positively associated with these measures of firm performance, but also that actually using them is significantly negatively associated. Whether similar findings will emerge regarding the effects of nonunion grievance procedures on firm performance is unknown, but the paucity of empirical knowledge about this relationship provides an obvious research opportunity for industrial relations scholars—perhaps especially because, as Colvin, Klaas, and Mahony make clear, the volume of employment disputes and attempts at dispute resolution involving nonunion employees and firms has greatly surpassed the volume involving unionized employees and firms.

Chapter 5, by John S. Heywood and Uwe Jirjahn, analyzes the determinants and consequences of performance-based pay. As the authors point out, performance-based, or incentive, pay has long-standing historical roots. It was, among other things, a staple of scientific management, but during much of the 20th century it became displaced—in thought and practice—by time-based pay in the forms of hourly wages and annual salaries. As the 20th century drew to a close, however, new pressures for and concepts of performance-based pay emerged, and these have continued into the early 21st century. For purposes of their analysis, Heywood and Jirjahn distinguish individual performance-based pay from group performance-based pay, and do so with respect to both determinants and consequences. In addition, and especially notable, the authors provide new evidence on a resurgent form of performance-based pay, namely, piece rates.

Theoretically, individual-based performance pay, such as merit plans, piece rates, and commissions, provides strong incentives for workers to perform, principally by exerting greater effort and, in the case of high-productivity workers, by sorting themselves into jobs for which they (or their performance) is rewarded. Heywood and Jirjahn succinctly review some of the conceptual and practical limitations of the performance-inducing property of incentive pay: the trade-off between insurance and incentives, which requires compensating differentials for risk-averse workers; limited employer ability to punish workers paywise for poor performance, which leads to rents for some workers; the withholding of effort and productivity-enhancing ideas and the restriction of output by workers who fear an employer's ratcheting up performance standards, though such behavior may be countered by cooperative, trust-building worker involvement in the design of incentive schemes; and the limited applicability of performance pay to work that involves multitasking. As the authors also point out, these and other related problems of implementing individual-based performance pay in practice reflect what Kerr (1975) dubbed "the folly of rewarding A when hoping for B." Thus, individual incentive schemes have resulted in stockbrokers providing fraudulent information to customers to boost sales; mechanics exaggerating automobile repairs to increase their own earnings; military recruiters, paid by volume, signing up poor-quality recruits; and public schools explicitly rewarding teachers for retention but at the cost of increased student course failure, low average student attendance, and no increase in achievement. To overcome these problems, more comprehensive supervisory assessments of individual worker productivity are often recommended. While some empirical evidence supports this recommendation, especially when nonmanagerial workers perform complex, multifaceted jobs, other evidence questions the validity and reliability of such assessments in light of frequent halo effects, recency effects, and central tendency when rating scales are used to assess performance. Indeed, formal performance appraisal systems have been shown to be subject to systematic (rather than episodic) perverse incentives that typically result in upwardly skewed ratings for individual workers (Lewin and Mitchell 1995).

These concerns about individual-based performance pay carry over to group-based performance pay, including small group incentives, gain sharing, and profit-sharing plans. Even more than individual-based performance pay, group-based pay requires cooperative, trustful employer–employee relationships. But as Heywood and Jirjahn show through case examples, formal modeling, and empirical findings, workers operating under one or another type of group incentive scheme nevertheless often seek to maximize their individual utility and thereby engage in shirking or free-riding behavior. Such tendencies may be curbed, and even eliminated, when technology and the organization of work make workers highly interdependent, when group incentives are based on long-term performance, or when group-based performance pay provides specific incentives for group self-monitoring and peer pressure to perform. But even these practices are subject to sharply contrasting views and judgments about their effectiveness. Perhaps the strongest evidence of relatively effective group-based performance pay comes from studies of profit sharing that find that this arrangement stimulates workers to help each other on the job, perform work more flexibly, and build trustful relationships with each other, with management, and even with customers. However, profitability is often influenced by exogenous events over which workers and work groups have little or no control so that even well-functioning, high-performing work groups may find that there are few or no profits to share.

Moving on, Heywood and Jirjahn give particular attention to piece rates as a form of individual-based performance pay and conclude that empirical evidence drawn from several nations largely supports theoretical propositions about this incentive arrangement. In particular, more productive workers do sort themselves into work paid by the piece; variance in output is greater among piece rate–paid workers than among wage- and salary-paid workers; the greater the variance in worker ability, the greater the gain to the firm from sorting more productive workers into piece rate schemes; and piece rate usage is inversely related to the costs of monitoring work and, in turn, positively related to organizational size. Moreover, there is rather strong evidence that because of their relatively shorter expected work tenure and lower labor force attachment, women are significantly more likely than men to sort themselves into individual-based piece rate work—and, correspondingly, are significantly less likely than men to sort themselves into team-based, team-compensated work. Using data from the United States, Australia, the United Kingdom, Hong Kong, and Germany, Heywood and Jirjahn clearly show that "establishments with larger shares of women are more likely to use piece rates." By contrast, the authors' conclusion about the role of unions in piece rate pay and performance pay more broadly is decidedly more mixed. While unions have long been thought to oppose all forms of individual performance pay, Heywood and Jirjahn cite evidence and examples, including German works councils and co-determination, of unions supporting piece rates and other forms of individual performance pay provided that cooperation with and trust in management are relatively high. In this regard, the authors conclude that "the sum of the contradictory evidence across countries and units of observation makes it seem unlikely that the decline in unionization observed in many countries will universally cause a large increase or decrease in the use of piece rates and commissions."

When it comes to the consequences of individual performance pay, perhaps the key question of interest is the extent to which that pay enhances establishment or firm performance. Econometric studies using economywide or industry samples of establishments and firms are only modestly useful for answering this question, say Heywood and Jirjahn, in part because the findings are mixed and in part because most of the extant studies are cross-sectional and therefore do not use fixed-effects performance estimation. Case studies and examples, which by their nature feature deep analysis of performance pay in individual firms, also do not provide an overriding conclusion about the effects of piece rates and other individual-based performance pay schemes on organizational performance. Studies of piece rate usage in automobile glass production and tree-planting firms report large productivity gains associated with the use of piece rates, while a detailed study of a shoe manufacturing company found that elimination of piece rate pay was associated with a significant profitability increase. Additionally, and perhaps ironically, there is evidence that the use of piece rate pay reduces gender and racial wage differentials as well as differences in performance evaluation, with the latter finding attributed to piece rates (and performance pay more broadly) being more objective and verifiable than time-based pay in terms of the output and quality measures on which piece rates are based.

Regarding the determinants of group-based performance pay, Heywood and Jirjahn's review of extant research finds that, contrary to theoretical prediction, the use of profit sharing is not inversely related to firm size, and in fact some studies report a contrary finding. Other variables, such as employee participation in decision making, multitasking, worker skill and education, and the degree of uncertainty facing the firm, are found to be positively associated with the use of profit sharing. As with individual-based performance pay, unions have typically been thought to oppose the use of group-based performance pay generally and profit sharing in particular, but recent studies using U.S. and European data variously find that unions' attitudes toward profit sharing have changed considerably, that some unions explicitly support the use of profit sharing, and that the supposed negative association between unionization and profit sharing disappears when this relationship is studied longitudinally. When it comes to the consequences of group-based performance pay, studies of profit sharing are once again in the forefront and typically find significant positive associations between the use of profit sharing and firm performance. Various interaction analyses suggest that the effects of profit sharing on firm performance are enhanced when profit sharing is combined with the use of work teams and other high performance–type work practices. Similarly, a study set in the United Kingdom found that the interactions between equal employment opportunity practices and both profit sharing and employee stock ownership plans (ESOPs) were associated with significant productivity improvement. French and German studies of profit sharing find that this particular group-based performance pay practice is significantly inversely associated with employee absence from work. Still other studies strongly suggest that the firm's industrial relations climate, measured by trust, fairness, and reciprocity, "may be crucial for the incentive effects of sharing schemes." This is, of course, a very similar conclusion to the one that these authors reached regarding the effects of individual-based performance pay on establishment and firm performance.

Toward the end of their chapter, Heywood and Jirjahn provide important new evidence on the determinants of piece rates using a unique German data set that permits the analysis of management's and workers' desires for piece rates. These data were obtained from a four-wave panel of German manufacturing establishments and were pooled for the purpose of conducting a partial observability approach. Descriptive statistics show that piece rates were used by almost 27% of these establishments, no doubt reflecting the positive association between works councils and piece rates in Germany, and in fully 67% of the establishments where workers participated in decisions about large investments. Initial Probit analysis found a significant negative association between worker participation in investment decisions and the use of piece rates in these German establishments. However, partial observability analysis found that this relationship was the result of two opposing forces, namely, workers' desire for piece rates, which is enhanced by their participating in investment decisions, and management's desire to avoid piece rates, which is also enhanced by worker participation in investment decisions. Regarding other variables of interest in this study, the share of blue-collar workers was associated with increased worker desire for piece rates, while coverage by a collective agreement was associated with increased management desire for piece rates. Organizational size had opposite effects on management and worker desires for piece rates, being positively associated with management desires and negatively associated with worker desires. A high share of female workers, by contrast, was positively associated with both management's and workers' desires for piece rates. Whether these findings are generalizable beyond Germany is a tantalizing but as yet unaddressed question.

In conclusion, Heywood and Jirjahn point out that there is substantial variation in the characteristics of performance pay wherever such pay is practiced. A key challenge to researchers is to learn more about the match of such characteristics to each other, to the nature of the workplace and its workers, and to the performance of the organization. To do so effectively requires that the multiple, typically separate, literatures on performance pay be combined and that studies go beyond focusing on one particular incentive scheme, such as piece rates or profit sharing.

As the authors put it, "Future research should provide a more systematic comparison of schemes and the circumstances under which each scheme is successful."

Chapter 6, by David I. Levine and David Lewin, introduces and analyzes a newly developing issue in U.S. industrial relations, namely, managerial misclassification. This issue is in one sense straightforward: it involves the claim that employees holding jobs with managerial titles and who are paid salaries rather than hourly wages are in fact primarily performing employee work rather than managerial work and therefore are entitled to overtime pay under U.S. labor law for the "excess" hours they work while employed as managers. In another sense, or several senses, however, this issue is anything but straightforward. Companies contend that their employees who hold jobs with managerial titles were selected to be and voluntarily chose to become managers do indeed perform primarily managerial work, and are evaluated and potentially additionally compensated based on their performance as managers. These misclassification-related overtime pay claims have been pursued during the last decade or so through litigation under the long-standing federal Fair Labor Standards Act (FLSA) as well as state wage and hour laws, especially in California, and thus appear to be largely a legal issue. From a scholarly perspective, however, these claims raise a variety of analytical and methodological considerations that are systematically addressed in chapter 5.

The first managerial misclassification claim was filed in California in 1994 and, as the data compiled by the authors show, scores of such claims have been filed since. Most cases involve large retail chains, ranging from the big box–type that offers thousands of varied products to supermarkets offering primarily food products to more specialized electronics, home furnishings, and rental car companies. Both large and small restaurant chains have also been prominently featured in managerial misclassification cases, and still other cases involve insurance, bottled water delivery, and moving equipment rental companies. In each instance, employees who held or in some circumstances still hold jobs carrying managerial titles seek overtime pay for the hours they worked or work beyond 40 in a week under the FLSA and beyond eight hours in a day under California law. In analyzing the legal process that governs these claims, Levine and Lewin observe that an individual plaintiff's potential damages are small relative to the cost of filing and pursuing a lawsuit, which means that lawyers are unlikely to take on an individual plaintiff's case. Instead, claims of managerial misclassification are pursued on a class action basis, and it is the determination by a court of whether a putative class meets the appropriate legal tests that has been

the main battleground between plaintiffs, defendants, and their representatives. If a class of plaintiffs becomes certified, as has typically
occurred in managerial misclassification cases, the ensuing battle is over
the merits of the claim and the determination of damages. In this regard
and as Levine and Lewin clearly show, class certification in a managerial
misclassification case is almost always followed by a "voluntary" negotiated settlement rather than a court trial.

The core question addressed, however, is why managerial misclassification lawsuits have exploded. The authors' answer runs roughly as
follows. Most such lawsuits have been filed against large, successful
companies whose business strategies have primarily emphasized
growth—revenue growth, in particular, but also and consequently
growth of locations, operations, and employment. Accompanying such
rapid growth are systematic efforts to develop national and even global
brands, to manage supply chains more efficiently, including through the
use of computerized information systems and related technologies, and
perhaps most of all to specify and replicate standard operating procedures (SOPs) in all locations and facilities. A key consequence of these
initiatives is, in turn, increased centralization of decision making,
whereby local store and facility managers make fewer decisions, and
regional, divisional, and headquarters-level managers make more decisions. Stated differently, over time the independent judgment and discretion exercised by lower-level managers who work for large retailers
(and certain other businesses) decline as these businesses grow and as
decision-making responsibility becomes more centralized. Hence, to the
extent that managerial misclassification has actually occurred, it is the
result of strategic business decisions, often successful decisions, rather
than a result of purposive attempts on the part of employers to avoid
overtime pay.

Also contributing to the phenomenon of managerial misclassification
and the rise of managerial misclassification lawsuits are the compensation practices of large retail and related companies. As Levine and
Lewin point out, in most of these companies lower-level managers are
eligible for incentive compensation based on the performance of the
locations and facilities they "manage." While some such incentive plans
feature stock options, stock ownership, and profit sharing, most common
among them is the bonus plan. Typically a bonus for, say, a store manager and perhaps for associate and department managers as well is based
on the difference between budgeted store operating costs and actual
store operating costs or, more narrowly, between budgeted labor costs
and actual labor costs. While conceptually there are myriad ways a store
manager can reduce actual compared to budgeted operating or labor

costs, centralized decision making means that a store manager cannot decide to change store operating hours or negotiate new contractual terms with a vendor or stock fewer goods. What a store manager can do, however, is exercise "independent" judgment and discretion in determining how many hourly wage workers to employ, the number of hours they will work, their work shifts, and the number of hours that the manager himself or herself will work. Because the manager is salaried, his or her additional work hours are not compensated per se, meaning that a bonus-eligible store manager has a potentially powerful incentive to substitute his or her labor for that of hourly paid workers. To the extent that a store manager is able to engage in such labor substitution, actual store labor costs will be reduced relative to budgeted store labor costs and the manager's bonus payment will be larger. Moreover, the rigorous performance evaluation systems, practices, and standards typically used with store managers by large retail and related companies further encourage them to work long hours. But as store managers engage in this type of behavior, they increase the proportion of their work that is nonmanagerial, perhaps to the point where they are primarily performing employee work—which is, of course, the underlying claim in managerial misclassification cases.

There are counterarguments to this managerial misclassification story, however, and these are reviewed in some detail by Levine and Lewin. For example, "if the labor market for low-level managers is competitive and if such managers are relatively mobile, then any effort by one employer to make these managers work unusually long hours will result in managerial quits, imposing a cost on the employer. Should that happen, the employer will have to revise compensation practices, either by raising pay or by reducing the incentives for low-level managers to work long hours." Additionally, the aforementioned incentive compensation story may be alternatively interpreted to mean that the companies in question are paying until the job is done rather than paying by the hour, which constitutes a rather different accountability story, in which employers accept that low-level managers will work long hours and perform some employee work but still primarily perform managerial work. Further, retail enterprises in particular are in effect service businesses that experience unpredictable waves of customers, deliveries, and exogenous events over which they have no control, such as weather-related or customer health emergencies. In these circumstances, low-level managers will from time to time be called upon to perform nonmanagerial work, but this does not necessarily mean that such work predominates. Still further, many businesses have adopted management by wandering around and customer relationship management policies and practices in which lower-level managers are expected, indeed required, to spend some of their time directly interacting with employees and customers, including occasionally actually performing employee work. Time spent in these ways, however, is (arguably) management rather than employee work.

The authors also pay particular attention to agency relationships in the context of managerial misclassification cases and to the role of social science expertise in such cases. To illustrate, plaintiffs' counsel work on a contingent fee basis in managerial misclassification cases, meaning that they are not compensated for their efforts unless they win. While winning in the context of litigation is popularly conceived of as receiving a favorable court decision (either by judge or jury), Levine and Lewin's data indicate that only one California-based managerial misclassification case has to this point actually proceeded through trial to a verdict. All other cases have been settled before or during trial, and plaintiffs' attorneys received a portion of the monetary settlements. The larger point here is that plaintiffs' attorneys have a clear incentive to search for managerial misclassification cases in which to represent plaintiffs—an incentive that is particularly strong in California, where it is relatively easy to obtain class certification in a managerial misclassification case. Attorneys who represent defendants in such cases do not work for contingent fees; they bill clients directly for services performed and receive payment irrespective of who wins the case and what settlement is reached. In these circumstances, it appears that defendants' attorneys have an incentive to pursue managerial misclassification cases up to and perhaps through the start of a trial but not to completion. While arguable, this interpretation of the incentives for attorneys to represent defendant companies in managerial misclassification cases is supported by leading law firms' extensive marketing and advertising of such services, especially through the Internet, in this specialty area.

Regarding the use of social science expertise in managerial misclassification cases, Levine and Lewin show that this has become widespread, perhaps especially because the courts, notably in California, have encouraged or otherwise been sympathetic to it. The most frequently used methods have been surveys of former or current employees holding managerial titles, followed by observational studies. Surveys in this context are intended to elicit data on how low-level managers spend or spent their time at work, in particular performing specific managerial and nonmanagerial tasks. Unsurprisingly, surveys conducted on behalf of plaintiffs are typically conducted among former low-level managers, and surveys conducted on behalf of defendants are typically conducted among current low-level managers. In both instances, there are certain well-known threats to the validity and reliability of the resulting data, mainly because these surveys are conducted in the context of adversarial legal proceedings rather than for basic research or independent study. In contrast to often retrospective and always self-reported survey data, observational studies are designed to obtain data on the work actually performed by low-level managers through direct observation. Here, ostensibly independent experts typically observe and record the work tasks performed by full populations or samples of low-level managers as well as the time spent performing those tasks. Because access to workplaces is controlled by employers, observational studies are virtually always conducted on behalf of defendants in managerial misclassification cases. Threats to the validity and reliability of such observational studies differ notably from the same threats for surveys, but they may be mitigated by careful design, repeat observations, and the use of multiple observers. Nevertheless, when proffered by plaintiffs' experts, the data obtained through applied social science research methods in managerial misclassification cases typically show that low-level managers mainly perform or performed nonmanagerial (that is, employee) work, with a notably small standard deviation. By contrast, when proffered by defendants' experts, the data obtained through social science research methods typically show that low-level managers mainly perform managerial work, but with a notably large standard deviation. More plainly stated, the findings of plaintiffs' experts invariably support the plaintiffs' position, and the findings of defendants' experts invariably support the defendants' position. Although the experts on both sides may in fact be capturing and highlighting different elements of low-level managers' work life reality, it is at least equally plausible that the adversarial context of litigation and the payment for expert services by one or the other party to litigation strongly shape the findings adduced from the application of social science research methods to disputes involving claims of managerial misclassification.

Levine and Lewin conclude their chapter by offering public policy recommendations regarding managerial misclassification and its regulation. They argue strongly that any improvements in policy should be based on a grounded understanding of the market failure or injustice that such policy is intended to address. Using transaction cost analysis as a point of departure, the authors observe that the specification of "bright lines" regarding the levels of annual compensation separating those who do from those who do not qualify for overtime pay makes good sense, and in this respect recent changes in federal and California-specified annual worker compensation levels to qualify for overtime pay seem appropriate. However, they also recommend that attorneys' fees in managerial misclassification cases be set as a proportionately declining share of voluntary settlements in such cases; that unrealistic weekly and monthly tests of the work tasks performed by employees holding managerial titles to determine if they are eligible for overtime pay be eliminated (largely to reduce employer uncertainty); that the reclassification of one group of low-level managers as hourly employees not be ratcheted up to change the exempt status of other groups of managers; and that the courts require plaintiffs and defendants in managerial misclassification cases to jointly rather than separately undertake employee surveys and observational studies. Levine and Lewin also recommend that employers periodically conduct organizational analyses to determine on a relatively more *ex ante*, proactive basis whether changes in business strategy, supply chain management, branding, and organizational structure have altered the work performed by low-level managers. By failing to do so, employers will continue and likely be even more fully pressed to engage in reactive, litigation-spurred defense of their employment and compensation practices for low-level managers.

Chapter 7, by Teresa Ghilarducci and Charles Jeszeck, analyzes the shift in the United States from firms to workers regarding risk and responsibility for retirement income security—a shift that began relatively recently but has become far more pronounced even more recently. The authors initially examine the details of this shift as they pertain to Social Security and personal savings, but then focus the bulk of their attention on private pension arrangements. Thereafter, Ghilarducci and Jeszeck draw out key implications for workers of the changing private pension scene, propose some policy reforms based upon these implications, and provide main conclusions based on their overall analysis.

That the U.S. population and hence the workforce is aging is well known, as is the markedly increased life expectancy for both men and women. The latter in particular should be good news—who can be against longer life?—but the challenges of this key demographic trend for retirement and retirement income planning are readily apparent, especially if the average age of retirement changes little if at all. As Ghilarducci and Jeszeck point out, retired U.S. workers are spending more time than ever before in retirement, which from actuarial and retirement income–support perspectives flies in the face of the assumptions that underlie enactment of the original Social Security Act. It is one thing to finance and pay benefits to retirees who are expected, on average, to live for a few years, but quite another to do so for retirees expected to live for 15 or even 20 years beyond retirement. Being a price-indexed benefit plan, Social Security mitigates and perhaps eliminates the risk that retirees' purchasing power will be eroded by inflation;

this obviously works to the benefit of current retirees. But with a declining ratio of workers to retirees, a ratio that is expected to decline from 3:1 to 2:1 during the next quarter century, either the Social Security taxable wage base or the tax rate, or both, will have to increase to fund benefits for future retirees—including the so-called baby boomers who will shortly be retiring en masse. This is hardly a new problem, in that Social Security has always involved income transfers from younger workers to older retirees. But what is new, as Ghilarducci and Jeszeck observe, are the consequences for Social Security financing emanating from recent, unexpected, and rising income inequality. In particular, earnings above the Social Security taxable-base wage cap are now growing faster—much faster—than earnings subject to the Social Security tax so that fewer revenues are and will be available to pay Social Security retirement benefits. Though this problem conceivably could be solved by traditional methods of raising the Social Security taxable-base wage cap and/or increasing the tax rate, this seems unlikely. Rather, pressures are mounting for the restructuring—meaning the reduction—of Social Security benefits and, even more, for the creation of individual retirement accounts that would be "managed" by individual workers rather than by the federal government. The latter proposal bears a striking resemblance to the relatively recent advent of 401(k) accounts in which workers manage their own money in place of firms' managing these workers' pension accounts/benefits. But if no political action is taken in this regard, a possibility not to be discounted, then the preretirement income replacement rate represented by Social Security benefit payments to the average individual will, as Ghilarducci and Jeszeck make clear, decline from about 41% at present to about 30% over the next two decades—raising the specter of a rising proportion of retirees living in poverty.

Declining Social Security retirement income presumably could, in part or in whole, be offset (that is, increased) by personal savings, but Ghilarducci and Jeszeck's analysis indicates that this is extremely unlikely. Whereas in 1980, U.S. workers were saving about 10% of their income annually, today they are saving none. This zero U.S. savings rate contrasts markedly with the rates of most other advanced nations, and it means that the ability of future retirees to supplement Social Security benefits will, on average, be meager to non-existent. Instructively, the older, higher U.S. savings rate was largely a function of investment in and payments to defined benefit (DB) pension plans, but as these plans have given way to defined contribution (DC) benefit plans and to 401(k) plans the savings rate has fallen accordingly—and precipitously. Further, and according to Ghilarducci and Jeszeck, forecasted savings rates under 401(k) and other voluntary saving plans have been significantly higher than actual savings rates under these plans. To illustrate, only one third of workers who responded to a 2004 survey indicated that they were "on track" to achieve as much as a 70% target preretirement income replacement rate during retirement. Indeed, in this same survey, only about two out of five respondents indicated that they had even thought about calculating savings needed for retirement. Not surprisingly, it is higher income earners who are most likely to have thought about planning their income stream during retirement and taken action, including seeking professional tax counseling.

During the second half of the 20th century, private pension plans provided the second largest source of income to retirees and elderly households, roughly 20% of all such income. But those plans were almost exclusively of the DB type, and, as Ghilarducci and Jeszeck show, such DB plans have rapidly become replaced by DC and 401(k) plans. By 2005, only about 21% of U.S. private sector workers were covered by DB pension plans, though perhaps another 43% or so were covered by DC plans, which represented a marked increase over the data reported a half-dozen years earlier. But whatever their type, pension plan coverage data tell only part of the story about income actually received by retirees and prospective retirees. Consider, for example, the apparently rising incidence of both DB and DC plans that allow retirees to take their benefits in a lump sum. This option appears especially popular among both current retirees and workers planning for retirement. While such popularity may reflect a careful calculation that retirement benefits taken as a lump sum will enable recipients to augment their savings substantially and "outlive" their retirement, compared to receiving a stream of benefits during retirement, there is perhaps an equally plausible argument to be made that when taken, these lump sums will be mostly or completely spent in the short term—in effect, treated as bonus-type disposable income. Whichever of these or other explanations holds sway empirically, there is little doubt that firms with pension plans much prefer to have their retirees take their benefits in lump sums rather than in multiyear payment streams (that is, annuities). Once lump-sum retirement benefits are paid, firms can remove such payments from their long-term liability accounts and appear better positioned for the future in terms of financial performance. These trends away from DB and toward DC plans, 401(k) plans, and even lump-sum over income-stream payments are, of course, significantly associated with the decline of unionism and collective bargaining in the United States, as Ghilarducci and Jeszeck also make clear.

Among the implications for workers of rapidly changing retirement income arrangements, those involving 401(k) plans are perhaps the most important, especially because this particular savings plan is likely to be the only one used by newer, smaller, younger firms (so-called entrepreneurial enterprises). Named after a provision of the U.S. Internal Revenue Code, a 401(k) plan basically involves workers' saving their own money, specifically by deferring a portion of their wages or salaries until retirement. In this regard, workers alone decide whether and to what extent their employers should "pay me now or pay me later," though employers typically offer their employees specific advice in this regard. In any case, recent data on savings rates under 401(k) plans show that for a median annual salary of $45,000, the median annual salary deferral was less than $1,900, or about half of the savings rate recommended by most financial advisers and plan administrators. If projected to retirement, this actual savings rate would yield only about an average annual 3% preretirement income rate. Further, the popularity of 401(k) plans stems in large part from the fact that workers can borrow against plan balances during the life of the plan—and many of them do. Indeed, because labor mobility is higher under 401(k) plans than under either DB or DC pension plans, 401(k) plan accumulations are often used to finance job changes and job searches. As Ghilarducci and Jeszeck put it, "401(k) plans may actually serve as severance plans that help alleviate the costs associated with being out of work and changing jobs." Further, the default risk associated with DB pension plans that was cushioned by passage of the 1970 Employee Retirement Income and Security Act (ERISA), which also created the Pension Benefit Guarantee Corporation (PBGC), is not nearly as strong when it comes to DC pension plans and 401(k) plans. Stated differently, and in keeping with a main theme of chapter 7, retirement plan income risk has shifted considerably, perhaps dramatically, from employer to employee. This theme is further illustrated by the riskier investment practices that attend DC pension plans and 401(k) plans compared to DB plans, especially when it comes to requirements—determined solely by the employer—for such investment, and by the nonannuity feature of most DC and 401(k) plans compared to DB plans.

Regarding public policy implications of their analysis, Ghilarducci and Jeszeck argue for encouraging pension benefit plans that combine the best features of DB and DC plans, especially cash balance plans under which employers rather than workers bear the investment risk and plan sponsors guarantee specific returns on employer contributions insured by the PBGC. Such cash balance plans can also be structured to provide annuity payments to retirees rather than simply offering the lump-sum option. Further, the authors propose an expansion of multi-employer pension plans, which serve to protect the retirement income benefits of workers employed by firms that experience financial difficulty or even bankruptcy. Conceptually, the same recommendation can be made for nonprofit and public organizations that experience financial difficulty, if not bankruptcy. Still further, Ghilarducci and Jeszeck propose that the Federal Savings Thrift Plan under which the 401(k) portion of federal employees' pension plan contributions is matched by the employer be extended to private sector DC pension plans, which, among other things, should raise worker demand for participation. Finally, the authors offer several other proposals for strengthening DC pension plans per se, including taxing early withdrawals, providing incentives for annuitizing DC plan payments, limiting the investment of DC plan funds in the stock of the company employing the workers who participate in the plan, and providing PBGC-like insurance for such plans. Taken together, these recommendations can be viewed as a call to protect workers from what has become something of a free-for-all or, in the authors' words, a "wild west," when it comes to retirement income and income security for the U.S. workforce.

Chapter 8, by Sophie Mitra and David Stapleton, provides a wide-ranging analysis of disability and return to work among the disabled in the United States. In reviewing employment trends over the last quarter century or so among persons with disabilities, for which the main data come from the U.S. Bureau of Labor Census Current Population Survey (CPS), the authors find that while employment rates for working age people without disabilities show a procyclical pattern, rates for working age people with disabilities have increasingly become unconnected to the business cycle. In particular, the rates have fallen and continued to fall during economic expansions and contractions that occurred during the 1990s and the early 2000s. Regarding work hours and type of work, there is considerable evidence that workers with disabilities are far more likely than workers without disabilities to be employed in contingent work, especially part-time work, and to work at home, including via telecommuting, and these differences have enlarged in recent years. Contingent work arrangements offer the benefit of flexibility to the disabled, but they come at the cost of lower wages, benefits, and job stability compared to work arrangements for the nondisabled. Mitra and Stapleton also review research on employment discrimination against persons with disabilities. Such discrimination may take various forms, including pure prejudice, but because statistical evidence shows that workers with disabilities are less productive than workers without disabilities, prejudice is not the only factor influencing the employment, work arrangements, and compensation of the disabled. Surveys typically find that "a substantial share of employers believe that employer, supervisor, and co-worker attitudes are a significant problem" when it comes to hiring persons with disabilities, and in a set of 13 laboratory studies, 10 found that evaluators were highly pessimistic about the future performance and promotion potential of workers with disabilities. Studies of wage differentials between persons with and without disabilities have typically concluded that a substantial portion of such differentials are due to discrimination; however, these studies (like studies of male–female and minority–majority group wage differentials) have not been able to fully control for unobserved characteristics that may be associated with disability (e.g., the ability of individuals to work quickly or intensively for long periods).

Over the past three decades, the institutional environment for the employment of persons with disabilities has changed considerably, with four separate national laws having been enacted by Congress. In this regard, Mitra and Stapleton pay particular attention to the impact on persons with disabilities of the 1990 Americans with Disabilities Act (ADA) and of selected disability benefit programs, notably Social Security Disability Insurance (SSDI) and Supplemental Security Income (SSI). It is well known that laws can have unintended consequences and sometimes even consequences opposite of those intended, and early studies of the ADA concluded that this law had negative effects on the employment of persons with disabilities, especially men. This key finding was attributed to employers' desire to avoid the reasonable accommodation and employment termination provisions of the ADA. Later studies, however, take issue with these conclusions and with how they were methodologically adduced. For example, one of these later studies used a modified definition of disability that included people who said that their functional limitations in daily life did not prevent them from working, and found that this group's employment position improved following passage of the ADA. Another study differentiated individuals with long-term disabilities from individuals with short-term disabilities and found that the decline in employment of people with long-term disabilities substantially predated passage of the ADA. Still another study found no employment decline among people with disabilities in U.S. states that had ADA-like laws in place prior to passage of the ADA; it also found that the short-term negative effects of the ADA's reasonable accommodation provisions on employment of the disabled dissipated as employers learned to adjust to the provisions.

SSDI and SSI are "two large federal disability programs [that] directly serve the population of persons with disabilities and affect their employment" situation. SSDI payments are based on individuals' past employment, whereas SSI is a welfare program that makes payments to those meeting the disability test and who have income and assets below specified thresholds. Both programs are aimed at persons with relatively severe impairments. During the two-year period ending in 2002, the number of SSDI and SSI recipients more than doubled, and there is considerable empirical evidence showing that expansion of these income support programs is significantly associated with the employment decline of persons with disabilities. Amendments in 1984 to the Social Security Act (SSA) that loosened the eligibility requirements for receiving SSDI and SSI payments and that expanded the pool of contingent applicants who could qualify for benefits by quitting their jobs to apply for them are thought to have particularly contributed to the employment decline of persons with disabilities. These declines as well as increases in SSDI participation have been especially pronounced among people with mental illnesses and people with musculoskeletal conditions, and those with low skills whose benefit levels increased relative to their wages as a consequence of indexing SSDI benefits to economywide wage growth. While these effects may be judged negatively by some, Mitra and Stapleton observe that they are not necessarily undesirable from a public policy perspective. Rather, "declines in the productivity of people with disabilities may be considered to be a social cost of such expansions . . . to be weighed against the possible social gains." The more challenging policy question, these authors say, is whether it is possible to provide income support to the disabled in a way that encourages rather than discourages their efforts to support themselves.

Mitra and Stapleton turn their attention next to empirical research on the factors influencing the return to work of the disabled. Among the positive factors in this regard are prior full-time (as compared to part-time) work, returning to the preinjury employer (where a worker became temporarily or partly disabled through a work injury), union membership, and relatively high education. Among the negative factors are relatively high workers' compensation benefits, worker age, and receipt of SSDI and SSI benefits. This last finding is hardly surprising given that SSDI imposes a 100% "tax" and the SSI a 50% tax on the disabled who return to work and earn above the Substantial Gainful Activity (SGA) dollar limit, meaning that disability benefits are reduced dollar for dollar above this limit, and the SSI imposes a 50% tax in this regard. While various amendments to the SSA as well as certain special and temporary programs, including an earnings disregard experiment, have sought to ease the return of the disabled to work, the long-standing basic (implicit tax) penalties imposed on earnings from work that are above specified SSDI and SSI benefit limitation levels continue to provide powerful disincentives for the disabled to actually return to work. It may well seem paradoxical, even contradictory, for the disability determination process under U.S. law to center on the inability to work while at the same time the SSDI and SSI programs offer certain incentives and programs intended to encourage beneficiaries to work. But as Mitra and Stapleton observe, "since the establishment of SSDI in 1956 and SSI in 1972, return to work has been an integral component of both programs." Understandably, therefore, U.S. public policy toward the disabled has shifted between periods when benefit provision and expansion have dominated and periods when benefit containment and return to work have dominated. A recent example of the latter is the Ticket to Work and Work Incentives Improvement Act (1999), which provides return-to-work "tickets" to SSDI and SSI beneficiaries that can be redeemed at local vocational rehabilitation agencies and other employment service providers and which revises SSA reimbursement of such service providers in ways intended to increase exit of benefit recipients from SSDI and SSI. Though the Ticket to Work program is in its early stage, the participation rate has been low and the anticipated invigoration of the market for vocational rehabilitation services has not yet materialized.

Disability management, a term that has relatively recently come into fashion, refers to various programs and activities intended to prevent disabilities from occurring, and when they do occur to minimize their impacts on employers and employees. In a fundamental sense, then, disability management is aimed at job retention. Mitra and Stapleton analyze disability management in the context of two particularly relevant U.S. laws, namely, the Family and Medical Leave Act (FMLA) and the aforementioned ADA. The FMLA covers establishments employing 50 or more persons and guarantees that employees who must cease work for health reasons, including disability and maternity, may take up to 12 weeks of medical and family leave without pay and retain their jobs. In 2000, about 16.5% of U.S. workers took leave under the FMLA, most for reasons other than disability or maternity. Under the ADA, employers must provide reasonable accommodations to employees with disabilities provided that these accommodations do not impose undue hardship on business operations. Empirical research finds that such accommodations are significantly associated with job retention and with the postponement of application for disability benefits. Related research shows that about 30% of workers with disabilities were accommodated by their employers prior to enactment of the ADA and that accommodation was significantly negatively associated with employee voluntary turnover. Beyond reasonable accommodations, per se, job retention services, whether provided by vocational rehabilitation agencies or employers themselves, are a potentially important component of disability management. In a recent random control trial study of job retention service intervention—specifically, identification of needed job accommodations, vocational counseling, and education and self-advocacy—conducted by a state vocational rehabilitation agency among a sample of private sector employees with arthritic conditions, the intervention was associated with significant reduction and postponement of job loss. Employer provision of job retention services, which is concentrated among large firms, has not yet been subject to systematic empirical inquiry, but anecdotal examples suggest that such services also reduce voluntary turnover and other job loss among employees with nonsevere disabilities. Determining whether and to what extent these types of interventions and services reduce application by the disabled for SSDI and/or SSI benefits represents an obvious and important research opportunity for those interested in disability management.

In sum, Mitra and Stapleton conclude that "the recent employment experience of working age people with disabilities is discouraging." This is in part because the employment rate of persons with disabilities relative to those without disabilities fell during the entire boom period of the 1990s—though this behavioral phenomenon was most likely due to reduction in eligibility standards for entry to the SSDI and SSI rolls rather than to an increase in impairment of the disabled. But it is also due in part to what Mitra and Stapleton label the federal government's predominant "caretaker" approach to working age people with disabilities, based on an outmoded, narrow view of disability as an exclusively medical issue. That the eligibility rules of SSDI and SSI (not to mention Medicare and Medicaid) discourage work and most likely more than offset the pro-work effects of the ADA support this caretaker interpretation. By contrast, the improved economic position of single mothers in the United States under welfare reforms instituted in the 1990s offers a possible benchmark for shifting from a caretaker to a "pro-work priority" policy toward the disabled.

The eighth and final chapter in this volume is not a paper in the conventional sense but, instead, a summary and integration of a roundtable discussion of key contemporary industrial relations issues. The roundtable members—Adrienne E. Eaton, Thomas A. Kochan, David B. Lipsky, Daniel J.B. Mitchell, and Paula B. Voos—were asked to address four main questions:

1. In view of the secular decline of unionism in the United States and abroad, what is the potential for the emergence and growth of other forms of worker representation?

2. How can the growth of both high-performance work systems (HPWS) and alternative dispute resolution (ADR) systems best be explained?

3. Is human resource management (HRM) being crowded out by organizational behavior (OB) in similar fashion to the earlier crowding out of industrial relations (IR) by HRM?

4. What are the main benefits and limitations of government regulation of contemporary employment relationships?

Regarding worker representation, roundtable members were more or less in agreement that a resurgence of U.S. unionism, especially traditional "business unionism," was unlikely to occur any time soon or even in the longer term. The forces of globalization, deregulation, and technological change, which have combined to play an undeniably strong role in the decline of U.S. unionism, will continue apace and shape any new forms of worker representation. Whether and to what extent such new forms are emerging or will emerge was the subject of different views among roundtable members. Some members believe that alternative forms of worker "representation" are emerging and will emerge further, such as managerial networks and caucuses, professional associations, community unions, and even nongovernmental organizations (NGOs). Other roundtable members believe that U.S. workers will increasingly seek political action to serve their ends, in part at the national level and in part at state and local government levels. That such worker-initiated political action has already occurred is reflected in the enactment of numerous municipal-level and some state-level living wage ordinances, legislative efforts to require employers to provide health insurance, and interest groups lobbying for prevailing wage provisions for government-subcontracted service employees. A potential risk in this regard, pointed out by one roundtable member, is that there are presently in place various organizations that claim to speak for and thus represent workers but are not actually financed or controlled by workers. Also noted were two other forms of union substitution that have developed in the United States over the last few decades. The first consists of modern-day versions of company unions or "dependent" representation, most notably workplace teams, as well as semi-union practices like open door and grievancelike procedures for the resolution of workplace disputes. The second consists of the numerous antidiscrimination-in-employment laws, related human resource regulatory statutes, and wrongful discharge–type court decisions that provide various employee groups with voice-type mechanisms. Perhaps as a punch line of the responses to this question, one roundtable member observed that the claim advanced by some scholars of a pent-up unsatisfied demand for unionization is questionable because the data on which this view is based come from surveys that fail to ask nonunion workers about their desire for unionism *if they had to pay a particular cost to belong to unions.* From this perspective, value for cost is as relevant a decision calculus to worker decisions about whether to form or join unions as it is to the decisions of consumers about whether to buy particular goods and services.

Regarding the growth of both high-performance work systems (HPWS) and alternative dispute resolution (ADR) systems, roundtable members are not necessarily convinced that HPWS have in fact grown as much as popular and some scholarly accounts suggest, and in any case they argue that decisions to adopt such systems are based on the well-known criteria of cost reduction and productivity enhancement. That is to say, HPWS will be adopted and/or spread if they lead to net cost reduction or net productivity improvement, or both, relative to more traditional work systems. Further, even as some employers have undeniably adopted HPWS, other employers as well as some of these same employers have also adopted more vigorous labor cost–containment practices, most especially outsourcing on both domestic and international fronts. Such highly contrasting practices represent a certain dualism on the part of the management of U.S. firms, in which one set of core employees is managed as an asset on which HPWS expenditures can be conceived of as investments yielding a positive economic return (as measured by firm performance) and another set of peripheral employees is managed as an expense to be contained or reduced.[3] Analytically consistent with this view, one roundtable member pointed out that union avoidance is hardly the only factor contributing to the growth of HPWS. Instead, HPWS constitute a strategic initiative that enhances organizational and workplace flexibility, which more closely accords with contemporary worker preferences and organizational performance objectives. Such initiatives, however, have been considerably more prominent in nonunion than unionized enterprises. Roundtable members also for the most part judged the growth of ADR to be independent of rather than correlated with the growth of HPWS. For some roundtable members, the growth of ADR can also be explained in cost–benefit terms, meaning that ADR is a preferred alternative to the litigation of employment disputes. Particularly interesting in this regard are the choices that firms make regarding the type of ADR system to employ, and these choices vary widely, according to one roundtable member's research. Some firms have systematic ADR policies and practices in place, while others follow a more ad hoc approach. Some ADR systems emphasize arbitration, others emphasize mediation, and still others emphasize peer review. It is also clearly the case that ADR is principally practiced by nonunion firms, and one roundtable member estimates that about 40% of all large nonunion U.S. firms have one or another ADR system in place. Indeed, according to roundtable members, the growth of such ADR systems and practices appears to have well outpaced the growth of HPWS in the United States. Instructively, however, two roundtable members believe that there is a positive correlation between the growth of ADR systems and the growth of HPWS, largely because the former can be considered a component of the latter. This view is supported by empirical studies that incorporate internal grievance and related dispute resolution practices in larger conceptualizations and empirical measures of HPWS.[4]

Roundtable members' responses to the question about organizational behavior crowding out human resource management were more varied than their responses to any of the other questions posed. One person judged the question to reflect the internal politics of business schools (in which, today, OB is widely taught, HR is moderately taught, and IR is marginally taught). This same member judged the rise of HR to be largely a function of the decline of U.S. unionism rather than a function of new HR thought, but also observed that HR specialists will continue to be produced by U.S. educational institutions and be employed by firms because certain HR functional subspecialties cannot be outsourced. Another roundtable member emphasized the continuing functional role of HR in U.S. enterprises, noted that HR jobs are expected to grow more rapidly than the average growth of all other major functional jobs over the next several years, and argued that while OB studies may in the near future surpass HR studies as a focus of interest in leading business schools, HR will continue to hold sway in most of the graduate and undergraduate programs that "produce" HR staffers and professionals for U.S. businesses. Still another roundtable member quibbled with the notion that HR studies have supplanted IR studies, pointing out that IR studies are increasingly migrating from economics departments and business schools to sociology departments, where "much of the best new work on labor market outcomes is being done." A fourth person, one who has substantial interaction with HR executives and professionals, believes that HR has clearly supplanted IR in terms of both study and practice, and that HR subspecialties—in strategic planning, performance measurement, and organizational transformation—are growing in the attention and resources being devoted to them. Yet this same roundtable member observed that other functional executives, professionals, and staff specialists, not to mention supervisors and employees, typically have negative views of the HR function in their respective organizations. As he put it, "If OB is crowding out HRM, then I suspect a root cause is the ongoing tension between HR specialists and other constituencies in many organizations."

This view seems to accord with the judgment offered by the fifth roundtable member, that "the bloom is off the rose of 'strategic HRM.'" Underlying this judgment are data showing that only in a subset of large firms do HR executives play a truly strategic role, and even in these firms, not to mention most others, HR takes a clear backseat to finance. Further on this point, relatively more HR operational tasks have been outsourced or otherwise dispersed to contract firms than the operational tasks in finance and most other functional specialties. For this roundtable member, these realities should more fully inform the teaching of HR and the training of HR majors in U.S. universities lest those in charge of such education lose credibility. And yet this same person judges OB programs and specialists to be doing "no better" in terms of training the next generation of HR specialists, principally because OB graduates understand little about HR. Whether there is common ground for an OB–HR rapprochement in this regard is up to readers to decide.

In responding to the final question, about government regulation of employment relationships, roundtable members seemed largely in accord in, on the one hand, recognizing the limitations on government regulation of the employment relationship but, on the other hand, recognizing the need for and in some cases advocating such regulation. This is a rather remarkably balanced set of views given that all but one of the roundtable members were trained as economists. The most "macro" view of government regulation of the employment relationship was expressed by one person, who emphasized the effects of globalization on the efforts of any single nation to effectively regulate its own employment relationships. This roundtable member called particular attention to voluntary "codes of conduct" that are emerging in various nations, which provide a clear alternative to government regulation, and also observed that within the United States relatively more government regulation of the employment relationship is taking place at the state and local levels rather than nationally. Another roundtable member gave similar emphasis to nonfederal government regulation of the employment relationship in the United States, arguing that such regulation is responsive to worker needs and that it substitutes for declining unionism and collective bargaining. This same person, however, argued for increased flexibility in the enforcement of employment relationship regulation, in particular, a two-track approach in which firms that meet regulatory standards are given increased flexibility to fashion particular policies and practices, while firms that fall short of regulatory standards are more closely monitored. Yet another roundtable member provided a formal analysis showing that while purely competitive labor markets will provide an optimal matching of employer needs and employee preferences, and thus no government regulation is required, many labor markets are in fact characterized by monopsony, which does require the regulation of "less-than-optimal working conditions, benefits, safety, and pay." Such regulation, argued this roundtable member, could improve efficiency and also have certain other positive macroeconomic effects. An even more distinctive view of government regulation of the employment relationship was offered by a roundtable member who focused on the political dynamics of such regulation. This person showed via specific examples that supposedly antiregulation Republicans sometimes strongly support regulation, while supposedly proregulation Democrats sometimes oppose regulation; as he puts it, "it depends on whose ox is being gored." He went on to say that despite his training as an economist and wariness of the externalities often imposed by regulation, his real-world experience in dealing with many companies, unions, and employees suggests to him that some regulation of the employment relationship is required. Ironically, this roundtable member also believes that the substantial growth of employment relationship regulation that has occurred in the United States over the last several decades, which he judges to be largely a substitute for declining unionism and collective bargaining, "constitutes a bad deal for American workers." All of this was perhaps best put into perspective by the final roundtable member, who on the one hand catalogued the limitations of government regulation of the employment relationships but then, on the other hand, concluded that "the main benefit of government regulation is that it may be the best game in town." By this she primarily meant that government regulation can improve standards of work, especially when such standards are threatened by low-standard competitors in the same legal jurisdiction. But whether work standards of any particular nation, including the United States, can be effectively maintained let alone regulated in an increasingly global economy is perhaps the leading question and challenge of modern times.

Notes

[1] See, as examples, Chamberlain, Pierson, and Wolfson (1958); Ginsburg et al. (1970); Aaron et al. (1971); Kochan, Mitchell, and Dyer (1982); and Lewin, Mitchell, and Sherer (1992).

[2] These decisions are known as The Steelworkers Trilogy, largely because they all were rendered in cases involving the same union, namely, the United Steelworkers of America (USWA). For a succinct treatment, see Gould (1982).

[3] For more on this theme, see Lewin and Dotan (2006).

[4] See, for example, Huselid (1995).

References

Aaron, Benjamin, Paul S. Meyer, John Crispo, Garth L. Mangum, and James L. Stern, eds. 1971. *A Review of Industrial Relations Research, Volume II*. Madison, WI: Industrial Relations Research Association.

Chamberlain, Neil W., Frank C. Pierson, and Theresa Wolfson, eds. 1958. *A Decade of Industrial Relations Research, 1946–56: An Appraisal of the Literature in the Field*. New York: Harper.

Dunlop, John T. 1957. "The Task of Contemporary Wage Theory." In George W. Taylor and Frank C. Pierson, eds., *New Concepts in Wage Determination*. New York: McGraw-Hill, pp. 118–44.

Ginsburg, Woodrow L., E. Robert Livernash, Herbert S. Parnes, and George Strauss. 1970. *A Review of Industrial Relations Research, Volume 1*. Madison, WI: Industrial Relations Research Association.

Gould, William B. 1982. *A Primer on American Labor Law*. Cambridge, MA: MIT Press.

Hirchsman, Albert O. 1970. *Exit, Voice and Loyalty: Responses to Decline in Firms, Organizations, and States*. Cambridge, MA: Harvard University Press.

Huselid, Mark A. 1995. "The Impact of Human Resource Management Practices on Turnover, Productivity, and Corporate Financial Performance." *Academy of Management Journal*, Vol. 38, no. 3, pp. 635–72.

Kerr, Steven. 1975. "On the Folly of Rewarding A, When Hoping for B." *Academy of Management Journal*, Vol. 18, no. 4, pp. 769–83.

Kochan, Thomas A., Daniel J.B. Mitchell, and Lee Dyer, Eds. 1982. *Industrial Relations Research in the 1970s: Review and Appraisal*. Madison, WI: Industrial Relations Research Association.

Lewin, D., and Hilla Dotan. 2006. *The Dual Theory of Human Resources and Business Performance*. Working paper, UCLA Anderson School of Management.

Lewin, David, and Daniel J.B. Mitchell. 1995. *Human Resource Management: An Economic Approach*, 2nd ed. Cincinnati, OH: South-Western.

Lewin, David, Olivia S. Mitchell, and Peter D. Sherer, eds. 1992. *Research Frontiers in Industrial Relations and Human Resources*. Madison, WI: Industrial Relations Research Association.

CHAPTER 2

Collective Bargaining: Keeping Score on a Great American Institution

JOEL CUTCHER-GERSHENFELD
University of Illinois

STEPHEN R. SLEIGH[1]
International Association of Machinists and Aerospace Workers,
AFL-CIO

FRITS K. PIL
University of Pittsburgh

The decentralized approach to collective bargaining is a great American institution. Ideally, it serves four core functions in society. First, collective bargaining has been endorsed in public policy as the preferred vehicle by which wages, hours, and working conditions are to be established in the United States. Second, it provides a means to codify past workplace innovations into governing contract language. Third, it serves as a forum to signal and guide future strategic directions for workplace voice and workplace conditions. Fourth, it has taken on an emergent but major role in defending deferred claims such as pensions and retiree health care benefits.

The core thesis of this chapter is that the institution of collective bargaining is failing to deliver on its potential for codifying workplace innovation and setting future strategic directions. Further, it is experiencing great stresses and strains when it comes to delivering basic wages, hours, and working conditions, and it is finding it difficult to assure the pay-out of deferred claims. To use baseball, another great American institution, as a metaphor: It is the bottom of the ninth inning for collective bargaining as a social institution; it is down by a number of runs and at great risk if it cannot spark a rally.[2] In this metaphorical game, collective bargaining must succeed in the face of a triple threat: shifts in markets (particularly globalization, deregulation, and other factors intensifying competition), changes in the nature of work (including new technology, increased focus on knowledge and skills, and outsourcing dynamics), and the erosion of other, interwoven social institutions (including unions, employer-centered systems for health care and retirement benefits, and work–family dynamics). The consequences of a failure to "step up to the plate" and meet the challenges are substantial. While collective bargaining once provided an important check and balance in society, ensuring fair treatment in the workplace and the distribution of earnings that fueled a growing middle class, today collective bargaining is most notable by its absence.[3] We have, for example, seen a massive restructuring of the U.S. pension system and the future retirement health benefits of younger workers. This has happened, however, not through the give and take of bargaining, but through unilateral employer announcements. Bankruptcies decimated labor agreements over a decade ago in the steel industry, and they are now having the same effect in the airline and auto supply sectors. Similarly, fair treatment in nonunion workplaces is assured only where inappropriate actions are specifically prohibited under the law (and even then only where the employee is prepared to file a complaint or a lawsuit) or where an employer chooses to support alternative dispute resolution vehicles. The increasing polarization of wealth in this country has the potential to erase many decades of gains achieved through collective bargaining, making The American Dream more distant for the coming generations (Kochan 2005). Ultimately, there is the risk of what is termed a "race to the bottom," where wages and benefits are progressively diminished as work moves to low-cost providers in this country and abroad.

Collective bargaining has not, of course, disappeared. There are still approximately 23,000 private sector labor negotiations every year in this country and at least half again as many public sector negotiations. Notable instances can be found where parties do craft innovative agreements that deliver mutual gains, some of them featured in this chapter. These are exceptions, however, and often even these important initiatives rest on fragile foundations.

Our aim is to use a combination of quantitative data and qualitative case examples to outline the full scale and scope of the challenge facing collective bargaining as an institution in the United States. The focus is not on unions—a distinct but interwoven institution—but specifically on collective bargaining. We seek to foster research, debate, and action around this important institution that is presently at risk.

Collective Bargaining as an Institution

In 1935, "encouraging the practice and procedure of collective bargaining" was declared national policy in the United States (National

Labor Relations Act [29 U.S.C. §§ 151–169], Section 1. {§ 151.}). At that time, one of the architects, George Taylor, commented:

> Our government policy is obviously to raise collective bargaining to the status of a social institution, in accordance with the belief that the process provides the best democratic procedure for eliminating the basis for employee grievances as distinct from treating mere surface symptoms (Shils et al. 1979).[4]

To understand collective bargaining as a social institution, consider three key properties of institutions—they are emergent, embedded, and enduring.

Like all institutions, collective bargaining achieved its status in society over time. There was collective bargaining long before the passage of the National Labor Relations Act, and there was even supporting legislation at the state level that preceded the national legislation. In this sense, the institution is emergent in nature and the particular form has not been predetermined.[5] In fact, the initial form that emerged (bargaining oriented around craft unionism) shifted and expanded to accommodate a new form (bargaining oriented around industrial unionism) that matched the rise of the industrial revolution. Today, there are aspects of unionism that are oriented around professional development, community action, and other elements of what has been termed a global and knowledge economy. It remains to be seen if new forms of collective bargaining will again emerge to reflect these new realities.

Also, like other institutional arrangements, collective bargaining doesn't stand on its own. It is embedded in a range of additional institutions, including a market economy, concepts such as freedom of speech and freedom of association, democratic principles for individual and collective expression, and others. In particular, the future of collective bargaining is interwoven with that of labor unions, which have experienced a 50-year decline in membership.[6] The two institutional arrangements are distinct—craft guilds existed long before the practice of collective bargaining, and the links between unions and political parties, as well as many other union activities, are also distinct from collective bargaining. Also, there are collective negotiations that take place all the time in workplaces even in the absence of a union. Nonetheless, as we will outline, collective bargaining can only be understood embedded in its context as we enter a new century.

While the emergent and embedded aspects of institutions clearly continue to be applicable, they are combined with a third aspect that is more complicated. This concerns the way that institutions are enduring. Our very point is that collective bargaining is at risk of not enduring—of losing its standing as a viable social institution. Much has been written on the way that institutions perpetuate themselves,[7] but it is also possible for an institutional arrangement to fail at this task—particularly when there are shifts in the larger context or when alternative institutional arrangements emerge. In the case of collective bargaining, the larger context has shifted as a result of globalization, new technology, sectoral shifts, growth in right-to-work states, and new forms of work. Furthermore, alternative arrangements have emerged in the form of nonunion human resource management practices that provide individual employees with some degree of (nonunion) voice.

Table 1 provides data on the most important forces shaping collective bargaining from the point of view of today's labor and management chief negotiators. These data are taken from a 2003 national random sample survey of matched pairs of negotiators, commissioned by the Federal Mediation and Conciliation Service (FMCS; with data from an earlier 1999 survey as a comparison).[8] The respondents were asked to indicate which of 14 different forces had directly impacted their most recent negotiation. As Table 1 indicates, fringe benefit pressures had a heavy or moderate impact on the vast majority of negotiations. Pressure on work rules and domestic competition were also highly salient factors. International competition was also mentioned, but not as frequently as the forces listed in the table (it was cited approximately 27% of the time by union respondents and 20% of the time by management). On some of the most commonly cited forces, namely falling real wages, low trust, and fear of job loss, the views of labor and management were very different.

TABLE 1

Contextual Forces Moderately or Heavily Influencing Labor Negotiations Cited by Matched Pairs of Union and Management Negotiators in U.S. Private Sector Collective Bargaining

	Union, 1999 (%)	Union, 2003 (%)	Management, 1999 (%)	Management, 2003 (%)
Fringe benefit pressure	76.9	81.2	68.1	67.9
Work rule flexibility	54.4	54.1	57.7	55.6
Domestic competition	51.8	53.8	48.2	46.8
Falling real wages	72.2	62.5	37.2	31.8
Low trust	54.7	53.5	46.7	29.1
Fear of job loss	36.4	48.5	28.3	26.4
Pressure to upgrade skills	31.4	30.9	32.6	33.2

Source: Analysis conducted with data from the FMCS National Performance Review Surveys of 1999 and 2003. Access to the survey instrument and the data is available on request from the authors, with approval from the FMCS.

In a number of cases parties pointed to pressure to upgrade skills as an important force.

Given the forces that are influencing collective bargaining as an institution, a key question concerns how the process will adapt. It is our belief that collective bargaining is more than just a conduit for economic and social forces—that the process does matter. Thus, this investigation into how the institution is doing in this metaphorical ball game does take into account the larger context, but we are particularly concerned with what is happening on the playing field.

Delivering on the Basics—One Foul Ball after Another

How is collective bargaining doing when it comes to delivering on the basics—agreements about wages, hours, and working conditions that maintain or improve standards of living while not impairing competition? This is the first "batter up" in our metaphorical ninth-inning stand, and things do not look good. There has been one foul ball after another when it comes to basic collective bargaining practices and outcomes.

As is documented in a companion article,[9] the 2003 FMCS survey of union and management negotiators indicates problems with the most basic of collective bargaining outcomes: whether an agreement was reached. Approximately 10% of the negotiations surveyed in 2003 failed to reach an agreement—more than double the rate in similar surveys conducted in 1999 and 1996. This number represents a dramatic increase in negotiations involving an employer that has gone out of business, a bargaining unit that has been decertified, or a negotiation that has not settled for more than two years after expiration (the cutoff in the FMCS data set for classifying a contract as not settled).

Additionally, consider the contract expiration date, which traditionally served to focus negotiations toward agreement. Over half of the negotiations in the 2003 survey had not reached agreement more than 30 days after the expiration date. Increasingly, the union is unwilling to strike, for fear of replacement workers or other adverse consequences, while management is unwilling to lock out the workforce, for fear of disruptions in service and production. The 2003 survey data on settlements are presented in Table 2, broken out by four regions (selected as representative of distinct parts of the country). Delays in settlement and failure to reach agreement are key issues on the West Coast. However, there are also delays in almost half of the negotiations on the East Coast and in the Midwest, where collective bargaining is of longer standing.

TABLE 2
Settlements Reached and Timing of Agreements, by Region, Cited by Matched Pairs of Union and Management Negotiators in U.S. Private Sector Collective Bargaining

	Union, 1996 (%)	Union, 1999 (%)	Union, 2003 (%)	Management, 1996 (%)	Management, 1999 (%)	Management, 2003 (%)
Settlements of renewal agreements (first contracts excluded)	95.5	97.8	91.4	95.9	97.4	89.5
Early agreements (more than a month before expiration)	6.8	8.3	4.1	6.0	6.4	3.7
On time (within a month before or after expiration)	59.9	68.9	44.3	55.6	64.5	42.5
Late agreements (more than a month after expiration)	29.9	22.8	51.6	37.6	29.0	53.7

Source: Analysis conducted with data from the FMCS National Performance Review Survey of 2003. Access to the survey instrument and the data is available on request from the authors, with approval from the FMCS.

44

In fact, while union representation has declined from approximately 20% of the workforce in the early 1980s to 12.5% today, the decline in work stoppages has occurred at a much faster rate. Figure 1 presents data on work stoppages (strikes and lockouts) for bargaining units of 1,000 or more employees. It is clear that the role of overt demonstrations of power in collective bargaining has shifted.

Even though work stoppages are less common, negotiations are not necessarily less contentious or more productive. Indeed, there is evidence to suggest the opposite. Some of the most recent stresses in the process may reflect the cyclical pressures associated with the post-9/11 recession. For example, while approximately 95% of agreements in the 1996 and 1999 surveys included a wage increase, only 80% of the 2003 negotiations did, and there was a similar dropoff in the proportion of agreements with a benefit increase, with only about 45% of the most recent agreements featuring an increase in benefits compared to higher levels in prior surveys.[10] In the case of benefits, the pressures around health care costs and retirement benefits (pensions and other retirement benefits) are now part of a bargaining landscape that goes well beyond economic cycles.

To provide a closer look at these and other more traditional issues, we have compiled a unique analysis, which is presented in Tables 3 and 4. Table 3 presents data on whether a given outcome is reported as having ever been negotiated and included in an agreement between the union and management matched pairs. While there is general agreement between union and management on whether there has ever been a wage increase or a benefit reduction, union respondents are almost 30% more likely to report new language on workplace safety. Management, by contrast, is more likely to report a benefit increase. There is also some variation in how the parties perceive negotiations regarding wage reductions and wage freezes.[11] The data in Table 3 are a baseline for the analysis of new agreements achieved, as presented in Table 4.

Table 4 shows the cases in 2003 in which new language on a given issue was reported as proposed (by union and by management), with a third column indicating the percentage of cases in which both parties reported a new agreement on the issue. The third column of data represents the relative efficiency of the process—the proportion of cases in which language was both proposed and achieved. Thus, over 75% of the time, when a wage increase was proposed, some wage gain was achieved. By contrast, new language on benefits (increase or decrease), safety, and wage freezes was achieved only about 30% to 40% of the time that these issues were proposed. While parties may sometimes see it in their interest to make a proposal without expecting an agreement, we assume that

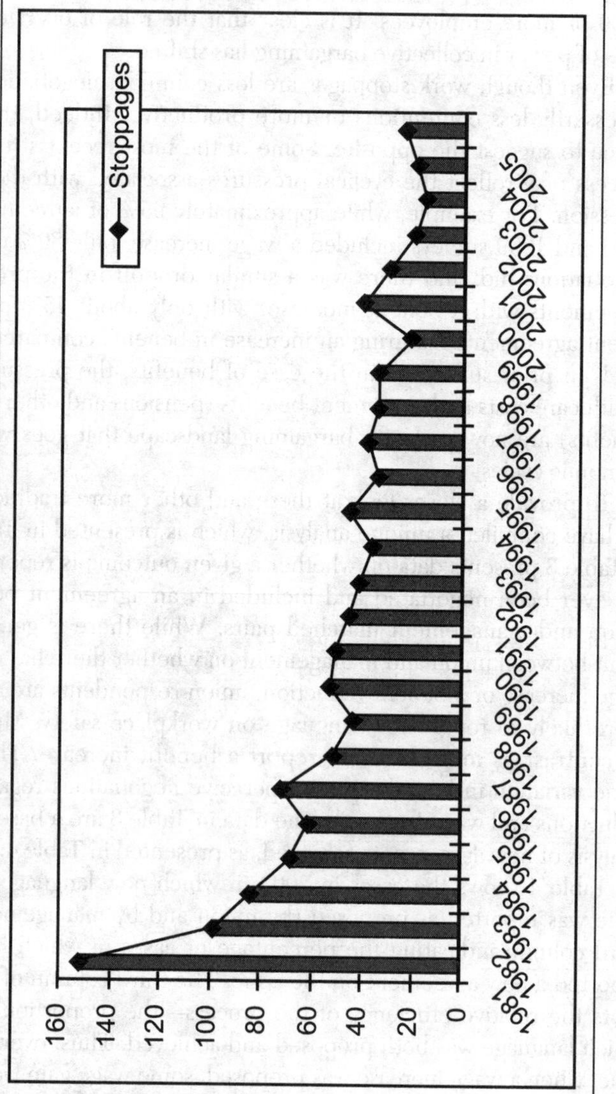

FIGURE 1
Work Stoppages by Year for Bargaining Units of 1,000 or More Workers

TABLE 3

Traditional Outcomes Reported as Having Ever Been Negotiated by Union and Management as Cited by Matched Pairs of Union and Management Negotiators in U.S. Private Sector Collective Bargaining

	Reported by union (%)	Reported by management (%)	Reported by union and management (%)
Wage reduction	17.2	12.8	2.7
Wage freeze	26.9	19.7	11.9
Benefit reduction	24.6	23.3	11.6
Wage increase	98.8	99.3	98.4
Benefit increase	57.8	73.1	44.5
Workplace safety	75.2	62.6	46.2

Source: Analysis conducted with data from the FMCS National Performance Review Survey of 2003. Access to the survey instrument and the data is available on request from the authors, with approval from the FMCS.

most of the time proposals are made with the hope of achieving some sort of agreement. While wage freezes and reductions in benefits or wages are clearly highly contentious areas where agreement may be difficult to attain, even proposals for new language on workplace safety are infrequently achieved. A well-functioning institutional forum would be one where parties can surface issues and, most of the time, find common ground. By this standard, collective bargaining is not performing particularly well on these traditional issues.

Behind the numbers in Table 4 are intense debates on the proportions of escalating health care costs to be borne by the employer and by

TABLE 4

Traditional New Language Proposed and Achieved in Labor Negotiations, Cited by Matched Pairs of Union and Management Negotiators in U.S. Private Sector Collective Bargaining

	New language proposed (reported by union and management; %)	New language achieved (reported by union and management; %)	Negotiations efficiency (%)
Wage reduction	3.3	0.2	6.1
Wage freeze	23.3	8.1	34.8
Benefit reduction	27.2	8.2	30.1
Wage increase	98.4	75.0	76.2
Benefit increase	73.7	25.6	34.7
Workplace safety	21.3	8.4	39.4

Source: Analysis conducted with data from the FMCS National Performance Review Survey of 2003. Access to the survey instrument and the data is available on request from the authors, with approval from the FMCS.

the employee, the increasingly strict requirements on retiree benefits accounting, the hard choices around protecting current wage and benefit levels at the expense of future hires, and the dynamics around new competitors in many industries that do not face the legacy costs carried by more established employers. These issues have resulted in recent high-profile strikes, including those at SBC Communications and the California Safeway supermarkets, as well as lockouts at Kroger and Albertsons in 2004. Tens of thousands of workers at the auto parts manufacturer Delphi are now facing a very uncertain future, with all of these tensions playing a central part in that situation.[12] None of the traditional aspects of negotiations constitute a strikeout, but neither do they represent much in the way of base hits. The process continues, but there is not much progress to report for labor or management—we are stuck with a succession of foul balls.

Enabling Innovation: Don't Count on Many Home Runs

In addition to its role in delivering traditional outcomes in wages, hours, and working conditions, collective bargaining has the potential to codify innovations that have emerged and to set the stage for new strategic directions. It is this innovative capacity that was a key focus of Kochan, Katz, and McKersie (1986), who indicated that only a combination of shop floor, collective bargaining, and strategic innovations would make it possible for industrial relations to reclaim its leadership role in shaping employment relations in this country. At the time, the alternative was for leadership to remain with a non-union human resource management (HRM) model that was playing an ever-stronger role in fostering frontline and strategic innovations. Today, both the "New Deal" industrial relations model and the HRM model are at risk in the face of what some have termed a "race to the bottom" that emphasizes the lowest common denominator for wages and benefits, with a primary focus on people as a cost to be minimized rather than as a resource that has the potential to create value and hence to be maximized.

In this context, let's consider the ability of collective bargaining to deliver agreements that are oriented around innovation and transformation. Table 5 reports baseline data on whether parties have ever reached agreements in a given relationship on potentially transformational issues important to labor and management, including work rule flexibility, new pay systems, work–family matters, joint committees, job security, employee involvement, and teams. As we saw with the more traditional outcomes, matched pairs of union and management respondents do differ in the degree that they report such agreements, with management more likely to report agreements for the first three and

TABLE 5

Transformational Outcomes Reported as Having Ever Been Negotiated by Union
and Management, Cited by Matched Pairs of Union and Management Negotiators in
U.S. Private Sector Collective Bargaining

	Reported by union (%)	Reported by management (%)	Reported by both union and management (%)
Work rule flexibility	47.8	57.3	34.1
Gain sharing, profit sharing	26.7	34.7	17.5
Work–family	29.0	37.1	17.1
Joint committees	37.3	25.2	17.1
Job security	34.1	20.8	10.3
Employee involvement	26.3	17.1	8.6
Teams	11.0	12.9	3.9

Source: Analysis conducted with data from the FMCS National Performance Review Survey
of 2003. Access to the survey instrument and the data is available on request from the authors,
with approval from the FMCS.

labor for the next three. Most of all, it is a relative minority of labor–
management relationships that have provisions on any of these subjects
in their agreements.

If we turn to relative efficiency of the process in delivering agreements on these issues, we see in Table 6 that most are just above a 50%
level of efficiency—the parties reach agreement slightly more than half
the time that these transformational issues are proposed. The record is a

TABLE 6

Transformational New Language Proposed and Achieved in Labor Negotiations,
Cited by Matched Pairs of Union and Management Negotiators in U.S. Private
Sector Collective Bargaining

	New language proposed (reported by union and management, in %)	New language achieved (reported by union and management, in %)	Negotiations efficiency (%)
Work rule flexibility	44.6	24.8	55.6
Gain sharing, profit sharing	19.2	10.1	52.6
Work–family	10.7	7.6	71.0
Joint committees	6.5	3.5	53.8
Job security	17.4	3.4	19.5
Employee involvement	10.8	2.1	19.4
Teams	1.1	0.6	54.5

Source: Analysis conducted with data from the FMCS National Performance Review Survey
of 2003. Access to the survey instrument and the data is available on request from the authors,
with approval from the FMCS.

bit better for work–family issues (around 70%) and much worse for job security and employee involvement (around 20%). Considering that most models of workplace innovation require a coupling of all of these issues, the variation in efficiency is a concern. Further, the agreements on most of these issues have declined compared with the 1999 and 1996 surveys (the exceptions being work rule flexibility and new pay systems; also, no data were collected on work–family issues in the earlier surveys). In all, it does suggest that collective bargaining is able to generate new language on many innovative matters—so a transformation enabled by collective bargaining is possible, but in terms of our baseball metaphor, it is more likely to be a series of base hits rather than any highly visible home runs.

In order to more fully understand the transformational dynamics, consider the data presented in Table 7 on new work practices in the automobile sector. These data are based on surveys of North American auto assembly plants conducted by the International Motor Vehicle Program (IMVP) in 25 U.S.-owned car factories in North America in 1994, and 23 in 2000. While the samples are not identical, what the figures do suggest is that there has been a general dropoff in the use of teamwork, a reduction in the number of workers involved in off-line quality improvement activities, and reductions in organizational practices associated with enhanced flexibility, skill development, and quality. Competitors in other parts of the world have dramatically increased their use of

TABLE 7
Workplace Innovation in U.S.-Owned Auto Assembly Plants, 1994 and 2000

	U.S.-owned plants in North America	
Work organization measure	1994	2000
Plants in regions with teams	35%	46%
Workforce in teams	49.4%	24.6%
Workforce in employee involvement or quality circles	32.8%	25.2%
Suggestions per employee	0.3	0.2
Suggestions implemented	41.8%	31.8%
Extent of job rotation in and across work groups on a scale of 1 (none) to 5 (frequent)	2.0	1.8
Responsibility for quality inspection/statistical process control on a scale of 0 (specialists only) to 4 (production workers only)	2.4	2.1

Note: Because our 1994 and 2000 samples are not identical for these measures, the figures represent only trends.
Data sources: Macduffie and Pil 1997; Pil and MacDuffie 1999; Holweg and Pil 2004.[13]

these same practices in the same period. This is further evidence of a trend away from integration across what Kochan, Katz, and McKersie (1986) termed shop floor, collective bargaining, and strategic levels.

There are, of course, instances where parties have achieved important innovations at the bargaining table that are connected to innovation at the workplace and strategic levels. In our next section, we will detail two case examples involving the use of interest-based bargaining methods. In both cases, process innovations have combined with substantive agreements that do confirm that innovation is feasible—even if it rests on fragile foundations in both cases.

To conclude our look at traditional and transformational collective bargaining outcomes, consider a key overarching outcome—the direction in which the overall union management relationship is headed. As Table 8 illustrates, about a third of union–management pairs report that things are improving. However, managers are the more positive, with an increasing proportion of managers reporting improvement. While the trend line for managers is in the positive direction, an increasing number of union respondents indicate worsening relationships and a decline in relationships that are improving. Consider also that 31.3% of union respondents report, in response to a separate question, that their relationship itself is somewhat or very adversarial, while just 15.6% of their counterpart managers have the same view.

Thus, we have a number of union–management pairs who have divergent views of the current state of their relationships and the direction of change. The majority, however, report that the relationship is not changing. If the relationship is in fact serving the interests of both parties, this could be a stable, beneficial situation. If, however, there are problems, as the earlier analysis suggests, the lack of change makes things even more problematic.

The overall perceptions reported in Table 8 are broken out by region in Table 9, and the patterns are highly variable. These data, which are from only the 2003 survey, indicate a much more positive view of the direction of change by both union and management in the New England region. There are also, however, a high proportion of union leaders in New England and on the West Coast who report that things are getting worse in their relationships—a much higher proportion than their counterparts in management. One finding that is particularly interesting is the high proportion of union respondents reporting improving relations in right-to-work states. In fact, only 10.2% of the union respondents in the right-to-work states report that their relationship is somewhat or very adversarial, which contrasts with 30.8% of union respondents in New England, 40.8% in the Midwest, and 51.2% on the West Coast.

TABLE 8
Perceived Direction of Change in Labor–Management Relations, Cited by Matched
Pairs of Union and Management Negotiators in
U.S. Private Sector Collective Bargaining

	Union, 1996 (%)	Union, 1999 (%)	Union, 2003 (%)	Management, 1996 (%)	Management, 1999 (%)	Management, 2003 (%)
Relationship improving	29.0	32.7	22.0	29.0	34.5	35.7
Relationship not changing	64.0	59.5	66.6	62.0	60.5	62.8
Relationship getting worse	7.0	7.8	11.4	9.0	5.0	1.5

Source: Analysis conducted with data from the FMCS National Performance Review Surveys of 1996, 1999, and 2003. Access to the survey instrument and the data is available on request from the authors, with approval from the FMCS.

Overall, there is important variation over time in perceptions about collective bargaining between union and management and across regions. Moreover, the trends are not favorable for this institution. It is not achieving the ninth inning production needed when it comes to the basics or when it comes to innovation, our first two metaphorical batters. We now turn to our third and final player—the new challenges facing the institution.

Collective Bargaining in Challenging Circumstances: Two Whiffs, a Bunt Single, a Double, and (At Last!) a Home Run

To highlight the complex dynamics that underlie the survey data, we will focus on five very challenging circumstances that push at the limits of collective bargaining as an institution: the representation of collective workforce interests in the context of a bankruptcy, contested first-contract negotiations, the sale of assets, an interest-based approach to negotiations on health care issues, and the effort to transform the bargaining process on a massive scale. For chapter co-author Steve Sleigh, the first three situations occupy enormous time and resources for his union, the International Association of Machinists and Aerospace Workers (IAM). Case examples will be presented for each of these situations. Two represent what might be considered complete failures, where the process has struck out. In a third example, bargaining produced a better outcome than a nonnegotiated settlement but still was very difficult for all parties—in baseball terms, a bunt single, where a bad situation has been made into something at least workable. The fourth example, the interest-based bargaining and health care negotiations case, might be

TABLE 9
Perceived Direction of Change, by Region, Cited by Matched Pairs of Union and Management Negotiators in U.S. Private Sector Collective Bargaining

	Union, New England[a] (%)	Union, Midwest[b] (%)	Union, West Coast[c] (%)	Union, right-to-work[d] states (%)	Management, New England[a] (%)	Management, Midwest[b] (%)	Management, West Coast[c] (%)	Management, right-to-work states[d] (%)
Relationship improving	42.2	9.6	11.1	48.1	52.5	28.2	32.3	31.7
Relationship not changing	41.1	82.2	71.8	48.1	47.5	69.0	68.1	68.3
Relationship getting worse	16.7	8.2	17.1	3.8	0.0	2.8	1.6	0.0

[a]New England is defined as Connecticut, Massachusetts, Maine, New Hampshire, New Jersey, New York, Pennsylvania, Rhode Island, and Vermont.

[b]Midwest is defined as Iowa, Illinois, Indiana, Michigan, Minnesota, Missouri, Ohio, and Wisconsin.

[c]West Coast is defined as California, Colorado, Montana, Nevada, Oregon, and Washington.

[d]Right-to-work states include Alabama, Arizona, Arkansas, Florida, Georgia, Idaho, Iowa, Kansas, Louisiana, Mississippi, Nebraska, Nevada, North Carolina, North Dakota, Oklahoma, South Dakota, Tennessee, Texas, Utah, Virginia, and Wyoming.

Source: Analysis conducted with data from the FMCS National Performance Review Survey of 2003. Access to the survey instrument and the data is available on request from the authors, with approval from the FMCS.

considered a double, and the transformation of the bargaining process on a massive scale may qualify as a home run.

Case 1: Bankruptcy Negotiations

Companies who file for Chapter 11 bankruptcy seek to reorganize and continue the business. Chapter 11 proceedings are meant to give the debtor company relief from creditors and give it time to come up with a plan of reorganization. In return, creditors, including unions with significant economic claims on the business, have privileged positions on a committee that gets to oversee the reorganization process. However, normal collective bargaining is thrown out the window by the presiding bankruptcy judge, who is charged with maximizing the value of the company as an ongoing concern. While negotiated settlements between labor, management, and other interested parties are preferred by the bankruptcy judge, the gavel belongs to the judge alone. Without a negotiated settlement the judge may terminate existing agreements and impose new terms.

Since September 11, 2001, nearly half of the commercial airlines in the United States have gone into Chapter 11 bankruptcy at one point or another. The combined effects of an economic downturn that became a recession, public fear of flying post-9/11, and the rapid rise of fuel prices created a sea of red ink that continues to hit the commercial airlines. "Bargaining" in such a situation is well described by two of co-author Sleigh's colleagues at the IAM:

> Faced with the choice of agreeing to a pay cut and keeping the other protections of the union contract, or having the agreement abrogated and thereby experiencing a pay cut and losing all other protections of a union contract, it should not be surprising that workers will "agree to" even draconian cuts in pay; the alternative is even worse (Roach and Almeida 2005).

In the airline industry, as with the steel industry earlier and auto parts manufacturing currently, Chapter 11–inspired labor cost cutting in one firm has led to a pattern of competitive price reductions that put pressure on other companies to cut their costs in order to survive. Once one firm in a competitive industry has a price advantage, others clamor for the same cuts. The spiral downward is hard to stop. After years of trying to "take wages out of competition," wages and benefits reductions are very much back in play: in baseball parlance, a strikeout.

Case 2: First-Contract Negotiations

The decline of union density is well documented, falling from nearly 40% of the private sector workforce in the 1950s to under 8%

today. As a result, more and more unions have come to understand that organizing new members is imperative to survival. Organizing workers who are fearful of employer retaliation is extremely difficult. Still, many employees do exercise their fundamental right to have a voice at work and, as the labor movement has promoted it, say "Union Yes!" Unfortunately, once a majority of workers make that statement, the battle for a collective bargaining agreement has just begun. For example, in December 2003 the IAM organized and won a representation election for the nearly 600 production employees at New Piper Aircraft in Vero Beach, Florida. Negotiations for a first contract commenced immediately and continued for nearly nine months. In August 2004, the IAM and New Piper were close to an agreement, but then not one, not two, but three hurricanes passed over, around, and through the New Piper facility.

For the next four months negotiations were put on hold as the company sought to rebuild its shattered factory. Negotiations restarted in January 2005, but little progress was made over the next six months. It was clear to observers that the company had determined that the longer it took to get an agreement the less support the union would have. In June 2005, the IAM informed New Piper that they were taking the last proposal made to the membership for a vote. That little bit of leverage forced the company to bargain seriously, and it made modest improvements for a proposed three-year agreement. Just prior to sending the proposed agreement to the employees for ratification, however, a decertification petition was filed. The contract was ratified, but the National Labor Relations Board ruled that a contract bar was in force since a ratified agreement was not in place at the time the petition was filed. In March 2006, more than 27 months after the union was elected by the employees to represent them, the IAM narrowly lost the decertification election.

This is just one case example, but it vividly illustrates a combination of management delays, unfortunate business circumstances, and the limits of traditional power tactics, all of which can undermine first-contract negotiations. When these first contracts prove hard to achieve, the very ability of collective bargaining to perpetuate itself is at risk. Despite many policy recommendations on this issue,[14] there has been gridlock at a federal level for many decades. In that sense, this is a metaphorical whiff, not just for this case, but also for the efforts to constructively engage this issue at a policy level.

Case 3: Negotiating an Asset Sale

The first two examples of "bargaining" in today's environment represent misses or whiffs for the union and workers they represent. The third example is a case of taking lemons and making lemonade, or at least something closer to acceptable! In the summer of 2004 the Boeing Company announced that it was putting its largest manufacturing facility for commercial airplanes up for sale. The Wichita, Kansas, facility was the biggest in a series of asset sales that Boeing had initiated three years earlier with the sale of its St. Louis manufacturing facility. The IAM and the engineers unit of the International Federation of Professional and Technical Employees (IFPTE) represented nearly 9,000 employees at the giant aerospace manufacturing facility.

After a competitive process the sale was awarded to an investment firm from Canada, the Onex Corporation, with little aerospace or manufacturing experience. A condition of the sale was successful negotiations with the IAM and IFPTE. Another condition was very aggressive cost savings back to Boeing. To achieve those savings Onex proposed significant reductions in pay rates, more shifting of health care costs to employees, the elimination of defined benefit pensions, and a host of other concessions.

After two months of negotiations a proposal was taken to IAM members that included many of these concessions. The proposal was rejected after a raucous meeting of nearly 4,000 very angry workers who were about to become former Boeing employees. The IAM and Onex then went into extended negotiations and came up with an innovative stock option program that would offset the wage reductions, and perhaps more, if the new company met or exceeded certain financial targets. With a new proposal in hand, and with a long-term commitment by Onex to grow the business, including participation in the IAM's multiemployer pension plan, IAM members overwhelmingly ratified the new agreement. The new company, Spirit Aerosystem, is a work in progress but so far largely a positive one. This may count as a bunt single in our metaphorical ball game.

Case 4: Interest-Based Bargaining and Health Care Cost Containment

Benefits issues—particularly health care—are having a paralyzing impact on collective bargaining negotiations around the country. The issue is, of course, larger than the unionized sector of the economy. As Peter J. Hurtgen, former director of the FMCS, observed, "Don't use the word 'solution' and the words 'health care' in the same sentence." Nonetheless, parties are finding themselves having to fashion responses to these larger forces at the bargaining unit, facility, or enterprise levels. Our fourth case illustrates how these dynamics intrude in efforts to use an interest-based, problem-solving approach to bargaining.

The case involves DTE, the gas and electric utility that serves southeast Michigan and other parts of that state, which was bargaining in

2004 with Local 223 of the Utility Workers (representing over 4,700 employees in a mix of trade, office professional, and gas operations). Well in advance of negotiations, the parties agreed to approach bargaining using what is termed an "interest-based" approach—avoiding locking in on positions and instead focusing on finding mutual gains agreements that address the underlying interests of each party. The context was challenging—there had been deregulation in the utility sector of the state, three separate contracts (for the electric, gas, and office professional workforces) were being combined into a single master agreement, and health care costs had been increasing (and the represented workforces were making minimal contributions to this cost).

The interest-based approach was evident at the outset in the establishment of six joint committees: contract consolidation, health and welfare benefits, pension/savings plan, safety, sick absence, and technology and training. This approach was enabled by joint training for both bargaining committees and for other key individuals on both sides who were likely to be involved in the negotiations as internal subject-matter experts or key stakeholders. The process itself involved the use of an external facilitation team[15] and a formal structure for examining each issue that included statement of the issue, review of relevant data, brainstorming on the interests of each side, brainstorming on options to consider, and then bargaining to agreement (taking into account the interests and the options).

Using this approach, the parties achieved mutual gains agreements on issues such as job security, safety, new technology, attendance, bidding on new jobs, the operation of the grievance procedure, workforce planning, and disability/workers compensation. In exploring the attendance issue, for example, the parties surfaced a common set of interests connecting attendance to work–family issues facing a population of many younger single mothers working in telephone call centers. On the issue of job security, management had prepared for union demands to limit subcontracting, but instead found itself engaged in a dialogue introduced by the union with the following opening questions from local president Jim Harrison:

> How can we ensure long-range workforce planning and implementation, increases in productivity, and utilization of represented employees? How can we ensure that our local union members are the workforce of priority and choice for this company?

Instead of a positional contest around potential subcontracting restrictions, the parties talked frankly about the strengths and limitations of the represented workforce relative to contractors. This led to agreements on advance union notification and input prior to outsourcing and contracting of work regularly and customarily done in the bargaining unit, but it also led to broader dialogue and action on work rules, flexibility, and other related matters. The parties also reached agreements supporting continuous improvement on safety, advance notice and skills training on new technology, improved processes for job bidding and posting, introduction of a problem-solving oriented approach to grievances, and a commitment to hire 350 new bargaining unit employees.

The problem-solving orientation became complicated, however, as the parties took on the issue of health care. The union came into the negotiations knowing that an increased contribution would be needed from its members to help defray what had been escalating costs that were all being absorbed by the employer. Still, the long list of desired adjustments in plans, benefits, and contributions suggested by the employer was both confusing and overwhelming to the bargaining committee. They were fearful that any such agreement would not be ratifiable. Further, there were continued complications around the quality of available data on the health care costs and usage rates. All of this had the parties making little progress on this critical issue for a few days, until the union surfaced an unexpected option. They proposed that members contribute a percentage of pay (1% for single employees, 1.5% for married employees, and 2% for married employees with children)—a simple formulation that was not hard to communicate, that had an equity component and a growth component, and that generated a substantial portion of the revenue that management sought. As the current director of human relations, Dennis Dabney, commented, "This was not anything that we had considered. Even though there was hard bargaining on this issue, the idea would not have surfaced if it weren't for the interest-based process that we have been following on other issues." Additional revenues were generated with a disease management program, plan consolidation, incentives for preventive care, health education, and many other adjustments.

Still, as the contract expiration approached, management was still seeking additional savings due to the intensified competitive context, while the union felt that there was not much more to give. In one emotional moment, the union listed dozens of joint productivity initiatives over the past decade that represented many millions of dollars of savings—all of which would be at risk due to member resentment of an overly concessionary agreement. The senior vice president of operations at the time, Ron May, confirmed the validity of the savings associated with all of these projects, making the moment even more poignant. Ultimately, the parties brought the wage issue into the discussion—a risky move if an agreement couldn't be reached. At the eleventh hour, an agreement was reached that allowed for some additional employee contributions (which provided benefit savings valued by the company and which also featured caps to limit total employee liability). These contributions were offset with an additional wage increase of approximately 1% in the first year (which was highly valued by the workforce). At this point, it was straight hard bargaining, but an agreement was finally achieved.

As an epilogue to the case, the parties found themselves six months into the new agreement, but with many provisions that were not being fully implemented. As a result, they established nine joint implementation teams and agreed that the full bargaining committees would meet every six months to take responsibility in an oversight capacity for these implementation efforts. After a year of joint implementation efforts, following a standardized joint alignment and implementation process, more than half of the agreements have been fully implemented, and the others are in various stages of review and action. The efforts have been recently complicated as industrial pressures are driving management to contemplate restructuring of some business operations. In terms of our baseball metaphor, the DTE story may count as a double—a success in applying a problem-solving process to bargaining, as well as a constructive engagement of health care issues, but continuing challenges in the linkage at strategic and workplace levels.

Case 5: Transformation of Negotiations on a Massive Scale[16]

Kaiser Permanente provides healthcare services to 8.2 million people in 18 states, which involves 30 medical centers, 431 medical offices, 11,000 physicians, and 110,000 employees who are represented by 10 different unions (with the Service Employees International Union [SEIU] being the largest). Beginning in 1996, a coalition of the unions came together with management out of recognition that deteriorating adversarial relations had the potential to be mutually destructive. A partnership was established, involving unions representing 81,000 employees (the two largest groups to stay out of the partnership are the northern California nurses and the Hawaii unions). Today, this partnership structure is organized around the framework in Figure 2.

While the initial partnership activities were not focused on collective bargaining, the 2000 negotiations were seen by both sides as a pivotal event. A comprehensive, interest-based approach was fashioned, which involved the coordination of timing for 31 separate local agreements and the establishment of a master national agreement. There were a total of approximately 200 union representatives and 200 management

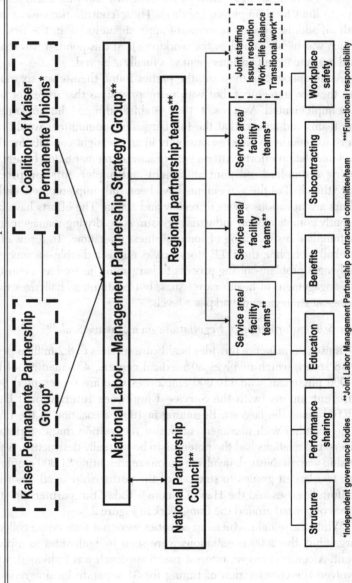

FIGURE 2
Kaiser Permanente Partnership Structure

Kaiser Permanente Partnership Group*

Coalition of Kaiser Permanente Unions*

National Labor—Management Partnership Strategy Group**

National Partnership Council**

Regional partnership teams**

Service area/facility teams**

Service area/facility teams**

Service area/facility teams**

Joint staffing
Issue resolution
Work—life balance
Transitional work***

Structure

Performance sharing

Education

Benefits

Subcontracting

Workplace safety

*Independent governance bodies   **Joint Labor Management Partnership contractual committee/team   ***functional responsibility

60

representatives in the subsequent 2001 negotiations. Their efforts were organized around seven major committees, each with various subcommittees. More than 20 external facilitators were engaged, some from the private firm Restructuring Associates and some from the FMCS.

The process initially faced skepticism by many on both sides, but that shifted as brainstorming surfaced many innovative options, which then led to agreements that were unprecedented in the healthcare sector. For example, the parties reached agreements on joint processes for tracking medical errors and near-misses—issues virtually taboo in the industry—as well as constructive processes for preventing recurrence. New language was agreed to on work–life issues, ongoing information sharing, technology adjustment, training and skills development, and performance sharing.

Other notable achievements in the early year of the partnership were the joint design and planning for the opening of a new hospital (Baldwin Park) below cost and on schedule; negotiation to restructure, save from closing, and turn around the performance of the Northern California Optical Laboratory; and the signing of an employment security and workforce adjustment agreement.

Following the 2000 negotiations, the parties took many of the ideas that surfaced in brainstorming during bargaining and began pursuing them as local partnership activities. Figure 3 provides an illustrative list of some of these projects. In each case, the project involves joint representatives and a structured process for problem solving. While these and

FIGURE 3
A Sample of More than 300 Local Partnership Activities Identified by Kaiser Permanente and the Coalition of Unions (with Geographic Area Indicated)

Workplace Safety (all regions)	Patient Safety (all regions)
SOS Committee (most regions)	Documentation Task Force (CO)
CARS Steering Committee (CO)	Music Guidelines (CO)
Chrysler Workgroup (CO)	Local Recognition Committee (CO)
Advice LMP Committee (MAS)	Tech Training Committee (NW)
Floor Staffing (NW)	After Hours Coverage (NW)
Social Design (NW)	EVS-Dirty Linen (NW)
Attendance Project (most regions)	Ambulatory Redesign (OH)
Work-Life Balance (OH)	Violence in the Workplace (OH)
Nursing Pathways (SCAL)	Optimal Office Practices (SCAL)
Service Excellence (SCAL)	Parking Task Force (SCAL)
Nursing Quality Improvement (SCAL)	New Model of Care Team (NCAL)
Bilingual Program (NCAL)	Supply Costs/Management (NCAL)
Contact Lens Assessment (NCAL)	Organizational Pride (NCAL)

other topics are highly compelling, the implementation of the 2001 agreement has been highly variable, with some projects producing notable successes and others falling short of expectations.

Negotiations of a second interest-based agreement took place in 2005, again with more than 400 representatives and the negotiation of a national master agreement, followed by various local agreements. Once again, a large group of facilitators has supported the process. This time, greater attention to implementation of provisions for improving performance, service quality, attendance, and other aspects of healthcare delivery has been integrated into the bargaining. What is most notable, however, is the continuity in approach relative to the first round of interest-based bargaining. While the ongoing relationship and negotiations will still benefit from continuous improvement efforts, the many dimensions of success lead us to classify this as a home run relative to the baseball metaphor. It may still be a long way from winning the game, but this is certainly a landmark negotiation.

Conclusions

We conclude this chapter with a final metaphorical batter still at the plate—and having a very tough at-bat. These five brief vignettes have highlighted the changed nature of collective bargaining today. In two examples, bankruptcy and first-contract negotiations, bargaining is a misnomer. There is no equality of power, no incentive for management to settle, and little reason for management to engage in the process. In the third example, an asset sale, the purchaser wanted the entity, so they were motivated to achieve a negotiated settlement. Of course the alternative for the union and workforce, a plant closure, made the union much more motivated to reach a negotiated settlement. In two additional examples we saw that innovation is possible and linkages to the strategic and workplace levels can be made.

To be clear, not all bargaining fits in these five categories. The IAM, which we drew on as a source for the first three case examples, negotiates nearly 1,000 agreements a year across a wide spectrum of industries and companies, both large and small and everything in between. The vast majority of these are not done in bankruptcy, as a first contract, or as an asset sale. While the IAM is proactive in supporting high-performance work systems where partnership structures can be established, these too do not represent the vast majority of negotiations. Still, the decline of union density, coupled with the lack of standing, experience, or enforcement of existing collective bargaining processes and the absence of a large volume of innovative efforts, has seriously eroded the institution of collective bargaining.

Public policy, in this case, has shortchanged collective bargaining. The patterns set in bankruptcy, first-contract negotiations, and asset sales impact all other bargaining. Without proper standing in bankruptcy or a meaningful requirement to reach agreement in either first contract or asset sales, collective bargaining becomes a one-sided affair with workers and unions on the short end of the deal.

We have seen that transformation of the U.S. industrial relations system depends on a combination of innovative substantive outcomes and constructive process improvements. These are found in only a minority of labor–management relationships. The process is moderately efficient in delivering on these innovations—when they are proposed—but not sufficiently so as to drive broad-scale transformation. Regional variation suggests that there may not be one single set of problems or solutions for collective bargaining in the United States. While some of the quantitative and qualitative findings presented in this chapter are certainly a product of the recent economic downturn, there is no question that we are also witnessing deterioration in the private sector. That is not to say there are no bright spots. For example, in case 3, we highlighted the success that IAM had in negotiating novel agreements using a stock option program to offset wage reductions, while cases 4 and 5 featured innovative process and substance in two high-profile situations. Similar examples can be found (for example) in efforts by unions to get board member seats, rights of first refusal on asset sales, successorship guarantees, and related matters.[17] Time will tell whether these strategies lead to successful outcomes for workers, employers, and communities. While union membership is shrinking overall, it should be noted that unions like the Service Workers International have become increasingly successful in organizing both smaller workplaces and those sectors of the economy undergoing the most rapid growth. The success in new sectors of the economy, and workforces that historically have proven hard to unionize, may prove to be another point of growth in this institutional landscape.

The decline in collective bargaining in the private sector raises serious questions about the voice of workers in today's workplace. While it has been argued that new work practices such as team work and quality improvement activities provide alternative mechanisms for workers to exert voice in their work lives, these do not constitute the collective input or the role supported and enabled by the institution of collective bargaining. In 1951 George Taylor warned that "the successful use of collective bargaining was dependent upon union and the management voluntarily giving reasonable weight to the broad public interest. . . . A general 'ganging up on the consumer' would be incompatible with the development of collective bargaining as a socially desirable institution" (Taylor 1951). Taylor's concern was that the parties would become too powerful at the bargaining table. While there is still the question of the public interest, today it shows up in new ways—such as teacher agreements with school boards that specifically address ways to improve educational outcomes, or police and fire agreements with municipalities that specifically address ways to improve public safety, or industrial agreements that specifically address environmental, quality, and other concerns, or healthcare agreements that specifically address issues such as medical errors, or agreements in any sector that specifically address work–life matters. In these types of agreements, the parties are utilizing the forum of collective bargaining to reach beyond issues of wages, hours, and working conditions and signal a mutual commitment to broader social concerns. Whether by these means or other methods, the key to seeing collective bargaining come out of this metaphorical ball game a winner will be its again achieving the status that George Taylor signaled—that of a socially desirable institution.

Notes

[1] Steve Sleigh formerly was with the International Association of Machinists and Aerospace Workers and is currently with The Yucaipa Companies.

[2] As we focus on a critical U.S. institution, we hope that the baseball metaphor adds a helpful counterpoint. We also note that for the first time since 1970, baseball players and management in 2002 reached a collective bargaining agreement without a strike or walkout—perhaps a good omen for collective bargaining as the line blurs between the baseball metaphor and the baseball reality.

[3] We are grateful to Betty Barrett for her insights on the absence of unions—of which this is one part.

[4] George Taylor, who went on to become a top industrial relations adviser to five U.S. presidents, made this comment at a Wharton Roundtable Conference in 1938.

[5] Many historians emphasize the social construction of institutional arrangements, noting alternative paths taken in other nations with very different consequences. See, for example, the way that Thomas Hughes (1993) traces the very different approaches to electrification in the United States and England.

[6] Unionization in the United States is at an all-time low of 12.5% in 2005 compared to 1953, when approximately one third of the workforce was represented by unions. The unionization rate of private sector employees is at 7.8%. (U.S. Department of Labor 2006). It is notable, however, that over 225,000 new workers were organized in 2005, stabilizing the unionization rate at the level of 2004.

[7] See, in particular, Robert Michels ([1915] 1962) and the key insights from what is termed the new institutionalism literatures in organizational behavior, sociology, and economics (for example, Powell and DiMaggio 1991).

[8] This portion of the chapter draws on the same data as our companion article, which come from a series of three stratified, national random-sample surveys of

matched pairs of private sector union and management negotiators. (For final reports on the surveys, see Kochan and Cutcher-Gershenfeld 1997; Kochan and Cutcher-Gershenfeld 2000; and Kochan, Cutcher-Gershenfeld, and Ferguson 2004.) The surveys were commissioned by the FMCS and conducted using a telephone survey protocol administered by the University of Massachusetts Survey Research Center in 1996, 1999, and 2003, with the sample drawn from the 30-day notices that parties provide to the FMCS before their contracts expire. In the 1996 survey, 1,557 union and management representatives (1,050 of them matched pairs) were interviewed between October and December, with a 74% response rate. In the 1999 survey, 2,004 union and management representatives (1,654 of them matched pairs) were interviewed between July and October. A subsample of over 400 public sector negotiations were surveyed in the handful of states where federal mediators also provide mediation support for state-level public sector bargaining units. In the 2003 survey, 1,718 union and management representatives (1,168 of them matched pairs) were interviewed between October 2003 and January 2004, with over 400 cases drawn from public sector and federal sector settings. A three-year sampling window was selected since the average contract duration is three years. In each round of data collection, we oversampled large employers and parties that had used mediation services. All results reported in this chapter are weighted to take into account the oversampling.

[9] See *Collective Bargaining in the 21st Century: A Negotiations Institution at Risk*, the companion article prepared for a general negotiations audience (Cutcher-Gershenfeld et al. 2006).

[10] While union and management gave similar responses on whether there was a wage increase, there was much more variation in their perceptions of whether there was a benefit increase, a perceptual difference that we examine in more detail shortly. In the 1996 and 1999 surveys, approximately 70% of union respondents and 55% of management counterparts reported a benefit increase. In 2003 the numbers were 45% and 43%, respectively—closer agreement between labor and management, but also a fall-off comparable to that found with wage increases.

[11] Note that in almost all instances, there are a number of matched pairs where one side reports an outcome that the other does not. This prompted follow-up calls to respondents, through which we learned that the disparities primarily reflect different perceptions of the same agreement. For example, a union respondent may report increased job security based on some provisions that are seen as enhancing it (such as a commitment to make new investments by management), while management will report having not made any specific job security guarantee. Similar dynamics were found on many items. As a result, some analysis of the data has involved a focus only on the cases where both sides agree that a provision was in the contract.

[12] The specific complications of negotiating in the face of bankruptcy will be addressed below.

[13] Also note that the fraction of workforce in teams is based only on plants with teams. The extent of job rotation is scored on a 1 to 5 scale, and the rotation policies are ordered as follows: 1. Workers are trained to do one job and do not rotate to other jobs; 2. workers are capable of doing other work tasks in their work group (or teams if teams are present), but generally do not rotate jobs; 3. workers rotate jobs frequently within their group, but not outside their group; 4. workers rotate jobs within their work groups and across work groups in the same department (body, paint, and assembly), but not across departments; and 5. workers rotate jobs within the work group,

across work groups, and across departments. Responsibility for quality control looks at four areas of responsibility: incoming parts, work-in-progress, finished products, and charting statistical process control (SPC) data. At one end of the spectrum, quality control staff can undertake these activities. At the other end of the spectrum, production workers (or no one) can do them. Other options include skilled trades, first line supervisors, and engineering staff.

[14] See, for example, U.S. Departments of Commerce and Labor 1994.

[15] Co-author Joel Cutcher-Gershenfeld served as lead facilitator, along with Betty Barrett.

[16] For more detail on this case, see McKersie, Eaton, and Kochan (2003) and McKersie, Kochan, et al. (2006).

[17] Examples of strategic linkages can be found, for example, in the United Steel Workers agreement with the International Steel Group. An example of the impact of parent guarantees is currently playing out with Delphi. GM consolidated its automotive components group into Delphi as a separate business unit within GM. In 1997, GM began disclosing separate financial information for the entity, and in 1998 incorporated it. GM spun off Delphi in 1999. GM's CEO at the time, John Smith, agreed to protect the interests of Delphi workers affected by the spinoff. In particular, GM provided assurances on postretirement benefits in the event Delphi ran into financial difficulty. This is proving to be extraordinarily costly for GM since Delphi entered chapter 11 in October 2005.

References

Cutcher-Gershenfeld, Joel, Thomas Kochan, John-Paul Ferguson, and Betty Barrett. 2006. *Collective Bargaining in the 21st Century: A Negotiations Institution at Risk*. Cambridge: MIT Working Paper.

Holweg, M., and F.K. Pil. 2004. *The Second Century*. Cambridge, MA: MIT Press.

Hughes, Thomas, 1993. *Networks of Power: Electrification in Western Society, 1880–1930*. Baltimore: Johns Hopkins University Press.

Kochan, Thomas A. 2005. *Restoring the American Dream: A Working Families' Agenda for America*. Cambridge, MA: MIT Press.

Kochan, Thomas A., and Joel Cutcher-Gershenfeld. 1997. *Final Report to the Federal Mediation and Conciliation Service on the National Performance Review Survey*. Washington, D.C.

————. 2000. *Final Report to the Federal Mediation and Conciliation Service on the Second National Performance Review Survey*. Washington, D.C.

Kochan, Thomas A., Joel Cutcher-Gershenfeld, and John-Paul Ferguson. 2004. *Final Report to the Federal Mediation and Conciliation Service on the Third National Performance Review Survey*. Washington, D.C.

Kochan, Thomas A., Harry C. Katz, and Robert B. McKersie. 1986. *The Transformation of American Industrial Relations*. New York: Basic Books.

MacDuffie, J.P., and F.K. Pil. 1997. "High-Involvement Work Practices and Human Resource Policies: An International Perspective." in T. Kochan, R. Lansbury, and J.P. MacDuffie, eds., *Evolving Employment Practices in the World Auto Industry*. Ithaca, NY: Cornell University Press, pp. 9–44.

McKersie, Robert, Susan Eaton, and Thomas Kochan. 2003. "Interest-Based Negotiations at Kaiser Permanente." MIT Sloan Working Paper No. 4312-03; Institute for Work & Employment Research Paper No. 05-2003.

McKersie, Robert, Thomas A. Kochan, Teresa Sharpe, Adrienne Eaton, George Strauss, and Mary Morgenstern. 2006. *Negotiating in Partnership: A Case Study of the 2005 National Negotiations at Kaiser Permanente*. Cambridge: MIT Sloan School of Management.

Michels, Robert. [1915] 1962. *Political Parties: A Sociological Study of the Oligarchical Tendencies of Modern Democracy*. New York: Dover.

Pil, F.K., and J.P. MacDuffie. 1999. "Organizational and Environmental Factors Influencing the Use of High-Involvement Work Practices." In P. Cappelli, ed., *Employment Strategies—Understanding Differences in Employment Practices*. New York: Oxford University Press.

Powell, Walter W., and Paul J. DiMaggio, eds. 1991. *The New Institutionalism in Organizational Analysis*. Chicago: University of Chicago Press.

Roach, Robert Jr., and Beth Almeida. 2005. "Response to *Airborne Distress*." *New Labor Forum*, Vol. 14, no. 2 (Summer), pp. 60–62.

Shils, Edward B., Walter J. Gershenfeld, Bernard Ingster, and William M. Weinberg. 1979. *Industrial Peacemaker: George W. Taylor's Contributions to Collective Bargaining*. Philadelphia: University of Pennsylvania Press.

Taylor, George. 1951. "National Labor Policy." *Annals of the American Academy of Political and Social Science*, Vol. 247 (March), pp. 185–194.

U.S. Department of Labor. 2006. *Union Member Survey* (USDL 06-99). January 20.

U.S. Departments of Commerce and Labor. 1994. *Fact Finding Report of the Commission on the Future of Worker Management Relations*. Washington, DC: GPO.

CHAPTER 3

The Political Economy of Employment Relations in the European Union

BERNDT K. KELLER
University of Konstanz

In this paper, selected issues of internationalization will be conceptualized as processes and problems of regional rather than global integration. In contrast to other regional economic blocs, such as NAFTA (the North American Free Trade Association), ASEAN (The Association of Southeast Asian Nations) and Mercosur, the European Union (EU) does not constitute solely a common market for services, goods, capital, and labor. Rather, the EU is also supposed to include a "social dimension" of its completed internal market or, in more recent political jargon, a specific "European social model." I deal with recent progress as well as remaining employment relations problems in developing and implementing the European social model, and I do so at the most relevant levels, namely, the company, or micro; the sectoral, or meso; and the interprofessional, or macro. The focus is the crucial interplay of national and European levels and not detailed comparisons of individual countries (i.e., member states). Thus, I do not intend to contribute to comparative industrial relations in a more traditional sense (Ferner and Hyman 1998), but instead focus exclusively on the supranational level. Similarly, my emphasis is not the historical aspects of European employment and industrial relations regulation but, rather, their present status and future perspectives.[1]

The major changes in the legal–institutional framework in general and in the specific modes of social regulation in particular are given special weight. In this regard, several regulatory regimes and stages of development, which partially overlap, have to be distinguished:

- regulatory minimalism and irrelevance of social policy and employment relations that prevailed in the 1950s and 1960s

- politically motivated strategies of strict and encompassing harmonization at the upper level of already existing national standards that dominated throughout the 1970s and until the mid-1980s
- more heterogeneous concepts of mutual recognition of standards existing at the national level and the setting of only statutory minimum European requirements and standards, which were supposed to be voluntarily surpassed at subordinate national, sectoral, or company levels, which were the most important principles operating between the late 1980s and mid-1990s
- the open method of coordination, which defines only very broad and general goals and depends on transnational coordination and which has been the leading regulatory paradigm in various policy fields since the late 1990s

The complicated interplay between processes of deregulation and liberalization at the national level and institution building at the European level constitutes the key for understanding the slow emergence of a specific system of what has frequently been called "multilevel governance." The principle of "subsidiarity," which has been revitalized for political reasons and was enshrined into the EU Treaty (Article 5) in the 1990s, has developed into the nucleus of the new core concept. It gives strict priority to purely voluntary framework agreements or collective contracts over any kind of legislative action, stresses the prime responsibility of the social partners instead of EU corporate actors for the establishment of regulatory rules, and favours strict decentralization of competencies at lower national, regional, and company levels over centralized decisions at the supranational level.[2]

There are various kinds of European measures and instruments—for example, regulation, directive, and recommendation—that differ fundamentally in their degree of binding power. As far as employment relations are concerned, the legal instrument of directives is of major importance. In reality, these binding means face not only well-known usual problems, but additional protracted problems as well. In this regard, we have to explicitly differentiate between short-term transposition from the European to the national level and long-term implementation at the subordinate sectoral or company level. In clear contrast to more conventional analysis, we also have to acknowledge that these later stages of the policy process are of equal importance for assessing overall results and final success (Anderson 2003). As one observer puts it, "Implementation may be seen not as a stage separated from policy-making, but rather as the continuation of policy formulation by other means. . . . [W]hat is technically implementation, constitutes the continuation of decision making, in the narrow sense, down to the lowest level because even the very basic standards of the Directive . . . may be reversed by enterprise-level agreement" (Falkner 1998:111). In other words, in later stages of the policy process, monitoring, evaluation of implementation procedures and results, and follow-up procedures are of major importance for the overall outcome to be taken into account and judged.

Directives have to be transposed from the European to the national level and become part of the *acquis communautaire*[3]; this procedure has to be finalized in a specified period, typically two to three years. Only after this necessary step has been completed can implementation procedures at the national level take place and establish rules for subordinate sectoral, regional, and company levels.[4] In contrast to fairly rigid regulations, directives are more flexible. One, they can consider existing legal and institutional differences between member states. Two, their specific, more informal customs and practices can be taken into consideration.

Furthermore, one must keep in mind that all kinds of European regulation have to be of a rather general nature or based on a broad common denominator because they cover markedly different systems of employment relations at subordinate levels. As a result, this necessary and integrated part of the overall political process provides national-level interest associations extensive opportunities for strategic maneuvering and political lobbying during the processes of decision making. These corporate actors are able to change the essence of European regulation to a considerable degree and adapt it not only to national peculiarities, customs, and practices, but also to their own specific interests. A high degree of heterogeneity is the likely result of these complex procedures.

The Micro Level: European Works Councils

The most important issue at the enterprise, or micro, level has definitely been worker participation in managerial decision making. Various regulations of employee involvement exist in the vast majority of EU member states, either on a legal or on a contractual basis. However, all these rules of corporate governance cover only the activities of enterprises within the boundaries of nation states. By definition, the rapidly growing number of multinational companies (MNCs) and their supranational activities cannot be included. Therefore, it was felt that a supplementary institution of collective "voice" was urgently needed for these key economic players at the supranational level.

In the early 1970s, first attempts at regulation sought to generalize one fairly developed type of worker participation at the national level and to introduce one, and only one, coherent, homogeneous system at the EU level. The well-known German system of joint decision making, or "codetermination," provided the blueprint. All these political efforts toward strict "harmonization" at the upper end of existing national standards were rather ambitious in their political motivation and far-reaching in their potential consequences. However, all of them failed completely because unanimous decisions were necessary in the Council of Ministers, which had to reach a final political conclusion, and member states were not willing to give up their specific legal–institutional frameworks and portions of their sovereign powers. Under this specific rule of political decision making, the veto power of individual member states was enormous and prevented any kind of transcendent European regulation, even as various efforts to find a common denominator were made throughout the 1970s and early 1980s (including the well-known Vredeling draft directives). The result was a complete and lasting political stalemate; this important issue was on the political agenda but not solved for many years.

First Phase: The Conclusion of Purely Voluntary Agreements

Since the mid-1980s, European works councils (EWCs) were established on a purely voluntary base. This took place only in a relatively small number of MNCs, first in state-owned French enterprises and later on in some other member states, such as Germany. The overall number of EWCs as institutions of joint regulation instead of unilateral decision making increased only slowly and never exceeded 30. This rather sluggish development taught the important political lesson that purely nonlegalistic, "neovoluntaristic" strategies of employment relations regulation cannot succeed in the long run; some type of mandatory (i.e., legislative) intervention was urgently needed (Hall et al. 1995).

Second Phase: The Directive and Politically Enforced Voluntarism

This lasting political stalemate was solved only after the Treaty on European Union—the so-called Maastricht Treaty—and its Protocol on Social Policy were adopted in late 1991. The "Council Directive 94/45/EC of 22 September 1994 on the establishment of a European Works Council or a procedure in Community-scale undertakings and Community-scale groups of undertakings for the purposes of informing and consulting employees" (European Council 1994) was adopted in September 1994 and had to be transposed by all member states within two years. The directive is valid for all MNCs independent of their country of origin's being a member state of the EU if they surpass the threshold of "at least 1000 employees within the Member States and at least 150 employees in each of at least two Member States" (Article 2).

Characteristic features of the directive are fundamental changes in the mode and instruments of regulation. In contrast to earlier, failed draft directives, this directive regulates only various procedural rather than substantive issues of employee involvement. Within this fundamental shift from materialization to proceduralization, all substantive arrangements have to be negotiated at the level of the individual MNC between the representatives of management and of labor. If these voluntary negotiations fail, certain minimum standards for a mandatory EWC, which are indicated in the so-called "subsidiary requirements" annexed to the directive, have to be introduced. Because of this primacy of negotiation, there is an enormous heterogeneity of rather different, quite flexible, tailor-made arrangements at the level of individual MNCs instead of the unitary, one-fits-all legal prescription one frequently finds at the level of individual member states.[5] Furthermore, in contrast to its predecessors, this new mode of regulation does not result in any kind of "upward harmonization" because it defines common minimum standards only and leaves ample room for the "management of diversity" at the enterprise level.

As already indicated, these statutory provisions have to be implemented within an indicated, limited period of time and can be surpassed on a strictly voluntary basis. The European Commission officially recommends voluntary agreements on higher standards of participation than the specified pure information and consultation, but it does not and cannot enforce their introduction at the level of individual MNCs; this new mode has been labeled "regulated self-regulation." It constitutes not the most ambitious but a fairly realistic approach toward social regulation.

Proponents of this new regulatory mode of defining statutory minimum standards ("Euro optimists") argued that it is rather innovative and promising in overcoming a long-lasting political stalemate and introducing the option to establish a flexible, genuine European body of representation with high potential for further development. Critics ("Euro pessimists") pointed out that this paradigm shift of regulation led not only to legislative minimalism, but to voluntary solutions at the lower end of already existing national regulation. Euro pessimists also observed the fact that more far-reaching rights beyond minimal opportunities for information and consultation exist only in a relatively small number of MNCs.

As noted earlier, directives constitute legally binding instruments of regulation that individual member states have to transpose from the European level to their respective national levels. They are free to choose specific means and instruments for transposition, but they have to stick to the specified time period—two years—and guarantee the complete coverage of employees. One of the major peculiarities of the EWC directive, which is somewhat difficult for non-Europeans to understand, is that all formerly concluded, purely voluntary agreements on information and consultation can be maintained without the existence of a legal basis if both sides agree to do so. This "favourability principle" applies to all agreements signed before September 1996— so-called Article 13 agreements—which was the specified end of the transposition phase. Within the relatively short period of two years there was a sudden, enormous increase in the overall number of concluded agreements to about 400.[6]

Third Phase: Legally Enforced EWCs

In obvious contrast to this unexpected rapid development during the transposition phase, only small numerical increases, so-called Article 6 agreements, have taken place since. These significant differences in quantitative growth can be explained by the fact that the procedural pre-conditions were less formalized and less complicated in the period before the directive became effective. Its Articles 5 and 6 specify in great detail all future procedures and prescribe, among other things, the establishment of a representative, special negotiating body (SNB) on the employees' side. The central management has to negotiate and conclude an agreement with this SNB on all relevant substantive details of information and consultation. Surprisingly enough, national and supranational unions (the European Industry Federations to be discussed later) are not explicitly mentioned in the directive. Nevertheless, they have played a prominent if not decisive role within these processes and have actively supported, if not launched, the establishment of numerous MNCs.

For various reasons it is difficult to provide precise numbers of MNCs and MNC employees covered by the directive. These numbers change because of corporate mergers and divestitures, but more basic is the underlying informational problem; there is no official reference source giving exact numbers of employees of individual companies.[7] Nevertheless, it appears that following the eastern enlargement of the EU in 2004, the total number of MNCs covered by the directive increased to about 2,200 (Kerckhofs 2006).

The somewhat surprising result after the first decade of the directive's existence is that the EWC agreement compliance rate, popularly known as the "strike rate," is only about one third of all MNCs and about two thirds of all MNC employees—the latter figure indicating that larger MNCs are considerably more likely than smaller ones to be in compli-

FIGURE 1
"A growing number of EWCs"

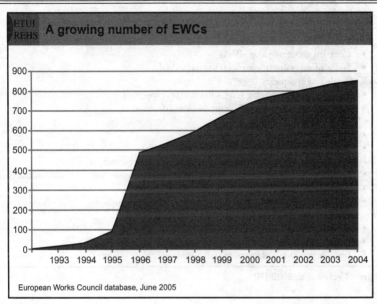

A growing number of EWCs

European Works Council database, June 2005

ance. Further, there are major differences in sectoral strike rates according to the extent of internationalization of production and strength of trade union organization (Marginson and Sisson 2004). All in all, one must conclude that serious and sometimes unexpected difficulties in developing and implementing EWCs still exist in the majority of cases. These varied difficulties, summarized in Table 1, operate on all sides of the table, so to speak, in that they include a lack of interest among employee representatives, lack of trade union capacity, and a low level of employer willingness to reach agreement.

One can argue, of course, that this type of quantitative analysis is neither sufficient nor illuminating because it does not tell us anything about the quality of employee involvement in managerial decision making. More qualitatively oriented comparative research in this area has focused on the everyday operation and activities of existing EWCs and has developed some preliminary EWC typologies (Lecher, Nagel, and Platzer 1999; Lecher et al. 2001, 2002). This work focuses on interactions between the EWC (employee representatives) and central management, between EWC members, between the EWC national employee interest representation and the workforce, and between the

TABLE 1

Factors Impeding EWC Initiatives

Lack of interest on the part of employee representatives
- Lack of knowledge
- Lack of Europeanization pressure
- Concern about negative effects
- Sense of excessive demands on the individual

Lack of trade union capacity
- Need to support existing EWCs has tied up capacities
- New prospects are more difficult and less attractive

Low level of employer willingness
- Declining number of employer initiatives
- Deterrent to workplace employee representatives

Absence of key preconditions in the field of employee representation
- Decentralized employee representation at national level
- Lack of effective employee representation
- Insufficient legal protection

Procedural factors
- Deterrent effect of complex procedure
- Difficulties in submitting application to employer
- Unclear provisions obstruct or stall initiatives

Source: Lecher et al. 2002:170.

(employee-side) EWC and trade unions. Within this analytical framework, four types are identified: the symbolic EWC, the service-oriented EWC, the project-oriented EWC, and the participation-oriented EWC. This typology does not represent a linear sequence but rather potential stages of development into more active and powerful bodies of interest representation; it also demonstrates the wide diversity of such bodies.[8]

In this regard, one must consider that the qualitative impact of employee representatives on management decision making has remained low in the vast majority of MNCs and has managed to surpass the minimum level of pure information and consultation only in a limited number of cases. More influential and powerful EWCs that could develop and become equal bargaining partners of central management are still the rare exception. So far only some have managed to negotiate about such "hard" issues as transnational corporate restructuring and outsourcing rather than focusing on such "soft" issues as codes of conduct. And European-level collective bargaining over so substantive an issue as wages remains elusive, even unrealistic.

In comparison with recent developments at the meso and macro levels, it may be argued that more progress toward a development of

"Europeanization" has been made at the enterprise level than at any other of the "multilevel" system of employment relations. To date, the directive on EWCs has been the most important institutional innovation and the first genuine institution of collective labor law at the European level. This is the basic reason why empirical research throughout the 1990s focused on EWC formation and potential future development of supranational forms of interest representation (Müller and Hoffmann 2001). Stated differently, EWCs constitute the most relevant social laboratory for transnational employment relations at the enterprise level.

This directive on EWCs should not be confused with another, more recent "Directive 2002/14/EC of the European Parliament and of the Council of 11 March 2002 establishing a general framework for informing and consulting employees in the European Community" (European Parliament and European Council 2002), which covers purely national companies with a certain minimum number of employees. It is remarkable to know that this directive's transposition and implementation has had major consequences only for a limited number of (old) member states, notably the United Kingdom and Ireland, which had not introduced legal or contractual regulation of employee information and consultation at the enterprise level (Hall et al. 2002; Sisson 2002). These varying institutional preconditions obviously demonstrate that not all member states necessarily face the same consequences of transposition and implementation in all individual cases of European framework regulation (Falkner et al. 2005). Furthermore, this variation explains the politically motivated resistance of some member states against any kind of European regulation that could lead to adaptation, let alone major changes in their national systems of employment relations.

In a related development, the more recent European Company Statute provides the option—but not the obligation—to establish a European company, called Societas Europaea (SE), to be governed by EC law instead of widely different national laws of individual member states. The potential savings of transaction costs that are presumed to take place in this regard appear to create strong incentives for the establishment of SEs despite the fact that a common taxation policy is missing. Moreover, this statute has been augmented by a "Council Directive 2001/86/EC of 8 October 2001 supplementing the Statute for a European company with regard to the involvement of employees" (European Council 2001) that specifies rules for various forms of compulsory employee involvement within the SE (Keller 2002). Despite these putative incentives, the overall number of officially registered SEs has remained quite low (European Industrial Relations Review 2005), and I will therefore continue to focus attention on EWCs.

Social Dialogues: Old Wine in New Bottles?

In various national contexts, social dialogues constitute frequently used instruments of policy making that attempt to include various private corporate actors (International Labour Organization 2006). Within the EU, this instrument, which is supposed to constitute a unique and indispensable component of the European social model, is of special importance for social policy in general and employment relations in particular. As far as corporate actors are concerned, it refers exclusively to the European peak association of management and labor—the "social partners" in Euro-jargon—and not to other actors in civil society, such as nongovernmental organizations (NGOs). Trilateral forms of the social dialogues include European public authorities, whereas bilateral forms encompass only the social partners. The same procedural arrangements can be applied at the macro (interprofessional) as well as at the meso (sectoral) level.

In contrast to occasional public statements and the politically motivated hopes of some, social dialogues should not be confused or identified with collective bargaining, which still occurs only at the national level. Strikes and lockouts as means of industrial action are explicitly excluded from social dialogues, and wages are not permitted to be a topic for negotiations within this specific EU legal framework (Article 137).

Certain recent attempts at purely voluntary transnational coordination of national collective bargaining can also be considered. These have taken place since the mid-1990s, but only on the union side and only in a few industries operating in cross-border regions (Schulten and Bispinck 2001). According to informally agreed-upon rules, nominal pay increases should be the sum of price increases and productivity growth. All in all, it seems fair to conclude that these efforts have not been overtly successful. Among others, they have been limited to a small number of countries and some selected sectors only (first of all, metalworking). At least some national unions have concluded collective agreements at lower increases than the core principle of productivity-oriented pay bargaining would suggest. Thus, they have deteriorated the opportunities of other unions.

From the perspective of labor unions, the introduction of the European Economic and Monetary Union (EMU) in the late 1990s altered the macroeconomic–institutional environment and increased the necessity of closer coordination in order to prevent downward pressure on working conditions in general and wages in particular. With the abolishing of national currencies, the former option of devaluation to increase competitiveness and to equalize asymmetric shocks ceased to exist. Further, labor market mobility in Europe has always been much lower than in other areas, notably the United States, and fiscal transfers between member states are legally excluded. Competitive pressures on national collective bargaining, especially wages and working hours, have thus increased significantly. In marked contrast to the vertical integration achievable through social dialogues, this strategy constitutes a specific form of horizontal coordination (Traxler 2003).

Social Dialogues at the Macro Level

First phase: The introduction of social dialogues in the mid-1980s. Social dialogues have taken place more frequently since the mid-1980s, initiated by Jacques Delors after he became president of the European Commission. He introduced them as new instruments of policy making in order to promote the "social dimension" of the single market (social dialogues "à la Val Duchesse"). The number of such dialogues increased slowly to about 40 "joint opinions" and covered a rather heterogeneous set of issues that went far beyond employment relations issues. All opinions or agreements resulting from these trilateral dialogues, which in contrast to some of the later stages always included the commission as a decisive third actor, were purely voluntary and had no binding consequences for the signatory parties. The complicated issues of transposition and implementation thus did not exist in this context.

The judgments of the social partners about this arrangement varied notably. Employers' organizations were quite satisfied with the arrangement because of its nonbinding nature, whereas unions tried hard to change its character fundamentally toward binding agreements. Supporters of the social dialogues continued to argue that they helped both parties get to know each other better and develop greater understanding of opposing positions, while critics emphasized that all results were nonbinding. This institutional arrangement of pure voluntarism continued into the next phase of development; however, this next phase was characterized by a greater incidence of binding agreements. (See Table 2 for a chronology of interprofessional social dialogues.)

Second phase: The Maastricht Social Protocol and Agreement. In the early 1990s, the commission fundamentally changed existing procedures of decision making. In particular it granted more autonomous rights and included the social partners more systematically in all processes of social policy formulation through social dialogue of a different nature. The Protocol on Social Policy and the Social Policy Agreement attached to the new Treaty on European Union—the "Maastricht Treaty"—introduced a

TABLE 2
Interprofessional Social Dialogues—Common Texts (Through 1993)

Title	Date
Joint opinion on the co-operative growth strategy for more employment	November 6, 1986
Joint opinion concerning training and motivation, and information and consultation	March 6, 1987
Joint opinion on the Annual Economic Report 1987/88	November 26, 1987
Joint opinion on the creation of a European occupational and geographical mobility area and improving the operation of the labor market in Europe	December 13, 1990
Joint opinion on education and training	June 19, 1990
Joint opinion on new technologies, work organization, and adaptability of the labor market	January 10, 1991
Joint opinion on the transition from school to adult and working life	April 5, 1991
Agreement of 31 October 1991	October 31, 1991
Joint opinion on ways of facilitating the broadest possible effective access to training opportunities	December 20, 1991
Joint statement on the future of the social dialogue	July 3, 1992
A renewed co-operative growth strategy for more employment	July 3, 1992
Joint opinion on vocational qualifications and certification	October 13, 1992
Recommendation on the functioning of interprofessional advisory committee	June 1, 1993
Joint opinion on the future role and actions of the Community in the field of education and training, including the role of the social partners	July 28, 1993
Proposals by the social partners for implementation of the Agreement annexed to the Protocol on social policy of the Treaty on European Union	October 29, 1993
Joint opinion on women and training	December 3, 1993
The framework for the broad economic policy guidelines	December 5, 1993

Source: Commission of the European Communities 2006a.

binding two-step consultation procedure for all its regulatory projects: first, "on the possible direction of Community action," and, second, "on the content of the envisaged proposal" (Articles 138 and 139; in 1997, the Maastricht Treaty was incorporated into the Amsterdam Treaty without major changes). Furthermore, it broadened the opportunity for the social partners to engage in contractual relations and to conclude framework agreements of a binding nature. If "both sides of industry" decide to negotiate voluntarily, the commission refrains for nine months from using any of its own activities for the duration of the negotiations. Thus, the social partners were granted a privileged status in political decision making that they did not previously have. Further, the basic mode of decision making in the Council of Ministers was changed from unanimity to qualified majority voting in selected policy areas, including working conditions, informing and consulting with workers, and modernization of social protection systems. The former veto power of individual member states became less important.[9]

The Union of Industrial and Employers' Confederations of the European Communities (UNICE), the European Centre of Enterprises with Public Participation and of Enterprises of General Economic Interest (CEEP) on the employers' side, and the European Trade Union Confederation (ETUC) on the employees' side are the most important, representative social partners and corporate actors for social dialogues (for details, see http://www.unice.org and http://www.etuc.org). The basic interests of these European federations of national peak associations in European regulation have long varied. ETUC has always favored various types of preferably binding social dialogues, believing that they would strengthen and further develop the social dimension of the internal market and prevent social dumping as one possible result of accelerated processes of economic integration. By contrast, UNICE has only reluctantly participated in social dialogue activities, preferably of the nonbinding type, doing so largely under the threat of legislative action by the commission. Thus, UNICE sought to prevent legislative measures and to maintain the status quo of nonexistent or minimal European regulation. Especially since issuing its report on future social policy, UNICE has vigorously opted for "more general social dialogue discussions" instead of one "restricted only to negotiating agreements at European level" (Union of Industrial and Employers' Confederations of the European Communities 1999:14).

Political expectations, especially those of trade unions, were quite high following the introduction of the institutional changes of the social protocol. A major breakthrough in European social policy making in general and in the development of European employment relations in particular was supposed to occur in the protocol's wake. However, after more then a decade, the impact of this institutional arrangement seems meager. In particular, the overall number of binding framework agreements concluded by the social partners themselves has remained low, with those that came into effect emphasizing parental leave (in 1995), part-time work (in 1997), and fixed-term work in (in 1999).[10] The majority of regulatory projects failed, either because the social partners decided not to launch voluntary negotiations or because their negotiations failed to reach agreement. In all these cases of semiprivate nondecisions, the commission had to take the initiative again in order to finalize its draft directive.[11] The commission's imminent but credible threat of legislative action ("either you negotiate or we'll legislate") created large pressure on the social partners, especially employer organizations, and the commission spurred the parties to negotiate on several occasions. As one scholar puts it, these apparently voluntary negotiations took place "in the shadow of the law" (Bercusson 1994:20).

It may therefore be concluded that the commission remained not only an important third corporate actor, but the political "prime mover," despite the fact that the social partners obtained more negotiation rights and greater autonomy. Going further, it may be argued that the basic modification in the mode of decision making, from unanimity to qualified majority in selected areas, proved to be of more importance than the change in the status of social partners and their options to achieve a higher, more binding quality of "negotiated legislation." (See Table 3 for a summary of results of the social dialogues at the interprofessional level.)

TABLE 3
Results of the Social Dialogues at the Interprofessional Level

Subject	Result of the social partners' consultation	Adoption of the regulation
European Works Council, 1993	Opinion following attempt at negotiations	Directive 94/45/EC
Reconciling working life and family life, 1995	Agreement on parental leave (December 14, 1996)	Directive 96/34/EC
Adaptation of the burden of proof in gender-based discrimination, 1995	Separate opinions	Directive 97/80/EC
Flexibility in working time and workers' security, 1995	Agreement on part-time work (June 6, 1997)	Directive 97/81/EC
	Agreement on fixed-term work (March 18, 1999)	Directive 99/70/EC
	Failure of negotiations on temporary work (May 2001)	
Prevention of sexual harassment at work, 1996	Separate opinions	No specific legislation because of member states' resistance
Worker information and consultation, 1997	Separate opinions	Directive 2002/14/EC
Protecting workers against employer's insolvency, 2000	Separate opinions	N/A
Modernizing and improving employment relations, 2000	Agreement on telework (May 2002)	N/A
Protecting workers against the risks connected with exposure to asbestos at work, 2000	Separate opinions	N/A
Safety and health at work for the self-employed, 2000	Separate opinions	N/A
Protecting employees' personal data, 2001	In progress	N/A
Anticipating and managing change, 2001	In progress	N/A

Source: Commission of the European Communities 2002a; author's additions.

As before, the sheer number of results does not necessarily constitute a valid indicator for reaching a balanced judgment of success or failure in this regard. Our empirical knowledge about processes of transposition and implementation remains substantially incomplete. Preliminary empirical studies indicate that not only delays in transposition but also various problems of implementation continue to exist in almost all member states (Falkner et al. 2005). It is therefore fair to conclude that the European "value added" remains limited. In particular, various provisions in and exemptions from the operative legislation create ample opportunities for evasion on subordinate levels.

Third phase: Most recent developments. In 2000, the Lisbon Summit articulated new, rather ambitious goals for the EU "to become the most competitive and dynamic knowledge-based economy in the world capable of sustainable economic growth with more and better jobs and greater social cohesion" (European Council 2000:2).[12] The so-called Lisbon strategy in general and the open method of coordination (OMC) in particular are presumed to be the principal instruments of a new phase of social regulation and to constitute new modes of European governance (Zeitlin, Pochet, and Magnusson 2005). The commission seeks to transfer the main responsibility for policy formulation to the social partners and to stress their independence and autonomous rights to reach binding framework agreements within the social dialogue structures that are supposed to be renewed and strengthened. In other words, the initiative for policy making and the responsibility to regulate specific issues are now supposed to be taken by the social partners and not by the commission itself; the commission will no longer set the parties' negotiating agenda.

In their official "joint declaration" issued just prior to the Laeken Summit in late 2001, the social partners agreed on their future role in European governance. In particular, they agreed on a work program for 2003 to 2005, which included such diversified instruments as framework agreements, opinions, recommendations, and statements, as well as some preliminary ideas for monitoring and follow-up. The social partners also announced their readiness for bipartite social dialogues.

To date, however, only a very few autonomous framework agreements have been concluded. The first was the "Framework of Actions for the Lifelong Development of Competencies and Qualifications" (European Trade Union Confederation, Union of Industrial and Employers' Confederations of Europe–UNICE/UEAPME, and European Centre of Enterprises of General Economic Interest 2002a), to be implemented by the open method of coordination. The agreements on telework (European Trade Union Confederation, Union of Industrial and Employers'

Confederations of Europe–UNICE/UEAPME, and European Centre of Enterprises of General Economic Interest 2002b) and work-related stress (European Trade Union Confederation, Union of Industrial and Employers' Confederations of Europe–UNICE/UEAPME, and European Centre of Enterprises of General Economic Interest 2004) are the most important results and test cases for this "post-Maastricht" period of policy making. These first examples of "new generation texts," such as codes of conduct, policy orientations, and guidelines, are also relevant because they will set the stage for all future processes of procedural structuring.

One fundamental continuing problem consists of the procedures for transposition and implementation. Basically (according to Article 139) there are two forms, the so-called legislative track "at the joint request of the signatory parties, by a Council decision on a proposal from the Commission," and the purely voluntary negotiation track "in accordance with the procedures and practices specific to management and labour and the Member States." From a legal perspective as well as the official view of the commission, these two options are intended to be equally important and applicable. In reality, however, their results differ significantly; of particular note, their coverage rates are quite dissimilar.[13] By definition, legislative action leads to a coverage rate of 100%, whereas voluntary procedures cover only the members of national associations. It is well known from comparative research that density ratios differ to a considerable degree between as well as within member states (Ebbinghaus and Visser 2000).

The legal instrument for extending collective agreements beyond the members of associations—the so-called *erga omnes* clause—exists in the majority of (old) member states but is not widely used in practice. In particular, it is ill suited to extending voluntarily concluded European agreements to implementation at lower levels.

It is therefore not surprising that the three aforementioned binding framework agreements reached during the mid- to late 1990s were implemented by legislative means (i.e., by a council decision and a following directive) in the vast majority of member states.[14] Under the new regulatory regime of purely voluntary framework agreements, however, member states cannot be expected to take legislative action to transpose the results from the European level to their respective national levels. In other words, the social partners' organizations themselves and not EU institutions will be in charge of transposing, implementing, and later monitoring the purely voluntary "new generation" texts. Thus, a qualitative shift from trilateral toward bilateral, and therefore autonomous, social dialogues has taken place, and the crucial political trigger of "bargaining in the shadow of the law" has faded.

In sum, it may be argued that there is a new trend or the revival of an old trend from "hard" and binding toward "soft" and nonbinding modes of regulation and European governance, which seems to favor employer interests more than the interests of unions and their members. The framework agreements on telework and work-related stress illustrate this fundamental change toward more "voluntaristic" arrangements. Further, these purely voluntary or autonomous agreements have to be transposed and implemented by the national social partners themselves without any legal support of the European institutions. The decisive question is, "Do the social partners' organizations have the actual power and opportunities to do so?" The answer, at least for the time being, is no, because the basic differences of interest continue to exist on both the vertical (national) and horizontal (cross-national) axes. To this point, hardly any major steps have been taken at the national level, and even in the most favorable circumstance national associations can at best only supply the voluntary compliance of their members. Furthermore, real sanctions for cases of noncompliance do not exist. In the same vein, the development and application of new instruments and procedures, not only for implementation but also for adequate monitoring and follow-up of concluded framework agreements, remain formidable tasks. All in all, it is likely that more diversified activities will take place within the new social dialogue structures, but that their results will be less binding for the social partners than under the regulatory regime of the Maastricht Treaty.

Social Dialogues at the Sectoral Level

Until recently, the commission considered its official communications on social dialogues at the macro level to be more important than those at the sectoral level, which was not given any special attention (Commission of the European Communities 1993, 1996).[15] Further, throughout the 1990s, not only political but also scholarly interest focused on macro-level social dialogues (Falkner 1998, Hartenberger 2001). It can be argued, however, that the opposite should be the case because agreements at the sectoral level tend to be relatively more flexible, if not tailor-made, and better able to cope with such issues as restructuring and training. In addition, collective bargaining continues to occur at the sectoral level in the majority of old member states (Traxler, Blaschke, and Kittel 2001; Marginson and Sisson 2004). Congruent with this reasoning, the commission, in one of its most recent official communications, shifted course and posited that the sectoral level "is the proper level for discussion on many issues linked to employment, such as working conditions, vocational training and industrial change, the knowledge

society, demographic patterns, enlargement and globalisation" (Commission of the European Communities 2002a:16–17).
First phase: Developments until the late 1990s. Sectoral social dialogues can be traced back to the 1970s and even the 1960s. For many years, they took place within two major institutional frameworks, namely, Joint Committees and Informal Working Parties. The Joint Committees were appointed by formal commission decisions, while the Informal Working Parties were launched by the social partners themselves, though both served similar purposes (Sörries 1999). There were two necessary preconditions for the establishment of sectoral dialogues (Keller 2003): the existence of long-term common policies, such as in agriculture and transport, and, later on the need to cope with the consequences of policies of privatization, liberalization, and deregulation, such as in telecommunication and postal services.

The number of included sectors grew gradually but remained relatively low. Further, some sectors with major importance for national economies, such as engineering and chemicals, remained completely excluded. Numerically, results increased slowly, with the number of social dialogue agreements reaching about 200 by the end of the 1990s. These covered not only or even primarily employment relations issues, but a heterogeneous set of policy areas, including industrial policy. Table 4 summarizes the institutional framework of the "old" sectoral social dialogues.

Opinions and judgments about the results of this long-lasting period were ambivalent, if not contradictory. Proponents of the existing forms, mainly employers and their interest associations, argued that both parties became more familiar with each other, promoted the exchange of

TABLE 4
Institutional Framework of the "Old" Sectoral Social Dialogue

Joint committees (JC)	Informal working parties (IWP)
Agriculture (1963)	Hotels, restaurants, cafes (1984)
Road transport (1965)	Sugar (1984)
Inland navigation (1967)	Commerce (1985)
Railways (1982)	Insurance (1987)
Fisheries (1974)	Banks (1990)
Maritime transport (1987)	Footwear (1991)
Civil aviation (1990)	Construction (1991)
Telecommunications (1990)	Cleaning (1992)
Postal services (1994)	Textiles and clothing (1992)
	Wood (1994)
	Private security (1994)

Source: Commission of the European Communities 1996.

information, and understood the opponent's positions better than without the existence of these dialogues. Opponents, especially unions and certain external observers, complained that sectoral social partners did not succeed at all in concluding binding framework agreements. In other words, there were no consequences of implementation for the signatory parties because of this purely voluntary character. Thus, it can legitimately be argued that sectoral dialogues never went beyond the "pre-Maastricht" stage of development of interprofessional dialogues. For some time, the commission remained undecided about this matter, but eventually it redefined its position in response to this type of harsh criticism.

Second phase: The restructuring by the Commission. Eventually, the commission decided to take a bold and rather unexpected political step toward institutional reform. It argued in its communication that the old structures "often hinder positive developments" and "have become over-institutionalised or have retained operational methods which have outlived their usefulness" (Commission of the European Communities 1998a:8). In its "Decision . . . Setting Up Sectoral Dialogue Committees Promoting the Dialogue Between the Social Partners at European Level," the Commission abolished all existing structures of Joint Committees and Informal Working Parties and went on to formulate explicit requirements for the establishment of new unitary, more harmonized "sectoral social dialogue committees" as "the key forum for consultation, joint action and negotiations" (Commission of the European Communities 1998b). In this regard, the social partners have to make "a joint request" and fulfill certain criteria of representativeness. The commission's political expectations were that the signatory parties would conclude framework agreements with binding consequences and thus overcome the purely informal character of the old structures.

The empirical consequences of this institutional reform are difficult to evaluate, both quantitatively and qualitatively. While there has been a modest increase in the number of included sectors to more than 30, comparison of the old with the new organizational structures indicates that literally all old diverse arrangements have been transferred into the new unified ones. In other words, the number of really new sectors (such as home furnishings) remains relatively small despite the overall numerical increase. It can therefore be convincingly argued that the new structure is hardly more than a rough continuation of the old, simply reestablished under the new frame of reference. The social partners managed to conserve their privileged status quo ante position and maintain the receipt of logistical and financial support from the commission, including simultaneous translation facilities, travel expenses, and secretarial services, for their activities.

One also has to take into consideration that the commission's official count of existing social dialogues is overtly optimistic. The criteria for the definition of what exactly constitutes a "sector" are vague. Some sectors, such as transport, are counted more than once.[16] Other included sectors, such as leather goods, are fairly small and not very important for their national economies. Further, the unequal distribution across sectors of the economy has remained uneven, and the results of recently established committees in such sectors as chemicals are unknown to this point. Table 5 summarizes the results of new and old sectoral social dialogues.

The sheer number of sectors constitutes only a rough indicator of success or failure. In terms of output, the number of concluded agreements increased for most of this period but not at all since the aforementioned full restructuring (Observatoire social européen 2004). In addition, existing agreements cover a wide variety of topics, notably industrial policy, which extends far beyond employment relations issues, and include ample evidence of political lobbying. Outcomes also differ significantly among sectors. The number of documents, one rough indicator of productivity, varies markedly, with some sectors, such as telecommunications and postal services, having many, and others having few or none (De Boer, Benedictus, and van der Meer 2005).

From a qualitative perspective, results are now more diversified, featuring various agreements, codes of conduct, joint statements, declarations, and recommendations. The officially criticized character of purely voluntary soft agreements, such as codes of conduct and recommendations, changed hardly at all after the restructuring became effective. In contrast to the hopes of and political pressure exerted by the commission, very few binding framework agreements are in place, and thus there are virtually no consequences for the sectoral social partners in terms of implementation and monitoring by the commission. In sum, major institutional restructuring has not reached the officially proclaimed goal of binding agreements, and prospects for achieving a critical threshold in this regard appear dim.

Third phase: Most recent development. A key contemporary issue involves representative corporate actors, especially at the sectoral rather than the interprofessional level. At the sectoral level, corporate actors are not ETUC and UNICE, but rather the European industry federations, which are confederations of national sectoral organizations on the employees' side and their sectoral counterparts on the employers' side. In some sectors, there are competing organizations on one or both sides. On the employers' side, sectoral organizations are frequently missing, and those that do exist are often unwilling or not

TABLE 5
Sectoral Social Dialogues—Old and New Structures

	New structure		Old structures		
	Joint request for a Sectoral Dialogue Committee	New dialogue	Joint committees	Informal working group	Nonstructured group
Agriculture	1		1		
Audiovisual	1	1			
Banking	1			1	
Chemical industry	1	1			
Civil aviation	1	1	1		
Cleaning industry	1			1	
Commerce	1			1	
Construction	1			1	
Electricity	1	1			1
Footwear	1			1	
Furniture	1	1			
Horeca	1			1	
Inland waterways	1		1		
Insurance	1			1	
Live performance (media)	1	1			1
Local and regional government	1	1			1
Mining (extractive industry)	1	1			
Personal services	1	1			
Postal services	1		1		
Private security	1			1	
Railways	1		1		
Road transport	1		1		
Sea fisheries	1		1		
Sea transport	1		1		
Shipbuilding	1	1			
Steel	1				
Sugar	1				1
Tanning and leather	1	1			
Telecommunications	1		1		
Temporary work	1	1			
Textiles and clothing	1			1	
Woodworking	1	1			1
	32	13	9	9	5

Source: Created from information in Commission of the European Communities (2004, 2006a).

mandated by constituencies to negotiate on their behalf. Further, these are not specialized employers' federations but instead general business federations whose concerns embrace representation of product market and economic interests far more than labor market and social interests. All in all, these organizations do not take the lead, preferring to take a "wait-and-see" position. On the employees' side, organizational substructures are less fragmented and therefore better suited to engaging in various social dialogue activities. There are 11 European industry federations in total (one example being the European Metalworkers' Federation), which are constitutionally integrated into ETUC organizational structures and basically willing to negotiate framework agreements within social dialogue contexts. But, as is evident, these federations often do not have an employers' counterpart willing to engage in such negotiations.

The persistent problem of representativeness has to be coped with because for reasons of legitimacy and effectiveness, the commission needs representative associations to consult and to initiate social dialogues. In its early communications, the commission officially defined certain criteria associations have to meet in order to be officially recognized as social partners and be granted the privileged status.[17] All in all, these criteria are quite broad, rather vague, and so flexible— malleable—in their interpretation and application to individual cases that they are widely open to administrative and political opportunism (Keller 2006).

If voluntary, binding bilateral framework agreements were concluded in the future, they will face exactly the same problems of transposition and implementation already noted in regard to their equivalents at the interprofessional level. These processes will completely depend on the aforementioned "voluntary route" and on the social partners as agencies. The European peak federations at the sectoral level, however, have neither the legal power nor the formal or informal authority to enforce the cooperation of their national affiliates in these protracted processes of soft implementation procedures.

The option of "positive sum games" constitutes a necessary precondition for agreements within existing social dialogue structures. However, the existence of this precondition cannot be taken for granted. If both sides of industry are not simultaneously interested in specific issues such as health and safety, training, and retraining, social dialogues cannot lead to positive (mutual) gains. Instead, these and other controversial issues will continue to be subject to distributive bargaining, or "zero sum games," and will defy solution in a presumed cooperative bargaining type of institutional context. It may therefore be concluded that the sector level is the "weak link" in European employment relations (Marginson 2005).

The European Employment Strategy: Europeanization of Employment Policy?

Until the mid-1990s, employment policy constituted a purely national responsibility and competence; the commission had no power in this field. The commission's white paper on "Growth, Competitiveness, Employment: The Challenges and Ways Forward into the 21st Century," issued in 1993 in a period of high unemployment, and the so-called Essen strategy, the implementation of results of the summit issued in late 1994, were the most important antecedents of a gradual change of existing principles of social regulation. After protracted efforts at political bargaining and a shift of political majority in some member states (such as France and the United Kingdom), the insertion of the so-called employment title into the Treaty of Amsterdam (Articles 125–130) changed the existing division of labor between actors at the national and supranational level to a certain degree. This political compromise introduced some new opportunities for intervention by the European authorities, who were now supposed to coordinate national employment and labor market policies without abolishing national autonomy in this policy area.

The 1997 Treaty of Amsterdam introduced new instruments of policy making, which initially became known as the "Luxembourg process" (following a special summit dedicated to employment issues) and later as the open method of coordination (OMC). Since then, the commission has attempted to broaden the options for application of OMC procedures far beyond employment policy into other heterogeneous policy areas in which national rights and prerogatives prevail, such as education and training, social protection, structural economic reform, and immigration policy. The basic idea is that the member states have to reach certain common European objectives but are completely free to select the means and instruments of implementation. Article 128 of this new mode of regulation includes the following:

- Annual employment guidelines to be adopted by the Council of Ministers that the member states "shall take into account in their employment policies" (European Community 1997:57).
- Annual reports by the member states "on the principal measures taken to implement its employment policy in the light of the guidelines for employment" (European Community 1997:57)—so-called national action plans.

- Involvement by the social partners at the national level in the establishment of the national action plans.

- A joint employment report by the council and commission, which makes use of various performance indicators and establishes benchmarks.

- If necessary, joint nonbinding recommendations to individual member states concerning their employment policies.

Thus, OMC is the prototypical example of the most recent paradigm shift in the mode of European governance. It basically consists of soft instead of hard law instruments and tools of policy making, without any binding consequences for member states or legislative measures to be taken. These "soft" policy tools include peer evaluation, recommendation, exchange of best practices, and experimental learning. Basic political rights and priorities remain determined at the national level, where an enormous, deep-routed diversity of institutions and policy legacies exists. Consequently, European institutions have only limited opportunities to coordinate national policies among different substantive areas.

The First Five Years

From 1997 to 2002, the commission established some 20 guidelines, which were condensed into four so-called pillars: adaptability, entrepreneurship, equal opportunities, and employability. A key problem in this regard is the differing interests of member states as well as of social partners with respect to both the guidelines and the pillars.[18] The integration of national and sectoral social partners, which was supposed to be reached by social dialogue provisions, varies to a considerable degree among member states and is basically limited to the formulation of national action plans, but it does not include their implementation, monitoring, and evaluation. Further, the involvement of European authorities remains fairly limited, and "hard" quantitative goals have not been formulated. A related problem is insufficient coordination with other policy fields of major importance, such as economic policy, monetary policy, budgetary policy, and wage policy, within the so-called macroeconomic dialogue, which was established in the late 1990s and ostensibly includes all major actors (Goetschy 2003).

The Second Five Years: Learning from Experience

During the first, more or less experimental, phase, only minor adaptations took place on an annual basis; however, major changes were introduced following a comprehensive evaluation of this phase (Commission of the European Communities 2002b). In particular, the

TABLE 6

The European Employment Strategy—A Comparison Between the Old Pillars and the New Guidelines Since 2003

European Employment Strategy, 1998–2003	European Employment Strategy since 2003
Four pillars	Three overall objectives
• strengthening **employability** through reducing the inflow into long-term unemployment; creating a more active labor market policy; developing a framework for training and lifelong learning; and facilitating the transition from school to work	• **full employment** with an overall employment rate of 70%, a rate of 60% for women and 50% for older workers (from 55–64), in the EU in 2010
• strengthening **entrepreneurship** through reducing costs and administrative burdens for business; promoting self-employment; promoting job creation in social economy and the local level; reducing the tax burden on labor; and reducing VAT in some labor-intensive sectors	• **improving quality and productivity at work** through instruments such as lifelong learning, career development, gender equality, health and safety at work, flexibility and security, and access to work; such agreements shall also be made through social dialogues
• strengthening **adaptability** through inviting social partners to negotiate about a modernization of work, heeding flexibility and security; responding to increasingly diverse forms of employment; and developing in-house training and investment in human resources	• **strengthening social cohesion and inclusion** through promoting access to quality employment for everyone who is capable of working, combating discrimination in the labor market, and preventing exclusion from work; these instruments shall also be used on a regional basis through the "open method of coordination"
• strengthening **equal opportunities** through talking gender gaps; reconciling work and family life; facilitating reintegration into labor market; and promoting the integration of disabled persons	These overall objectives are specified in 10 more detailed guidelines; the guidelines were amended in July 2005 to "Integrated Guidelines for Growth and Jobs."

Source: Created from information in Commission of the European Communities 2006b.

number of guidelines was reduced from 20 to 10, and the four pillars were replaced by three overarching objectives: full employment, improving quality and productivity at work, and strengthening social cohesion and inclusion. (Table 6 provides a summary comparison of the European employment strategy's old pillars and new guidelines.) Nevertheless, unemployment remained high in the majority of member states, and the overall contribution of the new employment strategy to combating high and persistent unemployment has been quite limited. Some new official goals, such as an increase in the overall employment rate across the EU to 70% by 2010, had to be abandoned because they proved to be too ambitious (Kok 2003). Further, efficient coordination of the guidelines and pillars with other policy processes, such as the macroeconomic dialogue, has been very difficult to achieve.

After several years of experience, it became clear that OMC has some specific strengths, including its organization as an iterative process, the possibility of creating learning opportunities for all participating corporate actors, and better exchange of information. OMC also has some major weaknesses, such as the absence of binding sanctions in cases of noncompliance with European targets, lack of additional financial and/or other incentives for member states, a very limited number of quantitative indicators, and the unequal integration of social partners into policy-making processes. Further, while OMC and the social dialogues at the interprofessional and sectoral levels share certain similarities, they have yet to be systematically coordinated or integrated. From a methodological perspective, causal impacts of the interplay between national and European levels and their corporate actors are difficult to detect, and measurable improvements attributable to the OMC are hard to isolate. At least in some national cases, procedural shifts in governance and policy making are more profound than substantive policy changes (Zeitlin 2005). Also, the application of the OMC as a means of self-regulation by both sides of industry is restricted to consensual topics with common interests and shared goals, such as health and safety. Unfortunately, this fundamental limitation means that OMC is not very well suited to dealing with core employment relations issues, and more broadly it may not, as the commission would have it, be "an extremely promising way forward" (Commission of the European Communities 2002b:18).

Conclusions and Perspectives

Genuine "European" employment relations consisting of an idealized coherent, horizontally and vertically interconnected, integrated system do not exist in practice and are not in the offing. Employment relations are one of those policy areas in which "conflict of interests between governments representing countries with advanced and less advanced economies and with divergent policy traditions and institutional structures are likely to make agreement on common European rules difficult or impossible" (Scharpf 1999:193). These problems are rendered even more difficult by the social partners at the national and European levels. If something like "European" employment relations comes into existence at all, it will most likely constitute a protracted mixture of national and supranational ingredients and developments (Keller and Platzer 2003; Marginson and Sisson 2004). In other words, a gradual and uneven "Europeanization" of national employment relations systems is more likely to take place without replacing prevailing national systems, only supplementing them in some respects.

Far-reaching movements toward strict convergence of existing national systems are unlikely to happen; instead, tendencies of continuity and path dependency of national employment relations will dominate. Some focal areas of social regulation, such as pay, rights of association, and industrial action, remain expressly excluded from community consideration in all versions of the treaties. Further, processes of institution building are protracted and take time to achieve even partial fruition. In the future, measures and instruments of horizontal coordination, as in the European Employment Strategy, will most likely dominate strategies of strict vertical integration.

From the beginning of integration there has always been a vacillation between phases of activity and stagnation in the development of the European social model and social policy. The Delors Commission of the late 1980s and early 1990s that was characterized by quantitatively *and* qualitatively far-reaching activities in interrelated fields of social policy and employment relations belongs to the past. In contrast to that period of revitalization, recent efforts toward the creation of the "social dimension" of the internal market are few in number and modest in substance; as one observer puts it, we have entered "an era of legislative abstinence" and "new modesty" (Kowalsky 2001:51).

So far, economic integration, or market making, is more advanced than social integration, or market correcting, despite all political plans to accelerate the latter. The commission argued in its white paper on social policy that within the European social model economic progress and social progress are inseparable. This political hope has not materialized in practice (Commission of the European Communities 1994; for comments see European Industrial Relations Review 1994a, 1994b, and 1994c). Indeed, it can be argued that despite certain developments since the early 1990s, such as a major increase in the number of EWCs, the gap between economic and social integration has deepened and widened precisely because of progressing economic integration. The completion of the common market in the early 1990s and the founding of the Economic and Monetary Union, which included abolishing national currencies and introducing a common currency and common interest rates among member states, are the most obvious indicators of the continuation of this structural imbalance.[19] Furthermore, these developments in the monetary and economic policy spheres have no functional equivalent in the social sphere.

The eastern enlargement of the EU in 2004, which increased the number of member states from 15 to 25, constitutes not only the most encompassing but also the most difficult of all historical enlargements.[20] This politically motivated decision will have long-term consequences for the character of the diverse EU polity in general and the development of European employment relations in particular. Several empirical studies conclude that the institutional infrastructure of the new member states, which is necessary for the transposition and implementation of any kind of EU regulation, is relatively weak and less developed than in the old member states (Ghellab and Vaughan-Whitehead 2003, Kohl and Platzer 2004). Existing interest organizations, especially those at the sectoral level, are quite weak in terms of available resources, notably manpower, finances, and mandates, and often compete with each other. They are hardly able, then, to participate in bilateral social dialogues. Moreover, density ratios differ considerably on both sides of industry and are much lower in the new member states than in the old. In contrast to the majority of old member states, collective bargaining in the new member states occurs not at the sectoral level in the form of multiemployer bargaining but rather at the company level. As a result, employer and employee collective bargaining coverage rates are significantly lower in the new member states.

All in all and looking ahead, processes of integration into a comprehensive European social model may be slowed, stopped, or even reversed as the diversity, heterogeneity, and fragmentation of national employment relation systems increase—an increase that will highlight rather than subordinate major institutional differences among European nations.

Notes

[1] A valuable source of detailed and most recent information is the European Industrial Relations Observatory, or EIRO <http://www.eiro.eurofound.eu.int>.

[2] It reads, "The Community shall act within the limits of the powers conferred upon it by this Treaty and of the objectives assigned to it therein."

[3] This is the sum of existing regulations at European level. This collection is binding for all member states and has to be part of their national rules and prescriptions. More recently, all new member states from eastern and central eastern Europe had to transpose the complete *acquis* before they were accepted.

[4] Article 249 of the EU treaty states, "A Directive shall be binding, as to the result to be achieved, upon each Member State to which it is addressed, but shall leave to the national authorities the choice of form and methods."

[5] It is illuminating to specify that, in empirical perspective, there are two basic patterns in the composition of EWCs that indicate a high degree of path dependency, and not of strict convergence, within this development at European level. The employee-only EWCs follow the Austrian–German national pattern, the joint management–employee EWCs the Belgian–French one.

[6] Marginson et al. (1998) provide the most detailed empirically based analysis of this period.

[7] The most reliable, continuously updated database is provided by the European Trade Union Institute, the research institute of the European Trade Union Congress <http://www.etuc.org/etui>.

[8] For summaries of existing empirical studies see Müller and Platzer (2003) and Marginson and Sisson (2004).

[9] The conservative government of the United Kingdom was not willing to accept any of these politically motivated changes and got a so-called "opt-out clause" from all labor legislation adopted under the protocol. This clause was abolished after new labor won the general election in 1997 and decided to opt back in.

[10] The more recent framework agreements on telework (European Trade Union Confederation et al. 2002b) and work-related stress (European Trade Union Confederation et al. 2004) are of a different qualitative nature and will be discussed later in another context.

[11] The most prominent example is the above-mentioned directive on EWCs. One side blamed the other for not launching negotiations, and the commission had to reintroduce its draft directive in order to finalize the pending project.

[12] More recently it turned out that the officially proclaimed goals were much too ambitious and had to be readjusted and reformulated (Kok 2003).

[13] Coverage rates indicate the percentage of employees whose working conditions, pay, and all other terms are defined by collective agreements. Figures refer to specific sectors or to the country as a whole.

[14] Denmark, the most relevant deviating case among the old member states, occasionally decided to make use of the "voluntary" route. This choice of strategy was in line with national "customs and practices" and was appropriate because of extraordinarily high density ratios on both sides, and therefore comparatively high coverage rates.

[15] Communications are official documents published by the commission in order to elaborate its present views and future strategies concerning social dialogues.

[16] The heterogeneous transport sector is represented by six committees (civil aviation, inland navigation, maritime transport, railways, road transport, and sea transport) and is counted six times.

[17] The organizations must "relate to specific sectors or categories and be organized at European level," "consist of organizations which are themselves an integral and recognized part of Member States' social partner structures and have the capacity to negotiate agreements," and have "adequate structures to ensure their effective participation in the work of the committees" (Commission of the European Communities 1998b:1,2). In 1998 and 2002 the commission launched so-called "studies of representativity" that were supposed to solve these problems.

[18] Among other issues, unions are mostly interested in employability, whereas the priority of employers' organizations is issues of entrepreneurship.

[19] All details concerning the political construction and economic consequences of the Economic and Monetary Union and the accompanying "Stability and Growth Pact," especially its 3% limit for public deficits, are beyond the scope of this chapter. Major changes toward a "softer" interpretation of the the pact's strict rules are likely to happen in the foreseeable future after some bigger member states have repeatedly violated these limits in consecutive years.

[20] The new member states are the Czech Republic, Cyprus, Estonia, Hungary, Latvia, Lithuania, Malta, Poland, Slovakia, and Slovenia. Bulgaria and Romania are supposed to follow soon.

References

Anderson, James E. 2003. *Public policy making*, 5th ed. Boston: Houghton Mifflin.

Bercusson, Brian. 1994. "The Dynamic of European Labour Law after Maastricht." *Industrial Law Journal*, Vol. 23, no. 1, March, pp. 1–31.

Commission of the European Communities. 1993. *Communication Concerning the Application of the Agreement on Social Policy (COM [93] 600 final)*. Brussels: Commission of the European Communities.

———. 1994. *European Social Policy: A Way Forward for the Union—A White Paper (COM/94/333 final)*. Brussels: Commission of the European Communities.

———. 1996. *Communication Concerning the Development of the Social Dialogue at Community Level (COM [1996] 448 final)*. Brussels: Commission of the European Communities.

———. 1998a. *Communication Adapting and Promoting the Social Dialogue at Community Level (COM [1998] 322 final)*. Brussels: Commission of the European Communities.

———. 1998b. *Commission Decision of 20 May 1998 on the Establishment of Sectoral Dialogue Committees Promoting the Dialogue Between the Social Partners at European Level (98/500/EC)*. Brussels: Commission of the European Communities.

———. 2002a. *Communication from the Commission: The European Social Dialogue, A Force for Innovation and Change (COM [2002] 341 final)*. Brussels: Commission of the European Communities.

———. 2002b. *Communication from the Commission to the Council, the European Parliament, the Economic and Social Committee and the Committee of the Regions: Taking Stock of Five Years of the European Employment Strategy*. Brussels: Commission of the European Communities.

———. 2004. *Communication Partnership for Change in an Enlarged Europe: Enhancing the Role of Social Dialogue (COM [2004] 557 final)*. Brussels: Commission of the European Communities.

———. 2006a. "Social dialogues text database." <http://ec.europa.eu/employment_social/dsw/dspMain.do?lang=en>. [Accessed January 26, 2006].

———. 2006b. "European Employment Strategy: Introduction." <http://ec.europa.eu/employment_social/employment_strategy/index_en.htm>. [Accessed January 26, 2006].

De Boer, Rob, Hester Benedictus, and Marc van der Meer. 2005. "Broadening without Intensification: The Added Value of the European Social and Sectoral Dialogue." *European Journal of Industrial Relations*, Vol. 11, no. 1, March, pp. 51–70.

Ebbinghaus, Bernhard, and Jelle Visser. 2000. *Trade Unions in Western Europe Since 1945*. London: Macmillan-Palgrave.

European Community. 1997. *Treaty Establishing the European Community*. Brussels: European Community.

European Council. 1994. *Council Directive 94/45/EC of 22 September 1994 on the Establishment of a European Works Council or a Procedure in Community-Scale Undertakings and Community-Scale Groups of Undertakings for the Purposes of Informing and Consulting Employees*. Brussels: European Council.

———. 2000. *Press release: Presidency Conclusions. Lisbon European Council, 23rd and 24th March 2000*. Brussels: European Council.

———. 2001. *Council Directive 2001/86/EC of 8 October 2001 Supplementing the Statute for a European Company with Regard to the Involvement of Employees*. Brussels: European Council.

European Industrial Relations Review. 1994a. "Social Policy White Paper: Part One." *European Industrial Relations Review*, Issue 248, September, pp. 13–18.

———. 1994b. "Social Policy White Paper: Part Two." *European Industrial Relations Review*, Issue 249, October, pp. 24–26.

———. 1994c. "Social Policy White Paper: Part Three." *European Industrial Relations Review*, Issue 250, November, pp. 28–31.

———. 2005. "European Company Statute State of Play." *European Industrial Relations Review*, Issue 383, December, pp. 22–25.

European Parliament and European Council. 2002. *Directive 2002/14/EC of the European Parliament and of the Council of 11 March 2002 Establishing a General Framework for Informing and Consulting Employees in the European Community*. Brussels: European Parliament–European Council.

European Trade Union Confederation, Union of Industrial and Employers' Confederations of Europe–UNICE/UEAPME, and European Centre of Enterprises of General Economic Interest. 2002a. *Framework of Actions for the Lifelong Development of Competencies and Qualifications*. Brussels: European Trade Union Confederation.

———. 2002b. *Framework agreement on telework*. Brussels: European Trade Union Confederation.

———. 2004. *Framework agreement on work-related stress*. Brussels: European Trade Union Confederation.

Falkner, Gerda. 1998. *EU Social Policy in the 1990s: Towards a Corporatist Policy Community*. London: Routledge.

Falkner, Gerda, Oliver Treib, Miriam Hartlapp, and Simone Leiber. 2005. *Complying with Europe: EU Harmonization and Soft Law in the Member States*. Cambridge, UK: Cambridge University Press.

Ferner, Anthony, and Richard Hyman, eds. 1998. *Changing Industrial Relations in Europe*, 2nd ed. Oxford: Blackwell.

Ghellab, Youcef, and Danieal Vaughan-Whitehead, eds. 2003. *Sectoral Social Dialogue in Future EU Member States: The Weakest Link*. Budapest: International Labour Organization–European Commission.

Goetschy, Janine. 2003. "European Employment Policy Since the 1990s." In Berndt Keller and Hans-Wolfgang Platzer, eds. *Industrial Relations and European Integration: Trans- and Supranational Developments and Prospects*. Aldershot: Ashgate, pp. 137–60.

Hall, Mark, Mark Carley, Michael Gold, Paul Marginson, and Keith Sisson. 1995. *European Works Councils: Planning for the Directive*. London: Eclipse.

Hall, Mark, Andrea Broughton, Mark Carley, and Keith Sisson. 2002. *Works Councils for the UK? Assessing the Impact of the EU Employee Consultation Directive*. London: Industrial Relations Services–Industrial Relations Research Unit.

Hartenberger, Ute. 2001. *Europäischer sozialer Dialog nach Maastricht: EU-Sozialpartnerverhandlungen auf dem Prüfstand*. Baden-Baden: Nomos.

International Labour Organization. 2006. *Infocus Programme on Social Dialogue, Labour Law and Labour Administration*. <http://www.ilo.org/public/english/-dialogue/ifpdial/sd/index.htm>. [Accessed January 26, 2006].

Keller, Berndt. 2002. "The European Company Statute: Employee Involvement—and Beyond." *Industrial Relations Journal*, Vol. 33, no. 5, December, pp. 423–44.

————. 2003. "Social Dialogues at Sectoral Level: The Neglected Ingredient of European Industrial Relations." In Berndt Keller and Hans-Wolfgang Platzer, eds. *Industrial Relations and European Integration: Trans- and Supranational Developments and Prospects.* Aldershot: Ashgate, pp. 30–57.

————. 2006. "Social Dialogues: The Specific Case of the European Union." In International Industrial Relations Association, ed. *"Social Actors, Work Organization and New Technologies in the 21st Century." International Industrial Relations Association 14th World Congress, September 2006, Lima, Peru,* Geneva: International Labour Organization, pp. 69–96.

Keller, Berndt, and Hans-Wolfgang Platzer, eds. 2003. *Industrial Relations and European Integration: Trans- and Supranational Developments and Prospects.* Aldershot: Ashgate.

Kerckhofs, Peter. 2006. *European Works Councils: Facts and Figures.* Brussels: European Trade Union Institute.

Kohl, Heribert, and Hans-Wolfgang Platzer. 2004. *Industrial Relations in Central and Eastern Europe: Transformation and Integration—A Comparison of the Eight New EU Member States.* Brussels: European Trade Union Institute.

Kok, Wim. 2003. *Jobs, Jobs, Jobs: Creating More Employment in Europe. Report of the Employment Taskforce Chaired by Wim Kok.* Brussels: Commission of the European Communities.

Kowalsky, Wolfgang. 2001. *Focus on European Social Policy: Countering Europessimism.* Brussels: European Trade Union Institute.

Lecher, Wolfgang, Bernhard Nagel, and Hans-Wolfgang Platzer. 1999. *The Establishment of European Works Councils: From Information Committee to Social Actor.* Aldershot: Ashgate.

Lecher, Wolfgang, Hans-Wolfgang Platzer, Stefan Rüb, and Klaus-Peter Weiner. 2001. *European Works Councils: Developments, Types and Networking.* Aldershort: Ashgate.

————. 2002. *European Works Councils: Negotiated Europeanisation—Between Statutory Framework and Social Dynamics.* Aldershot: Ashgate.

Marginson, Paul. 2005. "Industrial Relations at European Sector Level: The Weak Link?" *Economic and Industrial Democracy*, Vol. 26, no. 4, November, pp. 511–40.

Marginson, Paul, Mark Gilman, Otto Jacobi, and Hubert Krieger. 1998. *Negotiating European Works Councils: An Analysis of Agreements under Article 13.* Luxembourg: Office for Official Publications of the European Communities.

Marginson, Paul, and Keith Sisson. 2004. *European Integration and Industrial Relations: Multi-level Governance in the Making.* Houndmills, UK: Palgrave Macmillan.

Müller, Torsten, and Aline Hoffmann. 2001. *EWC Research: A Review of the Literature.* <http://users.wbs.warwick.ac.uk/irru/publications/warwick_papers>. [Accessed January 26, 2006].

Müller, Torsten, and Hans-Wolfgang Platzer. 2003. "European Works Councils: A New Mode of EU Regulation and the Emergence of a European Multi-level Structure of Workplace Industrial Relations." In Berndt Keller and Hans-Wolfgang Platzer, eds., *Industrial Relations and European Integration: Trans- and Supranational Developments and Prospects.* Aldershot: Ashgate, pp. 58–84.

Observatoire social européen. 2004. *Rapport final "Dialogue social sectoriel."* Brussels: Observatoire social européen.

Scharpf, Fritz W. 1999. *Governing in Europe: Effective and Democratic?* Oxford: Oxford University Press.
Schulten, Thorsten, and Rainer Bispinck, eds. 2001. *Collective bargaining under the Euro.* Brussels: European Trade Union Institute.
Sisson, Keith. 2002. "The Information and Consultation Directive: Unnecessary 'Regulation' or an Opportunity to Promote 'Partnership'?" *Warwick Papers in Industrial Relations* No. 67, Industrial Relations Research Unit, University of Warwick.
Sörries, Bernd. 1999. *Europäisierung der Arbeitsbeziehungen: Der soziale Dialog und seine Aktuere.* München; Mering: Hampp.
Traxler, Franz. 2003. "European Monetary Union and Collective Bargaining." In Berndt Keller and Hans-Wolfgang Platzer, eds. *Industrial Relations and European Integration: Trans- and Supranational Developments and Prospects.* Aldershot: Ashgate, pp. 85–111.
Traxler, Franz, Sabine Blaschke, and Bernhard Kittel. 2001. *National Labour Relations and Internationalized Markets: A Comparative Study of Institutions, Change, and Performance.* Oxford: Oxford University Press.
Union of Industrial and Employers' Confederations of the European Communities. 1999. *Releasing Europe's Employment Potential: Companies' Views on European Social Policy Beyond 2000.* Brussels: Union of Industrial and Employers' Confederations of the European Communities.
Zeitlin, Jonathan. 2005. "The Open Method of Co-ordination in Action: Theoretical Promise, Empirical Realities, Reform Strategy." In Jonathan Zeitlin and Philippe Pochet, with Lars Magnusson, eds. 2005. *The Open Method of Co-ordination in Action: The European Employment and Social Inclusion Strategies.* Brussels: Peter Lang, pp. 447–503.
Zeitlin, Jonathan, and Philippe Pochet, with Lars Magnusson, eds. 2005. *The Open Method of Co-ordination in Action: The European Employment and Social Inclusion Strategies.* Brussels: Peter Lang.

CHAPTER 4

Research on Alternative Dispute Resolution Procedures

ALEXANDER J.S. COLVIN
The Pennsylvania State University

BRIAN KLAAS
University of South Carolina

DOUGLAS MAHONY
University of South Carolina

Alternative dispute resolution (ADR) encompasses a range of procedures, such as mediation, arbitration, ombudspersons, and peer review, that provide alternative mechanisms for resolving disputes and conflicts, both in the workplace and in other settings. In the field of employment relations, recent years have seen a growing number and diversity of ADR procedures used, particularly in nonunion workplaces and in resolving employment law disputes (Ewing 1989; Feuille and Delaney 1992; Feuille and Chachere 1995; Colvin 2003a). Much of the past research on ADR has focused on the general question of what the most effective technique is for resolving conflicts. The assumption behind much of this research is that the primary goal of dispute resolution is simply the efficiency of resolution and that this is a goal shared by all parties. But dispute resolution does not occur in a vacuum, separated from other aspects of work and employment relations. Indeed, one of the initial questions to be addressed in evaluating ADR procedures is what they are an "alternative" to. Evaluating the impact of ADR procedures depends in large measure on how one evaluates the process that ADR is replacing. Furthermore, recent research is increasingly recognizing that ADR procedures can have a number of different outcomes for and impacts on different parties to a dispute. The impact of ADR procedures may be evaluated very differently for employers versus employees, but also for employees directly involved in disputes versus other employees in the same workplace.

We begin this chapter by reviewing the major developments that have led to the importance of and controversies over ADR in employment relations. Then we examine the distribution of ADR procedures and the determinants of their adoption. Next we look at the research on determinants and consequences of employee use of ADR, as well as the consequences for those employees' firms. Lastly, we address the growing body of research on decision making within ADR systems.

Developments within ADR: Why Should We Care?

A number of factors make ADR procedures of particular importance in contemporary American employment relations. The first of these is the limited extent of due process protections in the American workplace. The basic legal principle governing employment in the United States is "employment at will," which provides that an employer may fire an employee for good reason, bad reason, or no reason at all (Dunford and Devine 1998; Wheeler, Klaas, and Mahony 2004). Although partly tempered by the extensive body of employment discrimination law and more limited state-court exceptions, employment at will continues to be the governing legal principle for the vast majority of workplace disputes in the United States (Wheeler, Klaas, and Mahony 2004). In contrast to many European and other industrialized countries, there is no system of labor courts or employment tribunals to which an employee can turn for recourse in the event of a routine complaint of unfair treatment in the workplace that does not involve an allegation of discrimination.

At one time, it was plausible to think that the system of grievance procedures and labor arbitration based on collective agreements developed in the unionized setting would provide the general mode of workplace dispute resolution in the United States (Kerr et al. 1960). In the 1950s heyday of the New Deal industrial relations system, with around a third of the workforce unionized, it may have seemed reasonable to assume that the unionized workplace labor grievance-arbitration system would eventually spread to govern most workplaces and most disputes. However, with the decline of union representation to 12.5% of the workforce by 2005 (U.S. Bureau of Labor Statistics 2006), it is clear that, while important for this segment of the workforce, the labor grievance-arbitration system is not providing a general mechanism for resolving workplace conflicts. For this reason, the adoption of ADR procedures in nonunion workplaces, where the majority of employees are located, becomes especially important. For researchers, a key question is the degree to which nonunion ADR procedures can or do provide some degree of alternative to the grievance-arbitration procedures of the unionized workplace.

Perhaps surprisingly, given the employment-at-will principle, the second major factor driving developments in ADR is the growth and impact of employment litigation. Although American employment law is built around exceptions to employment at will, in the areas where exceptions exist, particularly for employment discrimination, legal disputes are characterized by a high intensity and resulting major impacts on employment relations (Colvin 2006).

Employment litigation in the United States can be viewed as a high-risk, high-stakes system of dispute resolution. The steps required for an employee to establish a valid legal claim are in many respects daunting, yet they hold a chance of yielding a substantial award against the employer. An employee seeking to make a legal claim against an employer must first ensure that the dispute involves one of the categories of discrimination that can be the subject of legal claims. Research on grievance procedures that allow both discrimination- and nondiscrimination-based grievances suggests that at most only 5% to 10% of workplace disputes involve discrimination (Lewin 1987), indicating that most employee claims will not pass even the first legal hurdle. Second, the litigation process itself is long and uncertain, with many employee claims being dismissed on preliminary motions before trial. Although each year more than 60,000 discrimination complaints are filed with the Equal Employment Opportunity Commission (EEOC) and more than 20,000 claims of employment discrimination in the courts, the total number of awards in the federal courts between 1994 and 2000 was only 1,298 (Eisenberg and Schlanger 2003; Clermont and Schwab 2004). In a study of how employment discrimination plaintiffs fare in the federal courts, Clermont and Schwab (2004) describe a "litigation pyramid" in which such plaintiffs are more likely than non-employment-case plaintiffs to have their cases dismissed based on a preliminary motion before trial, less likely to win at trial, and more likely to have judgments in their favor overturned on appeal. The average employee claim takes an average of 709 days to get to trial, some two and a half years (Eisenberg and Hill 2003). However, among employees who are successful, awards are substantial; in a segment of cases they have been very large, running into the millions of dollars. In a study of employment-discrimination verdicts in the federal courts between 1994 and 2000, Eisenberg and Schlanger (2003) found a median award of $110,000 but a mean award of $301,000, reflecting the strongly skewed distribution of awards, with a minority of very large ones inflating the mean figure.

Taken together these elements suggest a system that presents substantial barriers to success for an employee litigant, yet offers a small chance of obtaining a very large award. Conversely, for an employer, the system may seem to involve fighting off a large number of unmeritorious claims, in the sense that many are ultimately dismissed, yet require substantial legal expenses to obtain those dismissals (Estreicher 2001). In addition, the employer runs the ongoing risk of being subject to one of the few very large litigation verdicts, which may be expensive and attract negative publicity. From this perspective, ADR procedures that hold out the possibility of a simpler, faster, and cheaper mechanism for resolving potential legal claims, with the added benefit of avoiding negative publicity, hold very substantial attractions for employers (Stone 1999; Colvin 2001; Wheeler, Klaas, and Mahony 2004). For the employee, ADR that involves less time and expense in resolving a claim, particularly in the more typical cases where a mega-verdict is unlikely, could also hold significant attractions (Colvin 2001; Estreicher 2001). However, although the time, expense, and uncertainties in employment litigation create incentives for both employers and employees to favor the development of ADR, the two groups will not necessarily desire the same type of alternative. This became evident in the storm of controversy and disputes in the 1990s surrounding the development of employment arbitration as an ADR alternative to litigation.

The primary impetus for developing employment arbitration as an alternative to litigation came from a shift within the legal system itself. During the 1980s the Supreme Court in a series of cases reversed a longstanding skepticism among the courts toward using arbitration to resolve statutory claims (Stone 1999). These developments occurred outside the employment area and involved acceptance of the arbitrability of claims based on statutes in such areas as antitrust, RICO, and securities law. For employment law, the key extension of these decisions came in the 1991 case of *Gilmer v. Interstate/Johnson Lane*, 500 U.S. 20 (1991), where the Supreme Court for the first time held that a claim based on an employment statute, in this case the Age Discrimination in Employment Act, could be subject to arbitration. For employers, the *Gilmer* decision held out the possibility of adopting employment arbitration procedures that would replace the uncertainties and risks of large jury awards, with a simpler, faster procedure in which professional arbitrators would be unlikely to render mega-verdicts with large punitive and compensatory damage components (Colvin 2001; Estreicher 2001). Over the course of the 1990s, large numbers of employers began requiring employees, as a mandatory term and condition of employment, to enter into arbitration agreements covering any potential legal claim against the employer (Colvin 2004c).

For many employee advocates, the spread of mandatory employment arbitration was a disturbing development that threatened to undercut the protections contained in employment discrimination law (Stone 1996, 1999; Zack 1999). Criticism focused particularly on the combination in employment arbitration of the procedures being introduced as mandatory conditions of employment at the sole initiative of the employer; the resulting ability of the employer to determine the rules under which arbitration would occur, including the presence or absence of due process protections; and the role of the employer as a repeat player in arbitration against the one-time player individual employee (Bingham 1995, 1996, 1997). In a colorful analogy, Stone (1996) compared the new mandatory agreements to the old "yellow-dog" contracts through which employers in the early 20th century sought to bar employees from joining unions.

After a series of lower court decisions addressing the implications of the *Gilmer* decision, in 2001 the case of *Circuit City v. Adams*, 532 U.S. 105 (2001) resolved remaining doubts concerning the enforceability of arbitration agreements within employment contracts in favor of arbitrability. This reaffirmation of the enforceability of mandatory arbitration agreements and the absence of congressional action to reverse the Supreme Court decisions in this area have shifted the debate toward what standards for due process in the procedures should be required for arbitration agreements to be enforced (Leroy and Feuille 2003; Colvin 2004a; Wheeler, Klaas, and Mahony 2004). The courts have indicated a growing willingness to decline to enforce agreements lacking due process protections, based on the doctrine of unconscionability (Leroy and Feuille 2003). There have also been efforts in the professional dispute resolution community to establish due process standards for employment arbitration. In 1995 a coalition of groups, including the National Academy of Arbitrators, the American Arbitration Association, the American Bar Association, the American Civil Liberties Union, the Federal Mediation and Conciliation Service, the National Employment Lawyers Association, and the Society of Professionals in Dispute Resolution, developed a due process protocol setting out minimum standards for fairness in employment arbitration procedures (Dunlop and Zack 1997; Zack 1999). Although employers are not required to follow the protocol, the American Arbitration Association, a major arbitration service provider, indicated that it would follow the provisions in arbitrations that it administers (Wheeler, Klaas, and Mahony 2004). Enforcement of mandatory employment arbitration procedures continues to be among the most controversial issues in the ADR field. Empirical research has an important role to play in the debates. Later in this chapter we examine the growing body of empirical research on the extent, operation, and impact of employment arbitration procedures.

While legal and due process issues are important reasons to focus on developments in ADR, it should also be recognized that dispute resolution and workplace conflict management have potential implications for organizational performance. The impact of conflict and dispute resolution on organizational performance was notably demonstrated in a series of studies in the 1980s that showed a strong link between high levels of grievances and intense workplace conflict in unionized plants and poor levels of performance (Katz, Kochan, and Gobeille 1983; Katz, Kochan, and Weber 1985; Norsworthy and Zabala 1985; Ichniowski 1986). The studies focused primarily on the relationship between grievance rates and performance outcomes in unionized workplaces. Cutcher-Gershenfeld (1991) subsequently extended the analysis of the relationship between dispute resolution and organizational performance by including other aspects of conflict resolution. In particular, he found that both less-frequent conflicts and faster resolution of grievances at earlier, more informal stages were associated with higher performing, transformed patterns of workplace industrial relations. In studies of the relationship between human resource and industrial relations practices and organizational performance, both Arthur (1992) and Huselid (1995) similarly proposed aspects of grievance procedures as features of high-performance work systems. In each of these studies, however, the measures of dispute resolution proposed as forming an element of high-performance work systems were based on either the extent of access to or use of formal grievance procedures, in contrast to the idea in the previous studies that within formal grievance procedures more informal resolution of conflict is associated with better performance. Although these studies feature contrasting approaches to conceptualizing the relevant elements of dispute resolution, they all reinforce the importance of considering how dispute resolution procedures and activity affect organizational performance.

What Are Firms Doing with ADR?

When describing ADR procedures in the workplace it is first necessary to distinguish between union and nonunion workplaces. Grievance procedures in unionized workplaces have a distinctive history, structure, and role in labor relations as the primary mechanism for resolving disputes about the application of labor contracts (Lewin and Peterson 1988). By contrast, nonunion procedures are introduced at the initiative and discretion of employers, and their structures and roles vary widely with the different reasons for their adoption and the preferences and choices of management.

Union ADR Procedures

The system of labor arbitration for resolving disputes in unionized workplaces is in some respects itself an ADR procedure. Labor arbitration provides an alternative to industrial conflict, particularly strikes, as a mechanism to resolve disputes. This role is a primary justification in labor law for the strong deferral of the courts to arbitration procedures in resolving disputes in unionized workplaces. At the same time, labor arbitration is an alternative to the courts for resolving workplace disputes concerning the application of labor contracts (Stone 1981). However, while labor arbitration was developed as a flexible alternative procedure to industrial action and the courts, over time it has itself developed into a well-established, standardized set of procedures. Resulting concerns about the growing formalization, cost, and slow pace of modern labor arbitration have led to the expansion of ADR procedures developed as alternatives to traditional grievance and arbitration procedures in unionized workplaces (Feuille 1999).

The two most commonly used ADR procedures in unionized workplaces are expedited arbitration and grievance mediation. Expedited arbitration involves using simplified, less formal arbitration procedures directed at ensuring faster, less costly resolution of grievances (Zalusky 1976). The types of rule changes used in expedited arbitration include shorter, strictly enforced time limits for filing grievances; simplified presentation rules for arbitration hearings, such as limitations to written submissions; limitations on the length of arbitration hearings; use of a single arbitrator rather than a panel of arbitrators; time limits for the arbitrator to render a decision; and simplified decisions, such as a simple acceptance or rejection of the grievance.

Whereas expedited arbitration represents a simplified form of standard labor arbitration, grievance mediation provides a more genuine alternative to traditional procedures, with a mediation step being included before arbitration occurs (Feuille 1999). In an important study supporting the effectiveness of grievance mediation as an ADR procedure, Ury, Brett, and Goldberg (1988) examined the impact of grievance mediation in a coal mining workplace that was experiencing very high grievance levels and an inability to resolve grievances prior to arbitration. The introduction of grievance mediation in this setting led to a sharp increase in the resolution of grievances prior to arbitration, reducing the time and cost of grievance resolution, as well as improving the workplace relationship between the union and the employer. However, there is a paradox; although studies have shown strong positive impacts of grievance mediation, only around 3% of labor contracts include a step for it (Feuille 1999). Feuille argues that the explanation is that grievance mediation is a relatively fragile and limited process that works only where both parties are committed to it, whereas management in particular often prefers arbitration as a way to pressure unions to drop marginal grievances and as a more robust mechanism for ensuring resolution of difficult grievances.

Although expedited arbitration and grievance mediation are important ADR procedures in unionized settings, arguably more striking is the relative uniformity and continuity of labor arbitration and grievance procedures (Eaton and Keefe 1999). Grievance procedures culminating in labor arbitration and relatively similar in structure are found in almost all unionized workplaces and have changed relatively little in form or role over the last half-century—a statement that could not be made about many other aspects of labor relations. By contrast, when we turn to ADR procedures in nonunion workplaces, the most striking features are the variation and diversity in procedures and the high degree of change over time.

Nonunion ADR Procedures

A series of surveys over the last two decades suggest that half or more of organizations have some type of formal dispute resolution procedure for nonunion employees (Berenbeim 1980; Delaney, Lewin, and Ichniowski 1989; Edelman 1990; Feuille and Chachere 1995; Colvin 2003a; Lewin 2004, 2005). Modern ADR procedures in nonunion workplaces come in a variety of forms and structures. One broad differentiation is those where the ADR actor or decision maker determines a resolution of a dispute involving an employee and those where the ADR actor facilitates the resolution of the dispute. Arbitration is a classic determination-based ADR procedure, whereas mediation is a classic facilitation-based ADR procedure. Arbitration and mediation procedures are both found among ADR procedures in nonunion workplaces, but a number of additional types of determination and facilitation procedures are also employed.

Determination procedures. Determination-type procedures vary widely in their formality, due process protections, and decision makers. The most basic determination procedures involve employee appeal of complaints or grievances to a higher-level manager or managers, who then render a decision. The employee is typically instructed whom to initially direct the complaint to and whom the decision can be appealed to if the employee remains dissatisfied. These procedures may involve a number of steps, but in many, and likely most, nonunion procedures an individual higher-level manager is the final decision maker to whom the employee can appeal (Lewin 1993, 2005; Feuille and Chachere 1995). An obvious due process limitation of determination procedures is the lack of neutrality of the decision maker. Procedures that appeal to higher management can vary widely in their impact depending on the effort and attention managers put into their operation. In some basic "open door" procedures, employees are simply invited to bring their complaint to any manager, whose door will be "open" and who will attempt to resolve the problem (Feuille and Delaney 1992; Wheeler, Klaas, and Mahony 2004). Such procedures are obviously highly dependent on the goodwill of the individual manager contacted, and in some instances they may be so lacking in structure that they are little more than an informal procedure. Other determination procedures include those at IBM (which evolved out of an early open door procedure), where active investigation of disputes by higher-level management is directed from the CEO's office and involves substantial commitment of resources and rapid response to employee complaints (Ewing 1989). An important variation on the appeal to higher management procedures is the use of management appeal boards (Feuille and Chachere 1995). A panel of managers, typically three relatively senior executives, hears and decides employee complaints. An appeal board represents a more formalized approach to hearing and resolving disputes, involving substantially increased commitment of company resources in terms of the time of the executives on the board.

The most important recent innovation in determination-type procedures is the use of nonmanagerial decision makers. One type of procedure in this category is peer review panels, in which a majority of the panel that hears and decides employee complaints about unfair treatment in the workplace are employee peers of the grievant instead of managers (Cooper, Nolan, and Bales 2000; Colvin 2003a, 2003b, 2004a). Some review panels do exist where peer employees are a minority and managers the majority of panel members, but it appears that more procedures have a majority of employees (Feuille and Chachere 1995). Peer review panels got their initial impetus from a widely publicized model developed at a GE plant in the 1970s, where three peer employees and two managers sat on a panel to resolve grievances (Ewing 1989; Grote and Wimberly 1993). Over the 1980s and 1990s, peer review panels were adopted by increasing numbers of companies. In their 1992 survey of nonunion grievance procedures, Feuille and Chachere (1995) found that 5.1% of firms surveyed had either majority or minority peer review panel procedures. In a 1998 survey of telecommunications companies,

Colvin (2003a) found that 15.9% had peer review panel procedures. The higher incidence of peer review procedures in Colvin's study may partly reflect the more frequent adoption of these procedures as union substitution devices in an industry where there are relatively high levels of unionization and active organizing campaigns (Colvin 2003a).

Employment arbitration is the second major type of determination procedure involving nonmanagerial decision makers. As discussed earlier, employment arbitration received a major impetus from the Supreme Court's *Gilmer* decision in 1991, holding that claims based on employment statutes could be subject to arbitration agreements. Evidence indicates that adoption of employment arbitration procedures for nonunion employees spread rapidly following the *Gilmer* decision. In Feuille and Chachere's survey conducted in 1992, only 2.1% of respondent firms had adopted employment arbitration procedures (Feuille and Chachere 1995). By contrast, a 1995 survey by the Government Accountability Office found that 9.9% of companies subject to federal contractor reporting requirements had adopted employment arbitration procedures (General Accounting Office 1995). Further supporting the trend of growth, Colvin's 1998 survey of establishments in the telecommunications industry found that 16.3% had adopted employment arbitration procedures. A later 2003 survey of telecommunications industry establishments with a larger sample size, also conducted by Colvin, found a similar though slightly lower 14.1% incidence rate for employment arbitration procedures (Colvin 2004c).

Facilitation procedures. Two important innovations in nonunion workplaces are mediation and ombudspersons used in facilitation-type procedures (Bingham 2004; Wheeler, Klaas, and Mahony 2004). Mediation as a nonunion ADR procedure received an indirect boost from the expansion of employment arbitration in the wake of the *Gilmer* decision (Feuille 1999; Wheeler, Klaas, and Mahony 2004). Although arbitration may have advantages for employers compared to litigation, it still can involve substantial expense. Mediation may offer faster, cheaper resolution of disputes, with the added benefit that facilitation of a negotiated settlement of a dispute allows greater likelihood of being able to maintain a successful ongoing employment relationship (General Accounting Office 1997; Bingham 2004; Colvin 2004a). Although much greater attention has been paid to employment arbitration procedures, some evidence suggests increased adoption of mediation procedures used in conjunction with employment arbitration, typically as a prearbitration settlement step (General Accounting Office 1997; Colvin 2004a). Public agencies have also launched major initiatives to encourage mediation of employment discrimination disputes (Bingham 2004). At the federal level, the EEOC has launched extensive mediation programs (Lipsky, Seeber, and Fincher 2003; Bingham 2004), while at the state level the Massachusetts Human Rights Commission launched a mediation and arbitration program for employment discrimination claims (Kochan, Lautsch, and Bendersky 2002). Mediation has also been adopted by a number of public sector employers as a major component of ADR procedures for resolving employment disputes (General Accounting Office 1997; Bingham 2004).

In contrast to mediation, which generally involves using an external third-party neutral to resolve specific disputes, ombudsperson procedures involve establishing an office or an individual in a standing position in the organization to facilitate conflict resolution (Kolb 1987; Bingham and Chachere 1999; Bingham 2004; Wheeler, Klaas, and Mahony 2004). Ombudspersons can help facilitate the resolution of disputes between individuals in an organization through conciliation and mediation techniques. The role of the ombudsperson as a standing position can bring advantages in greater knowledge of organizational procedures and processes, as well as development of respect from management and employees through successful resolution of conflicts over time. On the other hand, an ombudsperson remains an employee of the organization and does not fulfill the same role as an external third-party neutral mediator or arbitrator (Cooper, Nolan, and Bales 2000). For this reason, a federal circuit court denied an employer's argument that an ombudsperson should receive the same privilege as a mediator against being required to testify in an employment discrimination case (*Carman v. McDonnell Douglas*, 114 F.3d 790 [8th Cir, 1997]). Systematic evidence is lacking on how widespread ombudsperson offices are.

Determinants of Firm Practices

With the virtual universality of labor arbitration and grievance procedures in unionized workplaces, the incidence of these procedures depends primarily on the extent of union representation. By contrast, given that adoption of ADR procedures in the nonunion workplace is at the discretion of management and, as outlined, various different types of procedures can be adopted, it is important to consider what factors influence the adoption of nonunion ADR procedures. A number of factors, both external and internal, come into play in explaining the adoption of and variation in nonunion ADR procedures. External pressures that may lead to the adoption of procedures include potential threats of union organizing and litigation pressures from the legal system. Internal influences include both general human resource management strategies and more specific conflict management strategies.

External Factors

Union substitution. In union substitution strategies, management in a nonunion establishment adopts employment policies similar to those of comparable unionized workplaces to reduce the relative attractiveness of unionization. Given that arguments about workplace justice and unfair treatment have been found to be particularly effective for unions in organizing drives (Bronfenbrenner 1997), management following union substitution strategies has a strong incentive to offer at least a partial substitute for the strong grievance procedures of unionized workplaces. This type of substitution was an important factor in the early development of nonunion ADR procedures. Many of the early procedures were responses to the labor arbitration and grievance procedures becoming common in unionized workplaces from the 1940s onward. A well-known example is the procedure adopted at Northrop Corporation in the context of substantial union organizing activity in the aircraft industry in the late 1940s, which included arbitration as the final step of a multistep grievance procedure closely paralleling what existed in unionized workplaces (Westin and Felieu 1988).

Although past accounts emphasized the role of union substitution in the development of nonunion ADR procedures (e.g., Berenbeim 1980), more recently some authors have questioned the continued importance of unionization threats given the decline in overall union representation (e.g., Feuille and Delaney 1992). However, the success of union substitution strategies is itself one of the plausible factors behind the decline in unionization rates, suggesting that these strategies could still be in wide use during a period of declining unionization. Research on the impact of union wage increases on nonunion wage setting has also shown that it is possible for union substitution strategies to play an important role even in industries where overall unionization is relatively low and concentrated in certain firms (Taras 1997). In a study specifically examining these effects on the adoption of nonunion ADR procedures, Colvin (2003a) found support for union substitution as a factor in the adoption of procedures in the telecommunications industry. Given that union representation and organizing activity in the United States tend to be concentrated in particular industries, these findings suggest that the role of union substitution in the adoption of nonunion ADR procedures is likely to vary by industry. As a result, rather than leading to uniform adoption of ADR procedures, union substitution is a factor likely to produce substantial variation in the adoption of procedures between different nonunion workplaces, depending on the level of unionization threat. Union substitution as a motivation is also likely to influence the type of nonunion ADR procedures that organizations adopt. In particular, the development and adoption of peer review panel procedures have been strongly associated with union substitution strategies. Indeed, the proto-typical peer review panel procedure adopted at a GE plant in the late 1970s was introduced directly as part of a union substitution strategy after a series of unsuccessful organizing drives at the plant (Ewing 1989). In a more recent example, the peer review procedure developed at the automotive parts manufacturer TRW was strongly influenced by the continued unionization threat in that industry (Colvin 2004a). More generally, in Colvin's study (2003a) of the adoption of nonunion ADR procedures in the telecommunications industry, union substitution was strongly associated with peer review panels, but not with other types of nonunion ADR procedures. Peer review panels offer a particularly useful union substitution tool for employers given that they allow employees to become involved in the process of remedying unfair treat-ment in the workplace (Colvin 2003a).

Legal pressures. Pressures from the legal system are the second major external factor leading to the adoption of nonunion ADR proce-dures. Among different types of procedures, employment arbitration is currently most strongly associated with litigation avoidance motivations, given the preclusive effect of arbitration agreements on employment law claims recognized by the Supreme Court in *Gilmer* in 1991 (Stone 1999). The likelihood that a company will adopt employment arbitration procedures depends on both its evaluation of the relative advantages of arbitration compared to litigation for resolving employment law claims and its evaluation of the level of litigation threat it is exposed to (Colvin 1999, 2003a). For example, some companies adopted employment arbi-tration procedures in direct response to increases in levels of litigation by employees, particularly in the wake of the rise in white collar employee downsizing in the early 1990s (Colvin 1999, 2004a). More generally, indicators of greater risk of litigation have been found to be associated with the adoption of employment arbitration procedures (Colvin 2003a).

In addition to the direct effect of the potential for litigation substitu-tion on the development of employment arbitration, legal pressures may also provide an incentive for adopting other types of nonunion ADR procedures. A substantial body of research by sociologists in the neoin-stitutional theory tradition has linked the expansion of employment discrimination laws and the adoption of nonunion grievance procedures by organizations (Edelman 1990; Sutton et al. 1994; Sutton and Dobbin 1996; Edelman, Uggen, and Erlanger 1999; Godard 2002). In explaining the relationships observed in their studies, these scholars emphasize the normative role of models of due process drawn from the legal system that are translated into the design of legalistic grievance procedures (Edelman 1990; Edelman, Abraham, and Erlanger 1992; Edelman, Uggen, and Erlanger 1999). A key component of this argument is the idea that direct or rational responses to the threat of litigation cannot explain the adoption of typical nonunion grievance procedures, since these procedures, unlike the employment arbitration procedures developed following *Gilmer*, would not bar employees from going to court (Edelman 1990; Sutton et al. 1994; Sutton and Dobbin 1996; Edelman, Uggen, and Erlanger 1999). The problem with this argument is its failure to recognize that even without having a legal effect of barring employees from going to court, nonunion ADR procedures can provide a substantial advantage to employers simply by leading to the resolution of disputes in the workplace that might otherwise provide the basis for a legal claim. A recent study comparing organizations in the United States and Canada found a significantly greater rate of adoption of nonunion grievance procedures in the United States, which was partly explained by greater concerns about litigation threats among the American employers (Colvin 2006).

Internal Factors

Human resource management strategies. In contrast to the external pressures of union organizing and litigation, human resource management strategies can provide an internal impetus to the adoption of nonunion ADR procedures. What are variously described as high-performance, high-involvement, or high-commitment work systems are claimed to enhance organizational performance by increasing employee commitment and involvement in the workplace (Walton 1985; Bailey 1993; Delery and Doty 1996; Ichniowski et al. 1996). Organizational justice theory suggests that nonunion ADR procedures may contribute to the performance of these systems by increasing employee justice perceptions and enhancing commitment to the organization (Sheppard, Lewicki, and Minton 1992; Folger and Cropanzano 1998). In an experimental study, Olson-Buchanan (1996) found that access to a grievance procedure increased employee willingness to continue working for their organization. In studies of high-performance work systems (HPWS), Huselid (1995) found that formal grievance procedures loaded on an HPWS factor, whereas Arthur (1992) postulated but did not find an association between formal grievance procedures and a high-performance cluster of work practices. More recently, a study using data from the Canadian Workplace and Employee Survey found that both the use of self-directed work teams and job rotation and an index of high-commitment practices predicted the presence of nonunion grievance procedures (Colvin 2004b). Among specific types of nonunion ADR procedures, Colvin (2003a) found a significant association between the adoption of self-directed work teams, one of the most characteristic HPWS practices, and the adoption of peer review procedures. Case study evidence suggests that HPWS strategies may also affect the design of specific procedural features, such as including stronger due process protections to avoid employee perceptions that the procedures are ineffective or biased toward management (Colvin 2004a).

  Conflict management strategies. Adoption and design of nonunion ADR procedures will also be influenced by the more specific conflict management strategies of management. Lipsky, Seeber, and Fincher (2003) argue that organizations adopt one of three broad categories of conflict management strategy, which they describe as the "Contend," "Settle," and "Prevent" strategies. Whereas organizations adopting a Contend strategy will be unlikely to adopt any type of procedure and simply oppose any claims against them, organizations adopting a Settle strategy will be more open to ADR procedures but will focus on simply resolving specific disputes as they arise. By contrast, organizations following a Prevent strategy will adopt systems that seek to proactively identify sources of conflict and prevent them from turning into costly disputes. A related idea that has gained prominence in the ADR literature is that organizations should develop integrated dispute resolution or conflict management systems (Constantino and Merchant 1996; Bendersky 2003). Advocates of this approach argue that these systems should provide employees with a range of options for resolving conflicts (Bendersky 2003). As with HPWS, conflict management strategies may interact with other factors in the development of nonunion ADR procedures. For example, strong litigation or union organizing pressures may help motivate an organization to follow a Prevent conflict management strategy. Similarly, concern for the effective resolution of employee grievances in an organization following an HPWS strategy may encourage the development of an integrated or complementary dispute resolution system.

Why Do Employees Use ADR?

  While employers may differ in why they implement ADR systems, such systems all function to provide employees with some form of voice in the workplace (Colvin 2003a). The voice offered by such systems may well be significant. However, it is important to note that ADR systems are typically used far less often than grievance systems in unionized organizations (Lewin 1990; Feuille and Delaney 1992). This relatively low rate raises questions about what factors encourage and what factors inhibit individual use of ADR within work organizations.

In examining the determinants of employee use of ADR systems, it is important to note that ADR utilization can take very different forms (Lewin 1987). For example, most ADR systems involve multiple steps, with the first step being relatively informal. Employees with concerns regarding whether they are being treated fairly or in a way that deprives them of their legal or contractual rights are encouraged to first address their concerns with their supervisors. Because of their informal nature, such discussions avoid public accusations regarding wrongdoing and allow for cooperative efforts to resolve concerns or problems. By contrast, later stages in ADR systems often involve appeals to a neutral party, such as a peer review board or an employment arbitrator (Colvin 2003b). At these later stages, the appeal is more formal and inevitably requires that claims be made public. Implied in taking such action is a statement about the perceived need for the intervention by a neutral party (Feuille and Chachere 1995; Bendersky 2003; Colvin 2004a).

We argue here that the determinants of ADR utilization vary with the form of ADR (Arnold and Carnevale 1997). Consistent with this argument, Olson-Buchanan and Boswell (2002) found that where the ADR process was more informal, employee loyalty was a more important determinant of usage than when the process was formal. Building upon their findings, we argue that the determinants of usage for the first stage in the ADR process will likely be very different from the determinants of usage at later, more formal stages in the appeal process. We begin by discussing factors likely to encourage or to inhibit use of the first step in the typical ADR system.

Initial-Stage Usage

The initial step in most systems of ADR is informal in nature. Employees are directed to communicate directly with their supervisors about any concerns they might have regarding how they have been treated by the employer (Lewin 1999; Colvin 2003a). The informal nature of this first step is a critical contextual factor (Sheppard 1984).

Figure 1 displays the likely determinants of ADR usage at the initial step. ADR usage is thought to be directly determined by employee perceptions regarding mistreatment, either by the employee's manager or by the application of organizational policy (Klaas 1989; Boswell and Olson-Buchanan 2004). However, the likelihood of an employee's actually perceiving mistreatment is, in turn, likely to be a function of employee attributes. Whether a decision is viewed as fair, inconsistent

FIGURE 1
Determinants of Initial-Stage ADR Use

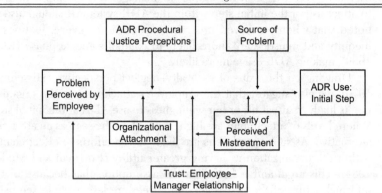

with past precedent, or a violation of organizational or legal policy is likely to depend on attitudes about the decision maker (Groth et al. 2002; Mayer and Gavin 2005). Where substantial mistrust exists in the employee–manager relationship, the manager's behavior is likely to be interpreted in light of that mistrust. Conversely, where there is substantial trust in the broader organization, decisions are less likely to be interpreted as violations of implicit or explicit agreements (Jones and George 1998).

While trust is likely to reduce the likelihood that an employee would perceive mistreatment, it is also likely that where such mistreatment is perceived, trust is likely to increase use of the ADR system, at least at the initial step. Because of the informal nature of the process at the initial stage, trust between an employee and his or her manager is likely to encourage the open discussion of concerns (Bendersky 2003). Trust is thought to emerge through a reciprocal social exchange process over time. Within that process (Coleman 1990; Jones and George 1998), trust emerges because each party observes the other demonstrate concern for the needs and interests of the other. As such, trust is likely to lead the employee to conclude that his or her manager will be responsive to the needs and concerns that might be addressed through the use of voice.

However, where the problem addressed is severe, trust is less likely to have an impact on whether an employee uses ADR in response to perceived mistreatment. Where the problem is severe, the employee may see little choice but to pursue the appeal through the various steps in the process as necessary (Arnold and Carnevale 1997). When the consequences of failing to gain satisfactory resolution of the perceived mistreatment outweigh concerns about managerial retribution for exercising voice, trust in the employee–manager relationship is unlikely to affect use of the initial step within the ADR system. It should also be noted that when perceived mistreatment is more severe, feelings of inequity and injustice are more likely to compel some response (Klaas 1989), making ADR usage more likely.

Drawing on the exit–voice–loyalty–neglect perspective (Hirschman 1970), we also suggest that the employee's attachment to the organization is likely to affect his or her willingness to use ADR at the initial step. Where levels of attachment are high, exit will not be seen as an attractive alternative. As such, employees are likely to see efforts to effect change within the organization as having greater utility (Freeman and Medoff 1984). This argument is based on the assumption that because of the informal nature of the first stage, employees are less likely to see using ADR as having negative implications for their prospects within the firm. Further, this assertion is consistent with the finding of Cappelli and Chauvin (1991) that grievance activity (in unionized firms) was higher in organizations paying above-market wages. The wages made it less likely that an employee would be able to obtain similar pay elsewhere, reducing the attractiveness of the exit option.

The nature and source of the perceived problem are also likely to play critical roles in determining how employees will respond to perceived mistreatment (Boswell and Olson-Buchanan 2004). Where the source of the mistreatment relates to broader organizational policy, employees are less likely to be reluctant to raise their concerns with their supervisor. Since the supervisor is not responsible for the perceived mistreatment, employees are less likely to be concerned about the supervisor being threatened by ADR use.

A final variable likely to be of importance relates to procedural justice perceptions regarding the ADR system itself (Feuille and Chachere 1995; Blancero and Dyer 1996; Folger and Cropanzano 1998). Even where there is limited trust between the manager and an employee, to the extent that the ADR system is seen as both effective and fair, employees are likely to be more willing to use it. While an employee may have doubts about his or her ability to resolve the problem at the initial step, confidence in the overall system may still lead the employee to use that step in response to perceived mistreatment.

Later-Stage ADR Usage

Somewhat different determinants are likely to be relevant to whether employees pursue their concerns in later stages of the ADR process. In most systems, the process becomes more formal as the

FIGURE 2
Determinants of Later-Stage ADR Use

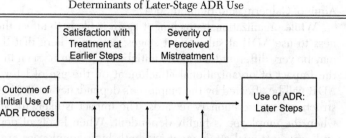

steps advance (Colvin 2004a). In addition, while some later steps in ADR systems clearly have a problem-solving focus (e.g., mediation), most formal systems culminate in quasi-judicial hearings (e.g., peer review boards or employment arbitration; Colvin 2003b). Further, the decision to use later steps in the process may often be seen as a direct challenge to the supervisor, particularly where the perceived mistreatment involves issues under supervisory control (Lewin 1990; Colvin 2003a, 2003b).

Because of these contextual factors, the determinants of usage at later stages of the ADR process are likely to differ from determinants at the initial step. Figure 2 displays a model depicting likely determinants of later-stage ADR use. As can be seen, whether perceived mistreatment leads to ADR usage at subsequent steps is likely to depend on how an employee perceives his or her treatment at earlier ones. These perceptions relate not only to the outcome resulting from the initial step, but also to perceptions regarding whether the employee was provided with sufficient voice at earlier steps. Here, the literatures on both procedural justice and interactional justice are likely to be relevant (Folger and Cropanzano 1998; Greenberg 2006). Beliefs regarding opportunities for voice at earlier steps are likely to be affected by both how earlier steps are structured and what information is shared with employees. Further, the interpersonal treatment when the employee initially raised concerns is also likely to affect perceptions regarding interactional justice and, in turn, perceptions regarding whether there were adequate opportunities to utilize voice mechanisms within the organization (Boroff 1991; Aquino, Galperin, and Bennett 2004).

While organizational attachment again is likely to affect the willingness to use ADR at subsequent stages, we argue here that the impact may be very different than at the initial step. As can be seen in Figure 2, the impact of organizational attachment on the use of later stages of ADR will be affected by the employee's dependency on the hierarchical structure for discretionary rewards. The impact is likely to be negative when the employee is highly dependent. When levels of dependence and organizational attachment are both high, employees are likely to be reluctant to directly challenge superiors in subsequent steps of the ADR process. Consistent with research showing that grievance activity can affect performance evaluations and other decisions involving some level of managerial discretion (Lewin and Peterson 1988; Klaas and DeNisi 1989), we would argue that employees may well be concerned about the consequences of openly challenging their superiors. While initial steps of ADR are more clearly designed to allow for constructive communication, subsequent steps involve a public challenge to prior decisions (Colvin 2004a). By contrast, the impact of organizational attachment on the use of later stages of ADR is likely to be positive in cases where the level of dependence on the hierarchical structure for discretionary rewards is low. For example, a positive effect is likely in cases where pay is determined more by group or team performance and/or where the individual does not anticipate competing for promotional opportunities.

Another variable likely to be important in predicting use of ADR at later steps relates to social support. In related literature examining who takes legal action against an employer after being terminated, Goldman (2001) found that social support was critical if the terminated employee was to interpret the employer's action as a potential legal violation. Goldman further suggested that social support was additionally critical given the confrontational nature of accusing a former employer of illegal discrimination. We argue that social support is also key at later steps within ADR. The formal nature of the ADR process combined with the necessity of publicly challenging superiors is likely sufficient cause for social support to be a critical component of this model (Groth et al. 2002). The issue of social support also highlights a key institutional difference between unionized grievance systems and ADR processes in nonunion settings. A union and its officers often provide needed social support to those considering action against an employer. Absent a union, social support must be provided by family, friends, and/or co-workers (Lewin 1987; Feuille and Delaney 1992; Colvin 2004a).

As can be seen in Figure 2, the nature and severity of perceived mistreatment are also likely to play an important role in determining employee responses at later ADR steps. For example, where an employee has been terminated, continued employment depends on the outcome of the ADR process (Bemmels 1997). So we would argue that when the perceived mistreatment is more severe, the employee is more likely to use subsequent ADR steps. A final variable identified in Figure 2 relates to procedural justice perceptions. As with decisions about whether to use ADR at the initial step, decisions about whether to use it at subsequent steps are likely to be affected by whether the system is seen as both effective and fair (Blancero and Dyer 1996). Related to this, norms about protecting employees from retaliation for using ADR are likely to be particularly critical.

Different Determinants for Different ADR Stages—Does It Matter?

The models we have discussed for using ADR at both initial and later steps raise interesting issues for organizations. Because of the informal nature of how issues are addressed at the initial step of ADR processes, we argued that factors such as trust in the employee–manager relationship will enhance the likelihood of an employee's using ADR to address perceived mistreatment. This would suggest that the initial stage may well be used to address a wide range of employment issues. It further suggests that where there is an effective employee–manager relationship, ADR may encourage both constructive communication between management and the employee and a sense of employee voice. However, the model presented here for ADR use at initial steps in procedures also raises questions about the voice mechanism being offered when there is a poor relationship between employee and manager. While we suggest that voice is still likely to be exercised when problems are severe, it is unclear if ADR would provide an effective forum for conflict resolution when trust in the employee–manager relationship is limited and when less severe problems are at issue.

The model we propose for ADR use at later steps in procedures suggests that there may be factors that inhibit ADR usage. Such factors are unlikely to be operative when the employee sees little risk associated with using ADR (e.g., when the employee is seeking to challenge termination) or perceives little dependency on the hierarchical structure for discretionary rewards. Where such conditions are not present, however, the model highlights why later stages of ADR may be less likely to induce the same level of open communication. This argument is premised on two assumptions: later stages in ADR almost inevitably involve a relatively direct and relatively public challenge to employment decisions by managers in the chain of command, and relatively few organizational cultures allow for such direct and public challenges to be viewed as constructive communication.

What Are the Consequences of Using an ADR System?

A critical question regarding ADR systems relates to the consequences for the individual employee of exercising voice through them. Does using an ADR system to address a problem or perceived mistreatment help to repair relationships between an employee and his or her managers? Does the exercise of voice within ADR prevent some of the behavioral consequences that would normally be associated with an employee's perceiving mistreatment? Or does effort by an employee to use systems of justice to change managerial behavior strain the relationship with managers in the organization? Do we observe retribution by managers and increased withdrawal by the employee?

Research examining the consequences for individuals of using ADR is relatively limited. To date, work in this area has emphasized one of two perspectives: the exit–voice–loyalty–neglect model or a model emphasizing managerial retribution in response to the exercise of voice.

ADR and the Exit–Voice–Loyalty–Neglect (EVLN) Model

Freeman and Medoff (1984) argued that differences in turnover between unionized and nonunionized firms might well be attributed to the voice provided by grievance systems required in most collective bargaining agreements. At the time of their seminal work, use of ADR in nonunion firms was more limited, making differences between union and nonunion firms in the access to voice mechanisms more significant. Drawing on the exit–voice literature, then, Freeman and Medoff (1984) argued that in nonunion firms employees would be less likely to see voice as a feasible alternative when conflict emerged in the workplace. In the absence of a viable voice mechanism, turnover would be more likely. By contrast, with collective bargaining the grievance system ensures that employees have an opportunity to exercise voice, reducing the attractiveness of the exit option. Consistent with the exit–voice model, unionization has been found to be associated across a number of settings with reduced turnover, controlling for wages and industry and organizational characteristics (Wilson and Peel 1991; Miller and Mulvey 1991). Further support in the unionized sector for the EVLN model is provided by research showing a relationship between greater strength of the grievance procedure and reduced turnover (Rees 1991).

Because the union–nonunion comparisons provide some evidence to support the EVLN model (Freeman 1980; Freeman and Medoff 1984), one might expect similar results from comparisons between nonunion firms with and without ADR. However, field data on the impact of ADR have to date produced only limited evidence to support the EVLN perspective. Batt, Colvin, and Keefe (2002) examined the impact of human resource practices and voice mechanisms on quit rates among telecommunications firms. While a marginally significant relationship was found between peer review and turnover, no significant relationship was observed between the use of nonunion arbitration and turnover rates, controlling for other components of high-involvement work systems. In addition, Delery et al. (2000) examined the determinants of quit rates among both union and nonunion trucking firms. One variable examined related to the proportion of employees involved with formal grievance procedures. After controlling for unionization, the grievance variable was not related to quit rates. However, given that the grievance variable may have been capturing employee use of the grievance process (as opposed to access to it), it is not clear whether this finding should be viewed as inconsistent with the EVLN model.

The modest support for the EVLN model in field studies examining ADR raises important questions. In the unionized sector, the collective bargaining structure provides strong institutional support for the grievance process, and it may in fact legitimize grievance behavior (Boroff and Lewin 1997). Is voice exercised in ADR systems viewed by employees as the same as grievance behavior exercised in the unionized sector? Or is there more variation among firms that have ADR in the actual effectiveness of their voice process, thus making it more difficult to examine the impact of effective ADR programs? Or perhaps the effect of ADR programs is tied to other high-involvement practices, thus making it difficult to isolate the contribution of ADR to lower turnover rates (Batt, Colvin, and Keefe 2002).

It is important to stress that the EVLN model does not argue that those who exercise voice are less likely to quit or engage in neglect behaviors than employees who did not exercise voice. Rather, it argues that an employee who perceives mistreatment is less likely to engage in exit or neglect alternatives if he or she uses the voice option (Boswell and Olson-Buchanan 2004). The exercise of voice may be an indication of workplace difficulties being experienced by an employee; where that is true, employees who exercise voice may actually be more likely to engage in turnover or neglect behaviors than those who do not (Katz, Kochan, and Gobeille 1983; Ichniowski 1986; Cutcher-Gershenfeld 1991). However, the employee who is experiencing some workplace difficulty is thought to be less likely to quit or engage in neglect behavior when he or she pursues the voice option (compared to when that option is not pursued).

Building on earlier work using the EVLN model, Olson-Buchanan and Boswell (2002) examined whether neglect behaviors are affected by use of voice. The more fully developed EVLN model argues that exit and voice are not the only responses to conflict. Employees can engage in a variety of neglect responses (e.g., absenteeism, reduced productivity), and these withdrawal responses can also be affected by the availability of effective voice mechanisms. Boswell and Olson-Buchanan (2004) found that perceived mistreatment, when it was personal in nature, was related to increased neglect responses. Interestingly, they found that whether the employee filed a grievance in response to the perceived mistreatment was not related to whether neglect responses were observed. In addition, in a laboratory study, Olson-Buchanan (1996) found that subjects who filed grievances engaged in more withdrawal behavior than did those who did not file grievances (even though they had access to a grievance system). Interestingly, though, this same study also found that subjects who experienced mistreatment and had access to a grievance system were less likely to exit than subjects who experienced mistreatment but did not have access to a voice mechanism.

While EVLN has received relatively consistent support when examining the impact of voice mechanisms in the unionized sector, the results are more mixed with regard to ADR. These relatively mixed results raise important questions for organizations and for future research. Does the impact of ADR vary with organizational characteristics or the design of the ADR system? What do firms need to do to get the same EVLN effect that is observed in association with unionized grievance procedures? What sort of due process protections are necessary? To what extent does the firm need to legitimize employee use of the ADR process (Klaas and Feldman 1993)?

In addressing such questions, it is important to consider both the nature of the conflict and the nature of the ADR process being used. For example, some ADR systems are designed primarily to function as alternatives to litigation. Employees who believe that their treatment violates a statutory or contractual provision can use the ADR system as an alternative to the legal system (Colvin 2004a). While such systems may well be functional for the organization and/or the employee, it is less clear whether they provide effective opportunities for voice about a wide range of employment issues. To the extent that they provide fewer opportunities for voice, questions might be raised about whether using them would be effective in reducing exit or neglect responses.

It may also be important for researchers to distinguish between the voice effects associated with use of ADR at early stages and at later stages. As noted earlier, the initial stages of ADR tend to be informal, with the focus on communication between employee and manager (Olson-Buchanan and Boswell 2002). Under what conditions does voice exercised in this more informal manner serve as an effective alternative to exit or neglect? Under what conditions does the salutary effect of exercising voice depend on being heard by more objective parties, and under what conditions does this salutary effect actually increase when voice is exercised more informally?

Retribution for the Exercise of Voice

In considering the consequences of exercising voice in an ADR system, it is important to also take note of the negative consequences for an employee that could result from managerial retribution. In studying the consequences of using a nonunion grievance procedure, Lewin (1990) found that filing a grievance was followed by lower performance evaluations as well as other negative outcomes in subsequent years. This finding is consistent with work in the unionized sector that has likewise showed that employees may experience negative consequences from using voice (Klaas and DeNisi 1989; Boroff and Lewin 1997; Lewin and Peterson 1999).

However, it is important to note that a grievance filed by an employee may reflect ongoing disagreement with a manager about how the employee should perform duties and/or how well those duties are being performed (Lewin 1999). In such cases, lower performance evaluations or other negative outcomes following grievance activity may not reflect retribution. If declining performance or behavioral problems ultimately led (because of action taken by management) to grievance activity, lower performance ratings in the subsequent year might be attributed to a continuing decline in performance.

Related to this, Boswell and Olson-Buchanan (2004) found in a study of staff employees in a university that, after controlling for perceived mistreatment, grievance filing behavior did not significantly explain attitudes and intentions relating to neglect or exit responses. This study did not examine the issue of managerial retribution (which would have required an assessment of managerial attitudes, assessments, or behaviors). However, it does raise the more general questions of whether managerial responses following grievance activity reflect continuing deterioration in the employee–manager relationship and whether grievance activity leads to retribution by the manager.

When examining the issue of retribution as a consequence of using ADR, therefore, it is important to consider the nature of the conflict and how ADR is being used. For example, is retribution equally likely when ADR is limited to presenting an employee's concerns to his or her manager, as opposed to pursuing ADR at levels above the manager? Further, how does the outcome of ADR use affect managerial behavior toward the employee who has used it? For example, does being over-ruled by a manager higher up in the chain of command or by a peer review board reduce the likelihood of retribution? Finally, little is known about how tendencies toward retribution might be affected by organizational norms about the legitimacy of using ADR.

Consequences for Firms from Using ADR

As we have discussed, a firm's decision to adopt an ADR system is frequently motivated by several factors. Accordingly, it is appropriate when evaluating ADR systems to consider multiple criteria. In light of the role played by union avoidance or substitution and by litigation avoidance in the motivation to adopt ADR, a suitable criterion for comparison and evaluation is the proportion of occurrences in which they produce rulings favoring the employer versus the employee. Likewise, the consequences of using ADR may be measured in terms of damages awarded. Moreover, the adoption of ADR, and of binding employment arbitration in particular, may significantly affect how an organization is perceived by its current and prospective employees. It is thus appropriate to examine the nature of ADR systems and how they might affect the organization.

Win Rates

Several researchers have examined published arbitration awards and found that the pattern of success for the employer varied considerably. In a recent review, LeRoy and Feuille (2001) reported a significantly greater incidence of the employer's prevailing in employment arbitration: the employer won in 61.8% of cases and the employee in 20.6%, with split decisions reached in 17.6%. In a study of employment arbitration cases published by the American Arbitration Association, Bingham (1998) reported employers prevailing in 79% of cases where the provisions of an employee handbook were involved. In contrast, when a case involved an individual contract of employment, the incidence of the employer's prevailing decreased to 31%.

Using data on employment arbitration awards gathered from multiple sources and covering the period between 1994 and 2001, Wheeler, Klaas, and Mahony (2004) found that overall the employer won 67% of the time. Consistent with Bingham's earlier work, the win rates varied with the nature of the case. Specifically, employers prevailed most often (70%) when the case involved an allegation of statutory discrimination and least often when the case involved an employment contract (44%) or when the burden of proof fell to the employer (40%).

In light of the role that strategies of union avoidance or substitution play in the impetus for ADR adoption, it is appropriate to briefly compare the outcomes of employment arbitration and labor arbitration. Looking only at labor arbitration cases where an employee challenged a termination, Wheeler, Klaas, and Mahony (2004) found that employers lost slightly more than half of the time (52%). In this instance, a loss for the employer is defined by the employee's being reinstated to his or her job, with or without back pay. Similarly, in their review of labor arbitration awards, Dilts and Dietsch (1989) found a near-even split in the aggregate win rates for employers (49.9%) and unions (50.1%). Interestingly, bearing the burden of proof lowered the aggregate win rate for each side down to 43%.

Research on labor arbitration awards reveals that the overall pattern of win rates for the employer varies with the nature of the case (Haber, Karim, and Johnson 1997). Specifically, employers prevailed least often (38.25%) in cases involving conditions of employment, followed by discharge cases (40.01%), then cases involving wages and hours (42.3%), while they were most likely to prevail (60.6%) when the case involved matters of arbitrability or cases involving promotions or demotions (56.9%).

Considering cases adjudicated in either the federal or state courts, the pattern of wins versus losses is confounded by the absence of data concerning those that do not reach a jury. By far the greatest proportion of cases are either settled voluntarily or decided on a motion for summary judgment by a judge. Indeed, one survey (Howard 1995) reported that between 79% and 84% of court cases involving an employment dispute were settled prior to final adjudication. In contrast, this same survey found that the percentage of settlements in employment arbitration cases ranged between 31% and 44%. The lower rate of settlement in arbitration is to be expected, as arbitration is often the final step in a multistep process in which most disputes are resolved at earlier steps (Colvin 2001). In addition to the possibility of settlement, significant numbers of cases are never adjudicated because many disputants are unable to secure legal representation. Indeed, some researchers estimate that employment attorneys agree to represent only 5% of the cases brought to them (Meeker and Dombrink 1993; Howard 1995). Nevertheless, there is a significant body of research examining the outcomes of employment disputes determined by the court system.

Looking at the federal courts, while the evidence from employment cases is somewhat mixed, there is a clear pattern of awards favoring the employer. For example, an examination of federal district court cases involving allegations of discrimination found that employers won 88% of the time for the period spanning 1996 to 2000 (Wheeler, Klaas, and Mahony 2004). In contrast, earlier studies showed that when a discrimination case went to trial, employers won 76% of the time in 1990 and 64.5% of the time in 1998 (Litras 2000). Thus, when compared to employment arbitration, the pattern of employment trial verdicts appears to be more favorable toward employers.

A significant drawback to relying on comparisons of this nature is that they do not consider the myriad systematic differences in the cases involved. To that end, Bingham and Mesch (2000) compared the decisions reached by labor arbitrators with those of employment arbitrators evaluating the same set of hypothetical cases. It was found that labor arbitrators were more likely to rule in favor of the employee than were employment arbitrators. Using a similar methodology, Wheeler, Klaas, and Mahony (2004) presented a variety of decision makers with an identical series of cases in which an employee was challenging a termination. Specifically, they compared awards favoring the employee across several different types of decision makers evaluating the same 12 cases. As expected, labor arbitrators were the decision makers most likely to rule in favor of the employee, 55% of the time. Human resource managers were second most likely to rule in favor of the employee, 46% of the time. Interestingly, at 45%, peer review panelists were nearly as likely as human resource managers to rule in favor of the employee. Jurors, who each had previously served in a case involving an employment dispute, ruled in favor of the employee just 38% of the time. Employment arbitrators ruled in favor of the employee least often: only 33% of the time when evaluating cases based on a just-cause issue, and 25% of the time when evaluating cases based on statutory claims (Wheeler, Klaas, and Mahony 2004).

Lastly, as an ADR mechanism, peer review systems tend to be well received by both managers and employees. From the perspective of an overall HR strategy, peer review systems tend to enhance employee perceptions of an organization's attractiveness while offering employers the potential to deliver objective and fair decisions (Wilensky and Jones 1994; Payson 1998). While there are only a few empirical investigations of peer review systems, some anecdotal evidence suggests that managers believe peer review panels result in more severe sanctions than had the decision been left up to the individual manager (Cooper, Nolan, and Bales 2000). However, Mahony, Klaas, and Wheeler (2005) found no significant difference between peer review and HR managers in willingness to rule for the employee. One study found that the implementation of peer review significantly reduced employee filings with the Equal Opportunity Commission (Wilensky and Jones 1994). In a comparison of procedures across workplaces, Colvin (2003b) found that among nonunion workplaces the percentage of disciplinary decisions subsequently reversed through grievance appeals was higher for both procedures with peer review panels (9.9% of all disciplinary decisions successfully appealed) and employment arbitration (11.1%) than for other types of nonunion grievance procedures (2.7%). This same study also found a significantly higher rate (17.3%) of successful appeals through grievance procedures in unionized workplaces (Colvin 2003b).

Awards

In addition to examining win–loss rates across different forms of dispute resolution, it is potentially informative to consider the amounts recovered by employees when they do prevail. In a recent survey of employment arbitrator awards, Estreicher (2001) reported a median award of $52,737 for cases determined prior to adoption of the Due Process Protocol, and $39,279 thereafter. In that same study, Estreicher references another review of American Arbitration Association (AAA) cases covering the period 1999 and 2000, which found a median award of $34,733. In an earlier study, Bingham (1998) found a mean award of $49,030 in a sample of 91 AAA cases decided during the period 1993 to 1995. As discussed earlier, for the period 1994 to 2000, the median award delivered by a jury in an employment discrimination case was $110,000 (Eisenberg and Schlanger 2003). While this amount for jury verdicts is substantially higher than the median award estimates for employment arbitrators, it is the possibility for the occasional large—often multimillion dollar—jury verdict that may pose the greater threat to employers and in practice be the more significant differentiator between outcomes from employment arbitration and court cases.

Organizational Outcomes

Considering that many employers adopt ADR processes as part of an overall HR strategy, it is appropriate to evaluate the effects these systems may have on other HR-related issues. To that end, two studies (Richey et al. 2001; Mahony et al. 2005) measured the effects of adopting employment arbitration systems on overall organizational attractiveness. Among potential applicants, the perceived desirability of an organization as a place to work was significantly reduced when the organization had in place a mandatory and binding procedure of employment arbitration (Richey et al. 2001; Mahony et al. 2005). Moreover, giving up the right to sue in employment disputes had a larger negative effect for minority applicants than for nonminority applicants. As both these studies suggest, the presence of mandatory employment arbitration may harm an organization's ability to attract and retain talent. The effects of those decisions become even more salient when the organization is attempting to attract a diverse workforce. The adverse consequences, however, may be mitigated. Indeed, Mahony et al. (2005) found the negative effects of mandatory employment arbitration are lessened when the procedures include strong due process protocols, similar to those advocated by AAA, or when they include just-cause protections. From the results of these two studies, it is clear that prospective employees are using the features of an organization's ADR system to make overall judgments about the employer.

Determinants of Outcomes from ADR

While it is informative to compare the likelihood of either the employer's or the employee's prevailing across dispute resolution forums, the underlying nature of individual cases affords the greatest predictive value. Research has shown that when evaluating employment termination cases, third-party decision makers are often influenced by a host of factors relating to the nature of the alleged offense and the contextual environment in which it occurred (Judge and Martocchio 1996; Vidmar 1998; Devine et al. 2001). This is in large part because decision makers are charged with restoring justice through imposing an appropriate sanction, and when the circumstances dictate they may be motivated to exact retributive justice (Vidmar 2001). That motivation occurs most often when harm is perceived to have occurred as the result of the offending party's deviation from accepted norms and obligations (Vidmar and Miller 1980; Deutsch and Coleman 2000).

Sanctioning decisions are further affected by the attribution process (Wood and Mitchell 1981). Several studies have consistently demonstrated that less-severe sanctions occur when the decision maker attributes the offending behavior to a cause beyond the employee's control (Abbott 1993; Judge and Martocchio 1996). The individual is seen as being less responsible or not responsible for the offense and thereby deserving of less punishment. Whether the terminated employee (the disputant) is appealing to management, a jury, or an arbitrator, he or she actively and deliberately attempts to alter the decision maker's impressions or to counter the presentation of otherwise damaging information.

In the process of managing these impressions, disputants often present extralegal information, including details not related to the merits of the termination. Disputants frequently present extralegal information with the intent of portraying themselves in a positive light or as being somehow less responsible or not responsible for the actions that resulted in their termination. Within the literature, several factors have been identified that affect attributions made by the decision maker (Klaas and Dell'Omo 1997).

Work History

While arbitral norms require that seniority be considered in labor arbitration hearings (Elkouri and Elkouri 1993), no such norms exist for employment disputes in the nonunion sector. Nevertheless, evidence from studies examining the role of extralegal information in employment tribunals suggests that impressions made by the disputant substantially affect the punishment received. In particular, evidence pertaining to the disputant's prior work history and performance, including absenteeism, disciplinary record, and/or seniority, has been found to influence disciplinary decisions across an array of dispute resolution forums, including labor arbitration, jurors, employment arbitration, and peer review (Wasserman and Robinson 1980; Reskin and Visher 1986; Simpson and Martocchio 1997; Eylon, Giacalone, and Pollard 2000; Wheeler, Klaas, and Mahony 2004). A similar bias in decision making has been found among managers and supervisors. For example, several studies of managerial decision makers found consistent evidence of the disputant's work history influencing the outcome, with those employees possessing a lengthy record of prior good performance receiving lesser penalties than those with relatively little tenure or with records of disciplinary infractions (Klaas and Wheeler 1990; Martocchio and Judge 1995; Mahony, Klaas, and Wheeler 2005). Overall, it appears that decision makers are more apt to attribute the cause of the disciplinary incident to factors beyond the disputant's control and to regard the disputant as worthy of rehabilitation when presented with evidence of a positive work record (Simpson and Martocchio 1997). In their comparative study, Wheeler, Klaas, and Mahony (2004) found that for all categories of decision makers, substantial weight was given to presence of a positive work record. Employees with favorable work histories were significantly more likely to receive favorable decisions than those with short or poor work histories, though the effect was weakest where employment arbitrators were the decision makers.

Provocation

Excuse making and justifications are two defensive behaviors intended to neutralize or mitigate the underlying adverse act or its consequences (Scott and Lyman 1968). Individual disputants may attempt to establish that they were indeed provoked by their supervisors (Abrams and Nolan 1985). In so doing, they claim that their poor performance or behavior is the direct result of the behavior or attitudes of another (Scott and Lyman 1968). Several studies have reported more lenient decisions among decision makers when presented with credible evidence in support of this defense. In decisions to reverse or reduce discipline, many labor arbitrators have cited managerial conduct as a contributory factor in the offense for which an employee was terminated (Stone 1969; Jennings and Wolters 1976; Bohlander and Blancero 1996; Lucero and Allen 1998). Klaas and Wheeler (1990) report a similar bias toward greater leniency among managerial decision makers, resulting in more modest discipline recommendations. Lastly, Wheeler, Klaas, and Mahony (2004) found a similar bias toward leniency among peer panels, jurors, HR managers, and labor arbitrators. Employment arbitrators appeared to give little weight to the employee's conduct being provoked.

Allegations of Employer Wrongdoing

In the absence of an explicit contract of employment, an allegation of discrimination often represents the only viable grounds for challenging a termination in an employment-at-will environment (Bales 1997). As a result, disputants often attempt to influence arbitrators' perceptions of them by claiming to be victims of discrimination. As performance appraisals tend to be subjective, their reliance on supervisory judgment often provides disputants opportunity to allege discriminatory bias in supervisors. While blaming someone else for the discipline predicament is an excuse behavior, the disputant need not deny the underlying poor performance. As with allegations of provocation, the disputant must demonstrate or persuade the arbitrator, through the presentation of evidence, that the negative evaluation of performance was "merely a pretext to effectuate his discriminatory attitudes" (Berrett and Kernan 1987:494). Evidence from published employment arbitration cases reveals that the success rate for disputants is modestly higher when brought before an employment arbitrator than when argued in federal courts, but not in state courts (Wheeler, Klaas, and Mahony 2004).

Nature of the Offense

Within the employment arena, termination is commonly viewed as the ultimate employer sanction. The literature on employee discipline and discharge shows that the decision to either reinstate or uphold a termination varies greatly with both the nature of the offense and with the strength of the evidence presented by the employer. Labor arbitrators, for instance, generally require a higher degree of proof when a grievant is challenging a termination than in cases involving lesser penalties (Elkouri and Elkouri 1993). The influence of the nature of the alleged offense on arbitration decisions is mixed. Labor arbitrators are more likely to reinstate a grievant terminated for dishonesty or poor performance than one terminated for other reasons (Labig, Helburn, and Rodgers 1985). Block and Stieber's review (1987), however, found that the discharge in cases involving poor performance, excessive absenteeism, employee threats or violence, incompetence, or negligence was significantly more likely to be upheld than in cases involving other offenses. While these reviews present contradictory findings, one possible explanation may center on the strength of the evidence presented.

When defending allegations of discriminatory discharge, for example, employers must demonstrate that the motivating factor behind the termination decision was not discriminatory in nature but rather driven by some other factor, such as employee wrongdoing or unsatisfactory work performance. Thus, in a case alleging poor performance, the likelihood of the employer's prevailing often depends on the ability to present documented evidence of the poor performance. Alleged offenses such as poor or unsatisfactory work performance are generally easily documented, and the employer's ability to prevail thus may hinge on the strength of the evidence put forth by the employer in an arbitration hearing. Indeed, weak or unsupported evidence of employee wrongdoing is among the most frequently cited factors used to justify a labor arbitrator's decision to reduce or reverse a disciplinary penalty (Karim and Stone 1988; Bohlander and Blancero 1996).

Procedural Compliance

Research on arbitral decision making yields a consistent pattern favoring the employee when evidence is presented of the employer's failing to follow stated procedures in the disciplinary process. Indeed, procedural noncompliance prior to a termination is frequently listed by labor arbitrators as the primary justification for overturning or lessening the penalty (Karim and Stone 1988; Bohlander and Blancero 1996; Lucero and Allen 1998; Simpson and Martocchio 1997). The employee was significantly more likely to prevail when able to demonstrate that the failure of the company to adhere to its stated disciplinary process had an unduly prejudicial effect on the employee's rights (Stone 1969; Karim and Stone 1988).

The weight assigned by labor arbitrators to procedural compliance is to be expected given the prevalence of the just-cause standard for discharge in the unionized sector. A similar pattern is evident, however, in decisions reached by juries, leading Berrett and Kernan (1987) to conclude that the courts appear to favor progressive discipline and employee notification of poor performance. In their review of judicial decisions regarding alleged wrongful termination, Dunford and Devine (1998) report that many courts in many states have adopted the position that procedures and policies outlined in an employee handbook may constitute an implied contract, particularly formal grievance procedures. Consequently, failure to follow progressive discipline may constitute a breech of the implied contract of employment. Procedural noncompliance may further negatively influence overall perceptions of organizational justice. Several researchers have found a consistent link between organizational justice perceptions and perceptions about an organization's grievance processes and appeal systems (Conlon 1993; Gordon and Fryxell 1993). Indeed, procedural compliance affects procedural justice perceptions regarding the sanctioning process (Lind and Tyler 1988). Among jurors involved in criminal cases, for example, evidence of procedural noncompliance resulted in reduced sanction decisions (Fleming, Wegener, and Petty 1999).

Klaas, Mahony, and Wheeler (2006) compared the decision-making policies of labor arbitrators with those of employment arbitrators and jurors. While the emphasis placed on procedural noncompliance varied in magnitude across the types of decision makers, there was a consistent increase in the likelihood of reversing a termination when the employer failed to follow stated procedures. Peer panelists, when presented with information that the company violated its own disciplinary procedures, were likewise more inclined to rule in favor of the employee (Wheeler, Klaas, and Mahony 2004). These findings, together with those from the jury decision-making literature, suggest that decision makers, even in the absence of a just cause standard, view procedural noncompliance as grounds for reversal of the termination.

Other Mitigating Circumstances

Disputants who present information concerning a recent traumatic life event do so with the intention of providing an alternative explanation for their poor performance (DeGree and Snyder 1985) or in an effort to garner sympathy from the decision maker. Self-handicapping in this way attempts to externalize the cause for the poor performance by attributing it to factors beyond the disputant's control. Empirical evidence from the impression-management literature supports the viability of this protective strategy to influence attributions about performance in evaluative settings (DeGree and Snyder 1985; Hirt, McCrea, and Boris 2003). A large and significant relationship between the presence of adverse personal problems and more lenient disciplinary outcomes was reported by Klaas and Wheeler (1990) in their study of managerial decision makers. In the case of poor performance, the introduction of evidence attesting to otherwise difficult or adverse personal circumstances—often a specific familial event such as protracted illness or death—is frequently cited by labor arbitrators in justifications for reducing or reversing discipline (Bohlander and Blancero 1996).

Conclusion

With the growth of alternative dispute resolution procedures, there is a danger of viewing ADR as a sui generis set of techniques to be examined in isolation from the broader issues of work and employment. From such a technique-based perspective on ADR, one could look at a procedure such as mediation abstracted from the workplace context and what it is serving as an alternative to. By contrast, a central insight of past industrial relations research is the interconnectedness of the range of different processes and activity that occur in work and employment relations (Dunlop 1958; Kochan, Katz, and McKersie 1994). Research on dispute resolution spans perspectives ranging from macro-level concerns about the roles of rising litigation and declining unionization in employment relations to such micro-level concerns as the nature of decision making within procedures and individual employee outcomes. Across this range of perspectives, the literature reviewed here illustrates how dispute resolution is connected to a broad range of issues in employment relations. Two themes running through this chapter help show these connections: the relationship between ADR and human resource management, and the relationship between dispute resolution in union and in nonunion settings.

ADR procedures are both influenced by and operate as part of the human resource management system of the firm. Adoption of ADR procedures is influenced by a firm's HR strategy; for example, firms employing high-performance work practices such as self-managed work teams are more likely to adopt related ADR procedures, such as peer review panels (Colvin 2003a). Use of ADR procedures by employees is in turn influenced by aspects of the HR system of the workplace (Colvin 2003b, 2004b). At the same time, the operation of ADR procedures will in turn affect other HR outcomes, such as employee loyalty, turnover, and the functioning of disciplinary systems (Boroff and Lewin 1997; Lewin 1999). Perhaps perversely, research indicating the frequency of managerial retaliation against employees who have lodged complaints against them through ADR procedures itself indicates the centrality of dispute resolution processes to relations of power and authority in the workplace (Lewin 1999; Lewin and Peterson 1999).

ADR procedures also need to be understood in relation to what they are serving as alternatives to. There is a particularly strong contrast between unionized and nonunionized workplaces in the area of dispute resolution procedures, yet the relationship between union and nonunion procedures is also important to understanding developments in the ADR area. Nonunion procedures have risen in importance with the secular decline in unionization levels, yet the expansion of nonunion ADR is also partly a response and contributing factor to declining unionization (Colvin 2003a). In evaluating the operation of nonunion ADR procedures, union counterparts continue to serve as a key point of comparison. For example, in understanding the operation of new employment arbitration procedures, comparisons to the decision-making processes of traditional labor arbitrators have proved particularly insightful (Wheeler, Klaas, and Mahony 2004).

Research on dispute resolution and grievance procedures was one of the central topics in past industrial relations research (Lewin and Peterson 1988). The review of the recent literature in this chapter indicates that with the growth of ADR, this continues to be a fertile area for current researchers. In particular, labor and employment relations research in the ADR area is developing insights that are relevant to such fields as human resource management, law, and organizational behavior. The challenge for future dispute resolution researchers will be to continue to take this broad perspective on ADR procedures and not become confined to a narrow focus on techniques.

References

Abbott, W.F. 1993. *Jury Research: A Review and Bibliography.* Washington, DC: American Law Institute.

Abrams R.I., and D.R. Nolan. 1985. "Towards a Theory of 'Just Cause' in Employee Discipline Cases." *Duke Law Review*, Vol. 1985, no. 3–4, pp. 594–623.

Aquino, K., B.L. Galperin, and J.R. Bennett. 2004. "Social Status and Aggressiveness as Moderators of the Relationship between Interactional Justice and Workplace Deviance." *Journal of Applied Social Psychology*, Vol. 34, no. 5 (May), pp. 1001–29.

Arnold, J.A., and P.J. Carnevale. 1997. "Preferences for Dispute Resolution Procedures as a Function of Intentionality, Consequences, Expected Future Interaction, and Power." *Journal of Applied Social Psychology*, Vol. 27, no. 5 (March), pp. 371–98.

Arthur, Jeffrey B. 1992. "The Link between Business Strategy and Industrial Relations Systems in American Steel Minimills." *Industrial and Labor Relations Review*, Vol. 45, no. 3 (April) pp. 488–506.

Bailey, T. 1993. *Discretionary Effort and the Organization of Work: Employee Participation and Work Reform Since Hawthorn.* New York: Columbia University.

Bales, Richard A. 1997. *Compulsory Arbitration.* Ithaca, NY: Cornell University Press.

Batt, R., A.J.S. Colvin, and J. Keefe. 2002. "Employee Voice, Human Resource Practices, and Quit Rates: Evidence from the Telecommunications Industry." *Industrial and Labor Relations Review*, Vol. 55, no. 4 (July), pp. 573–94.

Bemmels, B. 1997. "Exit, Voice, and Loyalty in Employment Relationships." In D. Lewin, D.J.B. Mitchell, and M.A. Zaidi, eds., *The Human Resource Management Handbook*. Greenwich, CT: JAI Press, pp. 245–59.

Bendersky, C. 2003. "Organizational Dispute Resolution Systems: A Complementarities Model." *Academy of Management Review*, Vol. 28, no. 4 (October), pp. 643–56.

Berenbeim, Ronald. 1980. *Nonunion Complaint Systems: A Corporate Appraisal*. New York: Conference Board.

Berrett, Gerald V., and Mary C. Kernan. 1987. "Performance Appraisal and Terminations: A Review of Court Decisions since *Brito v. Zia* with Implications for Personnel Practices." *Personnel Psychology*, Vol. 40, no. 3 (Autumn), pp. 489–503.

Bingham, Lisa B. 1995. "Is There a Bias in Arbitration of Non-Union Employment Disputes?" *International Journal of Conflict Management*, Vol. 6, no. 4 (October), pp. 369–97.

———. 1996. "Emerging Due Process Concerns in Employment Arbitration: A Look at Actual Cases." *Labor Law Journal*, Vol. 47, no. 2 (February), pp. 108–26.

———. 1997. "Employment Arbitration: The Repeat Player Effect." *Employee Rights and Employment Policy Journal*, Vol. 1, no. 1, pp. 189–220.

———. 1998. "On Repeat Players, Adhesive Contracts, and the Use of Statistics in Judicial Review of Employment Arbitration Awards." *McGeorge Law Review*, Vol. 29, no. 2 (Winter), pp. 223–59.

———. 2004. "Employment Dispute Resolution: The Case for Mediation." *Conflict Resolution Quarterly*, Vol. 22, no. 1–2 (Fall–Winter), pp. 145–74.

Bingham, Lisa B., and Denise R. Chachere. 1999. "Dispute Resolution in Employment: The Need for Research." In E. Eaton and J.H. Keefe, eds., *Employment Dispute Resolution and Worker Rights in the Changing Workplace*. Champaign, IL: Industrial Relations Research Association, pp. 95–135.

Bingham, Lisa B., and Debra J. Mesch. 2000. "Decision Making in Employment and Labor Arbitration." *Industrial Relations*, Vol. 39, no. 4 (October), pp. 671–94.

Blancero, D., and L. Dyer. 1996. "Due Process for Non-Union Employees: The Influence of System Characteristics on Fairness Perceptions." *Human Resource Management*, Vol. 35, no. 3 (Fall), pp. 343–59.

Block, Richard N., and Jack Stieber. 1987. "The Impact of Attorneys and Arbitrators on Arbitration Awards." *Industrial and Labor Relations Review*, Vol. 40, no. 4 (July), pp. 543–55.

Bohlander, George W., and Donna Blancero. 1996. "A Study of Reversal Determinants in Discipline and Discharge Arbitration Awards: The Impact of Just Cause Standards." *Labor Studies Journal*, Vol. 21, no. 3 (Fall), pp. 3–18.

Boroff, K. 1991. "Measuring the Perceptions of the Effectiveness of a Workplace Complaint Procedure." In D. Lewin and B.E. Kaufman, eds., *Advances in Industrial and Labor Relations*, Ch. 5, pp. 207–33.

Boroff, K.E., and D. Lewin. 1997. "Loyalty, Voice, and Intent to Exit a Union Firm: A Conceptual and Empirical Analysis." *Industrial and Labor Relations Review*, Vol. 51, no. 1 (October), pp. 50–63.

Boswell, W.R., and J.B. Olson-Buchanan. 2004. "Experiencing Mistreatment at Work: The Role of Grievance-Filing, Nature of Mistreatment, and Employee Withdrawal." *Academy of Management Journal*, Vol. 47, part 1, pp. 129–39.

Bronfenbrenner, Kate. 1997. "The Role of Union Strategies in NLRB Certification Elections." *Industrial and Labor Relations Review*, Vol. 50, no. 2 (January), pp. 195–212.

Cappelli, Peter, and Keith Chauvin. 1991. "A Test of an Efficiency Model of Grievance Activity." *Industrial and Labor Relations Review*, Vol. 45, no. 1 (October), pp. 3–14.

Carman v. McDonnell Douglas, 114 F.3d 790 (8th Cir, 1997).

Circuit City v. Adams, 532 U.S. 105 (2001).

Clermont, Kevin M., and Stewart J. Schwab. 2004. "How Employment Discrimination Plaintiffs Fare in Federal Court," *Journal of Empirical Legal Studies*, Vol. 1, no. 2 (July), pp. 429–58.

Coleman, J.S. 1990. *Foundations of Social Theory*. Cambridge, MA: Belknap Press.

Colvin, Alexander J.S. 1999. *Citizens and Citadels: Dispute Resolution and the Governance of Employment Relations*. Dissertation, Cornell University.

———. 2001. "The Relationship between Employment Arbitration and Workplace Dispute Resolution Procedures." *Ohio State Journal on Dispute Resolution*, Vol. 16, no. 3, pp. 643–68.

———. 2003a. "Institutional Pressures, Human Resource Strategies, and the Rise of Nonunion Dispute Resolution Procedures." *Industrial and Labor Relations Review*, Vol. 56, no. 3 (April), pp. 375–92.

———. 2003b. "The Dual Transformation of Workplace Dispute Resolution." *Industrial Relations*, Vol. 42, no. 4 (October), 712–35.

———. 2004a. "Adoption and Use of Dispute Resolution Procedures in the Nonunion Workplace." In D. Lewin and B.E. Kaufman, eds., *Advances in Industrial and Labor Relations*, Vol. 13, pp. 69–95.

———. 2004b. "The Relationship between Employee Involvement and Workplace Dispute Resolution." *Relations Industrielles/Industrial Relations*, Vol. 59, no. 4 (Fall), pp. 671–94.

———. 2004c. "Mandatory Arbitration and the Reconfiguration of Workplace Dispute Resolution." *Cornell Journal of Law and Public Policy*, Vol. 13, no. 3 (Summer), pp. 581–97.

———. 2006. "Flexibility and Fairness in Liberal Market Economies: The Comparative Impact of the Legal Environment and High Performance Work Systems." *British Journal of Industrial Relations*. Vol. 44, no. 1 (March), pp. 73–97.

Conlon, Donald, E. 1993. "Some Tests of the Self-Interest and Group-Value Models of Procedural Justice: Evidence from an Organizational Appeal Procedure." *Academy of Management Journal*, Vol. 36, no. 5 (October), pp. 1109–24.

Constantino, C.A., and C.S. Merchant. 1996. *Designing Conflict Management Systems: A Guide to Creating Productive and Healthy Organizations*. San Francisco: Jossey-Bass.

Cooper, Laura J., Dennis R. Nolan, and Richard A. Bales. 2000. *ADR in the Workplace*. St. Paul, MN: West Group.

Cutcher-Gershenfeld, J. 1991. "The Impact on Economic Performance of a Transformation in Workplace Relations." *Industrial and Labor Relations Review*, Vol. 44, no. 2 (January), pp. 241–60.

DeGree, Craig E., and C.R. Snyder. 1985. "Adler's Psychology (of Use) Today: Personal History of Traumatic Life Events as a Self-Handicapping Strategy." *Journal of Personality and Social Psychology*, Vol. 48, no. 6 (June), pp. 1512–19.

Delaney, John T., David Lewin, and Casey Ichniowski. 1989. *Human Resource Policies and Practices in American Firms*, BLMR #137. Washington, DC: U.S. Department of Labor.

Delery, John E., and Harold D. Doty. 1996. "Modes of Theorizing in Strategic Human Resource Management: Tests of Universalistic, Contingency, and Configurational Performance Predictions." *Academy of Management Journal*, Vol. 39, no. 4 (August), pp. 802–35.

Delery, J., N. Gupta, J. Shaw, G.D. Jenkins, and M. Ganster. 2000. "Unionization, Compensation, and Voice Effects on Quits and Retention." *Industrial Relations*, Vol. 39, no. 4 (October), pp. 625–46.

Deutsch, M., and P.T. Coleman. 2000. *The Handbook of Conflict Resolution: Theory and Practice*. San Francisco: Jossey-Bass.

Devine, Dennis J., Laura D. Clayton, Benjamin Dunford, R. Seying, and J. Pryce. 2001. "Jury Decision Making: 45 Years of Empirical Research on Deliberating Groups." *Psychology, Public Policy, and Law*, Vol. 7, no. 3 (September), pp. 622–727.

Dilts, David A., and Clarence R. Deitsch. 1989. "Arbitration Win/Loss Rates as a Measure of Arbitrator Neutrality." *The Arbitration Journal*, Vol. 44, no. 3 (September), pp. 42–7.

Dunford, Benjamin, and Dennis J. Devine. 1998. "Employment at Will and Employee Discharge: A Justice Perspective on Legal Action Following Termination." *Personnel Psychology*, Vol. 51, no. 4 (Winter), pp. 903–34.

Dunlop, John T. 1958. *Industrial Relations Systems*. New York: Holt.

Dunlop, John T., and Arnold M. Zack. 1997. *Mediation and Arbitration of Employment Disputes*. San Francisco: Jossey-Bass.

Eaton, Adrienne E., and Jeffrey H. Keefe. 1999. "Introduction and Overview." In Adrienne E. Eaton and Jeffrey H. Keefe, eds. *Employment Dispute Resolution and Worker Rights in the Changing Workplace*. Champaign, IL: Industrial Relations Research Association, pp. 1–26.

Edelman, L.B. 1990. "Legal Environments and Organizational Governance: The Expansion of Due Process in the American Workplace." *American Journal of Sociology*, Vol. 95, no. 6 (May), pp. 1401–40.

Edelman, Lauren B., Steven E. Abraham, and Howard S. Erlanger. 1992. "Professional Construction of Law: The Inflated Threat of Wrongful Discharge." *Law and Society Review*, Vol. 26, no. 1, pp. 47–83.

Edelman, Lauren B., Christopher Uggen, and Howard S. Erlanger. 1999. "The Endogeneity of Legal Regulation: Grievance Procedures as Rational Myth." *American Journal of Sociology*, Vol. 105, no. 2 (September), pp. 406–54.

Eisenberg, Theodore, and Elizabeth Hill. 2003. "Arbitration and Litigation of Employment Claims: An Empirical Comparison." *Dispute Resolution Journal*, Vol. 58, no. 4 (November 2003–January 2004), pp. 44–55.

Eisenberg, T., and M. Schlanger. 2003. "The Reliability of the Administrative Office of the U.S. Courts Database: An Initial Empirical Analysis." *Notre Dame Law Review*, Vol. 78 (August), 1455–96.

Elkouri, Frank, and Edna Elkouri. 1993. *How Arbitration Works*, 4th ed. Washington, DC: BNA Books.

Estreicher, Samuel. 2001. "Saturns for Rickshaws: The Stakes in the Debate over Predispute Employment Arbitration Agreements." *Ohio State Journal on Dispute Resolution*, Vol. 16, no. 3, pp. 559–70.

Ewing, David W. 1989. *Justice on the Job: Resolving Grievances in the Nonunion Workplace*. Boston, MA: Harvard Business School Press.

Eylon, Dafna, Robert Giacalone, and Hinda Pollard. 2000. Beyond contractual interpretation: Bias in arbitrators' case perceptions and award recommendations. *Journal of Organizational Behavior,* Vol. 21, no. 5 (August), pp. 513–24.

Feuille, Peter. 1999. "Grievance Mediation." In Adrienne E. Eaton and Jeffrey H. Keefe, eds. *Employment Dispute Resolution and Worker Rights in the Changing Workplace.* Champaign, IL: Industrial Relations Research Association, Ch. 6, pp. 187–217.

Feuille, P., and J.T. Delaney. 1992. "The Individual Pursuit of Organizational Justice: Grievance Procedures in Nonunion Workplaces." In G.R. Ferris and K.M. Rowland, eds., *Research in Personnel and Human Resource Management.* Stamford, CT: JAI Press, pp. 187–232.

Feuille, P., and D.T. Chachere. 1995. "Looking Fair or Being Fair: Remedial Voice Procedures in Nonunion Workplaces." *Journal of Management,* Vol. 21, no. 1 (Spring), pp. 27–42.

Fleming, M.A., D.T. Wegener, and R.E. Petty. 1999. "Procedural and Legal Motivations to Correct for Perceived Injustice." *Journal of Experimental Social Psychology,* Vol. 35, no. 2 (March), pp. 186–203.

Folger, R., and R. Cropanzano. 1998. *Organizational Justice and Human Resource Management.* Thousand Oaks, CA: Sage.

Freeman, R.B. 1980. "The Exit–Voice Tradeoff in the Labor Market: Unionism, Job Tenure, Quits, and Separations." *Quarterly Journal of Economics,* Vol. 94, no. 4 (June), pp. 643–73.

Freeman, R.B., and J.L Medoff. 1984. *What Do Unions Do?* New York: Basic Books.

General Accounting Office. 1995. *Employment Discrimination: Most Private-Sector Employers Use Alternative Dispute Resolution,* GAO/HEHS-95-150 Employment Discrimination Washington, DC: GAO.

———. 1997. *Alternative Dispute Resolution: Employers' Experiences with ADR in the Workplace,* GAO/GGD-97-157 ADR in the Workplace. Washington, DC: GAO.

Gilmer v. Interstate/Johnson Lane, 500 U.S. 20 (1991).

Godard, J. 2002. "Institutional Environments, Employer Practices, and States in Liberal Market Economies." *Industrial Relations,* Vol. 41, no. 2 (April), pp. 249–86.

Goldman, B. 2001. "Toward an Understanding of Employment Discrimination-Claiming: An Integration of Organizational Justice and Social Information Processing Theories." *Personnel Psychology,* Vol. 54, no. 2 (Summer), pp. 361–86.

Gordon, Michael E., and Gerald E. Fryxell. 1993. "The Role of Interpersonal Justice in Organizational Grievance Systems." In R. Cropanzano, ed., *Justice in the Workplace,* Mahwah, NJ: Erlbaum Associates, pp. 231–56.

Greenberg, J. 2006. "Losing Sleep over Organizational Injustice: Attenuating Insomniac Reactions to Underpayment Inequity with Supervisory Training in Interactional Injustice." *Journal of Applied Psychology,* Vol. 91, no. 1 (January), pp. 58–69.

Grote, Dick, and Jim Wimberly. 1993. "Peer Review." *Training* (March), pp. 51–55.

Groth, M., B. Goldman, S. Gilliland, and R. Bies. 2002. "Commitment to Legal Claiming: Influences of Attributions, Social Guidance, and Organizational Tenure." *Journal of Applied Psychology,* Vol. 87, no. 4 (August), pp. 781–8.

Haber, Lawrence J., Ahmad R. Karim, and J. Douglas Johnson. 1997. "A Survey of Published, Private-Sector Arbitral Decisions." *Labor Law Journal,* Vol. 48, no. 7, pp. 431–6.

Hirschman, A.O. 1970. *Exit, Voice, and Loyalty.* Cambridge, MA: Harvard University Press.

Hirt, E.R., S.M. McCrae, and H.I. Boris. 2003. "'I Know You Self-Handicapped Last Exam': Gender Differences in Reactions to Self-Handicapping." *Journal of Personality and Social Psychology*, Vol. 84, no. 1 (January), pp. 177–93.

Howard, William M. 1995. "Arbitrating Claims of Employment Discrimination." *Dispute Resolution Journal*, Vol. 50, no. 4 (Oct.–Dec.), pp. 40–50.

Huselid, Mark A. 1995. "The Impact of Human Resource Management Practices on Turnover, Productivity, and Corporate Financial Performance." *Academy of Management Journal*, Vol. 38, no. 3 (June), pp. 635–72.

Ichniowski, Casey, Thomas A. Kochan, David Levine, Craig Olson, and George Strauss. 1996. "What Works at Work: Overview and Assessment." *Industrial Relations*, Vol. 35, no. 3 (July), pp. 356–74.

Ichniowski, C. 1986. "The Effects of Grievance Activity on Productivity." *Industrial and Labor Relations Review*, Vol. 40, no. 1 (October), pp. 75–89.

Jennings, Ken, and Roger Wolters. 1976. "Discharge Cases Reconsidered." *The Arbitration Journal*, Vol. 31, no. 3 (September), pp. 164–80.

Jones, G.R., and J.M. George. 1998. "The Experience and Evolution of Trust: Implications for Cooperation and Teamwork." *Academy of Management Review*, Vol. 23, no. 3 (July), pp. 531–40.

Judge, Timothy A., and Joseph J. Martocchio. 1996. "Dispositional Influences on Attributions Concerning Absenteeism." *Journal of Management*, Vol. 22, no. 6, pp. 837–61.

Karim, Ahmad, and Thomas H. Stone. 1988. "An Empirical Examination of Arbitrator Decisions in Reversal and Reduction Discharge Hearings." *Labor Studies Journal*, Vol. 13, no. 2 (Summer), pp. 41–50.

Katz, H.C., T.A. Kochan, and K.R. Gobeille. 1983. "Industrial Relations Performance, Economic Performance, and QWL Programs: An Interplant Analysis." *Industrial and Labor Relations Review*, Vol. 37, no. 1 (October), pp. 3–17.

Katz, Harry C., Thomas A. Kochan, and Mark R. Weber. 1985. "Assessing the Effects of Industrial Relations and Quality of Work Life Efforts on Organizational Effectiveness." *Academy of Management Journal*, Vol. 28, no. 3 (September), pp. 509–27.

Kerr, Clark, John T. Dunlop, Fredrick Harbison, and Charles A. Myers. 1960. *Industrialism and Industrial Man.* Cambridge, MA: Harvard University Press.

Klaas, B.S. 1989. "Determinants of Grievance Activity and the Grievance System's Impact on Employee Behavior: An Integrative Perspective." *Academy of Management Review*, Vol. 14, no. 3 (July), pp. 445–58.

Klaas, B.S., and G.G. Dell'Omo. 1997. "Managerial Use of Dismissals: Organizational-Level Determinants." *Personnel Psychology*, Vol. 50, no. 4 (Winter), pp. 927–53.

Klaas, B.S., and A.S. DeNisi. 1989. "Managerial Reactions to Employee Dissent: The Impact of Grievance Activity on Performance Ratings." *Academy of Management Journal*, Vol. 32, no. 4 (December) pp. 705–18.

Klaas, B.S., and D. Feldman. 1993. "The Evaluation of Disciplinary Appeals in Nonunion Firms." *Human Resource Management Review*, Vol. 3, no. 1 (Spring), pp. 49–81.

Klaas, Brian S., Douglas M. Mahony, and Hoyt N. Wheeler. 2006. "Decision-Making about Workplace Disputes: A Policy-Capturing Study of Employment Arbitrators, Labor Arbitrators, and Jurors." *Industrial Relations*, Vol. 45, no. 1 (January), pp. 68–95.

Klaas, B.S., and H.N. Wheeler. 1990. "Managerial Decision-Making About Employee Discipline: A Policy-Capturing Approach." *Personnel Psychology*, Vol. 43, no. 1 (Spring), pp. 117–134.

Kochan, Thomas A., Harry C. Katz, and Robert B. McKersie. 1994. *The Transformation of American Industrial Relations*. Ithaca, NY: ILR Press.

Kochan, T.A., B.A. Lautsch, and C. Bendersky. 2002. "An Evaluation of the Massachusetts Commission Against Discrimination Alternative Dispute Resolution Program." *Harvard Negotiation Law Review*, Vol. 5, pp. 233–78.

Kolb, D.M. 1987. "Corporate Ombudsman and Organization Conflict Resolution." *Journal of Conflict Resolution*, Vol. 31, no. 4 (December), pp. 673–91.

Labig Jr., C.E., I.B. Helburn, and R.C. Rodgers. 1985. "Discipline History, Seniority and Reason for Discharge as Predictors of Post-Reinstatement Job Performance." *The Arbitration Journal*, Vol. 40, pp. 44–52.

LeRoy, Michael H., and Peter Feuille. 2001. "Final and Binding . . . But Appealable to Courts: Empirical Evidence of Judicial Review of Labor and Employment Arbitration Awards." Program Materials, 54th Annual Meeting, National Academy of Arbitrators, Sec. 2-A: 1–47.

———. 2003. "Judicial Enforcement of Pre-Dispute Arbitration Agreements: Back to the Future." *Ohio State Journal on Dispute Resolution*, Vol. 18, no. 2, pp. 249–341.

Lewin, D. 1987. "Conflict Resolution in the Nonunion Firm: A Theoretical and Empirical Analysis." *Journal of Conflict Resolution*, Vol. 31, no. 3 (September), pp. 465–502.

———. 1990. "Grievance Procedures in Nonunion Workplaces: An Empirical Analysis of Usage, Dynamics, and Outcomes." *Chicago-Kent Law Review*, Vol. 66, no. 3, pp. 823–44.

———. 1993. "Conflict Resolution and Management in Contemporary Work Organizations: Theoretical Perspectives and Empirical Evidence." In S.A. Bacharach, R.L. Seeber, and D.J. Walsh, eds., *Research in the Sociology of Organizations*, Vol. 12. Greenwich, CT: JAI Press, pp. 167–209.

———. 1999. "Theoretical and Empirical Research on the Grievance Procedure and Arbitration: A Critical Review." In A.E. Eaton and J.H. Keefe, eds., *Employment Dispute Resolution and Worker Rights*. Champaign, IL: Industrial Relations Research Association, pp. 137–86.

———. 2004. "Dispute Resolution in Nonunion Organizations: Key Empirical Findings." In Samuel Estreicher, ed., *Alternative Dispute Resolution in the Employment Arena*. New York: Kluwer, pp. 379–403.

———. 2005. "Unionism and Employment Conflict Resolution: Rethinking Collective Voice and Its Consequences." *Journal of Labor Research*. Vol. 26, no. 2 (Spring), pp. 209–39.

Lewin, D., and R.B. Peterson. 1988. *The Modern Grievance Procedure in the United States: A Theoretical and Empirical Analysis*. Westport, CT: Quorum.

———. 1999. "Behavioral Outcomes of Grievance Activity." *Industrial Relations*, Vol. 38, no. 4 (October), pp. 554–76.

Lind, E.A., and T.R. Tyler. 1988. *The Social Psychology of Procedural Justice*. New York: Plenum Press.

Lipsky, David B., Ronald L. Seeber, and Richard D. Fincher. 2003. *Emerging Systems for Managing Workplace Conflict*. San Francisco: Jossey-Bass.

Litras, Marika F.X. 2000. "Bureau of Justice Statistics Report on Civil Rights Complaints Filed in U.S. District Courts." *Daily Labor Report*, January 10, pp. E-5–E-17.

Lucero, Margaret A., and Robert E. Allen. 1998. "The Arbitration of Cases Involving Aggression Against Supervisors." *Dispute Resolution Journal*, Vol. 53, no. 1 (February), pp. 57–64.

Mahony, Douglas M., Brian S. Klaas, and Hoyt N. Wheeler. 2005. "Resolving Employment Disputes: Who Decides Just May Cost You Your Job." Presented at the 57th Annual Meeting of the Industrial Relations Research Association, Philadelphia, PA, January.

Mahony, Douglas M., Brian S. Klaas, John A. McClendon, and Arup Varma. 2005. "The Effects of Mandatory Employment Arbitration Systems on Applicants' Attraction to Organizations." *Human Resource Management*, Vol. 44, no. 4 (Winter), pp. 449–70.

Martocchio, Joseph J., and Timothy A. Judge. 1995. "The Role of Fairness Orientation and Supervisor Attributions in Absence Disciplinary Decisions." *Journal of Business and Psychology*, Vol. 10, no. 1 (Fall), pp. 115–38.

Mayer, R.C., and M.B. Gavin. 2005. "Trust in Management and Performance: Who Minds the Store While the Employees Watch the Boss?" *Academy of Management Journal*, Vol. 48, no. 5 (October), pp. 874–88.

Meeker, James W., and John Dombrink. 1993. "Access to the Civil Courts for Those of Low and Moderate Means." *Southern California Law Review*, Vol. 66, no. 5 (July), pp. 2217–31.

Miller, P., and C. Mulvey. 1991. "Australian Evidence on the Exit/Voice Model of the Labor Market." *Industrial and Labor Relations Review*, Vol. 45, no. 1 (October), pp. 44–57.

Norsworthy, J.R., and Craig A. Zabala. 1985. "Worker Attitudes, Worker Behavior, and Productivity in the U.S. Automobile Industry, 1959–76." *Industrial and Labor Relations Review*, Vol. 38, no. 4 (July), pp. 544–57.

Olson-Buchanan, J.B. 1996. "Voicing Discontent: What Happens to the Grievance Filer After the Grievance?" *Journal of Applied Psychology*, Vol. 81, no. 1 (February), pp. 52–63.

Olson-Buchanan, J.B., and W.R. Boswell. 2002. "The Role of Employee Loyalty and Formality in Voicing Discontent." *Journal of Applied Psychology*, Vol. 87, no. 6 (December), pp. 1167–74.

Payson, Martin. 1998. "A Jury of Peers." *Industry Week*, Vol. 247, no. 3 (December), p. 71.

Rees, D.I. 1991. "Grievance Procedure Strength and Teacher Quits." *Industrial and Labor Relations Review*, Vol. 45, no. 1 (October), pp. 31–43.

Reskin, Barbara F., and Christ A. Visher. 1986. "The Influence of Evidence and Extralegal Factors in Jurors' Decisions." *Law and Society Review*, Vol. 20, no. 3, pp. 423–38.

Richey, Brenda H., John Bernardin, Catherine L. Tyler, and Nancy McKinney. 2001. "The Effect of Arbitration Program Characteristics on Applicants' Intentions Toward Potential Employers." *Journal of Applied Psychology*, Vol. 86, no. 5 (October), pp. 1006–13.

Scott, Marvin B., and Stanford M. Lyman. 1968. "Accounts." *American Sociological Review*, Vol. 33, no. 1 (February), pp. 46–62.

Sheppard, B.H. 1984. "Third Party Conflict Intervention: A Procedural Framework." In B.M. Staw and L.L. Cummings, eds., *Research in Organizational Behavior*, Vol. 6, pp. 141–90.

Sheppard, Blair H., Roy J. Lewicki, and John W. Minton. 1992. *Organizational Justice: The Search for Fairness in the Workplace*. New York: Macmillan.

Simpson, Patricia A., and Joseph J. Martocchio. 1997. "The Influence of Work History Factors on Arbitration Outcomes." *Industrial and Labor Relations Review*, Vol. 50, no. 2 (January), pp. 252–67.

Stone, Katherine V.W. 1981. "The Postwar Paradigm in American Labor Law." *Yale Law Journal*, Vol. 90, pp. 1509–80.

———. 1996. "Mandatory Arbitration of Individual Employment Rights: The Yellow Dog Contract of the 1990s." *Denver University Law Review*, Vol. 73, pp. 1017–50.

———. 1999. "Employment Arbitration Under the Federal Arbitration Act." In A.E. Eaton and J.H. Keefe, eds., *Employment Dispute Resolution and Worker Rights in the Changing Workplace*. Champaign, IL: Industrial Relations Research Association, pp. 27–65.

Stone, Morris. 1969. "Why Arbitrators Reinstate Discharged Employees." *Monthly Labor Review*, Vol. 92, no. 10 (October), pp. 47–50.

Sutton, J.R., and F. Dobbin. 1996. "The Two Faces of Governance: Responses to Legal Uncertainty in U.S. Firms, 1955 to 1985." *American Sociological Review*, Vol. 61, no. 5 (October), pp. 794–811.

Sutton, J.R., F. Dobbin, J. Meyer, and W.R. Scott. 1994. "The Legalization of the Workplace." *American Journal of Sociology*, Vol. 99, no. 4 (January), pp. 944–71.

Taras, Daphne G. 1997. "Managerial Intentions and Wage Determination in the Canadian Petroleum Industry." *Industrial Relations*, Vol. 36, no. 2 (April), pp. 178–205.

Ury, W., J. Brett, and S. Goldberg. 1988. *Getting Disputes Resolved: Designing Systems to Cut the Cost of Conflict*. San Francisco: Jossey-Bass.

U.S. Bureau of Labor Statistics. 2006. *Union Members in 2005*. Washington, DC: Department of Labor.

Vidmar, Neil. 1998. "The Performance of the American Civil Jury: An Empirical Perspective." *Arizona Law Review*, Vol. 40, no. 4 (Fall), pp. 881–904.

———. 2001. "Retribution and Revenge." In V.L. Hamilton, ed., *Handbook of Justice Research in Law*. New Haven, CT: Yale University Press, pp. 31–61.

Vidmar, Neil, and David Miller. 1980. "Social-Psychological Processes Underlying Attitudes Toward Legal Punishment." *Law and Society Review*, Vol. 14, no. 3 (Spring), pp. 565–602.

Walton, Richard E. 1985. "From Control to Commitment in the Workplace." *Harvard Business Review*, Vol. 63, no. 2 (March/April), pp. 77–84.

Wasserman, D.T., and J.N. Robinson. 1980. "Extra-Legal Influences, Group Processes, and Jury Decision-Making: A Psychological Perspective." *North Carolina Central Law Journal*, Vol. 12, pp. 96–159.

Westin, Alan F., and Alfred G. Felieu. 1988. *Resolving Employment Disputes Without Litigation*. Washington, DC: Bureau of National Affairs.

Wheeler, Hoyt N., Brian S. Klaas, and Douglas M. Mahony. 2004. *Workplace Justice Without Unions*. Kalamazoo, MI: Upjohn Institute.

Wilensky, Ron, and Karen M. Jones. 1994. "Quick Response Key to Resolving Complaints." *HR Magazine*, Vol. 39, no. 3 (March), pp. 42–7.

Wilson, N., and M.J. Peel. 1991. "The Impact on Absenteeism and Quits of Profit-Sharing and Other Forms of Employee Participation." *Industrial and Labor Relations Review*, Vol. 44, no. 3 (April), pp. 454–68.

Wood, Robert E., and Terence Mitchell. 1981. "Manager Behavior in a Social Context: The Impact of Impression Management on Attributions and Disciplinary

Actions." *Organizational Behavior and Human Performance*, Vol. 28, no. 3 (December), pp. 356–78.

Zack, Arnold M. 1999. "Agreements to Arbitrate and the Waiver of Rights Under Employment Law." In A.E. Eaton and J.H. Keefe, eds., *Employment Dispute Resolution and Worker Rights in the Changing Workplace*. Champaign, IL: Industrial Relations Research Association, Ch. 3, pp. 67–94.

Zalusky, John. 1976. "Arbitration: Updating a Vital Process." *American Federationist*, Vol. 83, p. 4.

CHAPTER 5

Performance Pay: Determinants and Consequences

JOHN S. HEYWOOD
University of Wisconsin–Milwaukee

UWE JIRJAHN
University of Hanover

The simplification that labor is an undifferentiated input changes quickly as study of the labor market continues. First, the student learns that workers and firms make choices about the human capital invested in the worker and that these choices generate profound differences in labor market outcomes. Second, the student learns that even given the worker's human capital, the worker's effort, motivation, and commitment depend on the incentives the worker faces. Thus, far from being an undifferentiated input, labor's productivity depends, in part, on the structure of incentives created within the firm, incentives that are determined by managers, unions, and governments. While these incentives consist of everything from the leadership quality of management to the nature of shared workplace public goods, the most basic incentive remains the method of payment and the resulting structure of worker earnings. Altering the method of pay persists as a primary tool for encouraging employees to do the work they are hired to do.

Long a staple of scientific management, performance pay lost favor through much of the middle of the 20th century as academic articles in the United States trumpeted the "domination of time rates," unions fought for solidarity wages, and the centralized wage systems of continental Europe and Australia generated remarkable uniformity in earnings. Yet, just as everything old becomes new again, performance pay gained increasing attention in the final decades of the century. The original institutions that created and enforced the more nearly uniform earnings faced enormous pressure. Increased international competition, privatization, a protracted recession in Japan, and an emerging single market in Europe all contributed to this pressure. Private sector unionization in the United States fell below 8%, "new labour" did not fundamentally reverse Thatcherism, the Australian awards system was "deregulated," and European policy makers became concerned with labor market flexibility, a siren sound heard even in Japan. In this environment, leaders of both firms and governments grew increasingly interested in performance pay as a tool to increase labor productivity and to respond to changing external pressures. As in the period of scientific management, the expectation arose that an appropriate compensation system linking worker and firm objectives could be part of managing a workforce to create a competitive advantage or productive edge.[1] This expectation arose in settings and among professionals not typically associated with performance pay, including teachers, public sector service workers, and physicians (Rosenthal et al. 2005).

This chapter examines a variety of deviations from time rates of pay that, as a group, we label performance pay. On the one hand, such a label can be misleading, as even an hourly wage may have a performance standard as a requirement for continued employment (Lazear 2000). On the other hand, we persist in the label both because of its common usage and because we will strive to be explicit in separating the various types of incentive schemes. The next part of the chapter sets the stage and classifies types of performance pay. In doing so, it provides a general discussion of the theoretical promises and pitfalls associated with the different types of performance pay. While several alternative typologies exist, we organize our theoretical discussion largely around the distinction between individual-based and group-based schemes. Yet we consider distinctions such as that between subjective and objective performance measures. The third section reviews the empirical literature on the determinants and (intended and unintended) effects of performance pay in light of the theoretical considerations. Primarily, we discuss evidence on piece rates and profit sharing to illustrate the determinants of a typical individual-based and a typical group-based payment scheme.[2] To focus discussion and save space, other less commonly studied types of performance pay are only briefly discussed. The fourth section presents original estimations on the process of bargaining over piece rates in Germany. A final section concludes suggesting lines for future research.

Setting the Stage and Describing Performance Pay

Performance pay should be viewed as a general term covering any system that seeks to link pay to measured performance. However, we exclude discussion of job ladders, internal labor markets and promotion tournaments, and efficiency wages. While these may influence both performance and pay, they do so in a less direct fashion than most scholars identify with performance pay.

Nonetheless, there exists a wide variety of performance pay schemes. Schemes may differ in the functional form that links earnings and measured performance. Target-based schemes reward workers only if a certain performance goal is reached (Petersen 1992a). Pay is discontinuously linked to performance. Alternatively, schemes can be characterized by a continuous linear relationship between pay and performance. Holmstrom and Milgrom (1987) analyze the circumstances under which such a linear relationship is appropriate.

Furthermore, performance pay schemes differ in the performance measure used. First, measures may be either input- or output-related (Khalil and Lawaree 1995). Input-related performance measures relate to workers' actions or efforts, while output-related performance measures relate to owners' payoffs. Input-related measures for a salesperson include time spent, number of customers contacted, and new accounts created, while output-related measures include sales or profits (Raith 2004). Second, performance measures may be either objective or subjective (Baker, Jensen, and Murphy 1988). Objective measures are characterized by a low degree of discretion, as in a piece rate. Subjective measures, such as performance evaluations by superiors (e.g., evaluations of a worker's cooperativeness), entail a substantial degree of discretion. Finally, performance can be measured at different levels. Milkovich and Widgor (1991) distinguish between individual and group performance measures. Individual measures include merit plans, piece rates, and commissions. Group measures include small-group incentives, gain sharing, and profit sharing. Bonuses may be either individual or group.

In what follows, we organize our discussion around the distinction between individual-based and group-based performance pay. We will incorporate other aspects, such as the distinction between subjective and objective performance measures, into the discussion but use the level of the scheme as an organizing device.

Individual-Based Performance Pay

An individually assessed scheme offers the tightest connection between individual variations in performance and variations in pay. Hence, individual performance pay is usually thought to provide strong incentives for workers. First, workers are induced to exert high effort. Second high-productivity workers sort into jobs where they are rewarded (Lazear 1986).

A problem widely analyzed in the early theoretical literature is the trade-off between insurance and incentives. If a worker's performance depends not only on effort but also on random outside influences, performance pay involves income risk (Milgrom and Roberts 1992). First, markets and production technology are sources of randomness. Second, the measurement of performance can also be a source of randomness, especially subjective performance measures that depend on superiors' idiosyncratic perceptions. Third, a worker's ability to perform can itself be subject to random influences, such as weather or health problems. When performance pay involves income risk, risk-averse workers must receive compensating differentials. The stronger the link between performance and pay, the higher must be the differential. Hence, the employer will limit the intensity of the incentive scheme in order to reduce the compensating differential. This reasoning yields a clear prediction. The higher the variance of (measured) performance, the weaker the link between pay and performance. However, empirical tests of this prediction obtain mixed results (Prendergast 2002), suggesting that factors beyond the trade-off between insurance and incentives influence the design of performance pay.

An employer will also limit the intensity of performance pay if workers are subject to a limited liability (or wealth) constraint. Optimal incentives require that workers are both rewarded for good performance and punished for bad. Yet, with a binding limited liability constraint, workers cannot be punished for bad performance. Thus, incentives to exert effort can only be provided by higher rewards for good performance. This generates a rent for the workers. The employer faces a trade-off between limited liability rents and incentives. The higher the effort induced by the incentives, the higher a worker's rent. Interestingly, performance pay in face of a limited liability constraint has implications similar to those analyzed in the efficiency wage literature (Foster and Wan 1984; Laffont and Martimort 2002; Jirjahn 2006). Workers queue for jobs in which they can receive a rent, while employers are reluctant to invest in creating such jobs.

Performance pay also entails important dynamic aspects, including the ratchet effect (Gibbons 1987). Workers withhold both effort and productivity-enhancing ideas in the current period because they fear an increase in performance standards after a period of good performance. Such output restrictions will increase if group norms evolve and workers exert peer pressure on colleagues who exercise high effort (Levine 1992). A precondition for the ratchet effect is that the employer cannot credibly commit to a fixed performance standard. Several (partially opposing) ways to alleviate or overcome this problem have been suggested.[3] Short-term workers are less likely to fear ratchet effects because they are not affected by a future increase in performance standards (Milgrom and Roberts 1992). More importantly, cooperative employer–employee relations characterized by workers' involvement in the implementation, design, and change of incentives schemes may engender the trust and fairness that make performance pay feasible. Heywood, Huebler, and Jirjahn (1998) suggest this as the explanation behind their evidence that piece rates are more common in German workplaces with works councils. In Germany, works councils have strong codetermination rights with respect to the implementation and design of piece rates. In the next section, we will return to a detailed discussion on the role of industrial relations in adoption of performance pay.

Even without fear of ratchet effects, individual-based performance pay may not be appropriate for work characterized by multitasking (Holmstrom and Milgrom 1991; Baker 1992). In these situations workers must allocate their efforts across different tasks. In a world of incomplete contracting, the inability to reward every type of productive employee activity can result in counterproductive behavior. An emphasis on individual performance as measured by one or a few indicators causes workers to cut back on productive behaviors for which they are not rewarded. These behaviors include helping colleagues (Drago and Turnbull 1988), maintaining equipment, cultivating customer goodwill, striving for quality, and reducing chances of workplace injury (Freeman and Kleiner 2005). In addition to cutting back on productive behaviors, performance pay can cause workers to increase unproductive influence activities. Thus, Heywood, Huebler, and Jirjahn (1998) argue that workers in Germany who directly participate in investment decisions push for investments that allow increased output rather than increased efficiency when they are paid by a piece rate.[4]

These problems may all be seen as what Kerr (1975) called the "folly of rewarding A while hoping for B," and recent examples seem endless. Dun and Bradstreet faced large legal costs and extensive customer anger following a performance pay scheme that caused brokers to provide customers fraudulent information in order to make sales. Sears created an individual performance pay plan that caused their mechanics to exaggerate the repairs that customers needed for their automobiles in an effort to increase individual earnings (see Gibbons 1998 for more on these two examples). In the public sector, Asch (1990) found that military recruiters paid by their number of recruits signed up a lower quality of recruit. Eberts, Hollenbeck, and Stone (2002) compare two similar secondary schools in Michigan, one of which explicitly rewards teachers for retention and one of which retains a traditional earnings plan without merit pay. They found that the first school successfully increased retention rates relative to the second, but it also had an increased rate of course failure, lower average attendance, and no increase in achievement. While the rewarded performance measure increased, the ultimate success of the school fell. Folly indeed!

One possibility to alleviate the problems outlined in the previous paragraphs is to have supervisors make comprehensive judgments about the productivity of individual workers. This more complete assessment of productivity could evaluate helping others, learning new skills, participating effectively in groups, or cultivating good relations with customers. Indeed, Brown and Heywood (2005) show that such formal performance appraisal becomes more likely when jobs are complex and multifaceted. Their Australian data confirm that formal appraisal for nonmanagerial workers occurs where workers have greater control over the pace and variety of tasks. Such control allows wider variance in performance increasing the benefits from appraisal (and its link to pay).

But using evaluations for performance pay can generate its own folly. The difficult process of evaluating workers spawned concern with validity, reliability, and freedom from bias. The early focus was primarily on the role of the supervisor and the nature of rating scales. Researchers identified common errors made by supervisors, such as halo effects (a favorable overall rating based on outstanding performance in only a single duty), central tendency bias (rating all employees close to the scale midpoint irrespective of performance), and recency effects (placing too much emphasis on recent performance) (Milkovich and Newman 2002; Lewin and Mitchell 1995). More dramatically, the prejudices of the evaluator may enter the process. Elvira and Town (2001) confirm that the race of subordinates influences supervisors' performance evaluations. They found that white supervisors of both white and nonwhite subordinates typically give whites better ratings than nonwhites, even after controlling for productivity and demographic variables. This result is more disquieting when the evaluations form the basis of pay decisions. Workers with same productivity would have different earnings by race but also would have supervisory evaluations supporting the differences. Such an implication fits with a broader perspective that in less formal pay systems that depend on judgment, worker characteristics and the composition of the workforce play greater roles in determining compensation (Elvira and Graham 2002).

Added to the possibilities of honest mistakes and of prejudice is the possibility that performance measures will be strategically manipulated. Employers may underreport performance to save on wages (Prendergast 1999). Moreover, individual supervisors may use their discretion to reward only subordinates who provide private services or goods (Laffont 1990; Prendergast and Topel 1996). These services include flattery or loyalty to the superior's career concerns. Alternatively, the superior may rate all employees highly to demonstrate to those further up the hierarchy his or her outstanding managerial skills. A less productive superior may even favor unproductive subordinates to protect himself or herself from being replaced by productive subordinates (Friebel and Raith 2004). Also, a subordinate may strategically engage in influence activities that result in a positive evaluation but not necessarily in increased performance (Milgrom and Roberts 1988). Thus, in Prendergast's (1993) theory of "yes men," superiors favor proposals from subordinates that mirror their own opinions. This creates incentives for subordinates to make just such proposals. Strategic manipulation may be reduced if reputation concerns matter and interactions are long-term (Baker, Gibbons, and Murphy 1994). Additionally, the presence of organized labor in the appraisals may help with enforcement and reduce the incentives to manipulate the process.

This long list of "perverse incentives" (Lewin and Mitchell 1995) has some researchers suggesting alternative procedures. Edwards and Ewen (1996) present evidence that 360-degree appraisal is less susceptible to prejudice, bias, and strategic behavior. Such an appraisal typically involves not a single supervisor evaluating a subordinate but the participation of all those around a particular worker—above, below, and parallel. To date, such appraisals have typically been resource intensive and applied to managers. In addition, they are often intended as a developmental rather than evaluative tool (Antonioni 1996). Nonetheless, Brett and Atwater (2001) argue 360-degree appraisal has been associated with improved performance.

Despite the potential of such alternatives, we suggest that subjective performance evaluations cannot always avoid the folly of rewarding A while hoping for B. Indeed, the sum of practical concerns associated with operating a valid and reliable performance appraisal system and then using it to create a merit pay scheme has led one keen observer to quip that individual-based merit pay schemes "share two attributes: they absorb vast amounts of management time and resources, and make everyone unhappy" (Pfeffer 1998:115).

Group-Based Performance Pay

Many of the concerns identified for individual performance pay carry over to group-level performance pay. A limited liability (or wealth) constraint of the workers may still imply that workers cannot participate in financial losses. Hart and Huebler (1990) find that profit sharing in Germany does not substitute for the base wage but adds to it. Thus, employers may face a trade-off between limited liability rents and providing incentives in the case of profit sharing.

Cooperative and trustful employer–employee relations remain important for group-based schemes. Profit sharing will induce effort only if workers trust that managers pursue firm strategies and investments designed to increase financial performance. Moreover, workers must trust the accounting of profits. The movie industry suggests such trust may be unjustified (Cheatham, Davis, and Cheatham 1996). If actors' pay is based on the net profits of a film, the movie company can reduce labor costs by "creative accounting." In addition, smaller group-based performance pay can also be subject to the ratchet effect or speed-up concerns more commonly associated with individual piece rates (Meyer 1995).

While income risk is a general problem, individual- and group-based performance measures may differ in the degree of risk. Baker (2002) argues that the noise in performance measures increases with the level of the measure. Individual-based schemes primarily involve risks closely related to the worker's job. Profit sharing reflects all the factors influencing financial performance. This implies that employers will choose group performance pay only if its incentive advantages outweigh the disadvantage of an increased risk premium.

Yet, such an incentive advantage might seem unlikely because of the well known "$1/N$ problem." A worker who increases his productivity in response to a group reward receives only the share $1/N$ (where N is the number of workers in the group) of that increase back as a reward, with the remainder divided among the other members of the group. Using a simple analytical example we illustrate that the severity of the problem depends on the production technology and the design of the group-level incentives. We consider a group of N homogeneous workers. The group receives a share γ of total output

$$Q = \sum_{i=1}^{N} e_i \qquad (1)$$

where e_i denotes both worker i's effort and worker i's individual output with $e_i \in \{0,1\}$. The worker's utility depends on money income, y_i, and effort: $U_i (y_i, e_i) = y_i - C_i(e_i)$, where $C_i(e_i)$ denotes the disutility of effort function with $C(e_i) = ce_i$ and $\gamma/N < c < \gamma$. Let us first study a continuous and linear relationship between group output and income:

$$y_i = \frac{\gamma}{N} Q \qquad (2)$$

Workers' total welfare is

$$W = \sum_{j=1}^{N} U_j \qquad (3)$$

A socially optimal solution is that each worker exerts effort, $e_i = 1$, resulting in a positive increase in social welfare, $\Delta W = \gamma - c > 0$.

This yields total output $Q^\circ = N$ and utility $U^\circ = \gamma - c$ for each worker. Yet an individually rational worker considers only his or her own utility. Exerting effort under production technology (1) and pay scheme (2) results in a decrease of utility, $\Delta U_i = \gamma/N - c < 0$. Thus, $e_i = 0$ is the dominant strategy. A free-rider fully saves on a disutility of effort, while the income loss due to free-riding is small since the decrease in individual output is shared with colleagues. Workers could be better off if everyone exerts effort. Yet this is not individually rational.

A possible solution to the problem is a target-based incentive scheme (Holmstrom 1982; Petersen 1992a). Workers participate in output only if a certain goal is reached:

$$y_i = \begin{cases} \dfrac{\gamma}{N} \, Q \text{ if } Q \geq Q^\circ = N \\ 0 \text{ if } Q < Q^\circ \end{cases} \tag{4}$$

In contrast to (2), scheme (4) implies that exerting effort is a Nash equilibrium. Given that all colleagues exert effort ($e_j = 1$ for all $j \neq i$), worker i's own effort, $e_i = 1$, ensures that performance goal Q° is reached. This implies income $y_i = \gamma$ and utility $U^\circ = \gamma - c$. If worker i does not exert effort, Q° is not reached and i's income and utility are equal to zero. In contrast to (2), pay scheme (4) involves a more severe punishment of shirking. Under (2), one's own shirking implies only an income loss equal to $1/N$ of the reduction of worker i's individual output. Under (4), worker i also loses the share in the output produced by the colleagues if i free-rides and the group fails to reach Q°. Given that colleagues exert effort, worker i has an incentive to exert effort also. However, a potential problem associated with (4) is that free-riding by all team members is also an equilibrium. Coordination among workers may be required to ensure effort.

Further, the incentive effects of group schemes may depend on production technology. In a model by Adams (2002, 2006), effort is increasing in N if technology is characterized by interdependent worker productivity (teamwork). This contrasts with standard analyses showing that effort decreases in N (e.g., Kandel and Lazear 1992). Here we provide a simple analysis illustrating that for a given N, socially optimal effort can be achieved even under pay scheme (2) if technology is characterized by teamwork. Assume that the production function is given by

$$Q = N \prod_{i=1}^{N} e_i \tag{5}$$

If all workers exert effort, group output is $Q° = N$. If only one single worker free-rides, the team loses the entire output. Under this technology, there exists an alternative to the free-riding equilibrium. All workers exerting effort is also a Nash equilibrium, even if remuneration is based on scheme (2). Given that all of the colleagues exert effort, i's own effort, $e_i = 1$, ensures that $Q°$ is reached. This implies income $y_i = \gamma$ and utility $U° = \gamma - c$. If worker i free-rides, no output is produced and i's income and utility are equal to zero. Hence, even under scheme (2), worker i can increase utility by exerting effort given that colleagues also provide effort.

Technology (5) has the same consequence as the target-based scheme (4). Team production severely punishes free-riding since a single worker's shirking entails a drastic decline of group output and hence of income. This has practical implications. Holmstrom (1982) argues that an outside agent is required to enforce the target-based scheme (4). A hierarchical and centralized personnel management and the main banks in Japan or Germany may take this role (Aoki 1993). However, interdependent worker productivity can play a similar role. If teamwork makes it impossible to measure individual productivity (Rose 2002), group-based pay stands as the only alternative. This group-based pay will be more effective under team production since interdependent worker productivity helps to overcome the $1/N$ problem.

Other ways to solve the free-rider problem are discussed in the literature. MacLeod (1988) and Che and Yoo (2001) suggest that a worker may be deterred from free-riding in the current period by the anticipated loss of the co-workers' cooperation and effort in future periods. Hence, a situation characterized by high effort of group members can be the equilibrium over time (in a repeated game). This implies that group incentives are more effective under long-term employment relationships and stresses the role that group incentives play as part of clusters of complementary practices that include employment security and team production.

Kandel and Lazear (1992) examine the role of mutual monitoring and peer pressure in alleviating the $1/N$ problem. Peer pressure includes internal pressure through guilt and external pressure through shame or physical punishment when a worker is caught shirking by colleagues. However, peer pressure may decrease trust and cooperation between workers. As Kandel and Lazear (1992:805) note, "Less obvious is that workers in a firm with peer pressure may be worse off than those in one without it. While pressure guarantees higher effort, it does not guarantee higher utility because the pressure itself is a cost borne by all members of the firm."

As anecdotal evidence, Barron and Gjerde (1997) report that workers in Japanese-managed auto factories in North America explicitly asked management to provide regular absentee replacement workers in order to reduce what was perceived as excessive peer pressure on absent workers. Barron and Gjerde (1997) argue that the disutility imposed by peer pressure may cause workers to leave a firm providing profit sharing. This could happen if individually rational workers do not take into account the disutility their pressure imposes on co-workers, and so the overall degree of pressure is excessive. Ultimately, the costs of this externality are shifted to the firm. The firm must reduce the incentive intensity of the profit-sharing scheme to ensure that workers are attracted to the firm. Thus, excessive peer pressure may harm both the workforce and the firm.

However, other views contrast sharply about the effect of group-based incentives on trust, cooperation, and helping on the job. Drago and Turnbull (1988) compare the incentive effects of payment schemes based on individual performance and on group performance when the production technology is characterized by each worker's output depending on the worker's own effort and the help provided by colleagues. Individual payment schemes result in underprovision of cooperation, since helping on the job is not rewarded. In this situation, a greater output and higher worker utilities could be obtained if workers engaged in additional helping on the job. Profit sharing provides incentives for helping on the job since each worker's income depends, in part, on the output of colleagues.

Earlier work by FitzRoy and Kraft (1986) provides a model where a worker's utility depends not only on income and effort but also on the level of help in the workplace. The worker's utility and willingness to provide help increase with the average level of cooperation supplied by co-workers. Under payment schemes based on individual performance there exist two equilibria. Employees may be stuck in a Pareto inferior equilibrium in which no workers cooperate and so no worker has an incentive to provide help. The pareto superior equilibrium is characterized by mutual help and cooperation. An arbitrarily small profit-sharing arrangement shifts workers from the inferior noncooperative equilibrium to the superior cooperative equilibrium. The small profit-sharing arrangement induces a small amount of cooperation, but since cooperation enters the workers' utility functions, this small amount of cooperation facilitates a further increase in cooperation and so on. Thus, profit sharing acts as a catalyst in the move toward more mutual help, resulting in greater output and job satisfaction.

In contrast to FitzRoy and Kraft (1986) and Drago and Turnbull (1988), who both consider exogenously given worker utility functions, Rotemberg (1994) analyzes a two-stage game in which workers choose their utility functions at the first stage and provide effort at the second stage. Rotemberg identifies two conditions for choosing some degree of altruism. First, the income of a worker must depend on the output of co-workers. Second, a worker's own effort must increase the marginal productivity of co-workers' efforts. Given these conditions, workers commit to an altruistic utility function and provide a higher level of effort. The predicted positive effects on cooperation and helping on the job can be seen as examples of how group-based incentives may more closely align the objectives of individual workers and the firm. If workers perform multidimensional tasks, individual performance measures will likely be inadequate. Group schemes may reward helping other workers, building trustful relationships with customers, improving quality, and maintaining assets. While Holmstrom and Milgrom (1991) argue that firms may offer low-powered incentives to avoid the distortion from individual incentives, group incentives such as profit sharing stand as an alternative to both low-powered incentives and individual-based incentives. Even in the presence of a free-rider problem and high income risk, profit sharing may have advantages over both low-powered incentives and individual-based payment schemes (Jirjahn 2000). In contrast to low-powered incentives, profit sharing may elicit greater total effort even if the $1/N$ problem is not solved. In contrast to individual-based incentives, profit sharing provides incentives to exert effort in all activities that are relevant to the firm's current profit. Indeed, those studying the characteristics of highly flexible and productive firms often isolate the importance of group-level performance pay (Long 2001).

Finally, firms may need to provide incentives to workers to respond to random events. If production is subject to random influences and information on how to cope with these influences is available only on the shop floor, management will delegate the decisions about appropriate activities and effort levels to workers (Aoki 1990). After such delegation, input-related performance measurement based on monitoring is obviously not feasible. Incentives for flexibility may instead be provided by output-related performance pay (Prendergast 2002). However, different types of output-related pay may provide different incentives for flexibility. Drago and Turnbull (1991) show that profit sharing provides incentives to take into account both internal productivity shocks and external market conditions. Moreover, as discussed, individual-based incentives are likely to distort the allocation of effort if workers perform complex tasks. Thus, firms facing uncertainty and hence having an increased need for worker flexibility can be expected to adopt group schemes such as profit sharing (Jirjahn 1998).

Determinants and Consequences of Performance Pay

In this section we consider the determinants of various types of performance pay and their consequences. We discuss both underlying theory and the empirical evidence. We start with individual-level schemes and with the distinction of either input- or output-related performance measures.

Determinants of Individual Performance Pay

At its most simplified, with risk-neutral workers, the distinction between monitoring input (effort) and monitoring output blurs. If management can accurately and at little or no cost observe both worker input and output, the decision of which to monitor is irrelevant. A contract on effort that pays a salary and a contract on output that pays a piece rate both return first best efficiency. The crucial point is that this equivalence rarely exists. In many cases, monitoring effort may be highly costly. Employees may either work hard or pretend to work hard, and management cannot easily distinguish. Following Lazear (1986), imagine that management can identify output for each worker but only by paying a monitoring cost. Alternatively, management can avoid the monitoring cost and pay a salary. Thus, there exists a piece rate that directly reflects productivity and a salary that is entirely independent of productivity.

While this is a simple model, several implications are immediate. First, more productive workers will sort into piece rates, as only for them will it be worth paying (implicitly through reduced earnings) the monitoring cost. Second, the variance in output will be larger among those paid piece rates. Third, the greater the variance in underlying worker ability, the greater the gain to sorting out the more productive into the piece-rate scheme. Fourth, piece rates are less likely when the costs of monitoring output are high. A variant on this fourth prediction is that because piece rates involve fixed costs of establishment, per-worker monitoring costs are lower in large firms, making such firms more likely to use piece rates.

The basic notions from such a model receive empirical support. While issues of sorting and productivity will be covered when discussing the consequences of performance pay, we note that Petersen (1992b) confirms that piece-rate use is associated with greater variation in earnings. Similarly, Belfield and Marsden (2003) examine U.K. data, finding a robust positive association between the use of individual performance pay and earnings inequality. Indeed, the association between dispersion of pay and piece rates has been confirmed by Seiler (1984), Shearer (2004), Lazear (2000), and Freeman and Kleiner (2005). Moreover, the fourth prediction receives reasonable support, as Table 1 shows that in three of the five studies, establishment size emerges as a significant determinant of whether or not a plant adopts piece rates. This is also confirmed by individual data for the 15 countries of the European Union (Cowling 2001), which reveal that workers are more likely to receive

TABLE 1
Cross-Sectional Evidence on the Determinants of Piece Rates

	USA	Australia	UK	Hong Kong	Germany
Size	+	+	+	0	+
Capital intensity	NA	−	0	−	0
Technical change	NA	0	+	0	0
Managerial intensity	NA	+	−	−	NA
Women	+	+	+	+	+
Layoffs	NA	0	+	+	+
Tenure	NA	−	NA	NA	NA
Earnings slope	NA	NA	NA	−	NA
Promotion	NA	0	NA	NA	0
Competition	NA	+	0	0	+
Unionization	0	0	−	0	0
Joint Consultative Committee	NA	NA	0	0	NA
Works council	NA	NA	NA	NA	+
Part-time/casual	NA	−	−	NA	0

+ and − represent statistical significance in the direction indicated; 0 indicates insignificance; NA indicates "not applicable."
Sources: USA—Brown 1990; Australia—Drago and Heywood 1995; UK—Heywood, Siebert, and Wei 1997; Germany—Heywood, Huebler, and Jirjahn 1998; Hong Kong—Heywood and Wei 1997.

individual performance pay when they work in a larger establishment. There is, interestingly enough, some evidence in the EU data that the size effect is nonlinear, with workers in the very smallest establishments having a somewhat larger probability of receiving performance pay than those in the next larger category. This may reflect differences in the type of performance pay across the size distribution. Thus, some types of pay, say a sales commission, might be easy for a small establishment to adopt while others are not.

Most empirical estimates of the determinants of piece rates build from the predictions of the previous simple model, adding to them comparisons with alternative incentive schemes and recognition of institutional factors. Goldin (1986) presents a primary example of the former in her prediction that piece rates, as contemporaneous rewards, contrast with the strategy of using deferred compensation as an incentive to increase effort. Thus, those that are most likely to be motivated by Lazear-type deferred compensation (Lazear 1979, 1981) are workers with long expected tenure. Thus, Goldin argues that women because of their shorter expected tenure are likely to sort, and be sorted, into incentive schemes with contemporaneous rewards such as piece rates. A variant on this comes from the idea that women not only have shorter expected tenure but also have lower labor force attachment because of greater family responsibilities (Heywood and Wei 1997). This implies that women may be less suitable for team production situations in which absence has a greater cost and that are amenable to group incentive schemes. Women thus may be more likely to be observed in jobs without large elements of team production that are, in turn, more amenable to individual-based piece rates. Indeed, in evaluating German establishment data, Heywood and Jirjahn (2002) confirm that plants with large shares of women are more likely to use individual piece rates but that this doesn't carry over to group piece rates (that reward the productivity of a small group of workers). Moreover, the evidence suggests that group piece rates are associated with team production settings, and women are less prevalent in such settings.[5]

The evidence on the role of gender seems particularly strong. Studies from the five countries presented in Table 1 (the United States, Australia, the United Kingdom, Hong Kong, and Germany) confirm that establishments with larger shares of women are more likely to use piece rates. Using individual data from the United States, Geddes and Heywood (2003) confirmed that women are more likely to be paid piece rates but are less likely to be paid commissions. Following earlier work by MacLeod and Parent (1999), they suggest that commissioned sales work differs from piece rates in that commission sales involve a longer-term perspective and the worker is in a position of contact and trust with repeat customers. This provides the ability to influence the number and size of purchases, making commissions meaningful. Examples include manufacturing sales representatives and stockbrokers. This contrasts with a counter salesperson at a department store, who is less able to influence sales, does not have long-term relationships with buyers, and is unlikely to receive commissions. Thus, the seemingly similar circumstances of piece-rate work and commission work are actually different in terms of expected tenure. They also differ with regard to complexity. Piece rates are typically associated with simple and repetitive tasks, while commissions are associated with more complex selling relationships. Moreover, the pattern of commissions among sales workers gives a hint as to the future pattern in the United States. The most recent *Occupational Outlook Handbook* lists typical counter sales occupations as having employment that will increase faster than average, while occupations associated with commissions, such as manufacturing sales representatives, insurance sales representatives, and stockbrokers, are listed as growing at or below average. Thus as a share of all sales workers, that for workers on commission might be anticipated to fall.

Barth (1997) provides evidence on the general point that piece rates arise in situations where other incentive structures have greater costs or fewer benefits. She examines the firm-specific component of the return to tenure as evidence of the use of Lazear-type deferred compensation. She finds there are essentially no such returns for those paid piece rates. In other words, piece rates appear to substitute for deferred compensation as suggested by Goldin (1986).

A primary example of institutional frameworks influencing the use of performance pay includes the role of unions. Unions are presumed to object to variations in earnings across individuals and so resist this type of performance pay. They do this in the name of the solidarity wage and also in order to take wages out of competition. Moreover, it is much easier for unions to monitor base pay both to ensure that management meets contractual obligations and to compare earnings across plants and employers. In addition, unions will object to merit pay because of the potential for favoritism by supervisors (Brown 1990). Yet even piece rates can be subject to some supervisory favoritism, although presumably less, as managers assign workers to jobs, equipment, or times that make it easier to produce or unevenly enforce quality standards (Fang and Heywood 2006). Moreover, unions give workers the ability to resist piece rates that they fear because of ratchet effects, the tendency of management to lower the rate after workers have responded to an original rate with greater productivity.

While these arguments suggest that unions should be associated with reduced use of performance pay, a contrasting hypothesis is that unions act as an enforcement mechanism to reduce employer opportunism and to build cooperative employer–employee relations (Freeman and Lazear 1995; Hogan 2001). Thus, Heywood, Huebler, and Jirjahn (1998) argue that German works councils, with their codetermination rights, increase the trust workers have in any adopted performance pay, making such arrangements more likely. Similarly, Marsden and Belfield (2004) recently contended that teachers' unions in the United Kingdom have taken a procedural justice role in the design and management of performance-related pay for classroom teachers. Unions provide services to both union members and employers as they help to optimize performance pay.

However, the econometric evidence on the role of unions on individual performance pay is mixed at best and confused at worst. Certainly early case studies reveal strong union opposition to individualizing pay. Brown and Philips (1986), for example, attribute the decline of piece rates in California canneries to strong opposition by unions. Yet the econometric evidence in Table 1 reviewing establishment-level studies from five countries shows that only in the United Kingdom does the extent of unionization within the plant stand as a negative determinant of the use of piece rates. Not shown in the table are establishment evidence from Ng and Maki (1994) that unionization is a negative determinant of piece-rate use in Canada and more recent evidence from Long (2002) showing the opposite. Long does show that unionization is a negative determinant of the use of individual merit pay in Canada. Brown and Heywood (2003) found that changes in the extent of establishment unionization did not change the probability of adopting or dropping individual performance pay in Australia even as unionization played a role as a cross-sectional negative determinant. This might suggest that evidence of unionization as a determinant of individual performance pay merely reflects plant-specific effects. In other words, establishments that are unionized are less likely to have individual performance pay independent of the role of unionization. However, far more panel study estimations would be needed to confirm this suggestion.

As if the establishment-level studies were not muddy enough, a variety of individual-level studies have attempted to estimate the determinants of who is paid by individual performance pay. Using data from the United Kingdom, Booth and Frank (1999) showed that unionization is positively associated with a broad measure of performance pay for women and for men in the public sector while playing no role for men in the private sector. Yet the measure combines many types of performance pay. Using individual-level U.S. data, Geddes and Heywood (2003) found that while unionization plays no role in determining a broad measure of performance pay, it is a significant and negative determinant of being paid piece rates among those in craft and operative occupations and a negative determinant of being paid commissions in sales occupations.

This later evidence then links with the early case studies suggesting that uncovering the actual role of unions depends on examining narrow measures of performance pay and a set of workers and establishments in which the particular type of performance pay is a relevant choice. This is not to claim that unions genuinely object to individual performance pay and are effective in reducing its use. Rather, the state of the existing econometric evidence remains too blurred to draw a general conclusion and highlights the need for additional study using narrow definitions of performance pay and focusing on relevant samples.

Furthermore, the role unions play in the adoption of performance pay may depend on whether or not management and unions can build cooperative relationships. Regressions using only a simple dummy variable for unionization may not be very informative, as they can't capture whether employment relations are characterized by trust, reciprocity, and fairness. Heywood, Siebert, and Wei (1997) use British data to show that unionization is associated with reduced use of piece rates and at the same time show that unionized workplaces are more likely to have piece rates if managers report that relations with employees are "good."

More generally, Van het Karr and Gruenell (2001) show that European unions will often support variable pay when it is perceived to be transparent, fair, and jointly established and supervised.

Stronger evidence that worker representation can support the use of performance pay comes from Germany. German industrial relations are characterized by a dual representation through both unions and works councils (Huebler and Jirjahn 2003). While collective bargaining agreements are usually negotiated at the broad industrial level, works councils provide for establishment-level codetermination. Freeman and Lazear (1995) argue that works councils are more likely to build trust and cooperation when distributional conflicts are settled between unions and employers' associations outside the firm. Following from this, Heywood, Huebler, and Jirjahn (1998) show that works councils are positively associated with piece rates in establishments covered by collective bargaining agreements but not in uncovered establishments. This hints at an important interaction between sector-level bargaining and establishment-level codetermination in building cooperative relations. Jirjahn and Smith (2006) distinguish between works councils coupled with positive managerial attitudes toward employee involvement and those coupled with negative attitudes. They find that the use of piece rates is positively associated with the first regime but not the second. The sum of the contradictory evidence across countries and units of observation makes it seem unlikely that the decline in unionization observed in many countries will universally cause a large increase or decrease in the use of piece rates and commissions. The effects of declining unionization will likely depend on the industrial relations climate that existed before and after the decline in unionization.

Consequences of Individual Performance Pay

The object of individual performance pay is to align the interests of workers and firms. The degree to which this is accomplished varies dramatically, but one of the most basic issues remains the extent to which performance pay increases productivity.

The evidence on the link between performance pay and establishment performance in economy-wide samples remains mixed. Fernie and Metcalf (1995), Heywood, Siebert, and Wei (1997), and Belfield and Marsden (2003) point to significant positive associations between the use of performance pay and both productivity and financial performance, while Addison and Belfield (2001) found no association. Belfield and Marsden (2003) emphasize that the superior financial performance associated with performance pay is most evident when such pay matches the proper monitoring environment (low costs to monitor output, high costs to monitor input, low supervisory intensity, and so on). They also present evidence that over time managers move to install performance pay in matched monitoring environments and drop performance pay from unmatched monitoring environments, a process the authors identify as "experimentation." Yet, economy-wide cross-sectional analysis can only be suggestive. First, on the theory side, in equilibrium each firm should adopt the payment scheme that maximizes its profit (the eventual result of experimentation). As a result, cross-sectional regressions give no indication of the consequences for a representative firm adopting performance pay. Second, on the econometric side, panel data are required to hold constant individual establishment-specific effects on performance. Failure to use such fixed-effects estimators is likely to result in simply picking up correlations revealing that already profitable firms adopt performance pay but would have been highly profitable without performance pay. Concern with these points has led researchers to other field experiments and away from economy-wide data sets.

In a well-known case study, Lazear (2000) followed the consequences of the Safelite Glass Corporation, a large auto glass company, moving 3,000 employees from hourly wages to piece rates in 1994 and 1995. He measured a 44% gain in output per worker that was attributable to two equal-sized influences. First, the average worker produces more because of the incentive effect; second, the firm retains and hires the most able workers. These results confirm the anticipated consequence of increased effort from existing workers and positive sorting among potential workers. The evidence also suggests that quality did not suffer as a result of the piece-rate scheme (in part due to a new requirement that any defects must be taken care of by the worker that caused them for no additional compensation).

Shearer (2004) examined workers in a tree-planting firm that provides daily observations on individual worker productivity under both piece rates and time rates. He estimated the productivity gain associated with piece rates to be approximately 20%. Oettinger (2001) examined the variation in sales of stadium vendors, showing that higher commission rates were associated with higher sales after accounting for worker-specific fixed effects. When combined with the near unanimity that output-based pay is associated with higher pay (Seiler 1984; Lazear 2000; Parent 1999; Paarsch and Shearer 2000; Jirjahn and Stephan 2004;Heywood and O'Halloran 2005), two conclusions seem warranted. First, piece rates increase worker effort and the resulting output. Second, ratchet effects are not so severe that workers on piece rates do not retain a return on this increased effort.[6]

But before giving piece rates a strong recommendation, we recall the problems identified earlier with rewarding A but hoping for B. Freeman and Kleiner (2005) present a detailed case study of a shoe manufacturer's decision to eliminate piece rates. The authors emphasize that the increased productivity of a piece rate can come at too high a cost. Under piece rates, workers may skimp on quality, waste materials, and take greater risks. Moreover, fear of ratchet effects may make workers unwilling to share production-line knowledge with management. And perhaps most importantly, maintaining a functional piece-rate scheme requires adjusting the rate when technology or the product line changes. Such adjustments are costly. They require "reengineering the rate," may produce acrimony, and may reduce the incentive for workers to improve productivity because of both the uncertainty and the fear of ratchet effects.

Freeman and Kleiner show that the elimination of piece rates brought a new "bundle" of management practices, including just-in-time supply, a modular form of production with cross-trained workers in teams, and new efforts to reduce accidents. These practices, largely inconsistent with piece rates, were viewed as needed to expand the product line in order to compete with foreign manufacturers. In an event study using time-series data from the firm, the change away from piece rates lowered productivity but also lowered costs. The lower costs dominated, with the result being increased profitability.

Interestingly, the cross-sectional evidence in Table 1 shows that piece rates are more common when product market competition is most vigorous. More generally, the methodology of following individual firms' changing payment methods, while holding the firm constant, is not without difficulties. If we return to the idea of experimentation toward equilibrium, both firms adopting new performance pay schemes and those dropping existing performance pay schemes should increase profit by doing so. Put somewhat differently, neither the positive effects at Safelite Glass nor the negative effects at the shoe manufacturer hold a strong lesson for a randomly chosen firm.

When performance pay is based on output, it has the advantage of being more objective and verifiable. Regardless of whether tying pay to a particular output measure drives the desired behavior, it does reduce the chance for managerial favoritism. Elvira and Town (2001) make clear that one outcome of such favoritism can be racial and gender differences in managerial evaluation. In turn, worker earnings may reflect these differences. They confirm that white supervisors provide lower evaluations for nonwhites than for whites even when performance, as measured by the researchers, is identical. The use of an objective measure of output reduces the likelihood of such differences.

Heywood and O'Halloran (2005) provide an information model in which the use of piece rates increases the chance of authorities' detecting discrimination, thereby increasing the expected costs of discrimination and decreasing its extent. They test this with data from the National Longitudinal Study of Youth from 1998 to 2002 showing that the wage discrimination by race among those paid time rates is positive and significant but that the differential is nearly zero and statistically insignificant among those paid piece rates. Interestingly, the evidence also suggests that the racial differential among those paid bonuses is larger than that for those paid time rates. To the extent that such bonuses are the result of supervisory evaluation, this further supports the connection between payment methods and discrimination. Fang and Heywood (2006) provide further confirmation that the earnings differential associated with non-European Canadians vanishes for those paid piece rates and commissions. Jirhan and Stephan (2004) show that the gender differential in Germany is lower among workers paid piece rates than among those paid time rates. Moreover, Jirjahn and Stephan (2006) tie the payment of piece rates to more competitive product markets, providing a channel through which Becker's (1957) association between competitive product markets and reduced discrimination might flow. Thus, even as output-based pay increases the dispersion in outcomes and earning, it may lower racial, ethnic, and gender differentials.

Despite evidence that piece rates may reduce gender- and race-based wage differentials, individual performance pay itself may change general perceptions about the perceived fairness of compensation. Certainly, the advice to those actually setting pay highlights the importance of pay, as when Brown (1989) warns that "the prudent personnel manager devotes far less time to devising new pay incentives than to tending old notions of fairness." Performance-related pay violates basic notions of "pay for the job" and treating similar workers doing similar jobs similarly. This theme appears frequently in the complaints lodged by unions against performance-related pay (Issac 2001) and raises an efficiency concern. Those who perceive the pay system as unfair will be "demotivated" by the incentive structure it implements (Marsden and French 2002). Such concerns prompted Heywood and Wei (2006) to examine the influence of payment methods on job satisfaction. Using the National Longitudinal Study, they show that workers tend to report greater satisfaction when receiving performance pay. While not monolithic, these results suggest that performance-related pay, on average, does not result in sufficient unfairness as to reduce job satisfaction and so demotivate workers.

Determinants of Group Performance Pay

Prendergast (1999) reviews studies providing evidence for the $1/N$ problem in medical and legal partnerships. This evidence supports standard analyses showing that profit sharing becomes increasingly irrelevant in motivating workers as N increases. Hence, one would expect that larger firms would avoid using profit sharing, but most studies find either no significant association (e.g., Drago and Heywood 1995 for Australia, Heywood and Jirjahn 2002 for Germany, Kruse 1996 for the United States) or even a positive link (e.g., Jones and Pliskin 1997 for Canada). While fixed costs in the adoption of profit sharing might explain these results, Adams (2002, 2006) provides an alternative explanation. He argues that manufacturing firms in contrast to legal or medical partnerships have a higher degree of interdependent worker productivity. As discussed, team production may help overcome the $1/N$ problem. Moreover, if the degree of interdependent worker productivity increases with firm size, there may be a positive relationship between firm size and profit sharing. Larger firms are more likely to adopt profit sharing to provide incentives for workers to take into account production interdependencies.

Theory predicts that the complexity of tasks and multitasking should be associated with group rather than individual performance pay. There are several ways to measure multitasking in an empirical study. A skilled workforce, flexible work assignment, rotation among wide ranges of tasks, and a breakdown of occupational barriers as well as participation on the job and more autonomy through self-managing teams and employee-involvement groups are closely related to multitasking. Kruse (1996) finds that firms characterized by job enrichment, teamwork, or employee participation in decision making are more likely to introduce profit sharing. Long (2002) finds for Canada that high-involvement firms, firms with greater proportions of highly educated employees, and firms with work teams are more likely to have organizational performance pay. Estrin and Wilson (1993) show that employee participation is positively associated with using profit sharing in U.K. metalworking firms. Drago and Heywood (1995) find quality circles and productivity-improvement groups make profit sharing more likely in Australian establishments, whereas they have no significant impact on the use of piece rates. Brown (1990) and MacLeod and Parent (1999) show that complex jobs are less likely to provide individual-based performance pay.

Heywood and Jirjahn (2002) show that profit sharing in Germany is more likely (and individual piece rates are less likely) in establishments that require skilled blue-collar workers. Similarly, direct involvement of employees in investment decisions is positively associated with profit sharing but negatively associated with piece rates. Self-managed production teams raise the probability of profit sharing and other forms of group compensation but not individual-based performance pay. Jirjahn (2002) shows that profit sharing emerges as part of a broader package of policies that includes greater training, self-managed production teams, and programs to improve communication between workers and between workers and management. In contrast, piece rates emerge as part of a human resource management (HRM) system that does not rely on teams, improved communication, and training.

Profit sharing should be particularly valuable for firms facing high uncertainty and hence demanding high internal flexibility of their workers. Estrin and Wilson (1993) confirm a positive association between variability of profits and the use of profit sharing in U.K. metalworking firms. Similarly, Kruse (1996) shows that companies with higher variability of profits are more likely to adopt both profit-sharing plans and employee stock option plans (ESOPs).[7]

Evidence on the role of industrial relations is mixed. Empirical studies for the United States and the United Kingdom suggest that unions often oppose profit sharing (Lindop 1989; Eaton and Voos 1992). Unions might fear the dispersion of earnings across firms or see profit sharing as replacing unionization. However, recent evidence suggests that union attitudes toward profit sharing can change. Profit sharing may become a union objective in an era of concession bargaining when this profit sharing is important for the competitiveness of firms. In the United States, unions cooperated in the 1980s with the introduction of sharing schemes to increase employment growth (Bell and Neumark 1993). Correspondingly, Kruse (1996) shows that the negative link between unionization and profit sharing disappears in longitudinal data. Finally, institutional reports confirm that unions in several European countries take such schemes for granted and now bargain to assure their fairness and transparency (Van het Karr and Gruenell 2001).

Germany's dual system of worker representation is again interesting (Heywood, Huebler, and Jirjahn 1998; Heywood and Jirjahn 2002). On the one hand, establishments covered by collective bargaining agreements are less likely to use profit sharing, reflecting the general skepticism of German unions toward formal profit-sharing plans. Yet among establishments covered by collective agreements, those with works councils are more likely to have profit sharing. This result mirrors that obtained for individual-based performance pay and again highlights that works councils are more effective in building trust and cooperation when distributional conflicts are moderated by unions and employer associations outside the firm.

Consequences of Group-Level Performance Pay

Perotin and Robinson (2002) reviewed empirical studies on the productivity effects of profit sharing, concluding that the majority find positive effects. Given the $1/N$ problem, Prendergast (1999:41) remarks that "these results appear to be such a violation of standard agency theory." Yet some of the previous theoretical considerations suggest that group-level incentives may improve firm performance but that the effects are likely to depend on establishment characteristics, industrial relations, and other HRM practices. Several empirical studies confirm these profit-sharing interactions.

Mitchell, Lewin, and Lawler (1990) were the first to investigate the interaction of variable pay with nonfinancial participation. Kruse (1993) showed that adopting profit sharing positively influences short-run productivity and confirmed weak positive interaction effects of profit sharing with quality circles and information sharing. Cooke (1994) found that employee-participation programs contribute more to performance in unionized firms while the positive effect of profit sharing and gain sharing on performance is stronger in nonunion firms. Boning, Ichniowski, and Shaw (2001) showed that group incentive pay in the production lines of minimills raises output and that the use of teams coupled with group incentive pay raises output even further. Capelli and Neumark (2001) cast doubt on the productivity effects of so-called "high-performance work practices," but their estimates suggest that profit sharing and teams interact positively.

Fernie and Metcalf (1995) found for the United Kingdom a positive interaction of profit sharing and nonfinancial participation in unionized workplaces but a negative interaction in nonunionized workplaces. However, not only mere union presence but also a broader industrial relations climate characterized by trust, fairness, and reciprocity may be crucial for the incentive effects of sharing schemes. Perotin and Robinson (2000) examined the interaction of sharing schemes with antidiscrimination policies on establishment productivity in the United Kingdom. They found that ESOPs and deferred profit sharing tend to be associated with equal opportunity practices in generating productivity but that other forms of profit-related pay appear to negatively interact with those practices.

Fakhfakh and Perotin (2000) showed a positive productivity effect of profit sharing in France. They also showed that equipment is more efficiently used under profit sharing and that the positive effects of profit sharing are greater if employees have less strict supervision. FitzRoy and Kraft (1995) showed that profit sharing in Germany positively interacts with works council incidence. Jirjahn (1998) confirmed this positive productivity effect but only when coupled with self-managed production teams and the presence of works councils. Askildsen, Jirjahn, and Smith (2006) found that establishments with profit sharing are more likely to launch new products, to implement process innovations, and to invest in environmentally friendly production. This fits the notion that profit sharing provides incentives for flexibility and multitasking.

Wilson and Peel (1991) showed that profit sharing lowers absence in the United Kingdom. Heywood and Jirjahn (2004) showed a similar result for Germany, while Brown, Fakhfakh, and Sessions (1999) showed that profit sharing and ESOPs reduce absenteeism in France. These results may indicate that profit sharing induces peer pressure. Knez and Simester (2001) confirm a high degree of peer pressure induced by firm-wide profit sharing for employees at Continental Airlines, where employees actually monitored colleagues who called in sick. Freeman, Kruse, and Blasi (2004) provided survey evidence that profit sharing encourages workers to act against shirking behavior and thus to reduce the tendency to free-ride. Yet profit sharing induces worker actions against shirkers only if employees have a very positive view of management–employee relations.

Profit sharing may also provide incentives for cooperation and helping on the job. An econometric study by Drago and Garvey (1998) and an experimental study by Wageman and Baker (1997) failed to confirm this suggestion, but Encinosa, Gaynor, and Rebitzer (1997) found that the doctors in medical partnerships, as opposed to receiving earnings based on their individual contributions, report a significantly higher frequency of consulting one another about cases.

Heywood, Jirjahn, and Tsertsvadze (2005a) showed that for non-supervisory men profit sharing increases cooperation but that for those who highly value success on the job and for women, it has no influence on cooperation, and for supervisors it reduces cooperation. Heywood, Jirjahn, and Tsertsvadze (2005b) examined the impact of profit sharing on conflict with the boss. For nonsupervisory workers in excellent health, profit sharing reduces conflict with the boss, but for those who are not in excellent health and for supervisors, it does not. Hansen (1997) showed that while the performance of initially less productive workers improves under group schemes, the performance of more productive workers does not change. He speculates that group incentives induce high productivity workers to help improve the performance of less productive workers.

New Evidence on the Determinants of Piece Rates

In this section, we provide new evidence on the determinants of piece rates. We apply, for the first time, a partial observability approach to separately investigate the desires of management and workers for piece rates. Germany's unique system of codetermination and worker involvement makes this approach particularly appropriate.

As mentioned, German industrial relations are characterized by a dual structure of employee representation (Huebler and Jirjahn 2003). Works councils provide a highly developed mechanism for establishment-level participation, while collective bargaining agreements are usually negotiated at the sectoral level. While workers of each establishment vote to establish a council, the rights of the works councils are given by the Works Constitution Act (WCA). The WCA provides that the works council must agree to the implementation of any piece rate, making them the result of consultation and negotiation between management and workers.

Indeed, the high proportion of German manufacturing firms paying piece rates and premium pay may result from codetermination's reducing the fear of ratchet effects (Jirjahn 2002). In 1995, 26.6% of blue-collar men and 35.7% of blue-collar women were paid by piece rates or premium pay (Jirjahn 2002). Moreover, 18.2% of manufacturing workplaces offer piece rates and 16.1% offer premium pay, exceeding the German use of profit sharing (Heywood, Huebler, and Jirjahn 1998). This contrasts with U.S. microdata that reveal many more workers receiving profit sharing than piece rates (Parent 2002).

As piece rates in German firms with works councils result from negotiation, we should examine both the determinants influencing workers' desire for piece rates and the determinants influencing management's desire for piece rates. Some determinants may influence employees' desire and management's desire in opposite directions. Heywood, Huebler, and Jirjahn (1998) emphasize that workers receiving piece rates will use their ability to influence investment decisions to allow greater production and so earnings. Such influence activities, focusing on the quantity of output, benefit the workers but hurt efficiency and profitability. Thus management would try to avoid piece rates for workers with the ability to influence investment. But confirming this line of logic requires being able to separately estimate the behaviors of workers and of management.

The Partial Observability Approach

Altogether, the importance of codetermining piece rates requires separately estimating the determinants of the works council (woco) at establishment i desiring piece rates and the determinants of management (man) at establishment i desiring piece rates:

$$DES_{woco,i} = 1, \quad \text{if} \quad y_{woco,i} > 0 \quad \text{and} \quad DES_{woco,i} = 0, \text{otherwise}$$
$$DES_{man,i} = 1, \quad \text{if} \quad y_{man,i} > 0 \quad \text{and} \quad DES_{man,i} = 0, \text{otherwise} \quad (6)$$

where

$$y_{woco,i} = z_{woco,i} b_{1,woco} + x_{woco,i} b_{2,woco} + e_{woco,i}$$
$$y_{man,i} = z_{man,i} b_{1,man} + e_{man,i} \quad (7)$$

Thus, $DES_{woco,i}$ and $DES_{man,i} = 1$ are the dichotomous variables measuring the desire for a piece rate by the works council and by management and reflect the realization of the underlying latent variables $y_{woco,i}$ and $y_{man,i}$. Yet without detailed information on the true desires of both sides, statistical identification must be used to estimate the separate determinants. This is accomplished through variables unique to the works council or to management. Partial observability techniques (Poirer 1980; Abowd and Farber 1982) impose a structure on the equations above based on the underlying process. Thus, in the typical union or government queue model (Abowd and Farber 1982; Heywood and Mohanty 1995), employers choose from workers who previously identify a desire to work for unionized or governmental employers. This sequential process seems incorrect for bargaining over piece rates. Instead, codetermination gives each side the ability to stop the use of piece rates. Thus, observing a piece rate (PR) requires that both sides desire it:

$$PR_i = 1 \text{ only if } DES_{woco,i} = 1 \text{ and } DES_{man,i} = 1 \qquad (8)$$

As (2) makes clear these are probabilistic, the result becomes a bivariate probit with partial observability. Assuming independence of the errors, the probability of observing a piece rate is the product of the two sides' probability of desiring a piece rate:

$$\text{Prob}(PR_i = 1) = \text{Prob}(DES_{woco,i} = 1) \times \text{Prob}(DES_{man,i} = 1) \qquad (9)$$

Assuming a sensible choice of identifying variables in (2), one can recover separate estimates of the determinants of the two desires for a piece rate.

We emphasize that the object in testing is to recover information about circumstances of potential conflicts. Thus, as discussed, we anticipate that when workers participate in investment, management will be less likely to desire piece rates out of fear of influence activities on the part of workers. At the same time, workers would prefer piece rates as those same influence activities allow them to shape investments to increase their production and so earnings.

Data and Results

The empirical investigation uses the Hanover Panel, a four-wave panel of manufacturing establishments in the federal state of Lower Saxony. The data come from personal interviews with the owner, top manager, or head of the personnel department. The question on the use of piece rates is asked only in the first and the third waves. Therefore, the estimates are based on pooled data for the years 1994 and 1996. To ensure that negotiations play a role in the adoption of piece rates, the analysis is restricted to establishments having a works council.

TABLE 2
Variable Definitions and Descriptive Statistics (Mean, Standard Deviation)

Variable	Description
PieceRates	Dummy variable equal to 1 if the establishment uses piece rates in its production departments (.267, .443).
Women	Women as a proportion of all employees (.265, .220).
BlueCol	Blue-collar workers as a proportion of total employees (.655, .161).
BlueColSkilled	Skilled blue-collar workers as a proportion of total employees (.378, .233).
Turnover	Dummy variable equal to 1 if management feels employee turnover is too high (.023, .151).
EstabSize	Total employees in the establishment divided by 1,000 (.281, .942).
CollBarg	Dummy variable equal to 1 if the establishment is covered by a collective bargaining agreement (.812, .391).
ExpansionPlan	Dummy variable equal to 1 if management plans to increase the market share of the firm (.573, .495).
EmploymStabil	Dummy variable equal to 1 if the employment level at the end of the year is at least equal to that of the two previous years (.390, .488).
SalesConcentr	Sales of the six largest companies in each industrial sector as a share of total sales in the sector. Official German statistics from 1993 are matched to 32 industrial sectors identified by the survey (17.956, 15.222).
Teams	Dummy variable equal to 1 if workers are organized in production teams (.496, .500).
LatestTech	Dummy variable equal to 1 if the technology is of the most recent vintage (.347, .476).
ProfitShExecs	Dummy variable equal to 1 if executive managers have a profit-sharing plan (.531, .499).
ActiveOwner	Dummy variable equal to 1 if active owners are present in the establishment (.514, .500).
WrkrParticInInvest	Dummy variable equal to 1 if employees who will work directly with the investment (e.g., the machine) participate in decisions about large production investments (.670, .471).
Industry Dummies	10 broader defined industry dummies are included in the regressions.

The descriptive statistics are for establishments with a works council (N = 906).

Table 2 shows the definitions of variables and their descriptive statistics. Piece rates are used by 26.7% of the establishments. This relatively high percentage of establishments using piece rates reflects the positive association between works councils and piece rates. Furthermore, in 67% of the establishments, workers directly participate in decisions about large investments.

Table 3 presents the results from a simple probit model and from the partial observability model. The simple probit shows a negative association between workers' participation in investment decisions and the use of piece rates. The partial observability model shows that this results from two opposing influences. The opportunity to participate in investment

TABLE 3
Determinants of Piece Rates—Probit and Partial Observability Results

	Simple probit	Partial observability	
		Worker desire	Management desire
Constant	−2.738°°	−1.740°°	−1.178
	(6.109)	(2.010)	(1.454)
Women	1.419°°	1.033°°	1.580°°
	(5.089)	(2.295)	(3.245)
BlueCol	1.324°°	2.230°°	0.424
	(3.795)	(3.080)	(0.567)
BlueColSkilled	−0.226	0.328	−0.858°
	(0.940)	(0.616)	(1.799)
Turnover	.0746°°	1.145°°	
	(2.393)	(2.898)	
EstabSize	0.648°°	−0.621°	4.132°°
	(3.114)	(1.686)	(2.138)
EstabSize Squared	−0.061°°	0.069	−0.366
	(2.589)	(1.476)	(0.107)
CollBarg	0.427°°	−0.317	0.949°°
	(3.041)	(0.819)	(3.528)
ExpansionPlan	0.249°°	−.0285	0.703°°
	(2.428)	(1.185)	(2.863)
EmploymStabil	−0.297°°	−0.391°°	
	(2.762)	(2.302)	
SalesConcentr	−.0112°°	−.0075	−0.099
	(2.157)	(0.985)	(1.008)
Teams	0.003	0.114	−0.100
	(0.028)	(0.550)	(0.497)
LatestTech	−.1842°	−0.314°	
	(1.699)	(1.869)	
ProfitShExecs	0.272°°	0.400°°	−0.076
	(2.651)	(2.081)	(0.353)
ActiveOwner	0.031	−.369	
	(0.289)	(1.515)	
WrkrParticInInvest	−0.359°°	0.488°°	−1.352°°
	(3.403)	(2.067)	(4.029)
Industry dummies	Yes	Yes	
Chi-squared	184.3°°	251.4°°	
McFadden r-squared	.175	.220	
N	906	906	

The estimates are for establishments with a works council. T-statistics are in parentheses.
°Statistically significant at the 10% level.
°°Statistically significant at the 5% level.

177

decisions increases the workers' desire for piece rates, supporting the hypothesis that the opportunity to influence investments allows influence activities regarding the piece rate. Yet, if workers participate in investment decisions, it would be a folly to reward A (quantity) while hoping for B (appropriate establishment-wide decisions). Hence, management tries to avoid piece rates when workers participate in investment decisions in order to reduce the incentive to provide biased information. Indeed, the partial observability model confirms that the participation of workers in investment decisions reduces management's desire for piece rates.

Other results are interesting in their own right. A high share of blue-collar workers increases workers' desire for piece rates. This accords with the finding by Jirjahn and Stephan (2004) that workers with low potential earnings under time rates prefer piece rates. However, a high share of skilled blue-collar workers decreases management's desire for piece rates. If skilled blue-collar workers have to perform complex tasks, piece rates may not provide appropriate incentives.

Coverage by a collective agreement increases management's desire for piece rates. Works councils for which pay is set in collective agreements are less likely to engage in rent-seeking activities and are more likely to contribute to establishment surplus. Moreover, collective bargaining agreements often contain some regulations concerning the design of piece rate schemes that may facilitate negotiations with the works councils.

While most studies find a positive link between establishment size and piece rates, the partial observability model shows opposing influences on workers' and management's desire for piece rates. Establishment size positively influences management's desire for using piece rates, supporting the hypothesis that implementing piece rates involves substantial fixed costs. Yet establishment size negatively influences workers' desire for piece rates. One reason might be that workers in larger firms recognize that the hierarchy and size make informal monitoring less effective and allow them to reduce effort or require efficiency wages. Either may be preferred to piece rates. However, the simple probit estimates show that the influence of establishment size on management's desire dominates. Management may obtain the council's agreement by making concessions in other decision areas.

A high share of women exerts a positive influence on both desires. This supports the notion that women sort and are sorted into piece rates. Piece rate jobs may have less interdependent worker productivity, imposing lower costs on women who have disproportionate responsibility for household production. Alternatively, women may be more motivated by contemporaneous rewards than by deferred payments (Goldin 1986). Finally, piece rates may provide less opportunity for gender discrimination, making them more attractive to women.

Conclusions

The need for performance pay arises because worker effort tends to remain imperfectly observable and verifiable. Thus, optimal labor contracts cannot be written and enforced. In these circumstances, performance pay brings with it the promise of creating greater congruity between the objectives of workers and of the firm. This promise often remains unfulfilled as the incentives workers see remain an imperfect reflection of the ultimate organizational objectives. Nonetheless, in a variety of circumstances performance pay has prospered.

For relatively simple tasks in which quality can be easily checked, the use of piece rates remains a sensible way to conserve on monitoring resources and generate incentives. Much has been made in the literature of the role such incentives play in sorting workers, with the most productive workers moving into jobs with such incentives. While there exists empirical evidence that this is right on average, there is also evidence that the average may be composed of both positive and negative selection. Piece-rate workers may consist of both the best workers, who wish to do better than time rates allow, and the worst workers, for whom the productivity associated with the time rate is too great (Baland, Dreze, and Leruth 1999). Nonetheless, we emphasize that the complexity of the task for which a piece rate may be suitable and the willingness of workers to accept a piece rate appears to vary with the extent to which workers are involved in the establishment and oversight of the scheme. The relatively extensive use of piece and premium rates in German manufacturing reflects the codetermination process through which they are agreed upon. Yet the new empirical research presented in this chapter suggests that the process of codetermination leaves room for strategic behavior. Recognizing this, German workers involved in managerial decision making are more likely to prefer piece rates, but firms involving workers in decisions are less likely to prefer piece rates.

Individual merit pay that reflects supervisors' evaluations tends to exist where workers perform more complex and varied tasks. Despite the many problems associated with such evaluations, they remain the primary systematic way in which worker productivity is assessed (Jackson and Schuler 2003). While allowing greater flexibility in the range of activities and behaviors to be evaluated, the process also allows wide scope for the beliefs of supervisors to enter the process. This point is illustrated by recent evidence that race and ethnicity are more likely to influence earnings under such schemes than under more mechanical performance pay schemes, such as piece rates.

Group performance pay and broader profit sharing at the organizational level have emerged in the last several decades as an important element of high performance workplaces. Often viewed as part of the bundle of HRM practices that define such workplaces, this combination has been associated with firms with significantly more structural flexibility and multitasking. Such payment schemes are often tied to team organization and the performance of the team. As teamwork makes it difficult to measure an individual worker's productivity, individual-based performance pay may not be sensible. However, recent studies show that workers do not respond uniformly to group-based incentives. The effects of group performance pay and profit sharing depend on the type of worker and the work environment.

As even this brief conclusion suggests, there exists substantial variation in the characteristics of performance pay. The ongoing challenge for those studying these characteristics is to identify the match between them, the nature of the workplace and its workers, and the performance of the organization. This requires that the various strands of the literature on performance pay be combined. Existing studies often focus on one particular incentive scheme (e.g., only piece rates or only profit sharing). Future research should provide a more systematic comparison of schemes and the circumstances under which each scheme is successful.

Acknowledgment

The authors benefited from the opportunity to work together in the summer of 2005 at the University of Hanover and express thanks to all those who made that experience both fun and productive. Michelle Brown, David Lewin, and a reviewer deserve credit for improving this chapter.

Notes

[1] In her analysis of over 800 certified labor agreements in Australia, Brown (1997) identifies a series of broad and explicitly stated objectives that played varying roles in the decision to adopt performance pay. The objectives included attracting and retaining competent employees; providing a focus for formal training activities; promoting an achievement orientation, rewarding superior performance, and sharing the economic benefits of the resulting improved performance; promoting the achievement of organizational objectives by helping employees understand and participate in major performance areas; and promoting employee responsibility.

[2] In some instances piece rates may be based on group performance. Available evidence, however, suggests that group piece rates are used far less than individual piece rates (Heywood and Jirjahn 2002).

[3] Also see Carmichael and MacLeod (2000) and Kanemoto and MacLeod (1992).

[4] While worker involvement in the design of the piece rate may help overcome the ratchet effect, worker involvement in investment decisions may be counterproductive if workers receive piece rates.

[5] Alternative confirming evidence comes from less developed countries where women chose low-paying home work, uniformly paid by the piece, because such work provides the flexibility to fulfill family duties (Beneria and Roldan 1987).

[6] Indeed, Barkume (2004) confirms the earnings premium associated with performance pay even when holding constant pensions, shift differentials, overtime, and bonuses.

[7] Foss and Laursen (2005) use a sample of Danish firms to show that the variability of profits is positively associated with a broad measure of performance pay.

References

Abowd, John, and Henry Farber. 1982. "Job Queues and Union Status of Workers." *Industrial and Labor Relations Review*, Vol. 35, no. 3, pp. 354–67.

Adams, Christopher P. 2002. "Does Size Really Matter? Empirical Evidence on Group Incentives." Working Paper No. 252. Washington, DC: Federal Trade Commission.

———. 2006. "Optimal Team Incentives with CES Production." *Economics Letters*, Vol. 92, no. 1, pp. 143–48.

Addison, J.T., and C. Belfield. 2001. "Updating the Determinants of Firm Performance: Estimates Using the 1998 UK Workplace Employee Relations Survey." *British Journal of Industrial Relations*, Vol. 39, no. 3, pp. 341–66.

Antonioni, D. 1996. "Designing an Effective 360 Degree Appraisal Feedback Process." *Organizational Dynamics*, Vol. 25, no. 2, pp. 24–38.

Aoki, Masahiko. 1990. "The Participatory Generation of Information Rents and the Theory of the Firm." In M. Aoki, B. Gustafsson, and O.E. Williamson, eds., *The Firm as Nexus of Treaties*. Thousand Oaks, CA: Sage, pp. 111–39.

———. 1993. "The Informationally-participatory Firm." In Samuel Bowles, Herbert Ginitis, and Bo Gustafsson, eds., *Markets and Democracy: Participation, Accountability and Efficiency*. Cambridge: Cambridge University Press, pp. 231–47.

Asch, Beth J. 1990. "Do Incentives Matter? The Case of Navy Recruiters." *Industrial and Labor Relations Review*, Vol. 42, no. 3, pp. S89–106.

Askildsen, J.E., U. Jirjahn, and S.C. Smith. 2006. "Works Councils and Environmental Investment: Theory and Evidence from German Panel Data." *Journal of Economic Behavior and Organization*, Forthcoming.

Baker, George. 1992. "Incentive Contracts and Performance Measurement." *Journal of Political Economy*, Vol. 100, no. 3, pp. 598–614.

———. 2002. "Distortion and Risk in Optimal Incentive Contracts." *Journal of Human Resources*, Vol. 37, no. 4, pp. 728–51.

Baker, George, Robert Gibbons, and Kevin J. Murphy. 1994. "Subjective Performance Measures in Optimal Incentive Contracts." *Quarterly Journal of Economics*, Vol. 109, no. 4, pp. 1125–56.

Baker, G., M.J. Jensen, and K.J. Murphy. 1988. "Compensation and Incentives: Practice vs. Theory." *Journal of Finance*, Vol. 18, no. 3, pp. 593–616.

Baland, J., J. Dreze, and L. Leruth. 1999. "Daily Wages and Piece Rates in Agrarian Economies." *Journal of Development Economics*, Vol. 59, no. 2, pp. 445–61.

Baneria, Lourdes, and Martha Roldan. 1987. *The Crossroads of Class and Gender: Industrial Subcontracting and Household Dynamics in Mexico City*. Chicago: University of Chicago Press.

Barkume, Anthony. 2004. "Using Incentive Pay and Providing Pay Supplements in US Job Markets." *Industrial Relations*, Vol. 43, no. 3, pp. 618–33.

Barron, J.M., and K.P. Gjerde. 1997. "Peer Pressure in an Agency Relationship." *Journal of Labor Economics*, Vol. 15, no. 2, pp. 234–54.

Barth, Erling. 1997. "Firm-Specific Seniority and Wages." *Journal of Labor Economics*, Vol. 15, no. 3, pp. 495–506.

Becker, Gary S. 1957. *The Economics of Discrimination*. Chicago: University of Chicago Press.

Belfield, Richard, and David Marsden. 2003. "Performance Pay, Monitoring Environments and Establishment Performance." *International Journal of Manpower*, Vol. 24, no. 4, pp. 452–71.

Bell, L., and D. Neumark. 1993. "Lump Sum Payments and Profit Sharing Plans in the Union Sector of the United States Economy." *Economic Journal*, Vol. 103, no. 418, pp. 602–19.

Boning, Brent, Casey Ichniowski, and Kathryn Shaw. 2001. "Opportunity Counts: Teams and the Effectiveness of Production Incentives," NBER Working Paper No. 8306. Cambridge, MA: National Bureau of Economic Research.

Booth, Alison L., and Jeffrey Frank. 1999. "Earnings and Performance-Related Pay." *Journal of Labor Economics*, Vol. 17, no. 3, pp. 447–63.

Brett, J.F., and L.E. Atwater. 2001. "360 Degree Feedback: Accuracy, Reactions and Perceptions of Usefulness." *Journal of Applied Psychology*, Vol. 86, no. 5, pp. 930–42.

Brown, C. 1990. "Firms' Choice of Method of Pay." *Industrial and Labor Relations Review*, Vol. 43, no. 3, pp. 165s–82s.

Brown, Martin, and Peter Philips. 1986. "The Decline of Piece Rates in California Canneries: 1890–1969." *Industrial Relations*, Vol. 25, no. 1, pp. 81–91.

Brown, Michelle. 1997. "Performance Pay Choices: Evidence from Certified Agreements." *Journal of Industrial Relations*, Vol. 39, no. 3, pp. 349–68.

Brown, Michelle, and John S. Heywood. 2003. "The Determinants of Incentive Schemes: Australian Panel Data." *Australian Bulletin of Labour*, Vol. 29, no. 3, pp. 218–36.

————. 2005. "Performance Appraisal Systems: Determinants and Change." *British Journal of Industrial Relations*, Vol. 43, no. 4, pp. 659–79.

Brown, S., F. Fakhfakh, and J.G. Sessions. 1999. "Absenteeism and Employee Sharing." *Industrial and Labor Relations Review*, Vol. 52, no. 2, pp. 234–51.

Brown, William. 1989. "Company Pay Policies: The Art of Getting Change on the Cheap," Shirley Lemer Memorial Lecture, Manchester University. May 18, 1989. Mimeographed speech.

Cappelli, Peter, and David Neumark. 2001. "Do 'High-Performance' Work Practices Improve Establishment-Level Outcomes?" *Industrial and Labor Relations Review*, Vol. 54, no. 4, pp. 737–75.

Carmichael, H. Lorne, and W. Bentley MacLeod. 2000. "Worker Cooperation and the Ratchet Effect." *Journal of Labor Economics*, Vol. 18, no. 1, pp. 1–19.

Che, Y.K., and S.W. Yoo. 2001. "Optimal Incentives for Teams." *American Economic Review*, Vol. 91, no. 3, pp. 525–41.

Cheatham, C., D. Davis, and L. Cheatham. 1996. "Hollywood Profits: Gone with the Wind?" *CPA Journal*, Vol. 66, no. X 32–4.

Cooke, William N. 1994. "Employee Participation Programs, Group-Based Incentives, and Company Performance: A Union-Nonunion Comparison." *Industrial and Labor Relations Review*, Vol. 47, no. 4, pp. 594–609.

Cowling, Marc. 2001. "Fixed Wages or Productivity Pay: Evidence from 15 EU Countries." *Small Business Economics*, Vol. 16, no. 3, pp. 191–204.

Drago, Robert, and Gerald T. Garvey. 1998. "Incentives for Helping on the Job: Theory and Evidence." *Journal of Labor Economics*, Vol. 16, no. 1, pp. 1–25.

Drago, Robert, and John S. Heywood. 1995. "Choice of Payment Schemes: Australian Establishment Data." *Industrial Relations*, Vol. 34, no. 4, pp. 507–31.

Drago, Robert, and Geoffrey K. Turnbull. 1988. "Individual versus Group Piece Rates under Team Technologies." *Journal of the Japanese and International Economies*, Vol. 2, no. 1, pp. 1–10.

———. 1991. "Market Incentives and Work Incentives: The Question of Flexible Production." *International Economic Review*, Vol. 32, no. 1, pp. 77–83.

Eaton, A., and P.B. Voos. 1992. "Unions and Contemporary Innovations in Work Organization." In L. Mishel and P.B. Voos, eds., *Unions and Economic Competitiveness*. Armonk, NY: M.E. Sharpe, pp. 173–215.

Eberts, Randall, Kevin Hollenbeck, and Joe Stone. 2002. "Teacher Performance Incentives and Student Outcomes." *Journal of Human Resources*, Vol. 37, no. 4, pp. 913–27.

Edwards, M.R., and A.J. Ewen. 1996. *Providing 360 Degree Feedback: An Approach to Enhancing Individual and Organizational Performance*. Scottsdale, AZ: American Compensation Association.

Elvira, Marta, and Michael Graham. 2002. "Not Just a Formality: Pay System Formalization and Sex-Related Earnings Effects." *Organization Science*, Vol. 13, no. 6, pp. 601–17.

Elvira, Marta, and Robert Town. 2001. "The Effects of Race and Worker Productivity on Performance Evaluations." *Industrial Relations*, Vol. 40, no. 4, pp. 571–90.

Encinosa, W.E. III, M. Gaynor, and J. Rebitzer. 1997. "The Sociology of Groups and the Economics of Incentives: Theory and Evidence on Compensation Systems." NBER Working Paper No. 5953. Cambridge, MA: National Bureau of Economic Research.

Estrin, S., and N. Wilson. 1993. "Profit Sharing, the Marginal Cost of Labour and Employment Variability." Working paper, London Business School.

Fakhfakh, Fathi, and Virginie Perotin. 2000. "The Effects of Profit-sharing Schemes on Enterprise Performance in France." *Economic Analysis*, Vol. 3, no. 1, pp. 93–111.

Fang, Tony, and John S. Heywood. 2006. "Output Pay and Ethnic Wage Differentials: Canadian Evidence." *Industrial Relations*, Vol. 45, no. 2, 173–194.

Fernie, Susan, and David Metcalf. 1995. "Participation, Contingent Pay, Representation and Workplace Performance: Evidence from Great Britain." *British Journal of Industrial Relations*, Vol. 33, no. 3, pp. 379–415.

FitzRoy, Felix, and Kornelius Kraft. 1995. "On the Choice of Incentives in Firms." *Journal of Economic Behavior and Organization*, Vol. 26, no. 1, pp. 145–60.

FitzRoy, F., and K. Kraft. 1986. "Profitability and Profit-Sharing." *Journal of Industrial Economics*, Vol. 35, no. 2, pp. 113–30.

Foss, N.J., and K. Laursen. 2005. "Performance Pay, Delegation and Multitasking under Uncertainty and Innovativeness: An Empirical Investigation." *Journal of Economic Behavior and Organization*, Vol. 58, no. 2, pp. 246–76.

Foster, J.E., and H.Y. Wan. 1984. "Involuntary Unemployment as a Principal-Agent Equilibrium." *American Economic Review*, Vol. 74, no. 3, pp. 476–84.

Freeman, Richard B., and Morris M. Kleiner. 2005. "The Last American Shoe Man-ufacturers: Decreasing Productivity and Increasing Profits in the Shift from Piece Rates to Continuous Flow Production." *Industrial Relations*, Vol. 44, no. 2, pp. 307–30.

Freeman, Richard B., Douglas Kruse, and Joseph Blasi. 2004. "Monitoring Colleagues at Work: Profit Sharing, Employee Ownership, Broad-Based Stock Options and Workplace Performance in the United States." Discussion Paper No. 647. London: Centre for Economic Performance.

Freeman, Richard B., and Edward P. Lazear. 1995. "An Economic Analysis of Works Councils." In J. Rogers and W. Streeck, eds., *Works Councils: Consultation, Representation and Cooperation in Industrial Relations*. Chicago: University of Chicago Press, pp. 27–52.

Friebel, Guido, and Michael Raith. 2004. "Abuse of Authority and Hierarchical Com-munication." *RAND Journal of Economics*, Vol. 35, no. 2, pp. 224–44.

Geddes, Lori, and John S. Heywood. 2003. "Gender, Piece Rates, Commissions and Bonuses." *Industrial Relations*, Vol. 42, no. 3, pp. 419–42.

Gibbons, R. 1998. "Incentives and Careers in Organizations." *Journal of Economic Perspectives*, Vol. 12, no. 4, pp. 115–32.

Gibbons, Robert. 1987. "Piece-rate Incentive Schemes." *Journal of Labor Economics*, Vol. 5, no. 4, pp. 413–29.

Goldin, Claudia. 1986. "Monitoring Costs and Occupational Segregation by Sex: A Historical Analysis." *Journal of Labor Economics*, Vol. 4, no. 1, pp. 1–27.

Hansen, Daniel. 1997. "Worker Performance and Group Incentives: A Case Study." *Industrial and Labor Relations Review*, Vol. 51, no. 1, pp. 37–49.

Hart, Robert A., and Olaf Huebler. 1990. "Are Profit Shares and Wages Substitutes or Complementary Forms of Compensation?" *Kyklos*, Vol. 44, no. 2, pp. 221–31.

Heywood, John S., Olaf Huebler, and Uwe Jirjahn. 1998. "Variable Payment Schemes and Industrial Relations: Evidence from Germany." *Kyklos*, Vol. 51, no. 3, pp. 327–57.

Heywood, John S., and Uwe Jirjahn. 2002. "Payment Schemes and Gender in Germany." *Industrial and Labor Relations Review*, Vol. 56, no. 1, pp. 44–64.

———. 2004. "Teams, Teamwork and Absence." *Scandinavian Journal of Economics*, Vol. 106, no. 4, pp. 765–83.

Heywood, John S., Uwe Jirjahn, and Georgi Tsertsvadze. 2005a. "Getting along with Colleagues: Does Profit Sharing Help or Hurt?" *Kyklos*, Vol. 58, no. 4, pp. 569–85.

———. 2005b. "Does Profit Sharing Reduce Conflict with the Boss? Evidence from Germany." *International Economic Journal*, Vol. 19, no. 2, pp. 235–50.

Heywood, John S., and Madhu Mohanty. 1995. "Estimation of the US Federal Job Queue in the Presence of an Endogenous Union Queue." *Economica*, Vol. 62, no. 248, pp. 479–494.

Heywood, John S., and Patrick L. O'Halloran. 2005. "Racial Earnings Differentials and Performance Pay." *Journal of Human Resources*, Vol. 40, no. 2, pp. 435–52.

Heywood, John S., W.S. Siebert, and Xiangdong Wei. 1997. "Payment by Results Sys-tems: British Evidence." *British Journal of Industrial Relations*, Vol. 35, no. 1, pp. 1–22.

Heywood, John S., and Xiangdong Wei. 1997. "Piece Rate Payment Schemes and the Employment of Women: The Case of Hong Kong." *Journal of Comparative Economics*, Vol. 55, no. 2, pp. 354–72.

———. 2006. "Performance Pay and Job Satisfaction." *Journal of Industrial Relations*, Forthcoming.

Hogan, C. 2001. "Enforcement of Implicit Contracts through Unionization." *Journal of Labor Economics*, Vol. 19, no. 1, pp. 171–95.

Holmstrom, Bengt. 1982. "Moral Hazard in Teams." *Bell Journal of Economics*, Vol. 13, no. 2, pp. 324–40.

Holmstrom, Bengt, and Paul Milgrom. 1987. "Aggregation and Linearity in the Provision of Intertemporal Incentives." *Econometrica*, Vol. 55, no. 2, pp. 303–28.

————. 1991. "Multitask Principal Agent Analyses: Incentive Contracts, Asset Ownership and Job Design." *Journal of Law, Economics, & Organization*, Vol. 7, no. 1, pp. 24–52.

Huebler, Olaf, and Uwe Jirjahn. 2003. "Works Councils and Collective Bargaining in Germany: The Impact on Productivity and Wages." *Scottish Journal of Political Economy*, Vol. 50, no. 4, pp. 471–91.

Issac, J.E. 2001. "Performance Related Pay: The Importance of Fairness." *Journal of Industrial Relations*, Vol. 43, no. 2, pp. 111–23.

Jackson, S., and Schuler, R.S. 2003. *Managing Human Resources through Strategic Partnership* (8th ed.). Toronto: Thompson.

Jirjahn, U. 2002. "The German Experience with Performance Pay," in M. Brown and J.S. Heywood, eds., *Paying for Performance: An International Comparison*. Armonk New York: M.E. Sharpe, pp. 148–78.

Jirjahn, Uwe. 1998. *Effizienzwirkungen von Erfolgsbeteiligung und Partizipation: Eine mikroökonomische Analyse*. Frankfurt: Campus Verlag.

————. 2000. "Incentives for Multitasking: Fixed Wages or Profit Sharing?" *Economic Analysis*, Vol. 3, no. 2, pp. 137–48.

————. 2006. "A Note on Efficiency Wage Theory and Principal-Agent Theory." *Bulletin of Economic Research*, Forthcoming.

Jirjahn, Uwe, and Gesine Stephan. 2004. "Gender, Piece Rates and Wages: Evidence from Matched Employer-Employee Data." *Cambridge Journal of Economics*, Vol. 28, no. 5, pp. 683–704.

————. 2006. "Gender and Wages in Germany: The Impact of Product Market Competition and Collective Bargaining" In J.S. Heywood and J.H. Peoples, eds., *Product Market Structure and Labor Market Discrimination*. Albany, NY: SUNY Press, pp. 59–80.

Jirjahn, Uwe, and Stephen C. Smith. 2006. "What Factors Lead Management to Support or Oppose Employee Participation—With and without Works Councils? Hypotheses and Evidence from Germany." *Industrial Relations*, Forthcoming.

Jones, Derek, and Jeffrey Pliskin. 1997. "Determinants of the Incidence of Group Incentives: Evidence from Canada." *Canadian Journal of Economics*, Vol. 30, no. 4, pp. 1027–45.

Kandel, E., and E.P. Lazear. 1992. "Peer Pressure and Partnerships." *Journal of Political Economy*, Vol. 100, no. 4, pp. 801–17.

Kanemoto, Yoshitsugu, and W. Bentley MacLeod. 1992. "The Ratchet Effect and the Market for Secondhand Workers." *Journal of Labor Economics*, Vol. 10, no. 1, pp. 85–98.

Kerr, Steven. 1975. "On the Folly of Rewarding for A while Hoping for B." *Academy of Management Journal*, Vol. 18, no. 4, pp. 769–83.

Khalil, Fahad, and Jacques Lawaree. 1995. "Input versus Output Monitoring: Who Is the Residual Claimant?" *Journal of Economic Theory*, Vol. 66, no. 1, pp. 139–57.

Knez, Marc, and Duncan Simester. 2001. "Firm-Wide Incentives and Mutual Monitoring at Continental Airlines." *Journal of Labor Economics*, Vol. 19, no. 4, pp. 743–72.

Kruse, D.L. 1993. *Profit Sharing. Does It Make a Difference?* Kalamazoo, MI: Upjohn Institute.

―――. 1996. "Why Do Firms Adopt Profit Sharing and Employee Ownership Plans?" *British Journal of Industrial Relations*, Vol. 34, no. 4, pp. 515–38.

Laffont, J.-J. 1990. "Analysis of Hidden Gaming in a Three-Level Hierarchy." *Journal of Law, Economics, and Organization*, Vol. 6, no. 12, pp. 301–24.

Laffont, Jean-Jacques, and David Martimort. 2002. *The Theory of Incentives*. Princeton NJ: Princeton University Press.

Lazear, Edward P. 1979. "Why Is there Mandatory Retirement?" *Journal of Political Economy*, Vol. 87, no. 5, pp. 1261–84.

―――. 1981. "Agency, Earnings Profiles, Productivity and Hours Restrictions." *American Economics Review*, Vol. 71, pp. 606–20.

―――. 1986. "Salaries and Piece Rates." *Journal of Business*, Vol. 59, pp. 405–31.

―――. 2000. "Performance Pay and Productivity." *American Economic Review*, Vol. 90, pp. 1346–61.

Levine, David I. 1992. "Piece Rates, Output Restriction and Conformism." *Journal of Economic Psychology*, Vol. 13, no. 3, pp. 473–89.

Lewin, D., and Mitchell, D.J.B. 1995. *Human Resource Management: An Economic Approach* (2nd ed.). Cincinnati, OH: South-Western.

Lindop, E. 1989. "The Turbulent Birth of British Profit Sharing." *Personnel Management*, Vol. 21, no. 1, pp. 44–7.

Long, Richard J. 2001. "Pay Systems and Organizational Flexibility." *Canadian Journal of Administrative Sciences*, Vol. 18, no. 1, pp. 25–32.

―――. 2002. "Performance Pay in Canada." In Michelle Brown and John S. Heywood, eds., *Paying for Performance: An International Comparison*. New York: M.E. Sharp, pp. 52–89.

MacLeod, Bentley. 1988. "Equity, Efficiency, and Incentives in Cooperative Teams." In D.C. Jones and J. Svejnar, eds., *Advances in the Economic Analysis of Participatory and Labor-Managed Firms*, Vol. 3. Greenwich, CT: JAI Press, pp. 5–23.

MacLeod, B., and D. Parent. 1999. "Job Characteristics and the Form of Compensation." in S.W. Polachek, ed., *Research in Labor Economics*, Vol. 18. Greenwich, CT: JAI Press, pp. 177–242.

Marsden, David., and R. Belfield. 2004. "Unions, Performance-Related Pay and Procedural Justice: The Case of Classroom Teachers." Discussion Paper No. 660. London: Centre of Economic Performance.

Marsden, David, and Stephen French. 2002. "Performance Pay in the United Kingdom: The Case of the Inland Revenue Service." In Michelle Brown and John S. Heywood, eds., *Paying for Performance: An International Comparison*. Armonk, NY: M.E. Sharpe, pp. 115–47.

Meyer, M.M. 1995. "Cooperation and Competition in Organizations: A Dynamic Perspective." *European Economic Review*, Vol. 39, no. 3–4, pp. 709–22.

Milgrom, Paul, and John Roberts. 1988. "An Economic Approach to Influence Activities in Organizations." *American Journal of Sociology*, Vol. 94 (supplement), pp. S154–S179.

―――. 1992. *Economics, Organization and Management*. New York: Prentice Hall.

Milkovich, G.T., and J.M. Newman. 2002. *Compensation* (7th ed). Boston: McGraw-Hill Irwin.

Milkovich, G.T., and A.K. Widgor. 1991. *Pay for Performance: Evaluating Performance Appraisal and Merit Pay*. Washington DC: National Academy Press.

Mitchell, D.J.B., D. Lewin, and E.E. Lawler. 1990. "Alternative Pay Systems, Firm Performance and Productivity." In A.S. Blinder, ed., *Paying for Productivity*. Washington, DC: Brookings Institution, pp. 15–88.

Ng, I., and D. Maki. 1994. "Trade Union Influence on Human Resource Management Practices." *Industrial Relations*, Vol. 33, no. 1, pp. 121–35.

Oettinger, G. 2001. "Do Piece Rates Influence Effort Choices? Evidence from Stadium Vendors." *Economic Letters*, Vol. 73, no. 1, pp. 117–23.

Paarsch, Harry J., and Bruce Shearer. 2000. "Piece Rates, Fixed Wages, and Incentive Effects: Statistical Evidence from Payroll Records." *International Economic Review*, Vol. 41, no. 1, pp. 59–92.

Parent, Daniel. 1999. "Methods of Pay and Earnings: A Longitudinal Analysis." *Industrial and Labor Relations Review*, Vol. 53, no. 1, pp. 71–86.

———. 2002. "Performance Pay in the United States: Its Determinants and Effects." In Michelle Brown and John S. Heywood, eds., *Paying for Performance: An International Comparison*. Armonk, NY: M.E. Sharpe, pp. 17–51.

Perotin, Virginie, and Andrew Robinson. 2002. "Employee Participation in Profit and Ownership: A Review of the Issues and the Evidence." Working paper, Leeds University Business School.

Perotin, V., and A. Robinson. 2000. "Employee Participation and Equal Opportunities Practices: Productivity Effect and Potential Complementarities." *British Journal of Industrial Relations*, Vol. 38, no. 4, pp. 557–83.

Petersen, T. 1992a. "Individual, Collective, and Systems Rationality in Work Groups: Dilemmas and Market-Type Solutions." *American Journal of Sociology*, Vol. 98, no. 3, pp. 469–510.

———. 1992b. "Payment Systems and the Structure of Inequality: Conceptual Issues and an Analysis of Salespersons in Department Stores." *American Journal of Sociology*, Vol. 98, pp. 67–104.

Pfeffer, Jeffrey. 1998. "Six Dangerous Myths about Pay." *Harvard Business Review*, Vol. 76, no. 3, pp. 108–19.

Poirier, Dale J. 1980. "Partial Observability of Bivariate Probit Models." *Journal of Econometrics*, Vol. 12, pp. 209–217.

Prendergast, Candice. 1993. "A Theory of Yes Men." *American Economic Review*, Vol. 83, no. 4, pp. 757–70.

———. 1999. "The Provision of Incentives in Firms." *Journal of Economic Literature*, Vol. 37, no. 1, pp. 7–63.

———. 2002. "The Tenuous Trade-off between Risk and Incentives." *Journal of Political Economy*, Vol. 110, no. 5, pp. 1071–102.

Prendergast, Candice, and Robert H. Topel. 1996. "Favoritism in Organizations." *Journal of Political Economy*, Vol. 104, no. 5, pp. 958–78.

Raith, Michael. 2004. "Specific Knowledge and Performance Measurement." Discussion Paper No. 04-31. German Economic Association of Business Administration (Vallendar).

Rose, David C. 2002. "Marginal Productivity Analysis in Teams." *Journal of Economic Behavior and Organization*, Vol. 4, no. 4, pp. 355–63.

Rosenthal, M.B., R.G. Frank, Z.L. MA, and A.M. Epstein. 2005. "Early Experience with Pay-for Performance: From Concept to Practice." *Journal of the American Medical Association*, Vol. 294, no. 14, pp. 1788–93.

Rotemberg, J.J. 1994. "Human Relations in the Workplace." *Journal of Political Economy*, Vol. 102, no. 4, pp. 685–717.

Seiler, Eric. 1984. "Piece Rates vs. Time Rate: The Effect of Incentives on Earnings." *Review of Economics and Statistics*, Vol. 60, no. 3, pp. 363–76.

Shearer, Bruce. 2004. "Piece Rates, Fixed Wages and Incentives: Evidence from a Field Experiment." *Review of Economic Studies*, Vol. 71, no. 2, pp. 513–34.

Van het Karr, Robert, and Marianne Gruenell. 2001. "Variable Pay in Europe," European Industrial Relations Observatory, European Foundation for the Improvement of Living and Working Conditions. <www.eiro.eurofound.eu.int/about/ 2001/04/study/tn0104201s.html >. [Accessed March 22, 2005].

Wageman, Ruth, and George Baker. 1997. "Incentives and Cooperation: The Joint Effects of Task and Reward Interdependence on Group Performance." *Journal of Organizational Behavior*, Vol. 18, no. 2, pp. 139–58.

Wilson, Nicholas, and Michael J. Peel. 1991. "The Impact on Absenteeism and Quits of Profit Sharing and Other Forms of Employee Participation." *Industrial and Labor Relations Review*, Vol. 44, no. 3, pp. 455–68.

CHAPTER 6

The New "Managerial Misclassification" Challenge to Old Wage and Hour Law; Or, What Is Managerial Work?

DAVID I. LEVINE
University of California, Berkeley

DAVID LEWIN
University of California, Los Angeles

From the mid-1990s to the mid-2000s, roughly 1.3 million employees in California were members of class action lawsuits claiming they were deprived of overtime pay because their employers erroneously misclassified them as "managers." The total number of former and current employees represented in these class actions constitutes roughly 10% of California's private sector employment and is about as large as total union membership in the state.[1] These California-based lawsuits have been the leading edge of a national trend in managerial misclassification litigation under the Fair Labor Standards Act (FLSA). Outside of California, the pace of class actions rose from roughly a handful of cases filed annually in the mid-1990s to roughly 50 per year filed annually in the mid-2000s.[2]

Under the FLSA, managerial misclassification occurs when employees who hold job titles containing the word "manager" (or a synonym) and are paid salaries rather than hourly wages do not have management tasks as their "primary duties." As described below, California laws also require employees to spend more than half their time on "managerial" tasks to be classified as managers. If courts determine that misclassification exists, the misclassified employees are entitled to overtime pay for all of the hours they worked beyond 40 in a week (and beyond eight hours in a day in California). As we later elaborate, claims of managerial misclassification have been concentrated in the retail trade sector and typically involve employees holding relatively low-level managerial job titles outside of central headquarters; for example, "store manager" in small stores and "assistant manager" and "department manager" in larger stores.[3] We will refer to such employees as "low-level managers," using the term neutrally with respect to whether they are properly exempt from overtime pay requirements.

Legal Background and Litigation Trends

The Fair Labor Standards Act was passed by the U.S. Congress in 1938 and was subsequently replicated in part or in whole by laws enacted in most of the 50 states. Along with its other provisions, including those that established minimum hourly wages, the FLSA mandated overtime pay for most nonmanagerial workers. In distinctive language, the FLSA (and similar state legislation) refers to employees, presumably including managers, who are not covered by overtime pay provisions as "exempt" and to covered employees as "nonexempt."

The overtime provision of the FLSA specifically requires that private sector employers pay covered employees a 50% pay premium for hours worked beyond 40 in a week. With this requirement, the Congress (and the administration of President Franklin D. Roosevelt) reasoned that employers would hire more employees rather than pay a premium to current employees, thereby helping to reduce unemployment. A companion rationale was that newly hired employees would spend all that they earned, thereby stimulating aggregate demand and helping end the Great Depression.

During the latter part of the 20th century, public policy debates as well as administrative and court decisions involving the FLSA (and related state laws) typically focused on the industry and employment coverage of the overtime provision, including extension of that provision to the public sector, most notably in the cases of police officers and firefighters. It is only since the mid-1990s, however, that the focus of FSLA and especially state-level overtime pay enforcement has shifted to low-level managers that companies had long treated as exempt from overtime pay.[4]

While California is just one state, its $1.4-trillion gross state product makes it the fifth largest economy in the world, and its population of approximately 33 million is larger than the population of the smallest 21 states combined. Moreover, in California, unlike the rest of the nation, managers must not only have management tasks as their "primary duties," they must also actually spend more than half their time performing managerial tasks in order to be classified as managers and therefore be exempt from overtime pay requirements. Thus, if salaried retail store managers in California are stocking shelves, helping customers, or operating the cash register for more than half their work time and work more than 40 hours a week or eight hours a day, they are entitled to overtime pay—even if their "primary duties" are managerial.

The first cases reflecting this new challenge to old wage and hour law were filed during the mid-1990s in California courts, and that state remains the hotbed of the rapidly rising incidence of class action litigation over managerial misclassification.[5] By the mid-2000s, such cases, often involving large numbers of plaintiffs, had become common nationally. Within California alone, managerial misclassification cases have been filed against "big box" retailers including Home Depot, Office Depot, Office Max, Target, Best Buy, Smart & Final, and Wal-Mart. Other cases have been filed against large supermarket companies, such as Food 4 Less, and against more specialized chain retailers, including Radio Shack, Pier 1, Borders, Dollar Tree Stores, Pep Boys, Petco, and Rite-Aid. Numerous cases have also been filed against restaurants, including such large chains as Pizza Hut, Taco Bell, and Carl's Junior, and such smaller chains as Buca and Rubio's. Still other cases have been filed against insurance companies, such as Farmers Insurance; rent-a-car companies, such as Enterprise Rent-a-Car; moving equipment rental companies, such as U-Haul; and bottled water delivery companies, such as Yosemite Water. In short, managerial misclassification claims have been made against employers operating in many industries, and the number of such claims is likely to continue to grow.

The typical claim made by plaintiffs (or, more properly, their legal counsel) in a managerial misclassification case is that former and current low-level managers who held or hold such titles as "store manager," "assistant manager," or "department manager" perform largely nonmanagerial tasks, that is, tasks typically performed by hourly wage employees. Such low-level managers have been or are paid on a salaried basis and have been considered by their employers to be exempt from the overtime provisions of the FLSA and California law. If plaintiffs' claims prevail, however, they are considered non-exempt employees and are therefore owed overtime pay for all hours they worked beyond 40 in a week and, in California, beyond eight hours in a day during the time that they held "managerial" positions. The claims are typically made retroactively, for three years under the FLSA and four years under California law (the respective limitations on overtime claims under these statutes).

TABLE 1
Managerial Misclassification Cases Filed Under the FLSA and in California,
1998–2004

	1998	1999	2000	2001	2002	2003	2004	% Change, 1998–2004
FLSA								
Total cases filed	83	96	118	142	166	197	216	160
Total class action cases filed	76	87	102	127	148	173	207	172
Average size of class	723	844	946	1,233	1,576	1,745	1,922	159
California								
Total cases filed	71	82	101	122	141	170	183	158
Total class action cases filed	67	77	95	117	132	158	174	160
Average size of class	787	884	1,045	1,323	1,739	1,938	2,172	176

Note: Total number of former and current employees included in class action managerial misclassification lawsuits is 1,314,446 under the FLSA and 1,241,143 in California.

Sources: http://www.uscourts.gov/judiciary2005/juntablesC02jun05.pdf, p. 30 (and prior years 1998 to 2004); http://web.lexis-nexis.com/universe/form/academic/s_topiclaw.html?_m=9b2ab934dde0bdc1b17bba1599168c2&wchp=dGLbVlz-SkVA&_md5= bc55782f-49120027c547ffc497a69b69 (cases accessed from 1998 to 2004).

Although precise data on the volume of managerial misclassification lawsuits filed under the FLSA and state wage and hour laws are difficult to come by, Table 1 provides estimated data for such lawsuits filed between 1998 and 2004 under the FLSA and California law.[6]

During this period, the managerial misclassification cases filed annually under the FLSA and California law rose by about 160% each. The average size of the class represented increased more than 2.5 times between 1998 and 2004, again under both the FLSA and California law. Further, of the managerial misclassification cases pursued during 1998 to 2004, only about 2% of FLSA cases resulted in trial verdicts and only one California case resulted in a trial verdict (Table 2). The vast bulk of these cases were settled between the parties, typically without trial, but sometimes during a trial.

Regarding the relatively few managerial misclassification cases that were decided through trial verdicts between 1998 and 2004, plaintiffs won 65% of the FLSA cases and won the only California case (Table 3).

In the cases won by plaintiffs under the FLSA, the average per capita damages awarded increased markedly between 1998 and 2004, from $1,073 to $2,692. Though because of episodic reporting it is not possible to know fully the average per capita monetary award under

TABLE 2

Managerial Misclassification Case Status and Disposition Under the FLSA and in California, 1998–2004

	1998	1999	2000	2001	2002	2003	2004
FLSA							
Total Cases	83	96	118	142	166	197	216
Continuing cases	3.6%	8.3%	9.3%	28.9%	43.4%	69.5%	83.8%
Cases settled prior to class certification	7.2%	5.2%	3.4%	3.5%	3.6%	2.0%	1.4%
Cases with class certification	59.0%	63.5%	66.1%	50.7%	44.0%	19.8%	10.2%
Cases with class certification denied	15.6%	11.5%	15.3%	12.0%	6.0%	5.1%	3.2%
Cases withdrawn	6.0%	4.2%	2.5%	2.1%	1.2%	1.5%	0.5%
Cases dismissed	8.4%	6.3%	3.4%	2.8%	1.8%	2.0%	0.9%
Cases settled after class certification							
Without trial	49.4%	65.6%	56.8%	46.5%	39.8%	16.2%	8.3%
During trial	4.8%	6.3%	5.1%	2.8%	2.4%	2.0%	1.4%
Trial verdicts	2.4%	3.1%	2.5%	1.4%	1.8%	1.5%	0.5%
California							
Total Cases	71	82	101	122	141	170	183
Continuing cases	2.8%	6.1%	14.9%	29.5%	52.5%	65.3%	81.4%
Cases settled prior to class certification	7.0%	3.7%	4.0%	3.3%	2.1%	2.4%	1.6%
Cases with class certification denied	15.5%	14.6%	9.9%	9.8%	5.7%	2.4%	1.6%
Cases withdrawn	7.0%	6.1%	2.0%	3.3%	1.4%	1.8%	0.5%
Cases dismissed	9.9%	7.3%	2.0%	4.1%	2.1%	1.2%	0.5%
Cases with class certification	57.7%	62.2%	67.3%	50.0%	36.2%	27.1%	14.2%
Cases settled after class certification							
Without trial	50.7%	54.5%	60.4%	46.7%	32.6%	25.3%	12.5%
During trial	7.0%	7.3%	6.9%	3.3%	3.5%	1.8%	1.6%
Trial verdicts	0%	0%	0%	0.8%	0%	0%	0%

Sources: http://www.uscourts.gov/judiciary2005/juntablesC02jun05.pdf, p. 30 (and prior years 1998 to 2004); http://web.lexis-nexis.com/universe/form/academics/s_topiclaw.html?_m= 8bd2ab834dde0bdc1b17bba1599168c2&wchp=dGLbVlz-zSkVA&_md5= bc55782f49120027 c547ffc497a69b69 (cases accessed from 1998 to 2004). Continuing cases were ongoing as of June 2005.

managerial misclassification cases that were voluntarily settled by the parties, the data in Table 3 indicate that average damages received by plaintiffs in such settlements were considerably lower than the damages awarded through trial verdicts under the FLSA between 1998 and 2004. This is consistent with evidence from related areas of litigation, such as employment discrimination, in which larger per capita monetary

TABLE 3

Managerial Misclassification Trial Verdicts and Voluntary Settlements by Per Capita Monetary Damages Under the FLSA and in California, 1998–2004

	1998	1999	2000	2001	2002	2003	2004	Total
FLSA								
Total cases with trial verdicts	2	3	3	2	3	3	1	17
Trial verdicts for plaintiff	1	2	2	1	2	2	1	11
Trial verdicts for defendant	1	1	1	1	1	1	0	6
Average size of class	928	1,012	1,254	1,451	1,846	1,925	2,234	1,521
Average per capita damages in trial verdicts for plaintiffs	$1,073	$1,236	$1,531	$1,877	$2,066	$2,070	$2,692	$1,792
Average per capita damages in voluntarily settled cases*	$928	$1,004	$1,151	$1,234	$1,435	$1,489	$1,864	$1,301
California								
Total cases with trial verdicts	0	0	0	1	0	0	0	1
Trial verdicts for plaintiff	0	0	0	1	0	0	0	1
Trial verdicts for defendant	0	0	0	0	0	0	0	0
Average size of class	0	0	0	1,541	0	0	0	1,541
Average per capita damages in trial verdict for plaintiff	0	0	0	$2,310	0	0	0	$2,310
Average per capita damages in voluntarily settled cases**	$1,005	$1,179	$1,345	$1,798	$2,004	$2,158	$2,432	$1,703

*In a sample of 15 cases, 11 of them in California.

**In a sample of 41 cases drawn from published accounts and documents provided by plaintiffs' and defense counsel. For any of these cases that were also subject to voluntary settlements under the FLSA, the damages total in this row should be added to the damages total in the comparable row under the "FLSA" heading above to determine overall per capita damages.

Sources: http://www.uscourts.gov/judiciary2005/jun05/juntablesC02jun05.pdf, p. 30 (and prior years 1998 to 2004); http://web.lexis-nexis.com/universe/form/academics/s_topiclaw.html?_m=8bd2ab834dde0bdc1b17bba1599168c2&wchp=dGLbVlz-zSkVA&_md5=bc5578f2f49120027c547ffc497a69b69 (cases accessed from 1998 to 2004); documents from voluntarily settled FLSA and California managerial misclassification cases provided by plaintiffs' and defense counsel.

awards result from trial verdicts than from voluntary settlements. Also note from Table 3 that average per capita damages received by plaintiffs in managerial misclassification cases that were voluntarily settled between 1998 and 2004 doubled under the FLSA and increased about 2.5 times in California.

Because all but a handful of the California-based managerial misclassification cases involved alleged violations of both the FLSA and state law, the total payoff to a plaintiff in California is best represented by the sum of the average FLSA and average California awards. The average award in these cases typically is higher in California than in the rest of the nation because that state's damages formula is substantially more generous than the damages formula under the FLSA and under other states' overtime pay statutes.[7]

The Legal Process

Because individual damages in a managerial misclassification case are small relative to the cost of a lawsuit, lawyers are rarely willing to take on individual cases. As a result, almost all low-level managers involved in misclassification lawsuits are participants in class actions. A class action lawsuit has several phases: filing the case, certification of the class, merits, and determination of damages.

Initially, one or more potential plaintiffs search for counsel to represent them, or plaintiffs' counsel identifies a few (usually former) low-level managers willing to serve as "named plaintiffs." Typically, plaintiffs' counsel then adds a catch-all category to the filing that includes other current and former low-level managers who may also potentially claim that they were misclassified. Next, plaintiffs must convince the court to certify the class. For a class of plaintiffs to be certified, the court must find that common issues of fact or law predominate so that the court need not make individual inquiries into the facts of each case.

An employer faces a difficult challenge when arguing that common issues do not predominate in a managerial misclassification case. To win the merits portion of the case, an employer must claim that all of its workplaces obeyed the law, meaning that the vast majority of low-level managers were or are primarily performing managerial work. At the same time, and to defeat a motion for class certification, an employer must claim that there is large variation across its workplaces and low-level managers.

To determine the proportion of time that low-level managers spend performing managerial tasks—an essential "fact" for California law—an employer can analyze tasks using such methods as direct observation, surveys, and interviews.[8] But the challenge facing an employer who uses these methods remains the same, namely, to claim that all or most low-level managers spend more than half their work time performing (exempt) managerial tasks, while simultaneously claiming that these same managers vary so greatly in the tasks they do perform and in the amount of time spent performing them that it is not possible to generalize about low-level managers as a whole.[9]

By contrast, plaintiffs in a managerial misclassification case must first show that the employer has common policies across its workplaces. This claim is often straightforward to demonstrate in large companies that operate chains of stores or restaurants. It is more challenging, however, for plaintiffs to demonstrate that when these policies are translated into practice, the differences among workplace sales and employment, hourly employees' and upper managers' performance and reliability, and low-level managers' skills and preferences do not outweigh common issues of fact.

A key insight from organizational theory is that variations in workplace, employee, and upper management characteristics are not just challenges for lawyers trying to show that common issues predominate in a class action managerial misclassification lawsuit; these sources of variation are also challenges for a corporation's executives. Organizations with many similar workplaces typically implement particular systems to measure the performance of those workplaces and the people who manage them. These performance measures assist organizations in the allocation of resources, especially in response to characteristics unique to a particular product market, labor market, or workplace. For example, large retailers want to allocate more hourly employees to stores with higher customer demand, in part to provide the desired levels of customer service. In addition, such companies typically adjust the sizes of their workforces and the allocation of personnel to meet seasonal and other predictable shifts in customer demand, such as high demand during holidays and low demand during cold spells. This attempted optimization reflects top management's desire to maintain a consistent ratio of workplace resources to needs. Success in such optimization helps a company achieve its strategic objectives but, at the same time, makes it more difficult for that company to argue persuasively against class certification in a managerial misclassification case.

As an added benefit to the employer, if its performance management system allocates resources proportional to need, then store performance above expectations is more strongly related to store managers' skill, effort, and reliability. Large chain store companies typically use a variety of comparisons or benchmarks, such as prior store performance and nearby peer stores' performance, to factor out the level of performance in its specific stores that is attributable to exogenous factors. Consequently, incentives for managerial effort will be as uniform as company executives can make them across workplaces. However, this effort to make all performance goals equally challenging, that is, uniform, makes it still more difficult for an employer to successfully argue against class certification in a managerial misclassification case.

As shown in Table 3, plaintiffs win about two thirds of the managerial misclassification cases that go through trial to judicial verdicts. Yet, as shown in Table 2, over 90% of cases that achieve class certification settle prior to a court trial. There are two related reasons why most of these cases settle out of court. First, if both sides have common beliefs about the likelihood of prevailing at a trial, settling the case short of trial reduces transaction costs. Second, even if their beliefs diverge, risk-averse parties nevertheless have certain incentives to settle. For example, plaintiffs' counsels may have a particularly strong incentive to settle managerial misclassification cases prior to trial because they are paid only if their clients win their cases. Under the contingent fee arrangement that operates in these cases, plaintiffs' attorneys apparently receive between 25% and 35% of the monetary settlements.[10] On the defense side, while some models of management behavior assume that employers are risk-neutral, the potential monetary damages facing an employer, especially a large, well-known employer, can run into the tens or hundreds of millions of dollars.[11] Given the unpredictability of damages that juries and even judges may award, risk aversion also motivates company executives to settle managerial misclassification cases prior to trial.

As a managerial misclassification proceeds through litigation, a defendant employer (or, more properly, the defendant's legal counsel) almost always relies on declarations obtained from currently employed low-level managers, who typically say that they perform mostly managerial work and very little nonmanagerial (hourly) work. At the same time, plaintiffs' counsel relies on declarations obtained for the most part from previously employed low-level managers, who typically say that they performed primarily or largely nonmanagerial work and relatively little managerial work. In addition, and as noted earlier, some employers rely on data from surveys they have conducted or commissioned of currently employed managerial personnel to determine the relative amounts of time these personnel (say they) spend performing management versus nonmanagement tasks. Here, too, plaintiffs' counsel often does the same thing, relying on data from surveys that are usually administered only to former low-level managers but occasionally to current low-level managers as well. Also, as noted earlier, some defendant employers in managerial misclassification cases rely on data obtained from observational studies that they have conducted or commissioned, which involve directly observing the tasks performed and the time spent performing them by samples of currently employed low-level managers. Such data have apparently not been used by plaintiffs, however, because plaintiffs' counsel (or observational specialist) is unable to gain access to employers' workplaces in order to directly observe low-level managers at work.

If a class of plaintiffs alleging managerial misclassification is certified and the case actually goes to trial on its merits, a challenge facing the judge and/or jury is determining the veracity of evidence presented by the employer (or the employer's counsel) versus the evidence presented by plaintiffs (or plaintiffs' counsel). A defendant employer's evidence largely depends on testimony and data from currently employed managers, who have a clear incentive to answer questions in ways they believe their employer desires. Analogously, plaintiffs' counsel typically relies largely on evidence from former low-level managers, who stand to win thousands of dollars apiece if they provide answers their former employer does not desire. These incentives make both sides' testimony and related evidence suspect. Faced with this type of adversarial, win-lose decision context, it is not at all surprising that most parties to class action managerial misclassification cases have, despite lots of posturing, reached voluntary settlements rather than proceeding all the way though trial and verdict (see Table 2).[12]

Why Have Managerial Misclassification Lawsuits Exploded?

Organizational Size and Workplace Replication

From its roots in machine shops to Henry Ford's famous assembly line, the market-oriented strategy of product and service standardization led most businesses to adopt an organization structure featuring centralized decision making coupled with detailed instructions provided by supervisors and managers to those who actually carry out the work.[13] Indeed, for much of the 20th century, business enterprises across a wide range of industries grew and prospered by combining organizational hierarchy with work specialization. During the last quarter of the 20th century and influenced by increasing global economic competition, deregulation, and technological change, many of these same business enterprises changed their business strategies and organizational structures to decentralize more decisions (often accompanied by "delayering") and to increase team-based work. These changes were most evident in manufacturing businesses.

Among chain-type businesses that have been involved in recent managerial misclassification litigation, however, organizational hierarchy and work specialization remain common, all the more so as these enterprises grew larger. Such standardization may seem to be compromised, especially among national and multinational companies that separate strategy formulation and planning, which is centralized at headquarters, from strategy implementation, which occurs at dispersed local, national, and regional levels. But, in fact, such strategy implementation is typically carried out within and often closely guided by a common set of operational policies and procedures. Leading examples in this regard include Wal-Mart and McDonald's, both of which use standard sets of operating policies and procedures coupled with automation to create national, indeed, worldwide consistency of products and services. This consistency, in turn, forms the basis of very strong brands. Such enterprises are often referred to by strategy and organizational scholars as "replicator organizations"; they can be found in sectors as varied as insurance sales and mailbox stores.[14]

Replicator organizations have become increasingly important in the U.S. economy. While popular accounts often claim that small firms are at the forefront of job creation, the bulk of employment and employment increases are in large replicator organizations.[15] This is especially apparent in the retail trade sector, where a handful of large chain-type enterprises account for much more employment that do the tens of thousands of small retail businesses.

The combination of increased organizational size and a strategy of replication has several important effects on the organization of work in retail chains. In particular, as retail chains grow and replicate themselves, they typically centralize responsibility for a vast array of management decisions, including most selection of vendors, product pricing and discounts, advertising and promotion, inventory methods and controls, store operating hours, employee hiring and promotion policies, and more. Consequently, responsibility for management decision making moves from local establishments, such as stores, to central headquarters, thereby leaving fewer and fewer decisions in the hands of those who hold jobs carrying such titles as store manager, assistant manager, and department manager. From this perspective, companies that have to defend themselves against claims of managerial misclassification are vulnerable in large part due to their success, as attested to by growth and replication.

The growth of large retail and other chains is due, in turn, to several key factors, including changes in supply chain management, product markets and branding, and the diffusion of knowledge about successful replication. One of these factors is supply chain management, which has become a source of competitive advantage for many firms, most famously Wal-Mart.[16] Using computerized information systems, Wal-Mart as well as other global firms have learned to manage their supply chains to optimize the flow of products from the point at which factories produce them to the moment that customers select products from store shelves (and pay for them at cash registers).[17] Such global supply chains provide enormous economies of scale to those enterprises that can manage them efficiently.

The same global information technology that underpins global supply chain management also reduces the costs of centralized monitoring of dispersed workplaces by a company's headquarters. That is, if a supermarket company can monitor the flow of sodas or vegetables, it can also monitor how many of a store manager's performance reviews are behind schedule, how often employees are working unscheduled overtime, and the extent to which a store's actual labor costs deviate from budgeted labor costs for a work shift, day, week, or month. Indeed, this type of "electronic leash" makes it feasible for company headquarters to monitor hundreds of activities in a single branch, facility, or store, wherever it is located.

A second factor in the growth of large chains is the rise of national and global brands accompanied by use of media to advertise them, which provides additional potential economies of scale to large companies. Relevant to the focal issue of this chapter, brands with a broad geographic reach require consistency in advertising and promotion, which further serve to encourage centralized decision making. These brands also require consistency of customer experience, which additionally motivates companies tightly to control their branches. Although there are some regional variations, customers who step into a McDonald's, for example, know what to expect in terms of products and services whether those customers are in Indonesia, Israel, Ireland, or Iowa.

Global branding on the part of a firm can also make an ethical violation or scandal more costly because a single misbehaving manager can threaten a firm's global reputation. Firms with valuable brands are therefore especially concerned about regulatory, ethical, or public relations problems that can potentially tarnish the firm's image, reputation, and, ultimately, brand. This concern leads yet again to the centralization of decision making and to the close monitoring of local workplaces.

A third key factor in this story is the diffusion of knowledge of how to replicate successful organizations and workplaces. When McDonald's began to disseminate its Golden Arches to almost every corner of the globe, no company had ever built so many near-identical workplaces. Two generations later, there are many executives who have worked in replicator organizations and who can share the basic principles of replication. In addition, many professional consultants help companies implement more consistent practices across workplaces using combinations of detailed standard operating procedures (SOPs), training, monitoring, and incentives. As their title suggests, SOPs fundamentally reduce the discretion of local managers.[18]

The increased centralization of decision making in retail companies and other enterprises that have encountered managerial misclassification lawsuits has not, however, been accompanied by declining incentives for "managers" of local workplaces to work long hours. Rather, SOPs typically include detailed specifications and incentives for ensuring that all employees, including in local workplaces, work hard to achieve particular goals. In this regard, goals that are too hard will have little effect on employee job behavior because no amount of effort or overtime will lead to successful goal achievement. Similarly, goals that are too easy will also have little effect on employee job behavior because only a minimal level of effort with no overtime will lead to successful goal achievement. Hence, SOPs tend to emphasize what some organizational behavior specialists and labor economists refer to as "stretch goals."[19]

Even more to the point are the various methods that scholars and management practitioners have prescribed for reducing the variability of goals relative to resources. In this regard, replicator organizations typically set goals

1. based on past performance at the workplace,

2. based on unique features of each workplace,

3. customized for individuals so that the goals are "achievable yet challenging," and

4. based on performance relative to peer workplaces within the chain.

Similarly, SOPs are often used to reduce variation in the extent to which performance goals are challenging by benchmarking key dimensions of performance and requiring continuous improvement over time and versus competitors. From this perspective SOPs serve to reduce organizational slack, and the diffusion of these sophisticated monitoring and goal-setting specifications and methods ensures that the lack of discretion at local levels does not imply weaker incentives for working long hours.[20] The growth of large chain-type enterprises also increases incentives for employees to work long hours because, unlike their standalone brethren, such chains usually create internal labor markets. The possibility of promotion, in particular, provides incentives for employees and managers to work hard.

In sum, those enterprises that have been charged with managerial misclassification typically have in place business strategies that emphasize rapid growth. As these enterprises continue to implement their strategies, they grow still larger, use computerized information systems and related technologies to manage their supply chains more efficiently, develop national and even global brands, and specify SOPs to diffuse knowledge of how to replicate their operations in widespread locations. A key consequence of these strategic decisions is to further centralize organizational decision making, which means that headquarters, divisional, and regional managers gain decision-making power and control, and low-level managers within the workplace lose them. At the same time, these strategic and operational factors do not lessen and may even enhance incentives for low-level managers to work hard. The consequence of all this is that salaried low-level managers who work relatively long hours may perform predominantly nonmanagerial work which, in turn, generates claims of managerial misclassification.

Further, as replicator organizations grow and add still more workplaces, hundreds and sometimes thousands of low-level managers with similar or identical job titles are amassed, both nationwide and even within a single large state such as California. Such aggregations increase the likelihood of managerial misclassification cases being filed because, as we have noted, these lawsuits typically are of the class action type. Therefore, replicator organizations are much more susceptible to class action lawsuits than standalone workplaces.

Other Factors

While the growth of large replicator organizations demarcated by the strategic, organizational, and operational characteristics we have analyzed appears to be the main source of the rapid rise of managerial misclassification lawsuits, certain other factors may also be at work.

Compensation Practices

Low-level managers are usually eligible for incentive compensation in the form of stock options, stock ownership, profit sharing, bonuses, or combinations thereof. A bonus for a low-level manager (as well as for his or her immediate supervisor) is typically paid when the manager's store or facility spends less on labor costs than the company expected or budgeted. A profit-sharing payment, by definition, takes account of both revenue and cost; the larger the excess of total revenue over cost—that is, the profit margin—the larger the profit-sharing payment. Thus, managers eligible for bonuses or profit sharing have an incentive to reduce labor costs. One way of reducing such costs, especially from a top management perspective, is to make the base pay of lower-level managers a salary rather than an hourly wage. Because neither additional base pay nor overtime pay is required to be paid to managers who work longer than normal hours, such additional work by salaried managers does not raise a company's labor costs. Herein lies a strong incentive for companies to establish low-level, salaried managerial positions/job classifications and assign (and promote) certain personnel to them.

There are countervailing arguments in this regard. For example, if the labor market for low-level managers is competitive and if such managers are relatively mobile, then any effort by one employer to make these managers work unusually long hours will result in managerial quits, imposing a cost on the employer. Should that happen the employer would have to revise compensation practices, either by raising pay or by reducing the incentives for low-level managers to work long hours.

The mobility of low-level managers will not bring about efficient contracts, however, if such managers are faced with high quitting costs or if they did not expect to work "unusually" long hours, including performing nonmanagerial tasks, when they assumed their jobs. Low-level managers' costs of quitting may be especially large if all employers in a particular labor market use similar management and incentive compensation practices that induce long hours. Moreover, total compensation paid to low-level managers need not rise fully (to an efficient or market level) if such managers work long hours and build firm-specific human capital so as to signal their interest in possible promotion to still higher-level management positions.

Further, the incentive story being told here may be one of paying until the job is done rather than paying by the hour—which would also be consistent with an accountability story in which companies accept that low-level managers will work long hours and perform some nonmanagerial tasks in addition to managerial ones. Still further, retail enterprises are service businesses that experience varying waves of customers and deliveries and even occasional emergencies. Consequently, they may employ low-level managers not only to perform managerial tasks but also to respond to such unpredictable events. These arguments do not "prove" that all low-level managers perform substantial amounts of hourly paid work, but they do imply that compensating low-level managers through a combination of base salary and bonus (or profit-sharing) can be profitable, even if low-level managers earn more than hourly employees.

On balance, a store, restaurant, or facility manager who is potentially eligible to receive a bonus or profit-sharing payment has a strong incentive to work long hours and *not* to have subordinate hourly paid employees work long hours. When those subordinate employees do work long hours—specifically, beyond 40 in a week (and in California beyond eight in a day), they must be paid overtime for those hours. This raises labor costs, reducing the margin between budgeted and actual labor costs and ultimately reducing the bonus paid to the low-level manager. In such circumstances, low-level managers have an incentive to substitute their own labor for that of subordinate employees. Through that substitution, low-level managers increase the proportion of time spent performing nonmanagerial tasks and reduce the proportion spent on managerial tasks. This incentive is further reinforced to the extent that working long hours has a positive effect on the performance assessments (ratings)—and future promotions—of low-level managers. If all this occurs on a widespread and continuous basis, low-level managers may well claim that they are or have been misclassified and may pursue those claims through litigation. Such reasoning helps to explain why and how incentive compensation systems in replicator organizations contribute to the rapid rise of class action managerial misclassification lawsuits.

Customer Relationship Management Based on Managing by Wandering Around

As with many other types of enterprises, retail and restaurant businesses have adopted strong customer relationship management (CRM) policies, programs, and practices. These are intended to improve customer service and thereby increase both customer retention and revenue per customer. In this regard, many leading retail businesses stress the importance of low-level managers' spending a substantial share of their time interacting with customers in what might best be termed the store or restaurant frontline. Such time allocation may be analogized to and may have been adapted from the practice of "management by wandering around," pioneered by Hewlett-Packard (HP) several decades ago (Beer and Von Werssowetz 1982; Beer and Rogers 1995). Whereas HP sought managers who would regularly interact with employees at their workplaces in order to learn more about everyday operational, technical, and product development matters, large retailers and restaurant chains typically want their low-level managers to interact with customers in order to learn more about customer preferences and to demonstrate that they are providing good customer service. To illustrate, a supermarket store manager might lead a customer to the location of a particular food item or help a customer place purchased items into the car trunk. Or, a restaurant manager might deliver a food order to the customer's table or accept the customer's payment at the cash register. Whatever the underlying rationale, such management-by-walking-around-type customer service may well reduce the time that store, restaurant, and facility managers spend performing managerial tasks and increase the time they spend on nonmanagerial tasks—at least as these tasks are defined under the FLSA and California law.

Legal Factors

The explosion of managerial misclassification litigation in California is fueled in large part by the state's requirement that exempt managerial employees not only have managerial tasks as their primary duty (which is the FLSA standard), but also spend more than half their time performing managerial duties. Earlier we noted that hundreds of managerial misclassification cases have been filed in California since the first case was filed in 1994. Yet the basic contested issue in these cases, namely, how much time employees holding managerial titles spend or spent performing managerial versus nonmanagerial work, has remained the same over time, as have the arguments about whether a particular group of plaintiffs merited certification as a class. The likelihood of such certification appears to have increased in light of the California Supreme Court's 2004 decision in the Sav-On case (*Sav-On Drug Store, Inc. v. The Superior Court of Los Angeles County and Robert Rocher, et al.*, 2004). In light of these developments, it should by now be evident to any large company operating in California that low-level managers might well not be exempt from the state's overtime pay rules. Nevertheless, relatively few large employers operating in California appear to have reclassified their employees until confronted by managerial misclassification litigation (in other words, they have only done it involuntarily).

There are two broad classes of explanations for this failure of companies to reclassify low-level managers until sued. On the one hand, it is possible that large employers continued to believe that California law regarding overtime pay eligibility did not differ much if at all from the laws prevailing in other states, not to mention from the FLSA. Such a view may have been reinforced in companies where preliminary reviews of job descriptions, surveys, interviews, or observational studies indicated that their low-level managers were in fact performing predominantly managerial work.

On the other hand, there may have been a "business case" to deny overtime pay to low-level managers even if company executives believed that such employees were not exempt under California law. This business case may have been operative for four interrelated, mutually reinforcing reasons. First, any reclassification of existing low-level managers would likely trigger a lawsuit (or additional lawsuits) among former, and perhaps current, low-level managers seeking past overtime pay. Based on such reasoning, inaction regarding reclassification reduces the probability of a managerial misclassification lawsuit. Second, even if an employer knew that a managerial misclassification lawsuit was likely to be filed against it by former low-level managers, each day that passed without such a lawsuit's being filed meant that the statute of limitations eliminated one day of potential past damages. In this regard, employers may have judged salary-type pay (for low-level managers) to enable organizational performance goals to be achieved more fully and rapidly than hourly pay plus overtime for these same employees. Thus, some employers had incentives to continue paying salary without overtime pay to low-level managers even if these employers expected to reclassify low-level managers in the event of being sued. Third, an employer may have doubted that plaintiffs could win certification as a class in a managerial misclassification lawsuit, either because the employer was convinced that its low-level managers in fact performed predominantly managerial work or because the employer simply doubted plaintiffs' ability to prove that common issues of fact predominated over differences among its workplaces. Fourth, if in anticipation of a managerial misclassification lawsuit an employer "voluntarily" reclassified low-level managerial employees working in its California locations (e.g., stores), it might also have to reclassify its low-level managerial employees working in other states, with potentially large labor cost implications.

California's legal treatment of class certification in managerial misclassification cases is also relevant to the recent explosion of such cases there. Because it is relatively easy (due to judicial receptivity) for a plaintiffs' attorney to win class certification in these cases, particularly if the defendant is a large employer, plaintiffs' attorneys have especially strong incentives to represent low-level managers. Defendant employers and their attorneys, by contrast, are increasingly motivated to settle managerial misclassification cases voluntarily rather than proceed to trial. This reasoning implies that the damages awarded to plaintiffs from trial verdicts in California managerial misclassification cases are or will be larger than the damages allocated to plaintiffs from voluntary settlement of such managerial misclassification cases. While it is not possible formally to test this implication inasmuch as only one California managerial misclassification case has to this point proceeded all the way through trial to a judicial verdict, it is possible to approximate this differential between trial verdicts and voluntary settlements by using data from samples of cases that were settled before trial and during trial (that is, without judicial verdicts), respectively. In 41 cases that were settled before trial between 1998 and 2004, the average per capita damages received by plaintiffs were $1,703 (see Table 3), whereas the average per capita damages in 17 cases that were settled during trial were $2,310.[21] A simple chi-square test shows that the difference between these two amounts is

significant at p =< .01. Further, the managerial misclassification settlement data presented in Table 3 for cases decided under the FLSA (the
bulk of which are California-based) between 1998 and 2004 show average per capita damages of $1,792 in cases decided by trial verdicts, com-
pared to $1,301 in cases that concluded with voluntary settlements—a
difference that is also significant at p =<.01. These findings support the
proposition that trial verdicts as well as settlements reached during trials
are more costly than voluntary settlements of managerial misclassification cases and, as well, the proposition that relatively risk-averse defendant employers have a clear incentive to settle voluntarily rather than to
fully or even partially litigate managerial misclassification cases (propositions that likely apply outside of as well as inside California).

Still another aspect of California law that may have helped fuel the
growth of managerial misclassification cases is that the determination of
whether a particular work task is in fact "managerial" depends in part on
whether hourly employees also perform the task. The results of such a
determination can potentially lead to a cascade of managerial misclassification lawsuits. To illustrate, consider a company with numerous job
titles, each filled by employees who spend two thirds of their time performing tasks that are also performed by employees occupying lower-
level job titles. Further suppose that the top-ranking local-level job in
this company is store manager, next is assistant store manager, and next
is department manager, and that each of these is a salaried exempt job.
By assumption, department managers spend two thirds of their time
performing the same tasks as their subordinates. So if a lawsuit is initiated, the company will need to reclassify department managers as non-
exempt hourly employees and pay them overtime. After that
reclassification, the assistant managers (who, again by assumption, spend
two thirds of their time performing the same tasks as the department
managers) are now spending most of their time performing tasks also
performed by hourly employees. Should a court use this rule of thumb
for determining the exempt status of tasks performed by employees
holding managerial titles (as courts sometimes do), the assistant managers will also win their lawsuit and become hourly employees. The
same logic applies to the store manager and further up the chain of command. In other words, and unfortunately for the company, this argument
repeats for any rank, potentially even including the CEO!

Research Opportunities and Policy Recommendations

Having identified main dimensions of and analyzed key factors
influencing the rise of managerial misclassification litigation in the
United States during the late 20th and early 21st centuries, we now turn

to research opportunities and policy recommendations for dealing with this key issue. We pay particular attention to attorneys' incentives, theories of overtime pay regulation, reducing transaction costs, and problems in the law.

Attorneys' Incentives

In litigation involving claims of managerial misclassification, as in litigation generally, the contesting parties do not represent themselves; instead, each party is represented by counsel, that is, attorneys. A managerial misclassification case becomes a case when counsel for plaintiffs files a complaint of managerial misclassification with a court in a particular public jurisdiction. Counsel for the defendant responds by filing an answer to the complaint with the same court. If and as a claim of managerial misclassification proceeds, the litigation process typically involves the filing of and responses to an amended complaint or complaints, submission of and responses to interrogatories (written questions) posed by each party, specification by the court of a discovery period during which documents are solicited by each party from the other party, designation of fact witnesses, such as individual plaintiffs and officers of the defendant company, designation of experts by one or the other party or both parties, and conducting depositions of fact witnesses and experts. Following these stages of the litigation process, the court in the public jurisdiction in which the case was filed then determines if a class is certified—a decision that is then subject to appeals to higher level courts. Only if and after all of these hurdles have been cleared does a managerial misclassification case proceed to trial—unless it is withdrawn or settled voluntarily. All these components of the managerial misclassification litigation process are carried out by attorneys for each side, who serve as agents for their respective principals, that is, plaintiffs and defendant.

In the role of agent, plaintiffs' counsel typically receives compensation in the form of a fee that constitutes a percentage, typically between 25% and 35%, of a negotiated settlement or judicial damage award in favor of plaintiffs. On average, this fee percentage is slightly lower in larger settlements and is thus modestly inversely related to size of case. In the role of agent, defendant's counsel, by contrast, receives compensation in the form of periodic payments from defendant that are based on the hours worked by counsel on the case. Compensation to plaintiffs' counsel for serving as an agent is contingent on the outcome of a managerial misclassification case, whereas compensation to defendant's counsel is not. Further, if a managerial misclassification case concludes with a negotiated settlement, plaintiffs' counsel receives compensation for serving as an agent, but if such a case concludes with a judicial verdict for the defendant, plaintiffs' counsel receives no such compensation. So in terms of payoff for effort, the risk to plaintiffs' counsel is greater than the risk to defendant's counsel for representing principals in a managerial misclassification case.

In light of these realities, attorneys who represent plaintiffs have incentives to search—indeed, to troll—for managerial misclassification cases, especially those involving large employers. Such search behavior is likely to be more pronounced in managerial misclassification cases than in, say, employment discrimination or wrongful termination cases, given the relative ease of establishing a class action basis for a managerial misclassification lawsuit, and the tendency of courts (notably California courts) to certify plaintiffs as a class in managerial misclassification cases. The same realities also suggest that when plaintiffs' attorneys actually serve as agents for their principals in managerial misclassification cases, they will favor negotiated settlements over judicial awards. By contrast, attorneys who represent defendants in managerial misclassification cases appear to have incentives to pursue such cases through (but not completely through) trial rather than to reach negotiated settlements (or late-stage negotiated settlements).

That plaintiffs' attorneys may actively search for managerial misclassification cases in which to serve as counsel does not mean that some, perhaps many, low-level managers don't believe that they are or have been unjustly deprived of overtime pay. To the contrary, a core of such managers must believe just this if a managerial misclassification is to "have legs." What is likely in this regard, however, is that plaintiffs' attorneys act to enlarge the scope of and potential damages involved in a managerial misclassification case by actively searching for additional named plaintiffs and then vigorously pursuing a class action that includes some, perhaps many, unnamed additional plaintiffs. Further, it can be expected that, over time, plaintiffs' attorneys become more skilled at or simply more determined to sign up low-level managers to represent in managerial misclassification cases.[22] Thus, an interesting and potentially important research issue in this regard is distinguishing the proportion of truly aggrieved plaintiffs from marginally involved ones—those joining a managerial misclassification case solely in pursuit of a possible settlement.

Attorneys for defendant companies may not search for clients in managerial misclassification cases in a way directly analogous to that of plaintiffs' attorneys, but defense attorneys clearly make their services in this regard known to the broader business community and often trumpet their successes in representing companies in managerial misclassification cases. Indeed, large law firms that specialize in representing defendants in managerial misclassification cases have developed sophisticated marketing, advertising, and promotion programs intended to attract more client companies that face or may face claims of managerial misclassification.[23] This is not to say that defendant companies necessarily believe that they have unjustly deprived low-level managers of overtime pay, but rather that there is a very active market for legal services that many large law firms seek to provide and invest in providing to businesses facing claims of managerial misclassification. So a second interesting and potentially important research issue is determining how companies go about choosing law firms to defend them against claims of managerial misclassification. A companion issue is determining the extent to which companies, as distinct from the law firms that represent them, shape their strategies for defending against managerial misclassification lawsuits.

Theories of Overtime Pay Regulation

Ideally, the design of a "correct" overtime pay policy follows from a theory of the market failure or injustice that such a policy is intended to address, coupled with strong evidence in support of that theory. Although several rationales have been proposed to support overtime pay regulations, none has been rigorously linked to evidence demonstrating the magnitude of the problem. A constraint on requiring too much rigor from those proposing or supporting overtime pay rules is that the basic prediction of labor market theory is not met, in that there is not a consistent compensating differential for jobs with mandatory overtime (Ehrenberg 1989). At the same time, the lack of relatively high pay in jobs with mandatory overtime may be due to large numbers of workers' preferring long work hours and having (unobserved) lower hourly wages in alternative jobs.

With these cautions in mind, we now review some of the justifications for overtime regulation. The first laws that restricted hours of employment among male workers applied to railroads, where the objective was to reduce workplace accidents—a clear externality (Ehrenberg 1989). More recently in France, overtime pay rules based on the 35-hour week were implemented based on a theory of spreading the work and reducing unemployment, similar to the underlying motivation for adoption of the FLSA in the United States.[24] Such policies can lead to inefficiency, such as when there are fixed costs of commuting to work. At the same time, in regions with high unemployment, such inefficiencies can be partly or fully offset by reductions in socially costly unemployment and unemployment insurance.

Overtime pay rules can also help in reaching efficient contracts when there is imperfect information. Such rules provide a "default" contract that (if close to an optimal contract with full information) can be cheaper to implement than a case-by-case negotiation in which employees cannot easily monitor employer behavior. That is, in a world with no overtime regulation, many employees would need to negotiate detailed contracts with employers specifying regular hours, the circumstances in which overtime is permitted, and so on. A standard rule (i.e., law) can reduce these types of haggling costs even if the rule is often not optimal in specific cases. This form of regulation is particularly important when low-level managers might have poor information on the task mix and hours they will be working. For example, such employees might accept a job with a "manager" title but then be dissatisfied with resulting long work hours, including hours spent performing nonmanagerial tasks. And, if exit is costly, a standard rule or standard contract terms regarding overtime work and pay for these employees can reduce operating inefficiency.

Further, overtime pay regulation can help ameliorate a "rat race" in which people compete to work long hours, thereby making all workers worse off (Landers, Rebitzer, and Taylor 1996). At the same time, however, theories of rat races imply that strict regulation will either be avoided, as, for example, when workers surreptitiously take work home to win a promotion tournament, or will reduce base pay. Overtime pay rules may also reduce the rat race in consumption. To illustrate, if "keeping up with the Joneses" requires long hours of paid work, overtime rules may help undo the externality of conspicuous consumption (Frank 1985).

As we have noted, recommendations for improvement in public policy should be grounded in an understanding of the market failure or injustice that the policy is intended to address. Therefore, while we are cautious in endorsing proposals that might justify overtime regulations, we are also and perhaps especially cautious in endorsing proposals advanced by some for the complete removal of overtime pay regulations, and thus elimination of the managerial misclassification issue. Such proposals seem to us overdrawn. Labor markets, as with product markets and even capital markets, do not operate like the perfectly competitive market of introductory economics textbooks. It is plausible and highly likely that the mere existence of overtime pay regulation in many nations reflects a market failure or injustice that is not yet fully understood by economists or human resource and industrial relations specialists. Such lack of understanding limits our ability to provide advice for fully solving the problem of managerial classification.

It is clear that more research on managerial misclassification is needed. It would be especially helpful if we knew more about the extent to which employees holding salaried low-level managerial positions are satisfied with their positions and expected to work long hours when they took their jobs or, by contrast, believe that they have been duped into taking positions with fancy titles in which they perform largely routine tasks for long hours without overtime pay. In other words, the perceptions and opinions of low-level managers about their work need to be systematically obtained and assessed in order to reach informed judgments about allegations of managerial misclassification.

Reducing Transaction Costs

Even without a complete understanding of market failure or injustice, we know that current overtime pay regulations are flawed by high transaction costs. A good overtime pay rule requires that companies know when they are and aren't obeying the law. Thus, having salary cutoffs whereby those with low earnings are always eligible for overtime pay and those with high earnings are never eligible clearly makes sense. This is not a per se argument for any particular cutoffs or minimums regarding employee overtime pay coverage. Indeed, during the period from 1975 to 2004, the FLSA specified a minimum weekly salary of $250 and a minimum annual salary of $13,000 for an employee to be exempt from overtime pay (assuming that the employee also met the duties test specified in the law). At the start of that period, roughly 50% of U.S. employees earned less than $13,000 annually, whereas 30 years later only about 5% of U.S. employees earned less than $13,000 annually—thereby reducing the effectiveness of this bright line. Unsurprisingly, therefore, the FLSA was amended in 2004 to raise by about 80% the minimum weekly and minimum annual salary required for an employee to be exempt from overtime pay (as detailed in footnote 4). California's labor code presently specifies a monthly salary of $2,340, or $28,080 on an annual basis, as the cutoff point for an employee to be exempt from overtime pay provisions. Similar to the FLSA, California's labor code has been amended on several occasions to raise the overtime pay eligibility cutoff point.

These changes are consistent with the general principle of "bright lines" regarding annual pay level qualification for and disqualification from overtime pay. Hence, they should reduce the uncertainty faced and the transaction costs incurred by employers with respect to meeting federal and state (of California) overtime pay requirements. Unfortunately, and as this experience also shows, when nominal bright lines remain unchanged for long periods they become unrealistic. We therefore recommend that all federal and state eligibility cutoff points for overtime pay eligibility be indexed to overall wage inflation.

An additional source of transaction costs resulting from managerial classification cases is plaintiffs' attorneys' fees. As noted earlier, such fees rise more or less proportionately with size of class. While it is plausible that a large managerial misclassification case requires somewhat more work than a small one, litigating a case that involves 5,000 low-level managers as opposed to 50 does not require 100 times the work. We therefore recommend that courts set plaintiffs' attorneys' fees as a proportionately declining share of voluntary settlements, trial verdicts, and judicial awards in such cases. Adoption of this recommendation would reduce the incentive for plaintiffs' lawyers to file a lawsuit whenever there is a large class of plaintiffs, including and perhaps especially when the odds of plaintiffs' prevailing are low.[25]

Problems in the Law

Overtime pay rules should accord with the reality of contemporary workplaces. From this perspective, California law, which requires that overtime pay rules be met for each pay period, typically during a week or a month, imposes unrealistic obligations on employers. Few if any California employers operate in such a way as to be able to determine whether a low-level manager, on the one hand, primarily performed managerial tasks during the course of a year and is therefore not entitled to overtime pay or, on the other hand, primarily performed nonmanagerial tasks during a particular weekly or bi-weekly period, such as when store inventory was taken, and is therefore entitled to overtime pay. We therefore recommend that California's overtime pay law be amended to eliminate unrealistic weekly and monthly "tests" of the duties and tasks performed by managerial employees in determining their qualification for overtime pay.

Overtime rules must also meet tests of logical consistency. California's rule that the performance of a nonmanagerial task by a managerial employee can be used to argue that a particular managerial job itself is not managerial may well lead to the "unraveling" of the managerial exemption under California law, with successively higher level managerial jobs threatened with reclassification as nonmanagerial, hourly paid jobs. We therefore recommend that this law be amended to specify that the reclassification of one group of low-level managers as hourly employees does not change the exempt status of another group of low-level managers or of other groups of higher-level managers.

Incremental changes in the FLSA or in California's overtime law will not solve all of the problems raised by allegations of managerial misclassification. Earlier we noted that "management by walking around" is inherently a potpourri of tasks, such as when a store manager walks past a confused hourly employee and provides some on-the-spot training to that employee (a managerial task), keeps walking and picks up merchandise from the floor (an hourly task), and then helps an employee place or straighten packages of foodstuffs on store shelves (an hourly task, unless it is being done primarily to train the employee, in which case it may be a managerial task). There is no clear, unambiguous way to classify each of these tasks. Moreover, surveys or interviews of low-level managers to determine retrospectively how they spend their work time are prone to various self-reporting and recall errors, and thus may not validly distinguish between the managerial and nonmanagerial tasks actually performed by such "managers."

Alternative Approaches to Job Analysis

Companies facing claims of managerial misclassification typically hire large law firms to defend them. These law firms, in turn, often engage consultants to design and conduct surveys of low-level managers, and sometimes to design and conduct observational studies of low-level managers performing their work. In California cases, the surveys, whether conducted on behalf of plaintiffs or defendants, typically have been limited to former and/or current low-level managers who worked or work only in California, even when the defendant company is a large national (or global) enterprise. The strength of such studies is that the data apply to California and tend to be accepted by the courts; the weakness is that, as noted earlier, all of the respondents have a financial interest in the case and may therefore distort their responses.

When defendant companies have standard operating policies and procedures that apply to other states, as is common among large chain employers, an alternative methodology exists that is free from both sets of biases, namely, defendants could survey former low-level managers who worked outside of California. These respondents would have few incentives to distort their survey responses because they are not eligible for back pay under California settlements and they are no longer employed by the company in question. Indeed, plaintiffs' counsel could also survey this same group if defendant's counsel shared the relevant contact information.

Further, and as with surveys, job analyses based on observational studies of low-level managers conducted in managerial misclassification cases are tightly focused on—indeed, largely reactive to—litigation. Such observational studies are costly to companies because they for the most part focus on determining the tasks that low-level managers currently perform and the amount of time they spend performing them. These studies typically do not address fundamental factors affecting the types of work that low-level managers perform, including supply chain management, national/global branding, and organizational replication initiatives pursued by the managers' employers. In addition, such studies typically do not identify or analyze training and gaps in training of low-level managers or the opportunities for redesigning low-level managerial jobs. To systematically identify these factors and their influence on the types of work that low-level managers actually perform, defendant companies in managerial misclassification lawsuits should go beyond narrow observational studies to conduct what may best be referred to as proactively oriented organizational analysis.[26]

Even if a particular job analysis or observational study conducted to assist a company in its defense against a managerial misclassification claim is well designed for the company, it is not necessarily well designed for the court. Judges should experiment in this area by requiring plaintiffs and defendants in class action managerial misclassification cases to jointly undertake job analyses or observational studies, using agreed-upon designs, methods, and samples of low-level managerial jobs. To the best of our knowledge, this type of joint initiative has not been used in FLSA or California managerial misclassification cases, though it has been used successfully in union–management disputes and contract arbitration proceedings (Lipsky, Seeber, and Fincher 2003).

In sum, litigation is at best a noisy and at worst an invalid context for determining "truth" about the work performed by low-level managers. By the time a managerial misclassification case reaches the court, the parties in dispute have hardened their positions and typically use various arguments, studies, and methods to support their own and rebut the other party's arguments, studies, and methods. The defendant company and its attorneys have a vested interest in finding and showing that the company's low-level managers perform predominantly managerial work. Similarly, plaintiffs—typically former but sometimes current low-level managers—and their attorneys have a vested interest in seeking and obtaining damages as high as they can for alleged long hours of nonmanagerial work. In this type of adversarial proceeding, solutions to the larger issue of how to best regulate overtime hours and pay for low-level managers are unlikely to be forthcoming—just as minor patches to or changes in the FLSA and California law are unlikely to resolve this issue.

Until just recently, managerial misclassification occupied a relatively obscure corner of employment law, not to mention industrial relations research. At the same time, and as detailed in this paper, this single sphere of regulation is affected by globalization, work intensification and replication, innovations in supply chain management, and the rise of global brands—in short, by the whole suite of forces that affect most aspects of American companies, workers, and workplaces. As such, managerial misclassification provides a lens through which to observe the workings of these forces and how they affect employees, employers, and employment regulation for millions of low-level managers.

Further, the problems we have highlighted regarding current overtime pay and hours regulation are endemic, though with somewhat different characteristics and manifestations, in many other aspects of American workplace regulation. We need a great debate about how American workplaces and workplace regulatory policies (as well as schools and other institutions) should react to these forces of change—something akin to the vibrant debates about Fordism and Taylorism that occurred during the early and late stages of the 20th century, respectively. In such a great debate, moreover, the regulation of overtime work and pay should be addressed together with issues of skill formation, employee representation, equal opportunity, retirement income security, and other major issues of the day.

Notes

[1] Union membership data are from Milkman and Rooks (2003). The total number of members of California-based managerial misclassification class action lawsuits includes some people who worked at more than one of the employers being sued, so the total number of distinct employees covered by these lawsuits is somewhat less than 1.3 million.

[2] Based on our LexisNexis search of managerial misclassification cases filed between 1994 and 2005. Regarding LexisNexis searching: http://web.lexis-nexis.com/universe/form/academic/legalresearch.html?_m=8bd2ab834dde0bdc1b17b ba1599168c2&wchp=dGLbVlz-zSkVA&_md5=bc55782f49120027c547ffc497a69b69 is the general URL that enables readers to access the "Basic Legal Research" page, which contains various sections such as case laws, secondary literature, codes and regulations, and international legal materials. The best way to access any specific case is to use the "Get a Case" link under "Case Laws." By entering the parties to the case and/or the citation number, readers can access the case directly. For searching FLSA, overtime, or managerial misclassification cases, the link "Area of Law by Topic" under "Case Laws" URL is http://web.lexis-nexis.com/universe/form/academics/s_casecite.html?_m=8bd2ab834dde0bdc1b17bba1599168c2&wchp=dGLbVlz-zSkVA&_md5=bc55782f49120027c547ffc497a69b69. Further, readers can access newspaper articles/clippings, journal articles and reviews, and other sources regarding managerial misclassification and related legal matters by accessing "Legal News" and "Law Reviews" from the "Secondary Literature" section on the "Basic Legal Research Page." Because not all legal cases filed or decided are available in the LexisNexis database or other comparable databases (such as Westlaw), readers are encouraged to consult additional databases and sources, such as PACER.

[3] A major exception is a little known but highly provocative case in which 9,000 former and current U.S. Department of Justice attorneys filed a lawsuit against the department claiming that, under overtime requirements for federal government employees similar to those contained in the FLSA, they are entitled to overtime pay for the period 1992 to the present—and potentially for 1980 to the present! That case involves a claim of misclassification of professionals rather than misclassification of

managers, but the underlying issues are closely similar if not identical to those contested in managerial misclassification cases. These Department of Justice attorneys were certified as a class in November 2002, though to our knowledge the case has not proceeded further as of this writing. Other exceptions include the first California-based managerial misclassification case that went all the way through trial to a jury verdict, namely, *Crandall, et al. v. U-Haul* (2001), in which plaintiffs were former and current salaried location managers ostensibly in charge of local U-Haul facilities specializing in customer rental of moving vans, trailers, and trucks, and securities brokers who have recently filed misclassification lawsuits against Merrill Lynch, Morgan Stanley, Prudential Securities, and other brokerages claiming entitlement to overtime pay on the ground that they were (or are) hourly wage employees rather than exempt, commission-paid professional employees (King 2006).

[4] In addition to managers (or, as referred to in the FLSA, "executives"), some administrative and professional employees who are paid on a salaried basis are also exempt from overtime requirements. According to federal law, all exempt employees must earn at least $455 per week ($23,660 a year), be paid on a salaried basis, and regularly exercise independent judgment and discretion. In addition, to meet the executive exemption, the employee must manage two or more other employees and have managing as his or her primary duty. To meet the administrative exemption, the employee's primary duty must be the performance of office or nonmanual work directly related to the management or general business operations of the employer. To meet the professional exemption, the employee must engage in primarily intellectual work that requires advanced knowledge, must be highly creative, or must be a programmer. One other exemption is that anyone earning more than $100,000 a year is automatically classified as exempt. This complex law has numerous other provisions not elaborated here; further detail may be found at http://www.dol.gov/esa/regs/compliance/whd/fairpay/fs17a_overview.htm.

[5] The first California case alleging managerial misclassification of which we are aware was *Cooper v. Chief Auto Parts*, filed in 1994. Managerial misclassification cases can be distinguished from other recent cases alleging violations of the FLSA and California law, such as off-the-clock work, failure to provide employees with meal and rest breaks, excessive waiting time for separated employees to receive their final paychecks, and hours shaving (where low-level managers use a company's computerized systems to reduce—shave—recorded employee work hours). Examples of cases alleging off-the-clock work are *Plaintiffs v. Nordstrom* (1991), *Barton, et al. v. Albertson's* (1998) and *Thompson, et al. v. Albertson's* (2002); examples of cases alleging failure to provide meal and rest breaks are *Woods, et al. v. Dollar Financial Corp.* (2003) and *Pritchett, et al. v. Office Depot* (2005); examples of cases alleging waiting time violations are *Plaintiffs v. St. John's Hospital* (2003) and *Ward, et al. v. Albertson's* (2002); an example of a case alleging hour shaving is *Plaintiffs v. Denny's Restaurants* (2004).

[6] To address the rapid increase in class action overtime pay lawsuits and related concerns about the FLSA, the U.S. Department of Labor in 2004 promulgated new duties tests (last updated in 1959) and salary thresholds (last updated in 1975) to govern which employees are exempt from overtime pay provisions (see footnote 4 and the Department of Labor Fair Pay Overtime Initiative website at http://www.dol. gov/esa/regs/compliance/whd/fairpay/main.htm). According to the Employment Policy Foundation, "[s]implification of rules may reasonably reduce the number of case filings by one-third to one-half" (Illinois Hotel and Lodging Association 2004). This could save employers as much as $504 million in liquidated damages plus millions

more in reduced litigation-related costs. Further, on February 18, 2005, President George W. Bush signed the Class Action Fairness Act of 2005 (known as CAFA), a law that aims to move most class action employment lawsuits from state courts to federal courts.

[7] Under the federal FLSA, damages are calculated by applying a 50% overtime pay premium to hours worked beyond 40 in a week. By contrast, under California law, damages are calculated by applying a 150% premium to such hours—in effect, assuming that a "manager's" salary was paid based on a 40-hour work week. The formula is even more favorable to employees in California because the 150% pay premium is applied to the weekly salary divided by a 40-hour week. In contrast, the FLSA 50% premium is applied to the weekly salary divided by *actual* weekly hours. Finally, damages in managerial misclassification are more generous under the California overtime pay formula than under the FLSA formula because in these cases actual hours are always more than 40 per week.

[8] For an example of a direct observation study commissioned by one company to defend itself against a class action claim of managerial misclassification, see *Crandall, et al. v. U-Haul* (2001). For an example of an employee survey commissioned by a company to similarly defend itself, see *Collins, et al. v. Aaron Brothers, Inc.* (2001).

[9] Indeed, this challenge may be exacerbated by the use of and findings from such "expert" methods. For example, in the aforementioned *Collins, et al. v. Aaron Brothers, Inc.* case, the defendants' survey expert concluded that "[m]anagers vary greatly in the work they perform. . . . [I]t is therefore not possible to predict what one manager does based on what other managers, even in the same position, do" and that "[w]hen analyzed on a case-by-case basis, the majority of managers in each position perform predominantly exempt work" (Exhibit 3, pp. 2–3). From the perspective of a court attempting to determine if class certification is appropriate in a managerial misclassification case, these conclusions apparently amount to the employer's saying that low-level managers do *and* do not vary significantly in terms of the tasks they perform at work.

[10] We say "apparently" because there are no systematic data that bear on this point. The estimated 25% to 35% range of contingent fees for plaintiffs' counsels in these cases is based on discussions with selected plaintiffs' and defendants' counsel in managerial misclassification cases as well as perusal of certain proprietary documents in selected managerial misclassification cases that were voluntarily settled.

[11] In the case of Department of Justice attorneys who have sued the department for overtime pay (see footnote 3), potential damages are estimated to be $800 million if the beginning date of the case is 1992 and $1.2 billion if the beginning date is 1980.

[12] Also of relevance in this regard is that expected monetary benefits to plaintiffs from successful pursuit of a managerial misclassification case are typically much larger under California law than under the FLSA. As noted earlier, this is principally due to the different formulas for determining overtime pay between the FLSA and California law.

[13] See Taylor (1967 [1911]), pp. 30–67.

[14] On replicator organizations generally, see Winter (2002). On retail trade and fast food enterprises in particular, see Schlosser (2001), Love (1995), and Leidner (1993), who also discusses replicator organizations in the insurance industry.

[15] See http://www.bls.gov/ces/home.htm#data.

[16] See Ghemawat (1986); Ghemawat, Bradley, and Mark (2003); and Yoffie and Mack (2005).

[17] One of the side effects of these new technologies is an explosion of acronyms, including EDI (electronic data inventory), MIS (management information system), IP (Internet protocol), and ERP (electronic reporting protocol).

[18] For an example of SOPs in the context of a managerial misclassification case, see *Roberts, et al. v. Best Buy Co., Inc.* (2002).

[19] These observations are supported by psychological and economic models, including Locke and Latham (1990) and Lazear and Rosen (1981). They are also confirmed by empirical studies of goal setting, such as Knoeber and Thurman (1994), and the substantial literature surveyed in Locke and Latham (1990).

[20] Owner-operators of small "mom and pop" stores and restaurants face even stronger incentives than employees of chain-type businesses to work long hours—though such self-employed owner-operators are not, of course, legally entitled to overtime pay.

[21] We obtained these settlement data from attorneys representing plaintiffs and, in some cases, defendants, in California managerial misclassification cases settled between 1998 and 2004 as well as from the California Industrial Welfare Commission. For an example of the terms of settlement in a particular managerial misclassification case, see *Shields, et al. v. Starbucks Corp.*, No. 01-6446 (C.D. Cal. Dec. 17, 2002) (Cooper, J); class definition: persons employed by Starbucks as store managers and assistant store managers in California between June 20, 1997, and July 19, 2002, with plaintiffs alleging that they were denied overtime; settlement terms: $18,000,000 less (i) $4,500,000 in fees and expenses, (ii) $166,761 total to six named plaintiffs/class members in amounts ranging from $25,607 to $30,520, in lieu of payments they could otherwise obtain by filing claims, and for which they will give a broader release than other class members, and (iii) notice/settlement administration costs; valid claimants will be entitled to approximately $45 to $55 for each full-time week of employment (excluding any weeks spent on disability leave or an unpaid leave of absence), less any applicable payroll tax withholdings.

[22] Evidence in this regard may consist of successive managerial misclassification lawsuits filed by a particular firm of plaintiffs' attorneys against the same defendant company, and/or two or more firms of plaintiffs' attorneys joining forces as co-counsel in particular managerial misclassification cases. For examples of the former, see *Espinoza, et al. v. VCI Telecom* (2003) and *Garcia, et al. v. VCI Telecom* (2005). For an example of the latter, see *Pritchett, et al. v. Office Depot, Inc.* (2005). Additional evidence may consist of successive types of wage and hour lawsuits filed by a particular firm of plaintiffs' attorneys against the same defendant company—for example, a managerial misclassification lawsuit followed by a meal and break time lawsuit and/or a waiting time lawsuit.

[23] See, as examples, Littler, which labels itself "The National Employment and Labor Law Firm" (http://www.littler.com) and maintains the Littler Class Action Group, described as having "the breadth and depth of expertise to handle wage and hour disputes in all forms, including federal and state departments of labor" (http://www.littler.com/practiceareas/index.cfm?event=pubItem&pubItemID=11968 &childViewID=265), and Seyfarth Shaw (http://www.seyfarthshaw.com), which says, "One of the hallmarks of Seyfarth Shaw's employment law practice is our team-based

defense of wage and hour litigation. Our attorneys have litigated hundreds of complex wage and hour cases in the state and federal courts and with administrative agencies" (http://www.seyfarthshaw.com/index.cfm/fuseaction/practice_area.area_ of_concentration_detail/object_id/480fdebf-2417-4d45-be6b-8443cf271284/WageHour Litigation.cfm).

[24] Instructively, certain rationales for work hour restrictions and overtime pay, such as the goal of spreading work to the unemployed, are best met with a tax on overtime rather than with overtime payments to employees. This is because overtime pay encourages workers to supply overtime even as overtime pay discourages employer demand for overtime work.

[25] In general, attorney fees rise about 75% to 90% as rapidly as awards in large class action suits. It is plausible that a lower elasticity would suffice to provide high incentives for attorneys to choose cases more carefully and perhaps work even harder to win those cases. See Eisenberg and Miller (2004).

[26] This recommendation clearly applies to companies that have been charged with managerial misclassification, but perhaps even more to companies that have not (as yet) been charged. Organizational analysis is aimed at determining the extent to which supply chain management, national/global branding, and organizational replication initiatives have resulted in (or are explicitly designed to achieve) increased centralization of decision making. If and when it occurs, and following the reasoning presented in this chapter, more centralized decision making is highly likely to have reshaped low-level managerial jobs such that those who hold those jobs perform less managerial work and more nonmanagerial work than they previously did. If so, there may well be a fundamental business case rather than only legal justification for reclassifying some low-level managerial jobs as nonmanagerial jobs, the performance of which should be compensated by hourly wages rather than salaries.

References

Barton, et al. v. Albertson's Inc. (1998). U.S. District Court, District of Idaho, No. 970159SBLW (March 20).

Beer, M., and G.C. Rogers. 1995. "Human Resources at Hewlett-Packard (A)." Harvard Business School case #9-495-051. Boston: Harvard Business School, November 1.

Beer, M., and Richard O. Von Werssowetz. 1982. "Human Resources at Hewlett-Packard." Harvard Business School Case #9-482-125, May 6. Boston: Harvard Business School.

Collins, et al. v. Aaron Bros. (2001). Supreme Court of California, No. S095274 (February 28).

Cooper v. Chief Auto Parts, et al. (1995). Supreme Court of California, No. S045933 (April 13).

Crandall, et al. v. U-Haul International, et al. (2001). Los Angeles County Superior Court, No. S080691 (July 22).

Ehrenberg, R.G. 1989. "Workers' Rights: Rethinking Protective Labor Legislation." In D.L. Bawden and F. Skidmore, eds., *Research in Labor Economics*, Vol. 8, Part B. Washington, DC: Urban Institute Press, pp. 105–61.

Eisenberg, T., and G.P. Miller. 2004. "Attorney Fees in Class Action Settlements: An Empirical Study." *Journal of Empirical Legal Studies*, Vol. 1 (March), pp. 27–78.

Espinoza, et al. v. VCI Telecom (2003). Central District of California, No. 2CV04826JFWRZ (October 7).

Frank, R.H. (1985). *Choosing the Right Pond: Human Behavior and the Quest for Status.* New York: Oxford University Press.

Garcia, et al. v. VCI Telecom. (2005). Central District of California, No. 2CV04826JFWRZS (May 25).

Ghemawat, P. 1986. "Wal-Mart Store Discount Operations." Harvard Business School case #9-387-018. Boston: Harvard Business School, August 19.

Ghemawat, P., S.P. Bradley, & K. Mark. 2003. "Wal-Mart Stores in 2003." Harvard Business School case #9-704-430. Boston: Harvard Business School, September 18.

Illinois Hotel and Lodging Association. 2004. "New Labor Overtime Standards (May), p. 3. <http://www.stayillinois.com/members/innovations/Enews_May.htm.> [Accessed September 14, 2006].

King, A.G. 2006. "Is the System Broke or Are Brokers Gaming the System?" *Law.com*, February 15, 2 pp. <http://www.law.com/jsp/article.jsp?id=1139351651620.> [Accessed September 13, 2006].

Knoeber, C.R., and W.N. Thurman. 1994. "Testing the Theory of Tournaments: An Empirical Analysis of Broiler Production." *Journal of Labor Economics*, Vol. 12, no. 2, pp. 155–79.

Lazear, E., and S. Rosen. 1981. "Rank-Order Tournaments as Optimum Labor Contracts." *Journal of Political Economy*, Vol. 89, no. 5, pp. 841–64.

Leidner, J.R. 1993. *Fast Food, Fast Talk.* Berkeley, CA: University of California Press.

Landers, R.M., Rebitzer, J.B., and Taylor, L.J. (1996). "Rat Race Redux: Adverse Selection in the Determination of Work Hours in Law Firms." *American Economic Review*, Vol. 86 (June), pp. 3229–48.

Lipsky, D.B., R.L. Seeber, and R.D. Fincher. 2003. *Emerging Systems for Managing Workplace Conflict.* San Francisco: Jossey-Bass.

Locke, E.A., and G.P. Latham. 1990. *A Theory of Goal Setting and Task Performance.* Englewood Cliffs, NJ: Prentice Hall.

Love, J.F. 1995. *McDonald's: Behind the Arches.* New York: Bantam.

Milkman, Ruth, and Rooks, Daisy. 2003. "California Union Membership: A Turn-of-the-Century Portrait." In *The State of California Labor, 2003, Vol. 2.* Berkeley: University of California Institute for Labor and Employment, pp. 3–37.

"Nordstrom Settles Suit on Overtime; Employees to Receive More Than $20 Million" (1993). *The Washington Post*, January 12, p. C1.

Plaintiffs v. Nordstrom, Inc. (1991). Supreme Court of Washington State, No. W5473221 (March 30).

Plaintiffs v. St. John's Hospital (2003). Superior Court of Los Angeles County, No. CO454393 (February 15).

Plaintiffs v. Denny's Restaurants, Inc. (2004). Superior Court of Los Angeles County, No. CO278421 (April 26).

Pritchett, et al. v. Office Depot, Inc. (2005). U.S. Court of Appeals, Colorado, 10th Circuit, No. 050501 (August 18).

Roberts, et al. v. Best Buy Co., Inc. (2002). County of Contra Costa, California, No. CO201642 (September 22).

Sav-On Drug Store, Inc. v. The Superior Court of Los Angeles County and Robert Rocher, et al. (2004). Supreme Court of California, No. S106718 (August 26).

Schlosser, E. 2001. *Fast Food Nation.* Boston: Houghton Mifflin.

Shields, et al. v. Starbucks Corp. (2002). Supreme Court of California, No. S016446 (December, 17).

Taylor, F.W. [1911] 1967. *The Principles of Scientific Management.* New York: Norton.
Thompson, et al. v. *Albertson's, Inc.* 2002. U.S. District Court, District of Idaho, No.
   970159SBLWS (June 14).
Ward, et al. v. Albertson's, Inc. (2002). Superior Court of Los Angeles County, No.
   B161529 (December 3).
Winter, S.G. 2002. "Understanding Dynamic Capabilities," Working Paper 2002-05.
   Philadelphia: Wharton School, University of Pennsylvania.
Woods, et al. v. Dollar Financial Corp. (2003). Court of Appeals, California, 2nd
   Appellate District (September 14).
Yoffie, D.B., & B.J. Mack. 2005. "Wall-Mart, 2005." Harvard Business School case
   #9-705-460. Boston: Harvard Business School, January 4.

CHAPTER 7

Retirement, Pensions, and Managing One's Own Money

TERESA GHILARDUCCI
University of Notre Dame

CHARLES JESZECK
U.S. Government Accountability Office

Scarcely a week passes without a major media story on a new retirement nightmare: Social Security insolvency; pension plan terminations by Delphi, United Airlines, and other corporate household names; gyrating 401(k) accounts, some overloaded in stock from the worker's own employer; personal saving reaching another new low; eroding retiree health benefits. Large, trend-setting employers are forcing workers to assume greater risk and responsibility in funding their retirement. The shift in "R and R" will erode retirement income security. Most workers will never be able to efficiently accumulate enough assets in individual accounts and effectively choose payout options to provide a steady amount of income for life after retirement. Many of these prospective changes in retirement futures stem from declines in the presence of union contracts, a dramatic shift in presidential and congressional attitudes about government responsibility for social insurance, and the substitution of defined contribution or 401(k)-type accounts for traditional defined benefit pensions (McCaw 2004).

The concept of retirement is changing, to be sure, and over time American workers have been able to spend more time in retirement. In 1940, men at age 65 were expected to live 12.7 more years and women 14.7 more years. Life expectancy improvements have extended the average time spent by the average male worker in retirement from 11.5 years in 1950 to 18 years in 2003 (Government Accountability Office 2005b.) The largest increases in longevity occurred in the mid-1970s, when the effects of reduced smoking among men, Social Security benefit increases, and increased access to health care through Medicare had their salubrious effects. More time spent in retirement does not mean that retirement has to be reduced. There is a national debate about whether the nation can afford retirement given changes in longevity, and it is not one that we settle here. Clearly some workers will want to work longer, at least part-time. It is not clear that employers will provide the jobs older workers want. Older workers report that less physical strength is required of their jobs, but the jobs require more intense concentration and keen eyesight and involve more stress (Johnson 2004). All older workers want to work on their own terms, but that may not be possible if pension and retiree health care is less secure.

There is much opportunity for policy makers to reverse this deterioration of retirement income. In particular, policies should be designed to encourage more widespread coverage of pension plans, both defined benefit and defined contribution, and to extend the positive features of defined-benefit plans into the defined-contribution format. Policies should carefully define and sort out the appropriate risks and responsibilities employers and employees can bear.

The Erosion of the American Retirement Security System

We begin our discussion of the role of individual risk and responsibilities in providing retirement security with an analysis of the challenges facing each source of retirement income: Social Security, personal savings, and so-called occupational pensions, which can be either DB or DC plans. How the shift in risks and responsibilities manifests itself will determine each source's contribution to retirement security across income groups.

There has recently been increased focus on the declining availability of retiree health insurance and its implications for retirement security. A related issue that is also receiving attention is the role of housing as a critical asset in retirement (Bell, Carasso, and Steuerle 2005). While these issues are critical in the overall discussion of American retirement security, they are outside the scope of this paper.

Social Security

Covering virtually every American family, the cornerstone of national retirement security is Social Security. Social Security currently pays benefits to more than 47 million people, including retired workers, disabled workers, the spouses and children of retired and disabled workers, and the survivors of deceased workers. It is the largest single source of income for retirees (Social Security Administration 2004). The program has also been highly effective at reducing the incidence of poverty among the elderly, and disability and survivor benefits have helped millions of vulnerable families.

Social Security is a price-indexed DB plan that reduces the risks that retirees will "outlive" their finances, eliminates the risk that Social Security benefits' buying power will be eroded by inflation, and reduces the risk that one's dependents are left without income in the event of death, retirement, or disability. The problem is that Social Security is facing financial pressures that, left unchecked, could result in the program's being unable to pay future promised benefits. Under the Social Security trustees' intermediate assumption projections for 2005, unless some action is taken by 2043, the program will be insolvent, with program revenues sufficient to cover only about three quarters of total benefit costs, with additional but much smaller reductions occurring in later years. Over the trustees' entire 75-year projection period, the program's long-term actuarial deficit is estimated to equal 2.02 of the program's taxable payroll. This means the system would need an immediate tax increase or benefit reductions equivalent to 2.02% of total covered wage to maintain solvency over that period (Social Security Administration 2006).

In discussing Social Security's financial difficulties, the popular press often focuses on the relative sizes of the populations of covered workers and beneficiaries. This is an important parameter, as fewer people paying into the system to support a growing number of retirees will increase program costs, everything else equal. In 2006, the ratio of workers to retirees is approximately 3 to 1; it is projected to fall to approximately 2 to 1 by around 2030. While not as dramatic a decline as experienced by many European national pension systems, the trend is the same, with the program becoming more expensive.

However, focusing exclusively on the number of workers and retirees provides only partial information about the system's affordability. The system's finances are also influenced by the relative earnings of current workers and benefit levels of retirees. In this regard, the unexpected growth in wage inequality has adversely affected the system's finances. Social Security's progressive benefit formula returns higher benefits compared to contributions to lower income workers, and the share of lower income workers is growing. However, at the same time, since the Social Security payroll tax is capped and income to people with earnings over the cap has soared, revenue is not growing as fast as expected. The Social Security trust fund advisers in the 1980s never foresaw that, in the 1990s, earnings above the Social Security cap would grow faster than the income subject to the tax—this is an important contributor to the projected long-term financial gap (Diamond and Orszag 2003).

Although the Social Security system is in no immediate crisis, doing something now lowers the ultimate cost of repair and permits a phase-in of changes that could minimize disruption in benefit payments. In this context, the Congress, academics, and interest groups have proposed a variety of proposals to reform Social Security, ranging from a significant restructuring of benefits through the creation of individual accounts to a mere tweaking of the current system.

At the restructuring end of the spectrum are proposals in the Congress and from the presidential administration to create individual retirement accounts. Workers would manage their own Social Security accounts and be exposed to greater risk in return for both greater individual choices in retirement investments and, according to proponents, the possibility of a higher rate of return on contributions than what is available under current law. However, like similar developments already taking place in employer pensions and the workforce generally, workers would be required to take more responsibility for a number of key financial decisions that are currently made by plan sponsors or other institutions, including how much to save in an individual retirement account, how to invest, and the crucial decision about how to withdraw assets at retirement.

The individual account proposals range from those that add such accounts onto the current or traditional Social Security defined-benefit (DB) structure to others that carve out defined-contribution (DC) accounts by redirecting part of the current payroll tax and correspondingly reducing the traditional benefit. All proposals that do not raise taxes or cut benefits would make Social Security solvency problems worse, a result of the transition costs generated by creating individual accounts as the system continued paying benefits to current and near-term retirees while revenue was diverted to establish the new accounts.

Individual account systems can be designed so that contributions are mandatory or voluntary. Proposals differ in the manner in which accounts would be financed, the extent of choice and flexibility concerning investment options, the way in which benefits would be paid out (e.g., annuity versus lump sum), and the way the accounts would interact with the existing Social Security program. In any case, to the extent that all or a portion of the current Social Security benefit was replaced by an individual account, the government would be transferring some accumulation and payout risks to the individual worker.

At the tweaking end of the spectrum of individual-account proposals are various combinations of traditional revenue increases and cuts in traditional benefits. Cuts can be done, for example, by increasing the number of years used to calculate benefits, using price indexing instead of wage indexing to weight past earnings, reducing cost-of-living adjustments, raising the normal or early retirement ages, or reducing dependent benefits. Revenues can be raised by increasing the payroll tax, expanding the Social Security taxable wage base by raising the earnings cap, taxing more benefits, or covering the few remaining state and local government employees not in the system. Critics of proposals to cut benefits correctly argue that lower- and middle-income workers would be most affected. The poorest households rely on Social Security and public assistance almost exclusively—94% for the first quintile and 86% for the second—and have very little income from employer-based pension sources.

Though Social Security helps keep most retirees out of poverty, it is not sufficient to provide middle-class workers their accustomed standard of living. The system replaces about 41% of income for workers who earn average wages throughout their careers, although most planners recommend replacing 70% of preretirement income to maintain living standards sustained while working. The already low 41% replacement rate will fall in two decades to 30.5% as the benefit decreases due to the normal retirement age creeping up to age 67, which reduces income for those who collect at 65. Increases in income taxes and Medicare premiums also erode the value of the cash benefit (Munnell 2003).

In contrast, the elderly households in the top 20% of the income distribution obtain much more of their income from earnings and wealth—38 and 18.9%, respectively—compared to the middle-class elderly who obtain only 3.6% to 9.8% of their pension income from personal wealth. Table 1 shows the sources of retirement income, by percentage, coming to older households.

TABLE 1

Where Retirees Obtain Their Income: Percentages of Income by Source for Household Units with a Member over Age 55

	Quintile				
	First	Second	Third	Fourth	Fifth
Social Security (including Railroad Retirement)	82.9	84.5	67.5	47.6	19.9
Government and private employee pensions	3.2	6.3	14.5	24.9	20.4
Earnings	1.1	2.3	7.0	14.7	38.4
Income from assets (including savings from retirement accounts)	2.4	3.6	7.4	9.8	18.9
Public assistance and other sources	10.4	3.3	3.7	3.1	2.5
Total percent	100.0	100.0	100.0	100.0	100.0

Quintile upper limits are $9,721 (first), $15,181 (second), $23,880 (third), $40,982 (fourth).
Source: Social Security Administration (2004).

To ensure future retirement security while addressing Social Security's real financial challenges, reform must be coordinated with whatever changes are occurring in personal savings behavior and employer pensions. We turn next to personal wealth as a source of retirement income.

Personal Savings

For the first time since the Great Depression, at the end of 2005 Americans spent more than they received: American workers are now, on average, consuming all of their income and more. Just 20 years ago workers (ages 25 to 65) were saving 10% of their income (Munnell, Golub-Sass, and Varani 2005). At 0%, the United States ranks last among all industrialized countries in personal-savings rates, with rates being as high as 12% elsewhere (Bosworth and Bell 2005). The drop in the savings rate is a mystery to economists: we know that middle-aged workers save more than any other age group, and there are more middle-aged workers today than there were 20 years ago; the more education people have, the more they save, and workers are more educated than they have ever been; and most personal savings come from households in the top third of the income distribution, and this group has had the most income gains over the last decade (Bosworth and Bell 2005).

Though the reason for the lack of savings is an academic mystery, the fact that all household savings is now in the form of institutionalized, contractual "pension savings," including defined-benefit and defined-contribution plan assets, is well accepted and understood (Bosworth and Bell 2005; Munnell, Golub-Sass, and Varani 2005). American spendthrift consumption habits are legendary (household saving started to decline in the 1980s), but until the 1990s, contractual or institutionalized savings, again mainly pensions, helped stanch the red ink. Now a deep decline in contractual savings, especially by employer-financed defined-benefit pension plans, explains a large part of the decline in savings rate. It is worth exploring why employers cut their private defined-benefit pension contributions.

The regulatory framework governing the funding of private defined-benefit plans (Government Accountability Office 2005d) contributed to the decline in contractual savings because current funding rules allow employer plan sponsors considerable flexibility in making contributions, particularly when assets held by pension plans are rising rapidly.[2] Plan sponsors appear to have taken advantage of the rules during the run-up of the stock market in the late 1990s (Government Accountability Office 2005d). Other regulations designed to encourage plan sponsors to keep funding apace with liabilities include the variable rate premium (severely underfunded plans pay higher premiums to the government insurer, Pension Benefit Guaranty Corporation [PBGC]) and the additional funding charge (AFC) payment (payments are assessed against plans that become severely underfunded). Both the variable rate premium and the AFC had loopholes that allowed sponsors with underfunded plans to avoid making additional contributions or premiums. Additional factors contributing to reduced funding levels relate to corporate restructuring and mergers and acquisitions. Some analysts suggest that the imposition of an excise tax on overfunded plans during the late 1980s discouraged plan sponsors from making contributions afterward (Ippolito 2001). The consequence, estimated by the PBGC, is that private single employer defined-benefit plans had aggregate unfunded liabilities of $450 billion as of 2005.

This decline in defined-benefit pension saving means that employees will have to save more aggressively in voluntary 401(k) plans and other voluntary retirement savings vehicles. Unfortunately, the 20-year-old experience with 401(k) plans reveals that employees have been either unwilling or unable to fill the gap (Vanguard Group 2004; Munnell and Sundén 2004). A 2004 survey found that only one third of workers were on track to achieve the 70% target for retirement income replacement rate (Vanguard Group 2004). Though a full 90% of workers have thought about how much income they will need in retirement, only 41% have specific plans for obtaining the assets they need to produce that income. The survey also found that 40% of households risk not having enough income in retirement; they would need to double their savings rates or defer retirement until age 70 to avoid this problem. When it comes to planning for adequate retirement income, there is a large disconnect between thinking and doing. Financial education does not help much: only 40% of those who receive counseling or attend a financial education class change their saving behavior. In fact, planning itself may be on the decline! The percentage of workers who thought about calculating saving needs was as high as 53% in the late 1990s; then it to fell to 42% in 2004 (Employee Benefit Research Institute 2004).

There is little evidence that average- and lower-income workers have the resources and the capability to anticipate, manage, and save enough money to retire, or ever will. Generally, workers who report having reasonable expectations and who actively plan for retirement to meet those expectations have higher incomes in the first place. This relationship between income and retirement preparation is partially rooted in public policy. A major impetus for retirement planning stems from the tax code's exemption of income that is diverted into retirement accounts, such as 401(k) plans, Individual Retirement Accounts (IRAs), and similar savings vehicles. Since people in the higher-income quintiles have more income by definition and because income taxes are progressive, those people have the greatest financial incentive to take advantage of professional counseling to maximize their tax-preferred retirement savings.

The bottom line is that automatic institutionalized pension savings, particularly through defined-benefit plans, has been a critical source of personal assets for retirement purposes. To the extent that this savings continues to decline, the retirement prospects for many workers, particularly those with lower incomes, will continue to dim.

Private Pensions

After Social Security, private occupational pensions, including defined-benefit and defined-contribution plans, are the second largest source of retirement income, providing almost 20% of the income received by elderly households (refer again to Table 1). Since the research shows that contractual savings, particularly in defined-benefit pensions, seem to be an effective savings vehicle through which households can save for retirement, they would seem to be a key component in any strategy for ensuring that middle-class worker retain middle-class status in retirement. Yet a number of trends are challenging this role for pensions in Americans' retirement future.

The first challenge is that despite considerable federal tax incentives to employer-provided pensions, pension coverage has stagnated for the last decade, with participation of only about 60% of the workforce at any one time (Purcell 2005a). The tax expenditure for retirement funding was a full fourth of total annual Social Security contributions—$114 billion in 2004. Even more amazing, total household saving, at $102 billion, was lower than the federal pension tax expenditure (Bell, Carasso, and Steuerle 2005). The fastest growing portion of the retirement tax expenditures is for individual retirement accounts.

According to the U.S. Census Bureau's Current Population Survey (CPS), the share of workers (year-round and full-time) whose employers sponsor a pension plan has been slowly falling for years: most recently from 62.7% in 2003 to 61.8% in 2004. Coverage continues to be particularly low for low-income employees, younger employees, and part-time employees and among small employers (General Accounting Office 2001). The pension participation of employees who work full-time and for an entire year also fell from 54.1% in 2003 to 53.4% in 2004 (Purcell 2005a). The coverage rates are higher than actual participation rates because people can be disqualified from defined-benefit or defined-contribution plans by restrictions on years of service or hours of work per week; also, because participation in many defined-contribution plans, like 401(k) plans, is voluntary, some employees decide not to participate (i.e., decide not to reduce their take-home pay to fund their retirement; Purcell 2005b).

Although estimates of pension coverage vary depending on the data set that is used, the results are similar. The Department of Labor survey of private employers reports slightly increasing rates of pension coverage and participation. The 2005 National Compensation Survey shows that 60% of workers in the private sector have access to (i.e., are offered coverage in) a retirement plan of some sort and that 50% participate in a retirement plan. The comparable figures from the worker-based Current Population Survey for those in the same age range are 57% and 46%. The higher figures in the National Compensation Survey may be caused by employers' having better knowledge of who is covered than workers do. Also, many Current Population Survey respondents are not the actual worker but a spouse or other relative, who may not be knowledge-able about the employee's retirement plan. The bottom line is that regardless of the data set used, pension coverage is stagnating as a percentage of the labor force.

Although there are a number of causes for this decline, one con-tributing factor is a decline in collective bargaining. Collectively bar-gained compensation packages contain more employee benefits and other forms of nonwage compensation than do nonunion compensation packages. There are various mechanisms explaining the union effect on employee benefits. Unions may facilitate benefits by informing and edu-cating members about the importance of insurance and pensions (Budd 2004). Unions may also promote employee benefits relative to cash wages because unions represent the older worker rather than the mar-ginal, younger worker, who likely prefers cash to insurance. As shown in Table 2, union workers compared to all workers have almost twice the

TABLE 2
Pension Coverage by Sex, Income, and Union Status for Employees Working
More than 20 Hours per Week

	Male		Female	
	Union members	All workers	Union members	All workers
Low-income	70.67%	33.8%	69.8%	39.0%
Low middle-income	74.05%	55.2%	80.0%	64.2%
High middle-income	86.91%	75.1%	89.8%	78.7%
High-income	88.34%	80.4%	86.7%	82.2%

Source: Calculations from the U.S. Bureau of the Census, Current Population Survey (2003).

pension coverage rates for lower-income workers and over 10% more for higher-income workers.

Within the overall stagnation of pension coverage is the increasing dominance of defined-contribution (DC) plans over defined-benefit (DB) plans. The number of single employer DB plans has declined significantly, from about 95,000 in 1980 to fewer than 35,000 in 2002, while the number of active DB plan participants—employed workers covered by a DB plan—has declined as a percent of all national private wage and salary workers from 27.3 in 1980 to about 15% in 2002 (Purcell 2005a). This number excludes the 9 million active workers participating in multiemployer DB pension plans, but overall trends in multiemployer plans have mirrored the experience of single employer plans (see Government Accountability Office 2004a). There are fewer data on DC plans but, as of 2005, 43% of all private sector workers were covered by a DC plan, up from 36% in 1999. Table 3 shows percentages of private sector workers covered by pension plans.

It is crucial to note that pension coverage rates and participation rates are different. Though not explored deeply here, the gap between coverage and participation is smaller in DB plans because, with some exceptions for part-time or newly hired employees, coverage is largely universal within a workforce. In contrast, while DC plans may be offered to a large majority of a sponsoring employer's workforce, nonparticipation rates can be quite large, often averaging over 20% (Congressional Research Service 2004), and participation rates are likely even higher among lower-income workers.

Explaining the Shift of Defined-Benefit to Defined-Contribution Plans

Some commentators explain the trend away from DB plans and toward DC plans as an inevitable development in a global economy. Others view the change as the result of decisions that created a hostile environment for DB plans. The first view implies that DB plans are like dinosaurs, which became extinct when they did not evolve with a changing environment. The other view suggests that DB plans are like pandas, a worthwhile species endangered by shortsighted policies and decisions. The dinosaur interpretation argues that employees have come to prefer the 401(k)-type DC plan over the traditional DB plan because DC accounts are transparent, and workers can better understand their benefits. Indeed, DB plans are notoriously confusing; they often appear to analysts and policy makers as a mass of present values, current and termination liabilities, interest rates, and mortality tables. To even the most well-educated and interested employee, the DB present value is not easily known.

TABLE 3
Private Sector Workers' Participation in Pension Plans

Type of worker	Workers in all plans, 1999 (%)	Workers in all plans, 2005 (%)	Workers in DB plans, 1999 (%)	Workers in DB plans, 2005 (%)	Workers in DC plans, 1999 (%)	Workers in DC plans, 2005 (%)	All changes, 1999–2005 (%)	DB plan changes, 1999–2005 (%)	DC plan changes, 1999–2005 (%)
All workers	48	50	21	21	36	43	4.2	0.0	19.4
Nonunion	44	46	16	15	35	41	4.5	−6.3	17.1
Larger firms (>100 workers)	64	67	37	36	46	53	4.7	−2.7	15.2
Goods-producing	61	64	36	32	44	50	4.9	−11.1	13.6
Service industries	44	47	17	18	34	39	6.8	5.9	14.7
Full-time	56	60	25	25	42	50	7.1	0.0	19.0
Union	79	85	70	72	39	43	7.6	2.9	10.3
Smaller firms (0–99 workers)	34	37	8	9	27	32	8.8	12.5	18.5

Note: Ranked in descending order by growth of overall participation rates.
Source: National Compensation Survey, various years.

DC plans may be preferable to workers for additional reasons. One, workers can receive their benefits in a lump sum, a popular option despite the fact that many pension analysts believe that lump sum payouts represent poor retirement and saving policy, because taking a pension as a lump sum increases the potential for outliving one's savings.[3] In recent years, many DB plans have moved toward offering a lump sum option (DB plans of Delta Airlines and Continental Airlines pilots and the terminated DB plan of the Polaroid Corporation are some examples). DC plans also let participants borrow from their plans under limited situations, providing additional flexibility for financing homeownership and college education, although many financial planners would often question the soundness of such choices.

Yet, despite the popular wisdom, there is little evidence that DB pensions are stagnating because workers do not want them (Rappaport 2004). Rather, DC plans are, to many workers, a second-best option given the uncertainty and the lack of commitment to DB plans displayed by employers.

The "DB pensions are pandas" interpretation of the evidence is that DB coverage rates are stagnating because many companies are adopting DC plans to take advantage of temporary changes in accounting standards and the economy in order to lower pension costs, not to respond to worker preferences or to changes in labor processes and technology. Sponsors' pension costs are reduced by 401(k)-type plans because a substantial number of workers choose not to participate in a DC plan even when they essentially "leave money on the table" by foregoing the sponsor's contribution match. Between 2002 and 2004, had all eligible workers participated in their employers' 401(k) plans, employers would have had to contribute 26% more—for an annual total of $3.18 billion.[4]

The growth in DC plans has so far not raised overall pension participation. In 2005, employers reported that 43% of workers participate in DC plans and 21% in DB plans (see Table 3). If these shares were combined, 64% of the workforce would be in retirement plans, but only 50% are. If DC participation growth expanded access to pension plans rather than replacing or supplementing an already existing DB plan, then growing DC rates should have increased total pension participation rates. This has clearly not happened so far. Participation rates for all workers in all pension plans rose only 4.2% (Table 3), and DC participation rose 19.4%. Union workers (and workers in small firms) experienced the largest increases in pension participation rates—from 79% in 1999 to 85% in 2005—and this group had already started from a high base. Remarkably, this group also had one of the largest increases in DB coverage with small firm and service industry workers—70% to 72%—and a large increase in DC coverage, from 39% to 43%. Because unions almost always bargain DC plans to complement DB plans, we can be fairly certain that in this case, the increase in the DB rate boosted pension access. This relationship holds up in an evaluation of the correlation between general pension and DB participation rates. The correlation between the overall expansion of pension and DB participation rates is a strongly positive 79%. But the correlation between all pension and DC growth is a negative 10%. This means that groups with the highest growth rates in DC plans are not the most likely to experience a significant increase in pension access. The highest growth rate in DB coverage was 12.5%, for workers in small firms, and this group happened to also have the largest increase in overall growth rates—a boost of 8.8%. This evidence suggests that so far increases in DC plan coverage have not been correlated with increases in total pension coverage. The recently announced terminations of traditional DB plans and their replacement with 401(k) DC plans by IBM, Hewlett Packard, Motorola, and other major corporations further illustrate this finding.

Although the number of and total participation in DB plans continue to decline, such plans remain an important component of pension income and total retirement income. There is also some evidence that some new, smaller professional firms are forming DB plans (Frieswick 2002), although this at best may only slow the decline. Further, despite the declining number of DB plans and the increase in plan freezes among the remainder, a majority of Fortune 500 companies, especially in the pharmaceutical and manufacturing sectors, continue to maintain DB plans, which control trillions of dollars in assets. In the public sector, employers at all levels of government, the armed forces, public schools and universities, and hospitals continue to offer traditional DB plans. At least in the short run, many employers, public and private, will continue to sponsor DB plans.

Implications for Workers: Pension Design, Retiree Satisfaction, and Risk

We will describe next the changes in the distribution of "R and Rs," risks and responsibilities, as DB plans give way to DC plans in three key stages of retirement preparedness: accumulation, investment practices, and payout.

Accumulation Phase

The growth in 401(k) plans, and DC plans generally, implies a greater responsibility to accumulate assets at a sufficient level to provide adequate retirement income. So far, though, most participants have not done so. The median annual salary deferral into a 401(k)-type plan was just $1,896; an adequate savings rate would be twice that. (Financial planners recommend saving 12% of salary in a retirement account; $5,400 is required per year for workers earning the median salary of $45,000.) Further, the share of workers in 401(k) plans who say they cannot afford to save has risen from 15% in 1998 to 19% in 2003 (Purcell 2005b).

The several decades of experience with 401(k)-type plans (since 1978) are not encouraging to the hope that savings behavior will improve. The average size of DC account balances remains quite low. As of 2004, the mean value for 401(k) plans was $53,600 for near retirees, those ages 55 to 64, with a far lower median value of $23,000. These accounts may not seem small, but the annuities they would generate are. A $50,000 lump sum indexed for inflation would bring a 65-year-old less than $50 per month (Vanguard Group 2005). Low incomes, low savings, the potential to borrow from DC accounts, and the ability to consume the account balance when switching employers despite tax penalties are all likely suspects in the weak balance accumulation of DC plans. The average 401(k) account for someone nearing retirement is about $70,000—about enough to replace only 3% of an average income annually for the remainder of the retiree's life. Table 4 displays 2004 data for account balances by age of worker.

Why are workers not accumulating sufficient balances? Low incomes are one basic reason, but at least some individuals are hampered by human traits that interfere with asset accumulation. Desires for increased consumption, urges for immediate gratification, and the charming optimism people have that no financial emergency will befall them can lead to decisions that place more immediate priorities ahead of retirement saving. For example, even if people save a lot in their 401(k) plans, some tend to spend down or borrow against their savings for costs associated with job changes (over half of people with 401(k)s who change jobs spend their plan balances for health emergencies, home

TABLE 4
Values of Defined-Contribution Balances by Age of Worker in 2004

Ages of worker	Mean balance ($)	Median balance ($)
25–34	17,009	8,000
45–54	48,118	23,000
55–64	53,600	23,000

Source: Purcell (2005b).

purchases, and financing children's education. In 2004, seventy-two percent of workers have 401(k) plans that allow loans, which reduce accumulations; 10% of such workers with 401(k) savings have borrowed from their plans, and the median outstanding balance is $2,000 (Purcell 2005b). Such temptation is not only common, the ability to give in to it is popular among plan participants. The General Accounting Office (1997) found that the ability to borrow from one's 401(k) plan was a key incentive in workers choosing to participate in the plan.

That people can spend their 401(k) savings when they leave employment makes that vehicle, ironically, a problem in a mobile society. The seemingly attractive portability of 401(k) plans can become counterproductive for retirement saving; of plan participants who change jobs, half cash out their 401(k) monies rather than roll them over for retirement (Munnell and Sundén 2004). In such instances, 401(k) plans may actually serve as severance plans that help alleviate the costs associated with being out of work and changing jobs.

Other leakages from the 401(k) retirement vehicle also diminish needed accumulations. Many workers use 401(k) savings to pay for their children's education, household expenses, and housing needs. Although borrowing is often a consequence of broader weaknesses in the social safety net—low unemployment insurance benefits, the lack of health insurance, etc.—it nevertheless erodes the basic goal of pension plans, which is to help provide adequate retirement income.

The temptation regarding 401(k) borrowing applies not just to workers, but to policy makers as well. For example, Congress waived tax penalties for victims of Hurricane Katrina who withdrew assets from their 401(k) accounts. No one can deny the victims' financial desperation, but giving a devastated 45-year-old worker easier access to his or her 401(k) plan in autumn 2005 means possibly much lower income in 2025. Similarly situated victims who had defined-benefit accumulations will have more at retirement than 401(k) holders who borrowed from their plans in response to Katrina emergencies.[5]

Both DC and DB plan participants face default risk, which threatens adequate accumulation. Thousands of Enron employees and retirees collectively lost millions of dollars in their 401(k) plans when the firm, and its stock, collapsed. DB participants, while their benefits are partially protected by the Pension Benefit Guaranty Corporation (PBGC), the federal agency that insures benefits from DB plans, are not completely safe from such risk. Any employer sponsor could default on pensions, not pay early-retirement benefits, or stop valuable accumulations. Though the PBGC insures benefits from DB plans, which reduces the risk from employer default, the insurance does not cover all the benefits for high income workers, as the significant benefit reductions experienced by pilots at United and US Airways will attest. The PBGC insures benefits for single employer plan participants up to about $45,000 per year for a worker who retires at age 65. While this guaranteed benefit is correspondingly less for workers under age 65, it is something, compared to the situation for workers in a typical DC plan, who have no such protections at all.[6]

When workers and employers consistently contribute to 401(k) plans and there is no account leakage, there is a constant "accrual rate"—accumulation of assets at a constant rate—over the work lifetime. If a worker who continually participates in a DC plan wishes to continue to work for the current employer regardless of age, he or she keeps accruing benefits. In contrast, DB accruals increase sharply for older workers and then stop or slow down considerably when the worker reaches the plan's normal retirement age. Although the Department of the Treasury has recently issued regulations allowing the payment of "in service distributions"—receiving some pension benefits while still employed with a plan sponsor—everything else equal, there is less of an incentive to retire early under DC plans.

Workers also have to consider the risk that they may be separated from the employer sponsoring their pension plan, thus reducing the contributions to their plan. DC plans provide potentially greater protection than traditional DB plans from such unemployment risk. Under most DB plans, a worker's permanent separation from the covered firm prior to retirement can be disastrous for retirement benefits, because in most instances DB accruals for vested workers are frozen at the point of separation. This is a particular problem for young vested workers, who would be eligible for only a small benefit because of the low accrual patterns at younger ages in traditional DB plans. In the worst case, if a separated worker is not vested in the retirement plan, which typically requires five years of service, the worker receives nothing at retirement. Under a DC plan, vesting periods for employer contributions are typically far shorter, often only one year, and for employee contributions they are immediate. If a separated worker rolls over an account balance into another retirement account (but, as noted earlier, this is a big *if*, because many short-sighted workers use account balances for immediate consumption or other purposes), the DC benefit can still grow, even if the worker makes no additional contributions in future years.[7]

Investment Practices

DC plans place greater responsibility on the individual employee for choosing optimal investment strategies. In DB plans, professionals hired by the plan sponsor have that responsibility. Although some individual workers in DC plans pay for financial advice and although some sponsors may provide financial advice to their employees, many do not in fear of the liability for investment losses. In general, the evidence suggests that individuals in DC plans tend to make poor investment choices compared to DB plans, do not diversify enough, and trade either too much or too little.

Participants in DC plans also tend to have higher transaction costs, paying retail management fees for asset management while DB plan sponsors pay wholesale fees. The level of fees can crucially affect overall financial returns as workers are accumulating assets in their retirement portfolios: a fee of 1 percentage point can lower returns by 20%. In addition, individuals investing their own 401(k) plan assets select their asset allocations from a list of for-profit mutual funds, which are usually selected by the employer. The result is that typical fees charged to DC accounts can reduce account values by up to 21% to 30%, depending on the size of the account (Congressional Budget Office 2004).

DC plans also do not have the investment regulatory protections afforded to DB plan participants. For example, DB plan sponsors are typically prohibited from investing more than 10% of a plan's assets in the sponsor's own company, and the Department of Labor oversees a list of so-called prohibited transactions covering investment practices for DB plans. Participants in DC plans have no such protections, and sponsors also often provide the plan's matching contributions in the form of company stock. To the extent that DC participants may have a disproportionate amount of account assets in an employer's stock, they face the indirect but real danger that, should the employer experience a downturn, the company stock will decline in value at the same time that jobs and salary increases are at risk.

Payout Phase

DC and DB plans differ in the risks they present in the payout phase. "Longevity risk," or the risk of outliving one's money after retirement, is an important factor in DC plans. This risk can lead some retirees to severely restrict their spending, or to have a sudden drop in living standards at very old ages when the money runs out because they did not opt for a life annuity. A typical way to address longevity risk is to purchase an annuity that provides a steady stream of payments until the retiree dies. Social Security pays its old-age and other benefits in the form of an annuity.

Although DB plans can offer benefits as a lump sum (and an increasing number do), they are legally required to offer participants benefits as an annuity. The majority of DB plans still offer only that option. In contrast, although nothing prohibits sponsors from doing so, 401(k)-type and other DC plans have no requirement to offer participants an annuity option, and most DC plans pay out benefits in a lump sum. Unless initially provided their benefits in that form, the vast majority of retirees do not buy annuities with their retirement accounts, and they take on longevity, investment, financial, and inflation risks when they decide to take minimum distributions or any of the hundreds of other possible ways to spend down their financial assets. Even if a 401(k) plan participant chooses to purchase an annuity, DB plan sponsors can typically offer annuities more cheaply. The private annuities market remains quite small in the United States (General Accounting Office 1999). A participant seeking to purchase an annuity would find them to be expensive in the private market, due to adverse selection and the high administrative costs for small account balances. In fact, since retiree well-being is promoted as the primary public purpose for giving tax breaks for pension plans, a serious concern is the lack of an effective annuity market in the United States.

Annuities can provide real protection and peace of mind to retirees. Studies at Boston College (Bender and Jovan 2005) and by the Rand Corporation (Panis 2003) concluded that retirees are more secure and have a higher sense of well-being when their retirement income comes in the form of annuities. Annuities boost elderly persons' self-reported satisfaction by 6%, and having both a DB plan and a 401(k)-type plan boosts satisfaction even more, by 8%. However, having a 401(k)-type plan alone does not add to elderly persons' satisfaction. Being forced to retire decreased the level of satisfaction by 30%, and being in poor health by almost 20% (Bender and Jovan 2005). The reasonable interpretation is that the elderly would rather have an equivalent income coming from a DB plan or the combination of a DB and a DC plan, rather than just from a DC plan. This suggests that retiree satisfaction depends in part on minimizing risk, as well as on amount of income and wealth. This is borne out in the additional finding that having a supplement to Medicare or Medicaid health insurance coverage substantially increases satisfaction, even when the respondent is healthy.

Inflation is a payout risk that can pose a problem for both DB and DC plans. Annuities, if they are not inflation adjusted, have substantial inflation risk. Even a moderate annual inflation of 3% to 4% can halve the buying power of a 65-year-old's pension by the time he or she is 85. Yet few private-sector DB plans provide inflation-adjusted annuities. Retirees with a DC plan who receive good investment advice may be able to protect themselves from inflation through various investment strategies, although many retirees may be unwilling or unable to purchase such advice and even those who are may find it difficult to easily identify good investment advisers.

In sum, both DB and DC plans provide advantages to participants. With DB plans, the employer rather than the employee bears the risk of investment loss. In many ways, employers are often more able to bear this risk than individual workers. They typically have a longer time horizon, have more financial resources and larger account balances to invest, and can tap expert advice more easily. DB plans also typically pay annuities, and workers cannot access pension savings before retirement. Finally, DB plans are especially valuable to middle-aged workers, who are poised to experience the largest rates of accrual under traditional DB plans (Johnson and Uccello 2004). On the other hand, DC plans are attractive because they are well understood by workers and provide workers some control over their accounts. They also are portable, so to the extent that workers roll over their accounts, DC plans potentially provide some protection against the risk of unemployment. In addition, their constant accrual rates, while lower than the accrual rates received by older, long-tenured workers covered by a traditional DB plan, continue for as long as the employee continues to work, providing less of a disincentive to workers who wish to extend their careers beyond the plan's normal retirement age.

Public Policy Suggestions

The current debate over Social Security as well as the trends in pension design suggest that an implicit conflict exists between DB and DC retirement income vehicles and that increasingly, workers, employers, and the government must choose between the two. However, this is a false dichotomy. Ideally, workers should participate in both types of plans or at the very least have access to new plan designs that blend the strong suits of both.[8] Having both kinds of plans was common in the past, and even today, only a minority of workers covered by a DB have exclusive DB coverage, with most such workers also participating in a DC plan (Congressional Research Service 2004).

With the right kinds of policies, the United States can encourage plans with favorable characteristics of both DB and DC plans. For example, cash balance plans—which look like individual retirement or 401(k) accounts and whose values are expressed like them but for which employers invest the funds and bear all the performance risk—have increased in number over the last 20 years. In a cash balance plan, the sponsor guarantees a return on the employer's contributions and is obligated to pay the balance when the individual retires, and benefits are insured by the PBGC. Although cash balance plans express their benefit as an account total and often offer participants to take the benefit in a lump sum, cash balance plans are also required to offer an annuity option. In addition, the notional balances of the cash balance plans cannot be spent or borrowed against by the employee.

Cash balance plans have spawned considerable controversy. Over the last 10 years, many sponsors of traditional DB plans have converted them to cash balance plans. In many instances, workers, particularly older workers, lost expected benefits, as accrual patterns for cash balance plans favor younger employees over more senior ones (General Accounting Office 2000b). One recent district court case has ruled that such plans are age discriminatory, and the Internal Revenue Service has placed an effective moratorium on the applications for approval of cash balance plan designs (*Cooper v. IBM* 2003).

Yet it is not clear that there is anything intrinsically wrong with cash balance plans. Most of the controversy appears to stem from an unwillingness of at least some sponsors to provide sufficient transition protections to affected employees during plan conversions and with the general lack of generosity of the typical plan (Government Accountability Office 2005d). Cash balance plans, properly designed, could provide adequate benefits, for all workers and particularly for younger employees, and cash balance plans are under no requirement to offer a lump sum option. Some unions, like Communications Workers of America, have negotiated cash balance plans for some of their members.

The other major type of hybrid plan is over 70 years old: the DB multiemployer pension plan. Multiemployer plans, which cover approximately 20% of DB participants, exist in industries where workers are often skilled and mobile, such as mining, needle trades, trucking, and construction. TIAA-CREF, the largest pension plan in the United States, is a type of multiemployer plan that contains many DB and DC characteristics, covering research, university, and college professionals.

Through collective bargaining, US Airways and the union representing mechanics and other workers agreed to another DB plan after the old one was terminated in bankruptcy in the summer of 2005. When that single employer DB plan failed, the International Association of Machinists multiemployer plans stepped in as a replacement, offering better benefits than the airlines' proposed DC plans for the same contribution. The plan is more comparatively stable for the workers because it is a DB plan that includes the other airlines. These workers could lose their jobs at US Airways or any other airline, but as long as they obtain employment at another carrier participating in the plan, they could maintain active membership in the same pension plan.

In the late 1990s, a group of nurses in a New Jersey hospital finally achieved their longstanding demand to join the multiemployer pension plan of the hospital's operating engineers. Why a multiemployer plan? Why the operating engineers? The hospital had changed ownership so many times that each single-employer plan ended when another firm bought the hospital. The employees didn't move—it was the employers who were mobile. Joining the multiemployer plan—the only remaining plan at the site—allowed the nurses to build up credits in one DB plan and provide for a more secure retirement (Ghilarducci 2003).

Policy makers are concerned about individuals' ability to manage the new risks and responsibilities they face in planning their retirement, and the efficiency and equity implication is the $114-billion federal pension tax expenditure. So-called nondiscrimination rules require firms that provide benefits to higher-income employees to extend them to lower-income workers. However, despite these protections, lower-income DC plan participants still appear at a disadvantage. DB plans are often structured to automatically cover all workers and to pay benefits proportional to salary based on years of service. On the other hand, 401(k) plans tend to disproportionately benefit participants with higher incomes and more education because they receive better advice, have larger balances (and proportionately lower fees), and are more inclined to contribute to the plan (General Accounting Office 2004b). The median 401(k) balance for workers who earned $75,000 a year or more was $40,000, compared to $5,000 for workers who earned $25,000 a year or less. College graduates had account balances more than triple the $10,000 median for workers who did not graduate from high school (Munnell and Sundén 2004). The General Accounting Office (2001) analyzed how the increase in the contribution limits for DC contribution plans enacted in 2001 would be distributed. Only 8% of all DC participants would benefit from increasing the maximum contribution limit, and almost half of those people earned over $75,000 annually. DC plans tend to exacerbate existing income inequality among retirees. Besides being more financially able to contribute to DC plans, higher-income participants are also more likely to be well educated about investment issues generally and to have access to information about investment strategies and options.

There are, however, changes that can make DC plans more attractive to lower-income employees and encourage participation. For example, under the federal Thrift Saving Plan, the 401(k) portion of federal employees' pension plan, the employer match is structured so that all employees initially get 1% of their salary in the plan, regardless of their own contribution (even if it is 0). Such a requirement for private DC plans would likely dramatically increase participation, particularly by lower-income employees. The costs of the requirement would be somewhat mitigated because any new contributions would be tax deductible for the employer.

DC plans do have the advantage of greater portability. Even cash balance DB plans, touted for their benefit advantages to more mobile workers, generally have the same vesting requirements as traditional DB plans. The trick is to make DC plans function more like a pension. For example, incentives could be created to encourage DC plans to offer annuities and to discourage "leakage." New tax incentives could encourage annuitization, and perhaps private DC plan participants could be offered the right to purchase annuities at the same terms as those offered to federal or state employees. This could be coupled with some requirement for partial annuitization to ensure at least a poverty-level income, as was suggested during the Social Security reform debate. Taxes on early withdrawals could be increased substantially to further dissuade system leakages. Limits on the amount of company stock that can be held in an account and how much of an employer match can be offered as employee stock could be made comparable with the kinds of restrictions currently on DB plan sponsors. Finally, insurance proposals could be developed for DC plans to provide some benefit protections analogous to those enjoyed by participants covered in many DB plans. For example, it might be possible to offer participants some form of principal or benefit insurance, perhaps by the PBGC, in return for employees agreeing to certain guidelines regarding the investment of their accounts.

Conclusion

The U.S. system of retirement security is in transition. Though they never covered more than 40% of the workforce, private sector DB plans are declining. Social Security is under financial and political stress, and personal saving remains at record low levels. Proposals to transform the DB benefit of Social Security into a system of individual accounts have been fiercely debated since 1995. Despite their limitations in providing retirement benefits without significant reform, DC plans are here to stay, and they are likely to become the predominant plan design of the private occupational pension system, if they have not yet already become so. Given anemic savings rates among U.S. households, DC plans should be viewed in a positive light as potentially critical savings vehicles for retirement. In any case, the trends toward DCs and away from DBs are restructuring the retirement-income portfolio of U.S. workers. Both developments would require workers to actively manage their retirement investments and commit to accumulating assets solely for retirement purposes. Workers have to become more knowledgeable about investment choices and their needs over a much longer time horizon than most people are used to.

Too often the debate has been narrowly posed as an either/or proposition of DB versus DC. There is room, and in fact a need, for both types of retirement plans. At issue is how to foster the growth of both types and how to develop the incentives and regulatory protections to enhance the strengths of both while minimizing their deficiencies. At the minimum, it means addressing the real and long-term financial challenges facing Social Security in a way that protects and truly preserves its DB component. It means looking long and hard at how to ensure that DB plans are adequately financed and how to encourage new DB hybrid pension designs that do not harm the expected benefits of workers affected by sponsors' decisions to move existing plans to those designs. It means devising new incentives that at the very least do not push sponsors into exiting the DB system.

On the DC side, it also means a reconsideration of the "wild west," anything-goes regulatory framework that currently applies to these plans. Sensible protections that already govern the investment behavior of DB plan fiduciaries could be a good place to start, such as in the percentage of a portfolio allowed to be in company stock. Such a reconsideration also requires initiating a real dialogue among stakeholders on concerns like mandatory minimum contributions, incentives for at least partial annuitization, improved investment education, and some form of insurance on account balances. Ultimately, it matters less what vehicles we use to get to a reformed national system than simply that we ensure a secure retirement for all American workers and their families.

Notes

[1] The opinions expressed in this paper do not reflect the views of the U.S. Government Accountability Office.

[2] The federal Thrift Savings Plan (TSP) has often been cited as a possible model for providing a limited number of options that reduce risk and administrative costs while still providing some degree of choice to employees. However, a system of accounts that spans the entire national workforce and millions of employees would be significantly larger and more complex than TSP or any other system we have in place today (Government Accountability Office 2005c: p.15).

[3] In contrast, having access to stable sources of income, such as annuities (the form of payout that is required to be offered by DB plans), avoids this problem. In any case, hybrid DB plans, like cash balance plans, typically offer a lump sum feature as well as an annuity, and increasingly, many traditional DB plans are adding a lump sum option.

[4] In 2004, 56.4% of the private nonfarm workforce (133 million people) were offered a 401(k); only 72.9% participated, leaving about 20 million workers as

nonparticipants. That nonparticipation saved plan sponsors over $3,195,192,000, based on an average savings per nonparticipating worker of $156 (calculated by Choi, Madrian, and Laibson [2005] for a sample of over 800 employees). This number could be higher, since in one firm the employer saved over $250 per older worker who did not participate in the 401(k) even when eligible.

[5] The issue of temptation risk has also been a concern in the Social Security reform debate regarding individual accounts. Some analysts fear that future legislators will be unable to resist entreaties for participants to gain access to their individual accounts for similar worthwhile causes, leaving them with less for retirement.

[6] The PBGC has recently fallen into long-term financial difficulty for various reasons, including the termination of a number of large, underfunded plans by bankrupt sponsors. As of 2005, the agency had an accumulated deficit for its single employer program of over $22 billion. Like Social Security, the PBGC is not currently in crisis, but it faces insolvency down the road. The large deficit is not due immediately but is paid out in benefits over many years. However, premiums and accumulated assets are not sufficient to pay these benefits, and the current deficit can grow larger if, as expected, additional large underfunded plans are terminated by their financially weak sponsors. Furthermore, the benefits paid by the PBGC are not guaranteed by the federal government, although it is extremely likely that the government would pay them in the event that the PBGC became insolvent. Nevertheless, well over 90% of DB benefits owed to retirees by the PBGC are paid in full, and DB participants continue to enjoy far greater benefit protection than their DC counterparts. (See General Accounting Office 2003b and Government Accountability Office 2005d.)

[7] Recent proposals have been made to encourage automatic rollover of DC accounts when an employee changes jobs. (See Iwry and John 2006.)

[8] Cash balance plans, the great DB hope of the last decade, appear to be falling short of expectations. Legal uncertainties about their legality with regard to age discrimination appear to have eroded their popularity, at least among employers and some experts. (See General Accounting Office 2000c.)

References

Bell, Elizabeth, Adam Carasso, and C. Eugene Steuerle. 2005. "Strengthening Private Sources of Retirement Savings for Low-Income Families." Opportunity and Ownership Project Brief #5. Washington, DC: Urban Institute. <http:www.urban.org/url.cfm?ID=311229>. [Accessed May 6, 2006.]

Bender, Keith A., and Natalia A. Jovan. 2005. "What Makes Retirees Happy?" Issues in Brief #28. Boston: Center for Retirement Research, Boston College. <http://www.bc.edu/centers/crr/ib_28.shtml>. [Accessed May 6, 2006.]

Bosworth, Barry, and Lisa Bell. 2005. "The Decline in Saving: What Can We Learn from Survey Data?" Unpublished draft written for the 7th Annual Joint Conference of the Retirement Research Consortium, "Creating a Secure Retirement" (Washington, DC, August 11–12, 2005). <http://www.bc.edu/centers/crr/dummy/seventh_annual.shtml>. [Accessed May 6, 2006.]

Budd, John. "Non-Wage Forms of Compensation." Journal of Labor Research (Fall 2004): 598.

Bureau of the Census. 2006. Current Population Survey. <http://222.bls.census.gov/cps>. [Accessed May 7, 2006.]

Butrica, Barbara A., Howard M. Iams, and Karen E. Smith. 2003. "It's All Relative: Understanding the Retirement Prospects of Baby-Boomers." Working Paper #2003–21. Boston, MA: Center for Retirement Research, Boston College. <http://www.bc.edu/centers/crr/dummy/wp_2003-21.shtml>. [Accessed March 5, 2005.]

Carlson, Leah. 2005. "States Continue as Mainstay for DB Pensions." *Employee Benefit News*, June 1. <http://www.benefitnews.com/retire/detail.cfm?id= 7555&arch=1>. [Accessed May 6, 2006.]

Choi, James J., David Laibson, and Brigitte Madrian. 2005. "$100 Bills on the Sidewalk: Suboptimal Saving in 401(k) Plans." Prepared for the 7th Annual Joint Conference of the Retirement Research Consortium, "Creating a Secure Retirement" (Washington, DC, August 11–12, 2005). <http://www.bc.edu/centers/crr/ papers/Seventh_Paper/Choi2.pdf>. [Accessed August 15, 2005.]

Clowes, Michael. 2004. "The Long Road to Extinction." *Pensions and Investments*, Vol. 32, no. 16 (August 10), pp. 8–11.

Congressional Budget Office. 2004. *Administrative Costs of Private Accounts in Social Security*. Washington, DC: CBO. <http://www.cbo.gov/showdoc.cfm? index=5277&sequence=0>. [Accessed May 7, 2006.]

Congressional Research Service. 2004. *Retirement Savings and Household Wealth: A Summary of Recent Data, June 27, 2004*. Table 1, p. 4.

Congressional Research Service. 2004. *Pension Sponsorship and Participation: Summary of Recent Trends*. Report for Congress Number: RL30122, September 10.

Cooper v. IBM Pers. Pension Plan, F. Supp 2d. 1010 (S.D. Ill. 2003).

Diamond, Peter A., and Peter R. Orszag. 2003. *Saving Social Security: A Balanced Approach*. Washington, DC: Brookings Institution Press.

Employee Benefit Research Institute. 2004. *Will Americans Ever Become Savers? The 14th Retirement Confidence Survey, 2004*. Issue Brief #268 (April). Washington, DC: EBRI. <http://www.ebri.org/publications/ib/index.cfm? fa=ibDisp&content_id=496>.

Frieswick, Kris. 2002. "Honey, I Shrunk the 401(k)." *CFO Magazine*, August 1. <http://www.cfo.com/article.cfm/3005808?f=search>. [Accessed May 6, 2006.]

Gebhardtsbauer, Ron. 2004. "What Are the Trade-Offs? Defined Benefit Vs. Defined Contribution Systems." *AARP/CEPS Forum—A Balancing Act: Achieving Adequacy and Sustainability in Retirement Income Reform*. (Brussels, March 4, 2004). <http://www.actuary.org/pdf/pension/tradeoffs_030404.pdf>. [Accessed January 16, 2006.]

General Accounting Office. 1997. *401(k) Pension Plans: Loan Provisions Enhance Participation But May Affect Income Security for Some*. HEHS-98-5. Washington, DC: GAO.

———. 1999. *Social Security Reform: Implications of Private Annuities for Individual Accounts*. HEHS-99-160. Washington, DC: GAO.

———. 2000a. *Pension Plans: Characteristics of Persons in the Labor Force without Pension Coverage*. HEHS-00-131. Washington, DC: GAO.

———. 2000b. *Private Pensions: Implications of Conversions to Cash Balance Plans*. HEHS-00-185. Washington, DC: GAO.

———. 2000c. *Cash Balance Plans: Implications for Retirement Income*. HEHS-00-207. Washington, DC: GAO.

———. 2001. *Private Pensions: Issues of Coverage and Increasing Contribution Limits for Defined Contribution Plans*. GAO-01-846. Washington, DC: GAO.

————. 2003a. *Social Security Reform: Analysis of a Trust Fund Exhaustion Scenario Illustrates the Difficult Choices and the Need for Early Action.* GAO-03-1038T. Washington, DC: GAO.

————. 2003b. *Pension Benefit Guaranty Corporation: Single Employer Pension Insurance Program Faces Long-Term Risks.* GAO-04-90. Washington, DC: GAO.

Government Accountability Office. 2004a. *Private Pensions: Multiemployer Plans Face Short- and Long-Term Challenges.* GAO-04-423. Washington, DC: GAO.

————. 2004b. *Social Security: Distribution of Benefits and Taxes Relative to Earnings Level.* GAO-04-747. Washington, DC: GAO.

————. 2005a. *Social Security Reform: Analysis of a Trust Fund Exhaustion Scenario.* GAO-03-907. Washington, DC: GAO.

————. 2005b. *Private Pensions: Recent Experiences of Large Defined Benefit Plans Illustrate Weaknesses in Funding Rules.* GAO-05-294. Washington, DC: GAO.

————. 2005c. *Social Security Reform: Considerations for Individual Account Design.* GAO-05-847T. Washington, DC: GAO.

————. 2005d. *Private Pensions: Information on Cash Balance Pension Plans.* GAO-06-42. Washington, DC: GAO.

Ghilarducci, Teresa. 2003. "Delinking Employee Benefits from a Single Employer: Alternative Multiemployer Models." In David S. Blitzstein, Olivia S. Mitchell, Michael Gordon, and Judith F. Mazo, eds., *Benefits for the Workplace of the Future.* Philadelphia: University of Pennsylvania Press, pp. 260–84.

Ghilarducci, Teresa, and Wei Sun. "How Defined Contribution Plans and 401(k)s Affect Employer Pension Costs: 1981–1998." Unpublished paper. Submitted to the *Journal of Pension Economics and Finance*, January 1, 2005. <www.nd.edu/~tghilard; see #6 under "Recent Papers.">

Ghilarducci, Teresa, Wei Sun, and Steve Nyce. 2004. "Employer Pension Contributions and 401(k) Plans: A Note." *Industrial Relations*, Vol. 43, no. 2 (April), pp. 473–79.

Ippolito, Richard. 2001. "Reversion Taxes, Contingent Benefits, and Pension Funding." *Journal of Law and Economics*, Vol. 44 (Spring), p. 199.

Iwry, Mark J., and David C. John. 2006. *Retirement Security Project.* Washington DC: Brookings Institution, February.

Johnson, Richard W., and Cori E. Uccello. 2004. "Cash Balance Plans: What Do They Mean for Retirement Security?" *National Tax Journal*, Vol. 57, no. 2 (June), pp. 315–28.

Johnson, Richard. 2004. "Job Demand Among Older Workers." *Monthly Labor Review* (July) pp. 48–56.

McCaw, Daniel. 2004. "Strengthening Pension Security for All Americans: Are Workers Prepared for a Safe and Secure Retirement?" Testimony before the U.S. House of Representatives Committee on Education and the Workforce (February 25, 2004).

Mitchell, Olivia, S. Stephen P. Utkus, and Tongxuan Yang. 2005. "Turning Workers into Savers? Incentives, Liquidity, and Choice in 401(k) Plan Design." Working Paper No. W11726 (October). Cambridge, MA: National Bureau of Economic Research.

Munnell, Alicia H. 2003. "The Declining Role of Social Security." *Just the Facts on Retirement Issues*, JTF#6. Boston: Center for Retirement Research, Boston College.

Munnell, Alicia H., and Annika Sundén. 2003. "Suspending the Employer 401(k) Match." *Issues in Brief*, IB #12. Boston: Center for Retirement Research, Boston College. <http://www.bc.edu/centers/crr/ib_12.shtml>. [Accessed January 10, 2006.]

Munnell, Alicia H., and Annika Sundén. 2004. *Coming Up Short: The Challenge of 401(k) Plans*. Washington, DC: Brookings Institution Press.

Munnell, Alicia H., Francesca Golub-Sass, and Andrew Varani. 2005. "How Much Are Workers Saving?" *Issues in Brief*, IB #34. Boston: Center for Retirement Research, Boston College. <http://www.bc.edu/centers/crr/ib_34.shtml>. [Accessed December 10, 2005.]

National Compensation Survey. Various years: employee benefits in private industry, authors' computations from data available on the website. <www.bls.gov/ncs/ebs>

Panis, C. 2003. *Annuities and Retirement Satisfaction 2003*. RAND Labor and Population Program, DRU-3021. <http://www.rand.org/labor/DRU/DRU3021.pdf>.

Purcell, Patrick. 2005a. "Pension Sponsorship and Participation: Summary of Recent Trends" (Findings from the Domestic Social Policy Division). *CRS Report* #RL30122. Washington, DC: Congressional Research Service.

Purcell, Patrick. 2005b. "Retirement Plan Participation and Contributions: Trends from 1998 to 2003" (Findings from Domestic Social Policy Division). *CRS Report* #RL33116. Washington, DC: Congressional Research Service.

Rappaport, Anna. 2004. "Retirement Perspective: Exploding the Myth that Employees Always Prefer Defined Contribution Plans." May 20. <http://www.mercerhr.com/knowledgecenter/reportsummary.jhtml/dynamic/idContent/1138485>. [Accessed October 10, 2005.]

Social Security Administration. 2004. *Income of the Population 55 and Older, 2002*. <http://www.ssa.gov/policy/docs/statcomps/income_pop55/2002/index.html#toc>. [Accessed February 20, 2006.]

Social Security Administration. 2006. *Annual Report of the Board of Trustees of the Federal Old-Age and Survivors Insurance and Disability Insurance Trust Funds*. Washington, DC: SSA. <http://www.ssa/gov/OACT/TR/>. [Accessed May 7, 2006.]

Turner, John, and Dana Muir. 2005. "Longevity and Retirement Age in Defined Benefit Pension Plans." In John Turner and Teresa Ghilarducci, eds. *Work Options for Older Americans*. Forthcoming. South Bend, IN: Notre Dame Press.

Vanguard Group. 2004. *Expectations for Retirement: A Survey of Retirement Investors*. Valley Forge, PA: Vanguard Center for Retirement Research.

Vanguard Group. 2005. "Create Your Own Personal Pension Plan With an Income Annuity. <http://www.vanguard.com> [Accessed October 15, 2005.]

Watson Wyatt Worldwide. 2004. "Traditional Pension Plans Outperformed 401(k) Plans during Last Bear Market, Watson Wyatt Analysis Finds." Press release, November 22. <http://www.watsonwyatt.com/news/press.asp?ID=13953>. [Accessed February 20, 2006.]

Watson Wyatt Worldwide. 2005. "Recent Funding and Sponsorship Trends among the *FORTUNE* 1000." *Insider* (June). <http://www.watsonwyatt.com/us/pubs/insider/showarticle.asp?ArticleID=14750>. [Accessed February 20, 2006.]

Weller, Christian. 2005. *Ensuring Retirement Income Security with Cash Balance Plans*. Washington, DC: Center for American Progress.

Weller, Christian, and Edward N. Wolff. 2005. *Retirement Income: The Crucial Role of Social Security*. Washington, DC: Economic Policy Institute.

CHAPTER 8

Disability, Work, and Return to Work

SOPHIE MITRA
Fordham University

DAVID STAPLETON
Cornell University

Disability is a substantial phenomenon in the United States. Based
on the 2003 American Community Survey, 11.9% of the prime working-age population (ages 25 to 62) has a disability of some sort, including 6.9% who report a condition that limits the amount or kind of work
they can do, or work limitation (Weathers 2005). The disparity in
poverty status, employment, and earnings between persons with and
without disabilities is well established. The poverty rate among prime
working-age persons with any reported disability stands at 23.7%. It is
even higher for those with work limitations—29.6%—compared with
7.7% for those without disabilities (Weathers 2005). The employment
rate for men with disabilities is 43.4%, and for men with work limitations just 20.8%, compared to 87.1% for men without disabilities; the
corresponding percentages for women are 35.5%, 17.2%, and 72.2%,
respectively (Weathers 2005).

Understanding the labor market experiences of persons with disabilities is essential for persons with disabilities, disability advocates, and
policy makers alike. This chapter presents recent developments and
research findings regarding employment and disability. This topic is
broad; we will address selected issues that have recently been occupying
center stage in research and policy debates regarding disability, work,
and return to work. The first section reviews several important aspects of
the labor market experience of persons with disabilities, including
employment trends, working hours, and discrimination in hiring, retention, promotion, and compensation. The second section presents the
institutional background of the employment of persons with disabilities
and assesses how it may have influenced employment trends. The third
section presents recent research results on return to work, and the
fourth section focuses on disability management. The last section has

251

some concluding remarks and points toward new policy directions that may promote the employment of persons with disabilities.

Employment among Persons with Disabilities

Researchers need appropriate data to identify the population with disabilities and to measure its employment and the outcomes of disability and work policies. This has been challenging because disability is inherently difficult to define. Historically, definitions have been based on a medical model, under which disability is considered a characteristic of the individual and interventions center on solving the medical challenges the person faces. In contrast, the now widely accepted social model posits that disability results from the interaction between the individual and the individual's environment: persons with impairments are considered to have disabilities only if they are limited in their participation in society, for instance, through limited access to employment and education. Empirically, this has implications for following employment trends, work hours, and the type of work done by persons with disabilities.

Employment Trends

The United States Bureau of the Census, for instance, has developed criteria based on questions in the Current Population Survey (CPS) to measure the official employment rate, average household income, and poverty rates of the United States population by age, sex, race/ethnicity, and education. (See Table 1 for the list of acronyms used throughout the chapter.) The CPS includes measures of disability,

TABLE 1
Acronyms

Acronym	Definition
ADA	Americans with Disabilities Act
CPS	Current Population Survey
EPE	Extended Period of Eligibility
FMLA	Family and Medical Leave Act
LSVRSP	Longitudinal Study of the Vocational Rehabilitation Services Program
NHIS	National Health Interview Survey
SIPP	Survey of Income and Program Participation
SGA	Substantial Gainful Activity
SSA	Social Security Administration
SSDI	Social Security Disability Insurance
SSI	Supplemental Security Income
VR	Vocational Rehabilitation

which are based on work limitations. Burkhauser, Daly, et al. (2002) show that work limitation measures from the CPS significantly underestimate the number of persons in the broader population with impairments. In addition, work limitation–based definitions are likely to be sensitive to changes in the social environment of work, such as the strength of the economy, work incentives/disincentives created by public policy, and other policy initiatives, including the Americans with Disabilities Act. Controversy over the definition of disability has led some researchers to argue that the measures based on CPS work limitations cannot be used to reliably estimate the employment of working age persons with disabilities (Hale 2001). Nevertheless, Burkhauser, Daly, et al. (2002) and Burkhauser, Houtenville, and Wittenburg (2003) have shown that the employment trends of persons with work limitations measured in the CPS are very similar to those for the broader population of persons with impairments, based on the National Health Interview Survey (NHIS), as well as for the population of persons with functional limitations, based on the Survey of Income and Program Participation (SIPP). They conclude that, while imperfect, the CPS can be used to capture trends in economic success.

Figure 1 plots the employment rates for men and women with and without work limitations based on CPS data from 1981 through 2002. Figure 2 presents the employment rates for men and women with activity limitations based on NHIS data from 1970 through 2001. While looking

FIGURE 1
Employment Rates, 1981–2002, Based on CPS Data

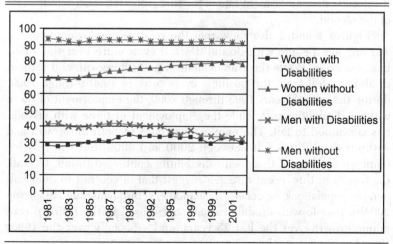

FIGURE 2
Employment Rates, 1970–2001, Based on NHIS Data

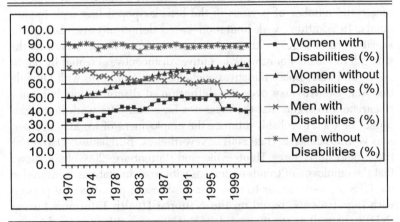

at the figures, it is important to keep in mind that during the periods covered, the United States experienced two major business cycles—1979 through 1989 and 1989 through 2000. Based on CPS data and confirmed with NHIS and SIPP data (Burkhauser, Houtenville and Wittenberg 2003), the employment rates of working age people with and without disabilities were procyclical over this first business cycle, falling over the recession years of the early 1980s and rising over the long period of growth from 1982 through 1989. However, the rise in the employment of those with disabilities was not as great as for those without, so over the decade the employment rate of the first group fell relative to the rate of the second.

Figures 1 and 2 also show that the relative employment rate of working age people with disabilities fell even more over the 1990s business cycle. While the employment of both those with and without disabilities fell from the business cycle peak of 1990 through 1993, during the growth years 1993 through 2000, the employment of those without disabilities rose while the employment of those with disabilities continued to fall. The employment rates of both those with and without disabilities fell between 2000 and 2003, but the relative employment rate of those with disabilities continued to fall. Overall, the results of this recent research suggest that in contrast to most vulnerable populations, especially single mothers (Burkhauser and Stapleton 2004b), people with disabilities have not shared in the fruits of economic growth over the last 25 years, and especially over the 1990s (Burkhauser and Stapleton 2004a).

Work Hours

For persons with disabilities who work, recent research has attempted to establish trends in work hours and type of work. In particular, much attention has been paid to the prevalence of part-time and contingent work among persons with disabilities. As noted by Oi (1978), "disability steals time." People with disabilities often need flexibility in work schedules or other job characteristics to deal with health concerns, therapy schedules, transportation, care, and other issues. Contingent, flexible, and part-time work arrangements, which often provide some flexibility in whether and when to work, may therefore be attractive to persons with disabilities. At the same time, there is an association between part-time and contingent employment on the one hand and less stable jobs with lower pay and benefits on the other (Kruse and Schur 2002; Schur 2002). A literature has recently emerged that looks at the incidence and nature of part-time employment among persons with disabilities and attempts to clarify whether persons with disabilities prefer or are constrained into part-time and contingent work arrangements.

Using data from the CPS from 1981 onward, Hotchkiss (2004b) finds that the rate of part-time work is increasing much faster among persons with disabilities than among persons without, and that this increase in part-time work is primarily voluntary. The author notes that part-time work may have become more attractive to disabled workers. The Occupational Information Network Database was used to look at descriptions for various jobs. It was found that relatively speaking, part-time jobs are not becoming qualitatively "more attractive." The author points to positive changes in policy as a possible cause for this increased part-time employment. Relevant changes include employers' accommodations for part-time work for disabled workers under the ADA, the extension of Medicaid benefits beyond Supplemental Security Income (SSI) eligibility through the Medicaid buy-in, and a 1999 increase in the earnings allowances for most SSI and Social Security Disability Insurance (SSDI) recipients.

In addition, using the 1995–2001 Contingent Work Supplements of the CPS, Schur (2003) shows that 44% of workers with work disabilities are in some contingent or part-time employment arrangement, compared to only 22% of those without work disabilities. Such jobs can allow SSDI recipients to stay under the earnings limit in order to maintain their benefits. However, the analysis showed this factor to be minor in the higher prevalence of these types of jobs among people with disabilities. Both the qualitative interviews and quantitative analysis identified health issues as the most important factor in explaining the high prevalence.

Home-based work, including telecommuting, is an additional form of flexible arrangement. Such work can be especially appropriate for people with mobility impairments or those who need to be near medical equipment. Analysis of the 2001 Work Schedules Supplement of the CPS shows that about one eighth (12.7%) of workers reporting work disabilities do home-based work for pay, significantly higher than the 8.4% figure for those not reporting work disabilities[1]. In addition, home-based work for pay increased more rapidly during the 1990s among people with work disabilities than among all other workers (Kruse and Schur 2002). The expansion in home-based work is driven largely by developments in computers and other information technology, which can have special benefits for people with disabilities.

Discrimination in Hiring, Retention, Promotion, and Compensation

As explained by Schur, Kruse, and Blanck (2005), employer discrimination against current or potential employees with disabilities may take different forms. Beyond wage discrimination (described below), personnel managers and supervisors may be personally uncomfortable around persons with disabilities, and this discomfort may be manifested in a reluctance to hire, retain, or promote. Employers may believe that a worker with a disability will not be well accepted by co-workers or customers and as a result will be less productive in some situations. In addition, employers may have stereotypes about the types of jobs that are appropriate for persons with certain types of disabilities, and they may have strong biases about the potential for further human-capital development of workers with disabilities.

Although much discrimination has its roots in simple prejudice, some is also statistical in origin. Because it is difficult to assess the capabilities of job applicants, employers look at any signals that, based on their knowledge, are correlated with productivity. Rightly or wrongly, most statistics suggest that workers with disabilities are less productive than workers without disabilities, so in the absence of more complete information about an individual applicant, an employer is likely to assume that an applicant with a disability will be less productive than an applicant without one, other things constant. Employers may also perceive that trying to assess the prospective productivity of a worker with a disability is particularly difficult, as productivity will vary with the particular disability, its severity, the exact requirements of each job, and the nature of potential accommodations. It may require more effort on an employer's part to make a good match between a worker with a disability and a particular job, and it may not be possible to adequately resolve uncertainty about a match's appropriateness prior to an actual employment commitment.

What empirical evidence exists regarding discrimination against persons with disabilities? A 1999 survey found that 22% of private sector employers reported that attitudes and stereotypes were a barrier to employment of people with disabilities in their own firms (Bruyère 2000). In addition, among employers who made changes to enhance the employment of people with disabilities, 32% said that it was difficult or very difficult to change supervisor and co-worker attitudes. A more recent nationally representative survey of private businesses found that 20% of employers said the greatest barrier to employment for people with disabilities is discrimination, prejudice, or employer reluctance to hire (Dixon, Kruse, and Van Horn 2003). These surveys show that a substantial share of employers believe that employer, supervisor, and co-worker attitudes are a significant problem. However, these results may underestimate the true extent of discrimination because "social desirability" bias discourages survey respondents from reporting prejudicial attitudes. There is also evidence that there are strong biases about the aspirations and potential for human-capital development. In 13 laboratory experiments, 10 found that evaluators were overly pessimistic about the future performance and promotion potential of workers with disabilities (Colella, DeNisi, and Varma 1998).

Finally, some researchers attribute a substantial share of the gap between the wages of persons with and without disabilities to discrimination. Baldwin and Johnson (2005) reached this conclusion in reviewing the dozen studies conducted in the past 15 years on wage discrimination based on disability (e.g., Baldwin and Johnson 2000). Among the variety of techniques used by these studies, several adjusted for productivity-related worker characteristics and then related the remaining gaps to measures of stigma for different types of disabilities. In general, however, it is not possible to determine what share of wage differences not explained by observable characteristics is due to discrimination rather than other unobserved characteristics that may be correlated with disability (e.g., the ability of the individual to work quickly or to work intensively for long periods).

The Institutional Environment

Various laws and programs are designed, at least in part, to positively affect the employment of persons with disabilities. The major laws over the past three decades are the ADA (Title I) of 1990, the Workforce Investment Act of 1998, the Individuals with Disabilities Education Act of 1997, and the Rehabilitation Act of 1973[2]. There are also myriad disability compensation programs, including employer-provided disability insurance, compensation programs for injury on the job (workers' compensation, veterans' compensation), means-tested programs (SSI, veterans' pensions), and the SSDI program. Some people with disabilities also receive cash or near-cash benefits from programs that are designed for larger low-income populations, most notably Temporary Assistance for Needy Families and food stamps. It is not possible to present a comprehensive picture of the institutional environment in this chapter. Instead we cover selected pieces of the institutional framework and how they may impact the employment of persons with disabilities, including one piece of legislation, the ADA, and selected disability benefit programs (workers' compensation, private disability insurance, SSDI, and SSI).[3]

ADA and Its Impact on Employment

The ADA, signed into law on July 26, 1990, and fully implemented over the subsequent two years, is the most important legislation affecting employer–employee relations for persons with disabilities. The ADA extended the same civil rights protections to individuals with disabilities as those already provided on the basis of race, sex, national origin, and religion. However, two features of the ADA make it qualitatively different than other civil rights protections. First, the membership of individuals in the protected class is much more difficult to determine. Any "qualified individual with a disability" is covered. The person must have "a physical or mental impairment that substantially limits one or more major life activities, has a record of such an impairment, or is regarded as having such an impairment." A person is qualified if he or she can perform the essential functions of the position in question, with or without reasonable accommodation. The exact meanings of the terms describing the protected class have been the subject of many court cases since the ADA's passage. Second, in addition to antidiscrimination provisions, the ADA requires most employers to make "reasonable accommodation" for disability in the workplace. Private establishments with 15 or more employees, state and local governments, employment agencies, and labor unions are all subject to the accommodation requirements. This requirement potentially imposes costs on the employer. In many instances these costs might be quite small relative to the employee's compensation, but some costs are potentially large and perhaps hidden (e.g., accommodations in scheduling).

The empirical research attempting to determine the ADA's effects on employment has produced mixed results[4]. A series of early studies linked the decline in employment of people with disabilities to the passage and implementation of the ADA. There are, in fact, plausible reasons why a law that was partly intended to increase employment of people with disabilities—by reducing employment discrimination, increasing access to the workplace, and changing perceptions about the ability of people with disabilities to be productive workers—could have the opposite effect. One reason is that employers can avoid the cost of potential litigation concerning termination and other personnel decisions simply by not hiring people with disabilities, a situation made feasible by the fact that it is very difficult to detect and litigate against discrimination in hiring. A second reason is that the ADA imposed costs on employers through its mandate for reasonable accommodations, providing additional motivation to avoid hiring employees with disabilities.

The timing of the initial decline in most employment statistics for people with disabilities appears to coincide with the passage of the ADA, lending substantial credibility to the hypothesis that the two are linked. Two largely independent analyses, using similar methods but different data sets, concluded that the ADA was the most likely cause of the decline. Using SIPP data, De Leire (2000) documents a decline in the employment of men with disabilities since the passage of the ADA, in particular in manufacturing, managerial, and blue-collar occupations. De Leire argues that employment rates for men with disabilities have fallen since the ADA was enacted and concludes that the reasonable accommodations mandate is a new barrier to employment. Using CPS data, Acemoglu and Angrist (2001) show a sharp drop after the ADA went into effect in the employment of persons with disabilities aged 21 to 39. They also found a post-ADA decline in the employment of men with disabilities aged 40 to 58, but no clear evidence of an effect on women aged 40 to 58.

More recent studies have reached very different conclusions, however. Kruse and Schur (2003) take issue with the definition of disability used in the studies by De Leire (2000) and Acemoglu and Angrist (2001). Presumably the impact of the ADA on employment would be greatest for those who would qualify as disabled under the act. The court's narrow interpretation of the ADA, and the inherent challenge in defining disability, makes it difficult for researchers to identify the relevant population to assess the law's effectiveness, and they may also mean that any effects of the ADA spill over to people with disabilities who do not meet the ADA definition. Kruse and Schur define disability outside the context of a self-reported work limitation, instead focusing on individuals' reported functional limitations in daily life activities. They narrow their group to people who say they are not prevented from working, arguing that they are most likely to meet the ADA definition of disability. They find that people in this group improved their relative employment levels in the early 1990s. This analysis does not address the fact that the proportion of persons with functional limitations who say they are not prevented from working declined during the same period.

Houtenville and Burkhauser (2004) differentiated individuals with "long-term" disabilities (disabilities reported in each of two CPS interviews conducted 12 months apart) from those with "short-term" disabilities (reported in just one of the two interviews). They find that the decline in employment for people with long-term disabilities began in the mid-1980s, several years prior to the passage of the ADA. Jolls and Prescott (2004) compared changes at the state level in the employment of people with disabilities before and after enactment of the ADA and analyzed three groups of states with respect to their disability rights laws pre-ADA: those that had laws with provisions similar to the ADA's antidiscrimination and accommodation mandates; those that had laws with antidiscrimination provisions only; and those that had no disability rights laws. The study found no employment declines for people with disabilities in the states with ADA-like laws, and only short-term declines in states with no laws or only antidiscrimination laws. After three to four years, however, differences across these three groups of states disappeared. The authors conclude that the introduction of accommodation mandates might initially have had a negative impact, while employers made workplaces accessible and learned how to provide accommodations, but once these initial employer investments were in place, any such impact disappeared. The antidiscrimination provisions of the ADA apparently had no impact, consistent with the findings from earlier research on the impact of the Civil Rights Act on the employment of African Americans (Leonard 1990; Donohue and Heckman 1991).

Social Security Disability Insurance and Supplementary Security Income

Beyond employer-provided disability insurance and workers' compensation, two large federal disability benefit programs directly serve the population of persons with disabilities and affect their employment: SSDI and SSI. SSDI entitlement is earned through past employment. Termination discontinues not only cash benefits but also Medicare benefits following an extended period of eligibility (Social Security Administration 2003). SSI is a welfare program, open to anyone meeting the disability test and having income and assets below thresholds. In both programs, disability is defined as "the inability to engage in any substantial gainful activity by reason of any medically determinable physical or mental impairment which can be expected to result in death or which has lasted or can be expected to last, for a continuous period of not less than 12 months" (Social Security Administration 2003). In addition, the definition specifies that for a person to be determined to be disabled, the impairment must be of such severity that he or she not only is unable to do previous work but is also unable to do any other kind of substantial work that exists in the national economy given his or her age, education, and work experience. The Social Security Administration (SSA) contracts with state disability-determination service agencies to determine whether applicants are disabled.

Since its inception in 1956, the SSDI program has gone through several phases of expansions and retrenchments, described in detail in Goodman and Waidman (2003). During the early and mid-1970s, the size grew sharply, leading to concern that the program was fiscally unsustainable and attracting persons with mild or moderate disabilities. The enactment of the Social Security Disability Amendment of 1980 marked the beginning of a retrenchment period. The amendment required the SSA to conduct continuing disability reviews of all recipients to assess whether they have medically recovered and to certify their continuing eligibility. In 1984, with the Disability Benefits Reform Act, "Congress loosened the reins again" (Goodman and Waidmann 2003). The act made it easier for persons with psychiatric impairments and chronic pain to qualify for benefits and made it more difficult for the SSA to terminate recipients based on medical recovery. In addition to regulatory changes affecting eligibility, the SSDI replacement rate (benefits paid relative to a measure of past earnings) for low-skill workers increased substantially in the 1980s and 1990s, because benefits are indexed to mean wage growth, and wages of low-skill workers grew at a below-average rate. Figure 3 presents the time series of the numbers of recipients (disabled only) on SSDI and SSI. The graph shows the different phases of expansions and retrenchments of the SSDI program that were described earlier.

There is substantial evidence that the expansions in the SSA's income support programs are the major cause of the employment decline for persons with disabilities. Bound and Waidmann (2002) found that the growth of SSDI tracks the employment of people with disabilities very closely at both national and state levels. Autor and Duggan (2003) showed that the number of SSDI recipients has responded to changes in eligibility criteria and program generosity. They also found that employment of people with disabilities became much more sensitive to the business cycle during the period after the 1984 amendments. They

FIGURE 3
Growth in Social Security Disability Benefit Rolls, 1974–2003

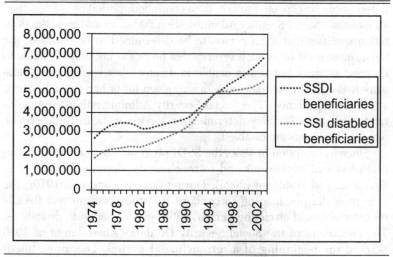

argue that the 1984 amendments expanded the pool of "contingent applicants," workers who might qualify for benefits if they were not working but who would have to quit their jobs to apply. Presumably some of these workers apply for benefits when they lose their jobs due to a recession. Autor and Duggan's hypothesis is further supported by Black, Daniel, and Sanders (2002), who found that SSDI applications became much more sensitive to the business cycle before the expansions, suggesting that when an economic downturn occurs, more workers with disabilities opt to exit the labor force and enter the SSDI program rather than return to work. Further support for this hypothesis is provided by Stapleton, Wittenburg, and Maag (2005), who inferred from an econometric analysis of SIPP data linked to SSA administrative data that about 15% of beneficiaries entering the SSDI rolls during the early 1990s were workers with disabilities who were induced to enter by the recession.

The evidence also indicates that the employment decline and increase in SSDI participation are both greatest for two groups of workers: those with conditions that were especially affected by the post-1984 changes in eligibility rules (mostly mental illnesses and certain musculoskeletal conditions) and those with low skills, whose benefit levels increased relative to their wages as a result of how SSDI benefits are indexed to wage growth. Finally, the recent finding by Houtenville and Burkhauser (2004) that the decline in employment for those with long-term disabilities began in the mid-1980s addresses this point more directly. To meet SSA medical eligibility criteria, an individual's condition must last for at least 12 months, so the employment statistics for those with long-term disabilities (i.e., at least 12 months) referred to earlier are more relevant to the role of the disability programs than other employment statistics; the latter invariably include a mix of people with short- and long-term disabilities. It appears that the decline in employment for the long-term group began shortly after the eligibility expansions were initiated.

Of course, the evidence about the effects of changes in the SSA programs on employment does not rule out other possible causes. After all, any change external to the SSA programs that reduces employment for people with disabilities is likely to increase the number who receive support from SSA programs. At the present time, however, there is no convincing evidence to counter the conclusion that expansions in SSA programs are the major cause of the decline in the employment rate of persons with disabilities. Although it may be the benefit expansions of the type witnessed after 1984 that reduced the employment of people with disabilities, that does not mean that such expansions are undesirable from a policy perspective. Declines in the productivity of people with disabilities may be considered to be a social cost of such expansions, but those costs have to be weighed against the possible social gains. Few would argue that those covered under the expanded eligibility definitions are worthy of public support, and improvements in their well-being may be a social benefit that more than outweighs the social cost. Perhaps the more challenging policy issue is whether it is possible to provide support to this same population in a way that encourages their efforts to support themselves, rather than discouraging them (Stapleton, O'Day, et al. 2005). This issue is becoming a pressing one as projected federal budget deficits threaten future funding for SSDI and SSI (Goodman and Stapleton 2005).

Employer-Provided Disability Insurance

Employer-provided disability insurance falls into three broad categories. *Sick leave* is paid time off while a person recovers from illness or injury that is not work related. *Short-term benefits* provide for salary replacement, often partial, for a 6- to 12-month period. Short-term benefits are calculated as a percentage of an employee's earnings or as a flat dollar amount. *Long-term benefits* are paid to employees who due to illness or injury are unable to work for an extended period. Long-term benefits start being paid after sick leave and short-term benefits expire. They generally continue until retirement, or for a period that varies depending on the employee's age at disability onset. In the United States, there are no federal statutory provisions for employer-provided disability insurance, but five states (California, Hawaii, New Jersey, New York, and Rhode Island) have introduced them. Except in these states, disability insurance benefits are provided voluntarily by the employer or as a part of the collective bargaining agreement negotiated by the employer and its unions. Workers may also buy individual disability insurance policies from insurance companies. Based on the Employer Benefit Survey for 2002–2003 (Bureau of Labor Statistics 2005), short- and long-term insurance cover 37% and 28% of private sector employees, respectively, and are more likely to be provided in medium and large firms than in small ones.

Levy (2004) used the Employer Benefit Survey and found that sick leave is a very common benefit in medium and large firms, and less common in small ones. Based on CPS data for 1993, Levy finds that sick leave and short-term and long-term disability benefits are more prevalent for highly educated workers, full-time workers, and prime-aged workers (26 to 64 years old). Another important finding of Levy's study is that there does not appear to be a clear trend in rates of private disability insurance coverage, which suggests that "in contrast with employer-sponsored health insurance, there is no cause for concern that private disability insurance coverage is eroding over time" (p. 13). On the other hand, a troubling finding is that workers without health insurance are also likely to lack private disability insurance. Levy's findings suggest that lacking private disability insurance is another important component of the ongoing debate on "the uninsured," which so far has focused on individuals without health insurance.

The typical private disability insurance policy replaces 60% or 80% of past earnings. Long-term disability insurance is "wrapped around" SSDI. For instance, if the long-term policy replaces 60% of the recipient's past earnings, but the individual qualifies for SSDI, then the SSDI payment is counted as part of the earnings replaced, thereby reducing the insurer's liability. In effect, SSDI provides a subsidy to private disability insurance, because insurers would have to charge higher premiums to provide the same coverage in the absence of SSDI. One effect of this arrangement is that, at some point during the life of a long-term claim, it is in the interest of the private insurer to help the claimant obtain SSDI benefits. Most policies require that the beneficiary apply for SSDI, and the insurer may provide assistance in the process. An interesting policy challenge is how to increase the incentive for private insurers to return the beneficiary to work so that the flow of workers from private insurance into the SSDI program is reduced.

Workers' Compensation

Each state and territory has its own system of workers' compensation that guarantees most workers coverage for medical costs and lost wages due to employment-related accidents or illnesses. Although federal law imposes some requirements, states and territories have a high level of discretion in the design and administration of their own systems. In almost all jurisdictions, employers may self-insure by demonstrating to the state or territory that they have adequate financial reserves to cover any potential claims; the exceptions are North Dakota, Wyoming, Puerto Rico, and the U.S. Virgin Islands. Several states that allow for self-insurance restrict it only to individual employers, while the remaining states allow employer groups to self-insure their members.

Like private long-term disability insurance, workers' compensation interacts with SSDI, but in a way that varies by state. In all states, if the combined total monthly benefit from SSDI and workers' compensation exceeds 80% of a worker's prior earnings, then either the SSDI or workers' compensation stipend must be reduced until the total benefit is just 80% of prior earnings. In 36 states, the SSDI payment is reduced, while in 14 states grandfathered under 1981 amendments to the Social Security Act, it is the workers' compensation benefit that is reduced. In these 14 states, the federal SSDI program provides an implicit subsidy to the state's workers' compensation program in the same way that it provides an implicit subsidy to private long-term disability insurance, as explained earlier.

Other Supports

Beyond the selected few disability benefit programs described earlier, many other programs provide support to persons with disabilities and may also impact their labor force participation. For instance, there are personal-assistance service programs financed through both public and private sources (e.g., personal funding or employer accommodations). Programs financed publicly (i.e., through Medicaid) that deliver such services are typically designed and implemented at the state level. Examples of personal-assistance services include help to accomplish daily activities (e.g., bathing, cleaning, preparing meals) or job-related tasks, communication, and transportation.

By far the most significant supports in terms of expenditures are for health care. Medicare is a public health insurance program for individuals ages 65 and over and persons with disabilities participating in SSDI. Historically, Medicare provides both hospital coverage (Part A) and supplementary medical insurance (Part B), and the 2004 Medicare Modernization Act included amendments to greatly expand coverage for prescription drugs. Medicaid is a federal–state matching program that provides medical assistance primarily to low-income and otherwise needy individuals, including persons with disabilities. Eligibility might be linked to SSI or Temporary Assistance to Needy Families. Expenditures to provide health care for working-age people with disabilities through Medicare and Medicaid are approximately of the same magnitude as expenditures for income support under SSDI and SSI (Goodman and Stapleton 2005). One major policy concern is that the rising cost of health care, accompanied by tightening of employer-provided health insurance benefits, has contributed to the decline in employment of people with disabilities. Although evidence of an impact is unclear (Hill, Livermore, and Houtenville 2003), there has been a significant effort to delink public health insurance benefits (Medicaid and Medicare) from income support benefits (SSI and SSDI). Most notably, provisions of the 1999 Ticket to Work and Work Incentives Improvement Act of 1999 and some earlier legislation encouraged (but did not require) states to implement Medicaid buy-in programs, under which workers with disabilities that would qualify them for SSI or SSDI can purchase Medicaid benefits at a heavily subsidized premium.

Besides programs targeted at persons with disabilities and health care, persons with disabilities may be eligible for a variety of mainstream programs. Food stamps increase the food purchasing power of low-income households by subsidizing purchases through coupons that can be used like cash at the grocery store. Section 8 housing programs provide substantial housing subsidies. The Low-Income Home Energy Assistance Program makes grants available to states and other jurisdictions to assist eligible households with energy costs. Significant transportation assistance is also available. It is important to note that the availability of these various supports varies tremendously by state and locality, and access is often difficult because the supports are part of a complex set of programs that are not integrated. In addition, most of these supports are conditioned in some fashion on earnings or income, which creates work disincentives and may add to the work disincentive effects of major disability programs such as SSDI.

Selected International Developments

Growth in disability benefit rolls and low employment rates for persons with disabilities are not the exclusive policy concerns of the United States. A recent volume from the Organisation for Economic Co-operation and Development (2003) concluded that work disincentives of benefit programs and the perception that disability is necessarily an obstacle to work are significant social problems; it recommended that the term *disabled* no longer be equated with "unable to work." Some countries have programs that seek to avoid work disincentives by disconnecting the traditional association of disability with work inability. One interesting country in this area is Great Britain (Mitra, Corden, and Thornton 2005), which has a benefit designed to help meet the extra costs incurred by persons with disabilities. Extra-cost benefits are noncontributory and non-means-tested and are available both to people who have and do not have paid work. The main extra-cost benefit, called the Disability Living Allowance, is paid to people with severe disability that results in personal care needs, mobility assistance needs, or both.

In addition, Great Britain has recently established a program to encourage persons with disabilities to work that lies outside the traditional disability benefit system: a Working Tax Credit is paid to a range of lower-income employed and self-employed persons, including persons with disabilities (disability element). The program is administered by the taxation authority. A person qualifies for a disability element of the working tax credit if they work for at least 16 hours per week, have a disability that puts them at a disadvantage in getting a job, or receive a qualifying benefit such as the long-term disability pension. The program attempts to encourage work among low-income households with disabilities and may thus prevent entries into the disability pension rolls or encourage exits through return to work by making work a better option than benefits. Outcomes of the working tax credit have not yet been evaluated, since it was only introduced in April 2003. Most countries, like the United States, focus on medical and vocational rehabilitation rather than incentives in their efforts to help people with disabilities return to work. We now turn to the literature on the subject of return to work.

Facilitating Return to Work

There have been various analyses of the factors that lead to return to work of workers who receive workers' compensation benefits and Social Security benefits. Worker, employer, disability, and benefit program characteristics can affect return-to-work outcomes. The results of these analyses are important in shaping policy debates on return to work.

Return to Work and Workers' Compensation

There are several well-established findings in the literature on return to work. Higher workers' compensation benefits are associated with a lower propensity to return to work, which shows that benefits produce work disincentives. In addition, older and less-educated workers are less likely to return to work (e.g., Fox, Borba, and Liu 2005). Other characteristics of employees and employers have been less studied but have nonetheless led to interesting findings. Fox, Borba, and Liu (2005) show that workers who worked part-time or for a partial year were less likely to return to work and were out of work longer than their full-time counterparts. Two studies (Butler, Johnson, and Baldwin 1995; Galizzi and Boden 2003) found that gender does not affect return to work, although Butler, Johnson, and Baldwin found that once women are back at work, they are more likely than men to have multiple spells of absences.

Butler, Johnson, and Baldwin (1995) also showed that labor unions appear to help workers return to work. However, relatively few of the disabled are likely to be assisted in this way due to the low and declining rates of unionization in the United States. Galizzi and Boden (2003) have shown that returning to the preinjury employer has a large negative impact on the duration off work after an injury, suggesting the importance of providing incentives for the preinjury employer to rehire the injured worker. The literature on return to work has paid much attention to a particular injury because of the high prevalence among older workers: back injury. Fox, Borba, and Liu (2005) find that workers with back injuries were out of work 35% to 198% longer than workers with inflammations, lacerations, and contusions, and they suggest that return-to-work programs that target back injuries present good opportunities for both employers and workers.

Return to Work and Social Security Benefits

SSDI and SSI have historically provided workers strong disincentives to attempt to reenter the labor market. Earnings of SSDI beneficiaries are reduced from 100% to 0% if earnings exceed the "Substantial Gainful Activity" (SGA)—the "benefit cliff." The benefit loss may be lower than or greater than earnings, as benefit payments may be below or above SGA. A trial work period does allow an SSDI beneficiary to earn an unlimited amount for nine months without losing benefits, but after that benefits are lost unless the beneficiary reduces earnings below SGA. SSI is more generous toward earnings, imposing an implicit tax of 50%. Further, even if earnings are above the level that reduces benefits to zero, but below a higher threshold, a beneficiary can retain Medicaid coverage and automatic reinstatement of SSI benefits should earnings fall. However, earnings above SGA can trigger a Continuing Disability Review, which could trigger benefit loss, and if an SSI recipient earns enough he or she will eventually lose eligibility for Medicaid benefits and for automatic SSI reinstatement in case of an earnings fall.

The literature on return to work and SSDI is limited. Worker characteristics have been found to influence return to work. Like in workers' compensation studies, several studies have shown that as workers age, they are less likely to return to work, and that workers with more education are more likely to go back to work (Muller 1992; Hennessey 1997; Schechter 1997). The reason for the limited literature on Social Security benefits and return to work is partly the apparent contradiction in terms. If disability determination is centered on the inability to work, it seems paradoxical that the SSDI and SSI programs offer work incentives and programs that are intended to encourage beneficiaries to work and potentially leave the rolls. Yet since the establishment of SSDI in 1956 and SSI in 1972, return to work has been an integral component of both programs. For instance, on August 1, 1956, as President Eisenhower signed the legislation establishing the SSDI program, he was quoted as saying, "We will endeavor to administer the disability [program] efficiently and effectively, [and] . . . to help rehabilitate the disabled so that they may return to useful employment." (Social Security Administration 2003:1). In this context, various aspects of SSDI have been put in place as means to encourage and support return to work. Since 1956, recipients have been allowed to work while staying on the rolls if their earnings are below a limit (the SGA level). In fact, the small literature on SSDI and return to work has shown that a significant portion of beneficiaries work: more than one in four beneficiaries work after benefit entitlement, though only 10% of all beneficiaries are considered substantial workers (Ycas 1996; Muller 1992). However, every year only about 0.5% of beneficiaries are terminated from SSDI due to return to work (Social Security Administration 2004).

Because the potential savings for the government are great if a beneficiary leaves the roll, a wide range of incentives and services have been aimed at returning disabled workers to work, beginning in 1960 with the trial work period. Further, certain Impairment Related Work Expenses are deducted from earnings before the SGA test is applied. In 1980, an extended period of eligibility (EPE) was introduced. The EPE takes place once the trial work period is completed and lasts for three years. During the EPE, benefits are withheld for those months in which earnings exceed SGA, but Medicare coverage continues (Social Security Administration 2003), and if earnings fall below SGA, benefits are automatically reinstated without a new application. Once the EPE is over, the person's SSDI benefit is terminated (assuming that the person continues to work). Hennessey and Muller (1994) found that few SSDI beneficiaries were aware of the program's incentives, and even among those who were, few reported being influenced to return to work because of them.

Earnings of SSI recipients are subject to the provisions of Section 1619 of the Social Security Act, which instituted the 50% offset provision described earlier. The offset applies only to earnings above an earnings disregard.[5] In addition, in most states all SSI recipients are categorically eligible for Medicaid, while in others most recipients meet eligibility rules. Medicaid rules vary by state, but until recently eligibility was jeopardized for almost all SSI recipients if earnings exceeded a threshold level—usually twice the maximum SSI benefit plus average Medicaid expenditures for the state's disabled Medicaid recipients. Typically, the percentage of disabled SSI recipients who have earnings, after disregard, above SGA has fluctuated around 6% (Social Security Administration 2004). One study showed that many SSI recipients with earnings above SGA restrain their earnings to keep them below the threshold that would make them ineligible for Medicaid and unable to automatically return to SSI should their earnings fall (Stapleton and Tucker 2000).

Ticket Act. In 1999, the Ticket to Work and Work Incentives Improvement Act in 1999-Public Law 106–70 (Ticket Act hereafter) was passed to specifically address the issue of low return-to-work rates for recipients. The Ticket Act addressed the health insurance issue by expanding the rules for state Medicaid buy-in programs and by increasing the extended period of Medicare eligibility for SSDI recipients from 3 to 7.5 years. Provisions of the Ticket Act also required the SSA to develop a process to expedite the reinstatement of former recipients who had returned to work should their earnings fall.

Ticket to Work Program. In addition, starting in 2002, the SSA rolled out the Ticket to Work and Self-Sufficiency program (Ticket to Work), which allows SSDI and SSI recipients who have been given return-to-work "tickets" to redeem their tickets with a vocational rehabilitation and other employment service provider of their choice among an array of approved public and private providers referred to as employment networks. The program, which is voluntary, was phased in nationally over three years. Before the Ticket to Work program, the SSA would reimburse state vocational rehabilitation agencies for services provided to a recipient if he or she achieved earnings above SGA for at least nine months after the completion of services, subject to certain payment limits. Under Ticket to Work, state vocational rehabilitation agencies can continue to use this traditional payment system, but they may opt to use one of two new systems with much stronger incentives for recipients to exit the SSI and SSDI rolls. Further, they must now compete with private providers, which are eligible to use either of the new payment systems, but which are not eligible to use the traditional system. Although the program has not been fully evaluated yet, an initial evaluation report (Thornton et al. 2004) has pointed toward several important implementation challenges. Initial participation in the Ticket to Work program is low, with less than 1% of recipients using their tickets, and the vast majority of participants are receiving services from state vocational rehabilitation agencies under the traditional payment system. While the Ticket to Work program was not envisioned as a way to move a large portion of SSI and SSDI recipients into work, participation rates are lower than expected. Thus far, the program has not generated the vigorous, innovative market for rehabilitation services that its designers envisioned.

Demonstrations. The SSA has also experimented with providing innovative employment services and supports through several large-scale return-to-work demonstration projects. For instance, Project NetWork, conducted between 1992 and 1995, provided SSI and SSDI recipients with intensive employment-focused case management. Later in 1998, the SSA together with the Rehabilitation Services Administration started the State Partnership Initiative project, awarding cooperative agreements to 18 states to develop innovative return-to-work programs for persons with disabilities, including SSDI and SSI recipients. Project NetWork had limited success. It did not reduce the reliance on SSI and SSDI benefits by statistically significant amounts for recipients, but it did for SSI applicants by about 2% (Kornfeld and Rupp 2000). In addition, Project NetWork increased average annual earnings per participant by 11% over the first two years, and essentially by zero in follow-up year 3. Results of the outcome evaluation of the State Partnership Initiative project are not yet available.

The Ticket to Work Act extends the SSA commissioner's authority to conduct demonstrations to examine the impact of implementing sliding-scale benefit offsets and a variety of innovative early interventions on the employment chances of SSDI applicants. Several demonstrations have been announced in that context, including the following: Benefit Offset (Four-State Pilot and Subsequent Demonstration), Early Intervention, Florida Freedom Initiative, Youth Transition, and Accelerated Benefits. However, progress in implementing these demonstrations has been slow, leading the Government Accountability Office (2004) to conclude that the additional demonstration authority of the Ticket to Work Act has so far been used to a limited extent.

Overall, the return-to-work prospects of SSDI recipients seem rather bleak: the work incentives that have been tried have not had a substantial effect, participation rates in return-to work programs and demonstrations have been very low, and innovations tested have not yielded strong results. One interpretation of this experience is that return to work for persons who receive permanent disability benefits may not be a realistic policy objective. Instead, interventions should take place before persons join the rolls or, going even further, before they lose or leave their jobs. This view is supported by recent research on the reservation wages of SSDI recipients. Using data from the New Beneficiary Data System, Mitra (2006) examines the reservation wages of a sample of SSDI recipients who report being willing to work if offered a job. Preliminary results indicate that the reservation wages of SSDI recipients are relatively high compared to the last wage earned before joining SSDI. Less than half of them would want a wage that is 80% or less of the last wage earned before getting onto SSDI. Because one would expect that this group on SSDI that has been out of the labor force for several years would suffer a wage cut in order to get a job, their probability to return to work and leave the rolls seems to be limited.

Another, complementary view is that past efforts have simply not adequately addressed the disincentive problem. For example, SSI's Section 1619 program, designed to reduce work disincentives, implicitly imposes a 50% tax on earnings. That's higher than the tax rates paid on earnings by the highest earners in our economy, applied to people who may be capable of earning the minimum wage or only slightly more. Further, it does not address the potential loss of in-kind benefits, such as food stamps (reduced by 30 cents for every dollar earned) or housing subsidies. Thus, it may take some combination of early intervention plus much stronger work incentives to substantially increase the employment and earnings of this population. During a period in which the retirement of the baby boom generation is likely to make fiscal stringency a long-term feature of the policy landscape, the challenge to policy makers is to develop feasible policies that address these issues *and* essentially pay for themselves.

Job Search

Job search is an important part of the return-to-work process for the unemployed with disabilities. Labor economics has a large literature on job search methods, their prevalence, and their effectiveness among the short-term unemployed. It has long been recognized that the informal channel of friends and relatives is the most effective way to find jobs (Holtzer 1987). The ineffectiveness of other routes, such as public employment services, has been demonstrated in several studies (e.g., Addison and Portugal 2001). These results are for the short-term unemployed in general, but Hotchkiss (2003) recently showed that they also apply to persons with disabilities. Based on CPS data, Hotchkiss finds that persons with disabilities use similar types of search methods as the short-term unemployed and that the relative effectiveness of different methods is the same.

The Hotchkiss (2003) results are based on CPS data, and the job search methods reported do not reflect whether the person used a vocational rehabilitation agency, which is a possible source of services for persons with disabilities. Schechter (1997) showed that SSDI recipients typically use three main job search methods: asking a friend, checking ads and contacting employers, and, in more than 20% of cases, using a lead from a vocational rehabilitation agency. Overall, except for the use of state vocational rehabilitation agencies, a job seeker on SSDI uses methods that are quite similar to those used by the short-term unemployed.

Of particular interest is the use of private employment agencies. Providing recipients a choice among a variety of employment service providers in addition to the traditional state vocational rehabilitation agencies is a major innovation of the Ticket to Work program. Included are private employment service providers that register for the program. To date, however, there is no evidence that the use of such providers is an effective job search method for SSDI recipients or persons with disabilities in general. In the broader literature on the short-term unemployed, few studies have addressed the effectiveness of private employment service agencies. Most early studies do not cover private employment service provision as a separate job search method (Holtzer 1987), perhaps because such agencies played a less important role at the time. Bortnick and Ports (1992) found that contacting a private provider has a positive impact for women's job search effectiveness but a negative one for men. More recently, Kuhn and Skuterud (2004) showed that contacting private providers does not have a statistically significant impact on job search effectiveness. It will be important as part of the evaluation of the Ticket to Work program to assess whether using private employment service providers is an effective search strategy for SSDI and SSI recipients.

Vocational Rehabilitation

Vocational rehabilitation services include job counseling, job training, and job placement. For many decades, the federal–state vocational rehabilitation (VR) program has been the traditional gateway for many persons with disabilities to access employment services. VR services are available to a wide range of persons with disabilities; about one quarter of state VR agency clients are SSDI and SSI recipients. Not every SSDI or SSI recipient is eligible for vocational services, however; applicants to the state agencies must meet eligibility criteria that vary from state to state. There have been significant criticisms of the VR program in the past two decades (e.g., Weaver 1994). These criticisms have continued to foster extensive discussion pertaining to the efficacy of public VR and the viability of the program's employment-related outcomes. Since the federal–state VR program was begun in 1920, it has been subject to many economic evaluations (Worrall 1988), concentrated on identifying the impact of service provision on participants' earnings outcomes. Unfortunately, many of the analyses have been hampered by data and methodological limitations. Recently, following the availability of new data sets at the state and federal levels, researchers have regained interest in evaluating the return-to-work performance of state VR services.

Dean and Honeycutt (2004) examined the impact of VR on participants' earnings using two enhanced data sources, one relying on administrative records collected for the state of Virginia and the other coming from a customized national survey, the Longitudinal Study of the Vocational Rehabilitation Services Program (LSVRSP). VR has a positive and statistically significant impact on earnings in roughly one third of the reporting periods, ranging up to $2,500 annually. However, these estimates are quite sensitive to the nature of the person's disabling condition, the choice of comparison group, and the type of econometric technique used to control for selection bias.

Also using the LSVRSP, Stapleton and Erickson (2004) compare return-to-work outcomes for two groups of state VR participants, those who received SSDI or SSI and those who did not. The latter consistently have better return-to-work outcomes than the former. Stapleton and Erickson show that part of the difference in outcomes is the result of differences in characteristics (demographic and human-capital characteristics and disability type and severity), but even after controlling for these factors in considerable detail, substantial differences remain, particularly with regard to earnings above SGA for at least nine months. One possibility is that much of the remaining difference is due to the work disincentives associated with SSDI and SSI, including their related health insurance benefits, but the study does not provide direct evidence on this point. If SSDI and SSI disincentives are an important determinant of poor return-to-work outcomes for recipients, however, then past criticism of the state VR performance might have been somewhat misplaced, because the disincentives are external to VR.

Disability Management

Regaining employment is very challenging after the onset of substantial impairment or acute episodes of chronic illness. Various obstacles need to be overcome in the process, including the deterioration of skills while unemployed and discrimination in hiring. There are opportunities to intervene before such barriers arise—that is, prior to job loss—through an array of approaches that have come to be known as "disability management."

Disability management is a broad term used to encompass a variety of activities and programs intended to prevent disabilities from occurring and/or to minimize their impact on employers and employees. The scope of disabilities that come under disability management is broad; it includes disabilities incurred on or off the job and physical as well as mental disabilities (including substance abuse). Disability management activities include claims management, return-to-work programs, wellness programs, employee assistance plans, medical clinics that are geared toward minimizing the effects of disability, and employee safety programs.

There are several key actors in job retention, including the employer, the employee, private disability or workers' compensation programs, and various government agencies. The employer's disability management strategy may include providing accommodations (e.g., flexible work schedules) and vocational rehabilitation services. The employee may request an accommodation when needed and may individually enroll in vocational rehabilitation services. Two laws, the Family and Medical Leave Act (FMLA) and the ADA, play prominent roles in retention policy in the United States. We review here the main aspects of the FMLA, employer accommodation under the ADA, and the provision of job retention services.

Family and Medical Leave Act

Since 1993, the FMLA has guaranteed that persons who must stop working because of their own health, maternity or disability, or to care for a relative (newborn child, ill child, ill spouse, or ill parent) may take up to 12 weeks of leave without pay and retain their jobs. The act applies to establishments of 50 or more employees. Based on a survey conducted in 2000, Waldfogel (2001) finds that 16.5% employees took leave under the act, and the employee's own health was the most commonly mentioned reason for taking leave; among those who took leave, only 7.8% reported that it was because of maternity or disability.

Employer Accommodations

Job retention is also an important part of the ADA. Under the ADA, the employer must provide *reasonable* accommodations to new and existing employees that would not lead to undue hardship on the business operation. Research has shown that job accommodations tend to promote job retention and postpone applications for disability benefits. Using the Social Security Survey of Disability and Work of 1978, Burkhauser, Butler, and Kim (1995) showed that in their sample, 30% of workers with disabilities were accommodated by their employers prior to the ADA. This result went against the commonly held view that accommodations were rare pre-ADA. In addition, they found that the risk of job exit is significantly influenced by employer accommodation. In another study of accommodation, Burkhauser, Butler, and Weathers (2002) used retrospective data from the first wave (1992) of the Health and Retirement Study matched with individual-level SSA record data on the generosity of SSDI benefits. Their results show that employer accommodation significantly slows a worker's application for SSDI benefits, suggesting that accommodation promoted job retention following the onset of a health condition.

Job Retention Services

Beyond employer accommodations, job retention can be promoted through services provided to persons with disabilities who are employed. Two major sources of job retention services are agencies that provide vocational rehabilitation, such as the state vocational rehabilitation agencies, and employers. There has been limited research on the effectiveness of job retention services, but results of a recent study appear to be promising. In a recent randomized controlled trial, Allaire, Li, and LaValley (2003) investigated the effectiveness of a job retention VR program. Eligibility criteria for the purposes of the program included a particular diagnosis of an arthritic nature, current employment, and some difficulty in doing work or expecting to have difficulty in the near future. All participants were from eastern Massachusetts and did not have severe functional limitations. The intervention tested was brief, consisting of three hours of services delivered by a rehabilitation counselor in two sessions. The three main areas of focus were identifying needed job accommodations, vocational counseling and education, and self-advocacy. The investigators found that VR services delivered during employment to persons with rheumatic diseases who were at risk for job loss both significantly reduced and postponed the incidence of job loss. Further research is needed into the effectiveness of such job retention services for persons with other types of disabilities, with severe functional limitations, and in a variety of labor market conditions.

Employers are also a source of job retention services. However, only large employers have enough employees to make a job retention intervention worthwhile. Often, such interventions are for workers with occupational injuries and illnesses. There is only anecdotal evidence regarding the efficacy of job retention services provided by employers, given that outcome data are collected sporadically and are considered proprietary (O'Leary and Dean 1998). In the United States, the government plays no role in providing and financing job retention services. In contrast, in Great Britain, the government is experimenting with providing job retention services through pilots targeting persons on short-term disability (statutory sick pay) (Mitra, Corden, and Thornton 2005). The employer-run short-term disability program, as a major pathway into the long-term government disability pension program, is a logical place to prevent future transitions onto the long-term disability rolls. Employees and self-employed people on sick leave for between six weeks and six months may volunteer to take part in the pilots. If they pass the screening test for eligibility, they are randomized to a health intervention, workplace intervention, combined intervention, or control group. External organizations provide the services. The intent is to provide job retention interventions at the earliest stage of disability (less than six months after the onset of a disability) and while persons are still employed. Results from this experiment are not available yet.

In the United States, such early job retention intervention before someone applies for SSDI would be challenging, as recent research has shown that only 14% of SSDI recipients received any kind of disability income in the year before they entered SSDI and that this disability income came from a variety of sources, including employer-provided temporary benefits, workers' compensation, and veterans' disability (Honeycutt 2004). Targeting future SSDI recipients therefore seems challenging in the United States context. Most of the participants of a job retention program, such as in the work of Allaire, Li, and LaValley (2003), may not apply, let alone qualify, for SSDI or SSI. It would seem worthwhile to investigate the potential cost effectiveness of job retention programs, as in Allaire, Li, and LaValley, especially if their effectiveness can be demonstrated for disabilities other than rheumatic ones and in a variety of labor market environments.

Concluding Remarks and Policy Implications

The recent employment experience of working age people with disabilities is discouraging. This is particularly true given that the passage of the ADA in 1990 was meant to usher in a new generation of policies that would more fully integrate working age people with disabilities into the mainstream of American life, including employment. The ADA is likely to have increased the percentage of workers with disabilities who were accommodated in the 1990s. In addition, persons who were accommodated were shown to have increased employment duration following disability onset. Despite this progress, the employment rate of persons with disabilities relative to those without disabilities fell over the entire 1990s business cycle, continuing a decline that has been observed in some studies since as early as the mid-1980s. The causes of this decline in relative employment are controversial. Nevertheless, the preponderance of the evidence suggests that it was not caused by an increase in the severity of impairments, nor by changes in the nature of work. The most likely causes were the substantial reduction in eligibility standards for entering the SSDI rolls that occurred in the mid-1980s as well as by the increase in benefits relative to market wages for low-skill workers. The unintended consequence of making nonwork pay was to discourage working age people with disabilities from taking advantage of the strengthening of their legal rights. This has led Stapleton, O'Day, et al. (2005) to talk about a "poverty trap" created by disability policies—one that limits the ability of people with disabilities to enjoy the fruits of economic growth and leaves many in poverty for the rest of their lives.

Historically, the federal government's provision of economic security for working age people with disabilities has been dominated by a caretaker approach, reflecting the outdated view that disability is an exclusively medical issue. The disability benefit system in the United States was not initially designed to promote employment and labor market retention. A glance at the federal budget shows that cash transfers and medical care expenditures (SSDI, SSI, Medicare, and Medicaid) dwarf expenditures for efforts to integrate those with disabilities into the labor force. And the eligibility rules for these programs discourage work and more than likely offset any prowork effect of the ADA over the 1990s. In contrast, the considerable improvement in the employment and poverty rates of single mothers after expansion of the Earned Income Tax Credit for low-income parents and the welfare reforms of 1996 shows that it is possible for government policy to shift from a caretaker to a prowork priority and to have a significant impact on a population that was "not expected to work."

There is a clear need to reform the disability benefit system so that it supports participation in society through employment. Our current knowledge of what is effective is insufficient to support a radical, almost-overnight policy transformation to a prowork policy, as was undertaken for low-income families. It is clear, however, that recently enacted policy changes and demonstrations such as those authorized in the Ticket Act are headed in the direction of transforming disability policy in a similar fashion. Future fiscal pressures make it extremely urgent to develop an approach to economic security that takes better advantage of the capability of people with disabilities so that lawmakers will have better options than simply cutting eligibility and benefit levels when those pressures become irresistible.

The research findings also suggest further scrutiny of the specific provisions of the ADA and their consequences. Researchers need to get past challenging the overall validity of the law as a tool for accomplishing its stated objectives, as some have done in the past, and instead consider how specific provisions of the law and its implementation might be improved. Researchers might, for instance, address how to refine the law's definition of disability in ways that will reduce future litigation, meet ADA objectives, and be amenable to measurement. They also might consider how refinements to the definition of "reasonable" accommodation and public programs to support accommodations would reduce employer costs and increase their incentive to hire or retain employees with disabilities. As the disability rights movement seeks to increase the social integration of people with disabilities, perhaps legal scholars should consider how the protection of their civil rights could be integrated with the civil rights protections for other groups.

By and large, the recent developments in disability research conform to the expectations of labor market theory on the disincentive effects of benefit programs. They also imply, however, that labor theorists and applied researchers need to think differently about disability than they sometimes have. Disability can no longer be conveniently equated with inability to work. There is no clear line between those who "can" work and those who "cannot," and a broad range of factors in the individual's environment determines how productive someone can be in conjunction with medical and other characteristics. The analysis of Autor and Duggan (2003) illustrates this point; they found that changes in disability income support policy reduced the natural rate of unemployment by encouraging people with disabilities to take themselves out of the labor force.

Notes

[1] These data are unpublished; they were calculated by Douglas Kruse, Rutgers University, and presented at a session on telework and disability of the Society of Industrial Organization Psychologists, Los Angeles, April 2005, organized by the Office on Disability and Employment Policy of the United States Department of Labor.

[2] For a review of the impact of these different legislations on employment, see Bruyère et al. (2002).

[3] For an analysis of the wide range of federal disability benefit programs, see Government Accountability Office (2005).

[4] For a review of different studies conducted on this issue, see Stapleton and Burkhauser (2003).

[5] This disregard, or the limit beyond which the 50% offset provision applies, includes a small blanket earnings disregard as well as disregards for Impairment Related Work Expenses and any Plan to Achieve Self Support.

References

Acemoglu, D., and J. Angrist. 2001. "Consequences of Employment Protection? The Case of the Americans with Disabilities Act." *Journal of Political Economy*, Vol. 109, no. 5 (October), pp. 915–57.

Addison, J.T., and P. Portugal. 2001. "Job Search Methods and Outcomes." Institute for the Study of Labor (IZA) (Bonn, Germany), Discussion Paper No. 349, August.

Allaire, S.H., W. Li, and M.P. LaValley. 2003. "Reduction of Job Loss in Persons with Rheumatic Diseases Receiving Vocational Rehabilitation." *Arthritis and Rheumatism*, Vol. 48, no. 11 (November), pp. 3212–18.

Autor, D.H., and M.G. Duggan. 2003. "The Rise in the Disability Rolls and the Decline in Unemployment." *Quarterly Journal of Economics*, Vol. 118, no. 1 (February), pp. 157–206.

Baldwin, M., and W.G. Johnson. 2000. "Labor Market Discrimination Against Men with Disabilities in the Year of the ADA 2000." *Southern Economic Journal*, Vol. 66, no. 3 (January), pp. 548–66.

———. 2005. "A Critical Review of Studies of Discrimination Against Workers with Disabilities." In W.M. Rodgers III, ed., *Handbook on the Economics of Discrimination*. Northampton, MA: Elgar.

Berkowitz, M., and D. Dean. 1998. "Facilitating Employment through Vocational Rehabilitation." In T. Thomason, J.F. Burton, and D. Hyatt. eds., *New Approaches to Disability in the Workplace*. Madison, WI: Industrial Relations Research Association.

Black, D., K. Daniel, and S. Sanders. 2002. "The Impact of Economic Conditions on Participation in Disability Programs: Evidence from the Coal Boom and Bust." *American Economic Review*, Vol. 92, no. 1 (March), pp. 27–50.

Bortnick, S.M., and M.H. Ports. 1992. "Job Search Methods of the Unemployed." *Monthly Labor Review*, Vol. 115, no. 12 (December), pp. 29–35.

Bound, J., and R.V. Burkhauser. 1999. "Economic Analysis of Transfer Programs Targeted on People with Disabilities." In O. Ashenfelter and D. Card. eds., *Handbook of Labor Economics*, Vol. 3C. Amsterdam: Elsevier Science.

Bound, J., and T. Waidmann. 2002. "Accounting for Recent Declines in Employment Rates Among Working-Aged Men and Women with Disabilities." *Journal of Human Resources*, Vol. 37, no. 2 (Spring), pp. 231–50.

Bruyère, S. 2000. "Disability Employment Policies and Practices in Private and Federal Sector Organizations." Ithaca, NY: Program on Employment and Disability, Cornell University.

Bruyère, S., W. Erickson, S. VanLooy, E. Sitaras, J. Cook, J. Burke, L. Farah, and J. Morris. 2002. *Employment and Disability Policy: Recommendations for a Social Sciences Research Agenda*. Paper presented at National Institute of Disability and Rehabilitation Research and American Psychological Association conference "Bridging Gaps: Refining the Disability Research Agenda for Rehabilitation and Social Sciences."

Bureau of Labor Statistics. 2005. Employee Benefits Survey. <http:data.bls.gov/cgi-bin/surveymost?eb>. [Accessed March 1, 2006.]

Burkhauser, R.V., J.S. Butler, and Y.W. Kim. 1995. "The Importance of Employer Accommodation on the Job Duration of Workers with Disabilities: A Hazard Model Approach." *Labour Economics*, Vol. 2, no. 2 (June), pp. 109–30.

Burkhauser, R.V., J.S. Butler, and R. Weathers. 2002. "How Policy Variables Influence the Timing of Social Security Disability Insurance Applications." *Social Security Bulletin*, Vol. 64, no. 1, pp. 1–32.

Burkhauser, R.V., M.C. Daly, A.J. Houtenville, and N. Nargis. 2002. "Self-Reported Work-Limitation Data: What They Can and Cannot Tell Us." *Demography*, Vol. 39, no. 3 (August), pp. 541–55.

Burkhauser, R.V., A.J. Houtenville, and D.C. Wittenburg. 2003. "A user's guide to current statistics on employment of people with disabilities." In D.C. Stapleton and R.V. Burkhauser, eds., *The Decline in Employment of People with Disabilities: A Policy Puzzle*. Kalamazoo, MI: W.E. UpJohn Institute for Employment Research.

Burkhauser, R.V., and D.C. Stapleton. 2003. "Introduction." In D.C. Stapleton and R.V. Burkhauser. eds., *The Decline in Employment of People with Disabilities: A Policy Puzzle*. Kalamazoo, MI: W.E. UpJohn Institute for Employment Research.

———. 2004a. "The Decline in the Employment Rate for People with Disabilities: Bad Data, Bad Health, or Bad Policy?" *Journal of Vocational Rehabilitation*, Vol. 20, no. 3 (Sept.), pp. 185–201.

———. 2004b. "Employing Those Not Expected to Work: The Stunning Changes in the Employment of Single Mothers with Children and People with Disabilities in the United States in the 1990s." In Bernd Marin, Christopher Prinz, and Monika Queisser, eds., *Disability Policy Under Review*, Hants, England: Ashgate.

Butler, R.J., W.G. Johnson, and M.L. Baldwin. 1995. "Managing Work Disability: Why First Return to Work Is Not a Measure of Success." *Industrial and Labor Relations Review*, Vol. 48, no. 3 (April), pp. 452–69.

Colella, A., A. DeNisi, and A. Varma. 1998. "The Impact of Ratee's Disability on Performance Judgments and Choice as Partner: The Role of Disability-Job Fit Stereotypes and Interdependence of Rewards." *Journal of Applied Psychology*, Vol. 83, no. 1 (February), pp. 102–11.

Dean, D., and T. Honeycutt. 2004. "Evaluating the Long-Term Employment Outcomes of Vocational Rehabilitation Participants Using Survey and Administrative Data." Report submitted to the Social Security Administration. New Brunswick, NJ: Disability Research Institute, Rutgers University.

De Leire, T. 2000. "The Wage and Employment Effects of the Americans with Disabilities Act." *Journal of Human Resources*, Vol. 35, no. 4 (Fall), pp. 693–715.

Dixon, K.A., D. Kruse, and C.E. van Horn. 2003. *Restricted Access: A Survey of Employers About People with Disabilities and Lowering Barriers to Work*. New Brunswick, NJ: Heldrich Center for Workforce Development, Rutgers University.

Donohue, J., and J. Heckman. 1991. "Continuous Versus Episodic Change: The Impact of Civil Rights Policy on the Economic Status of Blacks." *Journal of Economic Literature*, Vol. 29, no. 4 (December), pp. 1603–43.

Fox, S., P. Borba, and T. Liu. 2005. *Return to Work Outcomes of Injured Workers: Evidence from California, Massachusetts, Pennsylvania and Texas*. Cambridge, MA: Workers Compensation Research Institute.

Galizzi, M., and L.I. Boden. 2003. "The Return to Work of Injured Workers: Evidence from Matched Unemployment Insurance and Workers' Compensation Data." *Labour Economics*, Vol. 10, no. 3, (June), pp. 311–37.

Government Accountability Office. 2004. *Social Security Disability: Improved Processes for Planning and Conducting Demonstrations May Help SSA More Effectively Use Its Demonstration Authority*. GAO-05-19. Washington, DC: Government Printing Office.

———. 2005. *Federal Disability Assistance: Wide Array of Programs Needs to Be Examined in Light of 21st Century Challenges*. Report to Congressional Committees. GAO-05-626. Washington, DC: GAO.

Goodman, N., and D.C. Stapleton. 2005. "Federal Expenditures for Working-Age People with Disabilities." Working paper. Ithaca, NY: Institute for Policy Research, Cornell University.

Goodman, N., and T. Waidman. 2003. "The Role of Disability Insurance in Explaining the Recent Decline in the Employment Rate of People with Disabilities." In Stapleton and Burkhauser (eds)., *The Decline in Employment of People with Disabilities: A Policy Puzzle*. Kalamazoo, MI: UpJohn Institute for Employment Research.

Hale, T.W. 2001. "Lack of a Disability Measure in Today's Current Population Survey." *Monthly Labor Review*, Vol. 124, no. 7 (July), pp. 38–40.

Hennessey, J.C. 1997. "Factors Affecting the Work Efforts of Disabled-Worker Beneficiaries." *Social Security Bulletin*, Vol. 60, no. 3, pp. 3–20.

Hennessey, J.C., and L.S. Muller. 1994. "Work Efforts of Disabled-Worker Beneficiaries: Preliminary Findings from the New Beneficiary Followup Survey." *Social Security Bulletin*, Vol. 57, no. 3, pp. 42–51.

Hill, S.C., Livermore, G.A., and Houtenville, A.J. 2003. "Rising Health Care Expenditures and the Employment of People with High Cost Chronic Conditions." In D.C. Stapleton and R.V. Burkhauser, eds., *The Decline in Employment of People with Disabilities: A Policy Puzzle*. Kalamazoo, MI: Upjohn Institute for Employment Research, pp. 181–216.

Holtzer, J.H. 1987. "Job Search by Employed and Unemployed Youth." *Industrial and Labor Relations Review*, Vol. 40, no. 4 (July), pp. 601–611.

Honeycutt, T.C. 2004. "Program and Benefit Paths to the Social Security Disability Insurance Program." *Journal of Vocational Rehabilitation*, Vol. 21, no. 2, pp. 83–94.

Honeycutt, T.C., and S. Mitra. 2004. *Learning from Others: Temporary and Partial Programs in Nine Countries*. New Brunswick, NJ: Disability Research Institute, Rutgers University.

Hotchkiss, J.L. 2003. *The Labor Market Experience of Workers with Disabilities: The ADA and Beyond*. Kalamazoo, MI: UpJohn Institute for Employment Research.

———. 2004a. "A Closer Look at the Employment Impact of the Americans with Disabilities Act." *Journal of Human Resources*, Vol. 39, no. 4 (Fall), pp. 887–911.

———. 2004b. "Growing Part-Time Employment Among Workers With Disabilities: Marginalization or Opportunity." *Federal Reserve Bank of Atlanta Economic Review* (Third Quarter), pp. 1–16.

Houtenville, A.J., and R.V. Burkhauser. 2004. "Did the Employment of People of Disabilities Decline in the 1990s, and Was the ADA Responsible?" Research brief. Ithaca, NY: Research and Rehabilitation Training Center for Economic Research on Employment Policy for Persons with Disabilities, Cornell University.

Jolls, C., and J.J. Prescott. 2004. "Disaggregating Employment Protection: The Case of Disability Discrimination." Working Paper 10740. Cambridge, MA: National Bureau of Economic Research.

Kornfeld, R., and K. Rupp. 2000. "The Effects of the Project NetWork Return-to-Work Case Management Experiment on Participant Earnings, Benefit Receipt, and Other Outcomes." *Social Security Bulletin*, Vol. 63, no. 1, pp. 12–33.

Kruse, D., and L. Schur, 2002. "Non-standard Work Arrangements and Disability Income." Report to the Disability Research Institute, University of Illinois at Urbana-Champaign.

————. 2003. "Employment of People with Disabilities Following the ADA." *Industrial Relations*, Vol. 42, no. 1 (January), pp. 31–66.

Kuhn, P., and M. Skuterud. 2004. "Internet Job Search and Unemployment Durations." *American Economic Review*, Vol. 94, no. 1 (March), pp. 218–32.

Leonard, J.S. 1990. "The Impact of Affirmative Action Regulation and Equal Employment Law on Black Employment." *Journal of Economic Perspectives*, Vol. 4, no. 4 (Autumn), pp. 47–63.

Levy, H. 2004. "Private Employer-Sponsored Disability Insurance: Where Are the Gaps in Coverage?" Working Paper 10382. Cambridge, MA: National Bureau of Economic Research.

Mitra, S. 2006. "Social Security Disability Insurance, Reservation Wages and Return to Work." Working paper. Bronx, NY: Fordham University.

Mitra, S., A. Corden, and P. Thornton. 2005. "Recent Innovations in Great Britain's Disability Benefit System." In T. Honeycutt and S. Mitra, eds., *Learning From Others: Temporary and Partial Programs in Nine Countries*. Final report for the Disability Research Institute. Urbana-Champaign, IL: Disability Research Institute.

Muller, L.S. 1992. "Disability Beneficiaries Who Work and Their Experience Under Program Work Incentives." *Social Security Bulletin*, Vol. 57, no. 2, pp. 2–19.

Oi, W. 1978. "Three Paths from Disability to Poverty." Technical Analysis Paper No. 57. Washington, DC: U. S. Department of Labor.

O'Leary, P., and D. Dean. 1998. *International Research Project on Job Retention and Return to Work Strategies for Disabled Workers*. Study Report USA. Geneva: International Labour Organization.

Organisation for Economic Co-operation and Development. 2003. *Transforming Disability into Ability: Policies to Promote Work and Income Security for Disabled People*. Paris: OECD.

Schechter, E.S. 1997. "Work While Receiving Disability Insurance Benefits: Additional Findings from the New Beneficiary Followup Survey." *Social Security Bulletin*, Vol. 60, no. 1, pp. 3–18.

Schur, L. 2002. "Dead-End Jobs or a Path to Economic Well-Being? The Consequences of Non-standard Work for People with Disabilities." *Behavioral Sciences and the Law*, Vol. 20, no. 6 (Nov./Dec.), pp. 601–20.

————. 2003. "Barriers or Opportunities? The Causes of Contingent and Part-Time Work among People with Disabilities." *Industrial Relations*, Vol. 42, no. 4 (October) pp. 589–622.

Schur, L., D. Kruse, and P. Blanck. 2005. "Corporate Culture and the Employment of People with Disabilities." *Behavioral Sciences and the Law*, Vol. 23, no.1 (January), pp. 3–20.

Social Security Administration. 2003. *Annual Statistical Report on the Social Security Disability Insurance Program*. Baltimore, MD: SSA.

————. 2004. *Annual Report of the Supplemental Security Income*. Baltimore, MD: SSA.

————. 2005. *Statistical Supplement of the Social Security Bulletin*. Baltimore, MD: SSA.

Stapleton, D.C., and R.V. Burkhauser, eds. 2003. *The Decline in Employment of People with Disabilities: A Policy Puzzle*. Kalamazoo, MI: UpJohn Institute for Employment Research.

Stapleton, D.C., and W.A. Erickson (2004). *Characteristics or Incentives: Why Do Employment Outcomes for SSA Beneficiary Clients of VR Agencies Differ, on Average, from Those of Other Clients?* Research report. Ithaca, NY: Research and Rehabilitation Training Center for Economic Research on Employment Policy for Persons with Disabilities, Cornell University.

Stapleton, D.C., and A. Tucker. 2000. "Will Expanding Health Care Coverage for People with Disabilities Increase Their Employment and Earnings? Evidence From an Analysis of the SSI Work Incentive Program." In D. Salkever and Alan Sorkin, eds., *Research in Human Capital and Development*, Vol. 13, pp. 133–80. Stamford, CT: JAI Press.

Stapleton, D.C., B. O'Day, G.A. Livermore, and A. Imparato. 2005. "Dismantling from the Poverty Trap: Disability Policy for the 21st Century." Working paper. Ithaca, NY: Cornell University Institute for Policy Research.

Stapleton, D.C., D.C. Wittenburg, and E. Maag. 2005. "A Difficult Cycle? The Effect of Labor Market Changes on The Employment and Program Participation of People with Disabilities." Working paper. Ithaca, NY: Institute for Policy Research and Urban Institute, Cornell University.

Thornton, C., G. Livermore, D. Stapleton, J. Kregel, T. Silva, B. O'Day, T. Fraker, W.G. Revell, H. Schroeder, and M. Edwards. 2004. *Evaluation of the Ticket to Work Program*. Washington, DC: Mathematica Policy Research.

Trupin, L., and E. Yelin. 2003. *Impact of Structural Chance in the Distribution of Occupations and Industries on the Employment of Persons with Disabilities in the United States, 1970–2001*. Urbana-Champaign, IL: Disability Research Institute.

Waldfogel, J. 2001. "Family and Medical Leave: Evidence from the 2000 Surveys." *Monthly Labor Review*, Vol. 124, no. 9 (September), pp. 17–23.

Weathers, R. 2005. *A Guide to Disability Statistics from the American Community Survey*. Ithaca, NY: Disability Statistics and Demographics Rehabilitation Research and Training Center, Employment and Disability Institute, Cornell University.

Weaver, C.L. 1994. "Privatizing Vocational Rehabilitation: Options for Increasing Individual Choice and Enhancing Competition," *Journal of Disability Policy Studies*, Vol. 5, no. 1 (Summer), pp. 53–76.

Worrall, J. 1988. "Analysis of Benefits and Costs in Vocational Rehabilitation." In M. Berkowitz, ed., *Measuring the Efficiency of Public Programs: Costs and Benefits in Vocational Rehabilitation*, Philadelphia: Temple University Press.

Ycas, M.A. 1996. "Patterns of Return to Work in a Cohort of Disabled-Worker Beneficiaries." In J.L. Mashaw, V. Reno, R.V. Burkhauser, and M. Berkowitz, eds., *Disability Work and Cash Benefits*. Kalamazoo, MI: Upjohn Institute for Employment Research, pp. 169–87.

CHAPTER 9

Contemporary Issues in Employment Relations—A Roundtable

DAVID LEWIN, MODERATOR

For the 2006 LERA research volume, leading scholars were assembled in a roundtable for the purpose of eliciting their views on key contemporary industrial relations issues. The roundtable members were Adrienne E. Eaton, professor and director of labor extension in the Rutgers University School of Management and Labor Relations; Thomas A. Kochan, the George M. Bunker Professor of Management and director of the Institute for Work and Employment Research in the MIT Sloan School of Management; David B. Lipsky, the Anne Evans Estabrook Professor of Dispute Resolution and former dean of the School of Industrial and Labor Relations, Cornell University; Daniel J.B. Mitchell, the Ho-Su Wu Chair in Management in the UCLA Anderson School of Management and former director of the UCLA Institute of Industrial Relations; and Paula B. Voos, professor and chair of the Department of Labor Studies and Employment in the Rutgers University School of Management and Labor Relations. The key issues were posed as questions, and the responses are summarized below.

Lewin: In view of the secular decline of unionism in the United States and abroad, what is the potential for the emergence and growth of other forms of worker representation?

Lipsky: There are two fundamental forms of worker representation, I believe; one form I label "independent," the other "dependent." Unionism is clearly an independent form of worker representation that allows workers to establish and maintain an organization "of the members, for the members, and by the members." A principal characteristic of independent representation, therefore, is that the workers themselves control their representatives. There are several means by which workers can exercise such control, but two stand out: they can elect their representatives or, alternatively, they can hire them. In the vast majority of unions the officers are elected by the members, but in some unions business agents and administrators are hired by the organization. Indeed, in certain civil service and professional associations, top-level administrators ("executive directors") exercise more influence on the organization's policies and practices than do elected officers. A hallmark of independent worker representation is that the policy makers and administrators are ultimately accountable to the members of the organization.

Probably the best-known type of dependent representation is the so-called company union, but there are many other varieties of this form. Any organization or entity that purports to speak for (i.e., "represent") workers but is not actually controlled by workers is a form of dependent representation. Every student of labor relations knows that the Wagner Act banned company unions. That statute made it an unfair labor practice for an employer "to dominate or interfere with the formation or administration of any labor organization or contribute financial or other support to it." The Wagner Act virtually eliminated the company unions that were so prevalent during the 1920s. But in the last quarter of the 20th century, the increasing use of teams in American business enterprises once again raised the specter of company unionism. Teams have many of the characteristics of unions, but is there any doubt that they are really established, financed, and ultimately controlled by employers? (No!)

In the political arena, there are countless organizations that claim to represent the views of workers and their families. Some of them have been created by the labor movement (e.g., the AFL-CIO's Working America) and some are closely allied with it (e.g., the Alliance for Retired Americans). But it is quite evident that the vast majority of political action groups that claim to speak for American workers are neither financed nor controlled by them. To illustrate, consider the National Right to Work Committee, which asserts on its website (http://www.nrtwc.org/about/), "The members of the Committee are men and women—in all walks of life, from every corner of America, union members as well as nonunion employees—who, through their voluntary contributions, support the work of the Committee." This statement fails to mention that the committee is financed almost entirely by employers and business groups.

It is probably no coincidence that the relative decline of authentic unionism in the United States has been accompanied by a dramatic increase in the use of teams in American industry. Also, political action groups and other organizations allied with the labor movement have struggled to maintain their strength, while various entities that profess to act on behalf of workers but are actually financed by business and conservative interests have proliferated. In other words, for three decades or more dependent representation has been replacing the independent representation of American workers. I do not foresee a reversal of this trend in the immediate future because all the key factors that have contributed to this development—globalization, deregulation, technological change, and the rebalancing of political power—will continue to shape the future of worker "representation."

Eaton: I think we need to broaden our understanding of what a union is. For decades, scholars and trade unionists themselves have equated "union" with a collective bargaining agent, and the Wagner Act framework has limited our thinking in this regard. More recently, both of those groups have been reconsidering this narrow definition. In a recent article in *Labor Studies Journal* focused on "managerial unionism," Paula Voos and I harked back to Sydney and Beatrice Webb to argue for a return to an expanded definition of unionism. As we point out, "The Webbs broadly defined a union as a 'continuous association of wage-earners' for the purpose of maintaining or improving the conditions of their working lives" (Eaton and Voos 2004, p. 25). We further explored this notion through the lens of the Webbs's "methods of trade unionism," which included collective bargaining as well as mutual insurance and legal enactment, but then expanded it to include the contemporary concept of "skill development and career assistance."

We then used this broadened definition to frame a review of organizational types created by managerial employees to improve the conditions of their working lives. These include intraorganizational forms like networks and caucuses, cross-organizational forms like professional associations, and, in certain contexts, collective bargaining organizations. While our focus was on managerial workers, other scholars have applied many of these same ideas to other occupational groups, such as service workers (Cobble 1991), professional workers (Hurd and Bunge 2003), or any workers trying to survive in the more mobile and contingent labor markets of the contemporary era (Heckscher 2001; Osterman et al. 2001). In this regard, my Rutgers colleague, Janice Fine, has been studying community unionism and worker centers, which tend to be oriented around the needs of low wage and immigrant workers (see Fine 2006). Though, in my view, there are notable problems and shortcomings in noncollective bargaining forms of unions—for example, underinstitutionalization—there is also considerable appeal of these newer forms to workers themselves. Further, these are not isolated phenomena; there are substantial numbers of workers participating in all these different forms. An important question in this regard is whether these nontraditional forms of worker representation are interested in and can ally themselves with the more traditional labor movement, perhaps especially to create political power.

Mitchell: There have been nonunion methods of obtaining employee input into decision making for a very long time, ranging from the simple suggestion box to the elaborate worker representation and "company union" plans developed during and after World War I; the quality circles of the 1980s also fall into this category. Although there was much fuss during the 1990s about the Wagner Act's limitation on company unions as a broader constraint on worker participation, the Wagner framework is basically "don't ask; don't tell." That is, there are undoubtedly many nonunion representation arrangements that likely would run afoul of National Labor Relations Board (NLRB) scrutiny if complaints were made, but which don't actually do so because no one complains. Further, nonunion firms often have grievance arrangements ranging from informal "open door" policies to more formal voice-type systems. The public sector in particular has long had formal grievance systems as part of the larger civil service apparatus.

Outside of these particular microlevel arrangements, the legal system has provided another avenue for employee voice. In particular, the courts have evolved exceptions to the employment-at-will doctrine and, in some cases, provided avenues for "wrongful discharge" claims. In still other cases, clever attorneys are able to rework what might otherwise be considered employee grievances to fit into complaint mechanisms for programs such as Equal Employment Opportunity (EEO) and workers' compensation.

Some scholars have argued that, apart from the arrangements outlined above, there is a large, pent-up demand among American workers for something like European-style works councils. Freeman and Rogers's (1999) survey evidence in particular is often taken as proof of such latent demand. But the problem with this argument is that while workers undoubtedly will say that *at no cost* they would like more influence on decision making, the depth of such sentiment can only be gauged when there is an explicit, specified cost—in question form, "Would you be willing to have your pay cut by 10% in order to have a works council?" It is most unlikely that such cost-posing questions would produce evidence of strong latent worker demand for works councils or the like. To emphasize this point, consider that there are over 400 congressional districts in the United States, yet not one candidate that I am aware of has run for office on a platform of establishing works councils!

It is true that, absent employer resistance, the unionization rate in the United States would be substantially higher than it actually is. The gap between the public sector, in which almost 4 in 10 workers are union-represented, and the private sector, in which 1 in 10 workers are union-represented, is evidence for this proposition. Public employers are less resistant to unionization than private employers because public employers are subject to political constraints, are not exposed to pressures to maximize profits, and tend to operate in areas where market competition is not (much of) a factor. Consequently, public employers resist unions considerably less than do private employers.

The history of unionization in the United States is that key external events, such as the Great Depression, have been a major influence on unionization and on public policies related to employment more broadly; perhaps there will be such great events in the future. In particular, large-scale terrorist attacks, a world financial crisis if Asian central banks dump their dollar reserves, or the failure of pensions, health care, and Social Security to carry the safety net load for the retiring baby boom generation could trigger new forms of employee voice. My guess, however, is that whatever employee voice is triggered by such events will be expressed largely through the political channel.

Voos: If employees cannot use unions to express their distinctive interests and resolve the problems that they experience at the workplace, then I predict that they will attempt to improve their situation through other means. In democratic nations, it is likely that there will be added pressure for governmental solutions to common employee problems. These might include labor organizations that emphasize political rather than collective bargaining strategies or independent movements pressing for legislation in alliance with labor organizations. Recent examples in the United States include the numerous local movements for city and statewide living wages, legislative efforts (such as in California) to require employers to provide health insurance or (such as in Maryland) to contribute a certain proportion of compensation to health insurance, and interest groups (such as in New Jersey) lobbying for prevailing wage provisions for government subcontracted service employees.

Alternatively, employees may seek redress of their work-related frustrations through increased litigation and the courts. Some of this litigation involves individual employment discrimination cases, while other litigation involves collective or class action cases. A notable example is the recent successful effort to ensure that grocery delivery workers in New York City, many of whom are undocumented immigrants, are not misclassified as independent contractors but, instead, are paid employees subject to the minimum wage and overtime provisions of the Fair Labor Standards Act (FLSA).

Finally, in nondemocratic nations, lack of access to either independent union representation or legitimate political means of expressing discontent is likely to be associated with social unrest; China is a notable case in point.[1] While it is hard to know how much of the recent rash of protests in China are responses to employment problems as opposed to environmental concerns, land seizures, provision of health care, and other issues, the lack of both independent unions and democratic political parties in that nation seems clearly to be associated with manifest social unrest.

Kochan: Given the widespread desire for a voice at work, the void left by the decline of traditional unions will be filled in some way or another. Indeed, there is already a variety of "alternative" forms of voice and representation emerging among different groups. My own view is that these will evolve into a mixture of alternative forms, including but perhaps not limited to:

- Unions that develop new models and strategies for organizing and representing workers. Already we see unions like the Service Employees International Union (SEIU) and others that are organizing target groups, largely low-wage workers, through means that get around the election procedures of the NLRB through some mixture of corporate campaigns, community coalitions, neutrality agreements, and, in some cases, such as at Kaiser Permanente, partnership processes. Various combinations of these efforts will continue to be a source of new union members.

- Professional organizations that represent members without formal collective bargaining rights are playing key roles in many occupations. Physical therapists have been active in setting certification standards and providing continuing education, joining more traditional professional groups like doctors, lawyers, architects, and other health care personnel in providing such services. These forms of representation need to be counted in any estimate of percentage of the "represented" workforce in today's economy.

- Community groups, coalitions, and emerging institutions, such as the various worker centers, and ethnic groups, such as the Korean Immigrant Workers in Los Angeles at the low end and Indian and Chinese engineers and computer specialists at the high end.

- Nongovernmental organizations (NGOs) that put pressure on corporations to meet and monitor labor standards in their supply chains.

These forms are not mutually exclusive. Instead, there may be a mix of these models, such as community and ethnic group coalitions that work with unions to gain representation. Given this diversity of approaches, we need to stop equating "representation" with the number of workers covered under traditional forms of collective bargaining if we want to accurately measure, much less understand, the state of worker representation today and in the future. Finally, the wild card in predicting the future of worker representation involves the American public. If and when the American public wakes up to the fact that basic rights of representation are unfairly suppressed and the effects of this suppression hit home to them, they may demand more responsible behavior on the part of employers and government. This is what it will take for these and other forms of worker representation to grow to a large scale.

Lewin: How can the growth of both high-performance work systems (HPWS) and alternative dispute resolution (ADR) systems best be explained?

Mitchell: The question presumes that there is a substantial growth of both types of systems and that both are part of the same package. It's not clear to me that HPWS are in fact experiencing dramatic growth; usually the issue is posed as "low road" versus "high road." There is no theory that says that a particular industry might not feature dual equilibriums, that is to say that, low-road firms that compete mainly on low labor costs might co-exist with high road firms with better pay, benefits, and conditions. The issue turns on whether productivity gains that might come from high-road practices can offset low labor costs.

Demonstration projects involving low-skill manufacturing, such as the Sweat-X experiment in Los Angeles, do not provide evidence that in such sectors there is a high road payoff. On the other hand, firms that employ a substantial number of highly skilled professionals generally need to be concerned that their human assets don't walk out the door. Long-term labor force projections indicate slow growth in the share of managerial and professional workers, so one might expect high road practices to grow slowly, too. The key point is that this is a sectoral issue. What matters most are the production technology and the degree of reliance on highly skilled workers who are costly to replace.

Alternative dispute resolution is a separate issue. What is the process an alternative to? In the union sector, strike frequency appears to have fallen, particularly in the early 1980s, when the most dramatic losses of union membership occurred. It is not clear, however, that the decline in strike propensity reflects increased usage of traditional alternatives, such as mediation and/or interest arbitration. Within the union sector, we really have no reliable information as to whether such approaches as "med-arb" are in fact replacing traditional grievance and arbitration systems in rights disputes.

In the nonunion sector, because of the propensity to litigate and the erosion of at-will employment, use of such techniques as requiring employees to acknowledge at-will status, treating them as independent contractors, or requiring that employment disputes be settled through alternatives to courts is surely growing. Some of these responses are of questionable legality. That doesn't mean, however, that they are not being used and are not growing in usage.

Kochan: Union avoidance is part but not all of the explanation for the growth of HPWS and ADR. It is overly simplistic to see union avoidance as the *only* factor causing their growth. HPWS also have grown because they offer significant productivity and service quality benefits, and the majority of workers prefer them to more detailed and tightly constricted job designs. The problem is that they started first in nonunion settings and were used as union avoidance tactics. Therefore, union leaders were (and in some cases still are) slow to see their potential benefits for union members and union management relationships. Where unions have embraced and adapted these processes to union-management settings and are involved in overseeing their use, they can produce and have produced joint gains.

ADR is also a response to the growing costs of litigation. Here we have the same problem: unions have been slow to see how they could incorporate and champion ADR as a service to current and potential members. If unions took this more adaptive approach, ADR would not only spread more rapidly, but the due process standards that are needed for ADR to become a useful public policy tool would be more readily enforceable.

Eaton: I'm not convinced that the growth of HPWS that was well documented a decade ago has been sustained. I would go even further and speculate that there may be a decline in the overall use of these systems. As far as I know, there is no recent evidence for the prevalence of the practices commonly associated with HPWS. My sense of this is related in part to the steady decline in manufacturing in which, at least in the union sector (the sector with which I'm most familiar), many of these practices are quite well known if not common. Whereas 10 or 20 years ago management may have been interested in engaging the workforce and the union in reforming the production system, the pressures today seem to be pushing management heavily toward the off-shoring option. At the same time, there has been some growth in labor–management partnerships and the attendant use of high performance work practices in parts of the health care industry and in the public sector. Whether these initiatives can be sustained given the pressures those sectors are also under remains unclear. Perhaps, as a field, we should be asking today about the impact on HPWS of the erosion of high-quality health care and retirement benefits. In general, the "low road," as exemplified by Wal-Mart, remains a compelling alternative for some if not many companies and industries, although that model, especially at Wal-Mart itself, is encountering considerable public pressure and questions about its performance.

I'm more sanguine about the continued growth of ADR practices, although here again I have not seen any recent data indicating that growth has continued. In their literature review, Bingham and Chachere (1999) listed the most common reasons employers gave for the adoption of ADR, which were to reduce the risk, cost, and slow speed of litigation; respond to a changing regulatory environment that encouraged ADR; more strongly focus on the disputants' underlying interests rather than the validity of their positions; improve productivity through reducing unwanted absenteeism and turnover and increased organizational commitment; achieve greater confidentiality; and avoid unionization. A cursory review of these motivations suggests that there has probably been little change in most of them. The shifting legal framework may have undermined some practices, particularly mandatory arbitration, but overall it continues to provide encouragement to ADR. Looser labor markets in some industries and for many occupational groups may have decreased worries about employee turnover for some employers, but for many others (for example, in health care) employee retention remains an important goal. And, while union density still appears to be in long-term decline, there is also sufficient organizing activity in some sectors to keep union avoidance on the radar screen for many employers. In short, absent any evidence to the contrary, I hypothesize that ADR systems will continue to grow.

Lipsky: For the past decade, Ron Seeber and I have been conducting research on the rise of ADR (Lipsky and Seeber 1998; Lipsky, Seeber, and Fincher 2003; Lipsky and Seeber 2004, 2006; Seeber and Lipsky 2005). Our research has been based on a survey of the Fortune 1000 companies, a survey of the members of the National Academy of Arbitrators, on-site interviews with managers and lawyers at about 60 major U.S. corporations, and other data sources. In our research, we find that virtually all major

U.S.-based corporations nowadays use arbitration, mediation, or other third-party techniques to resolve workplace disputes. These techniques may be used either on an ad hoc basis or as a matter of policy. More specifically, we estimate that about 40% of the Fortune 1000 companies use ADR techniques as a matter of policy (Lipsky, Seeber, and Fincher 2003).

What accounts for the rise of ADR in the United States? Over a 30-year period, from 1963 to 1993, Congress passed at least two dozen major statutes regulating employment conditions. These statutes gave rise to new areas of litigation, ranging from sexual harassment and accommodation of the disabled to age discrimination and wrongful termination. More and more dimensions of the employment relationship were brought under the scrutiny of the judicial system and a multitude of regulatory agencies. Over time, litigants (especially employers) expressed increasing frustration with the legal system because of the long delays in resolving disputes, the costs associated with these delays, and the often unsatisfactory outcomes. Hence, they increasingly turned to ADR as a means of avoiding these costs and delays.

ADR is principally a phenomenon of the nonunion workplace. No informed observer of employment relations believes that the relative decline of unionism has been accompanied by a decline in workplace conflict. Nonunion employers realized that they had to devise a means of dealing with workplace disputes, and that relying on litigation clearly was not the answer. ADR had the great advantage over litigation of providing a faster, cheaper, and more efficient means of resolving employment disputes. Some employers, however, came to believe that using ADR was (also) an effective means of avoiding unionization. In the interviews we conducted with employers, a handful acknowledged that union avoidance was one of the main reasons why they turned to ADR.

Seeber and I also discovered, however, that there is a link between the growing use of HPWS and the rise of ADR. But to understand this link, one has to recognize that many U.S. corporations are moving beyond ADR toward the adoption of so-called integrated conflict management systems. Such a system does not simply feature the use of certain third-party dispute resolution techniques or even the adoption of a set of conflict resolution policies. Rather, an integrated conflict management system "introduces a systematic approach to preventing, managing, and resolving conflict that focuses on the causes of conflict within the organization" (Gosline et al. 2001, p. 8). In *Emerging Systems for Managing Workplace Conflict*, we wrote, "The reorganization of the workplace has had pronounced implications for conflict management in that a workplace conflict management system is the logical handmaiden of a high-performance work system" (Lipsky, Seeber, and Fincher 2003:68). In our survey of Fortune 1000 companies and our fieldwork, we discovered that a company that had adopted advanced workplace practices, such as team-based production, was more likely to have a conflict management system. While the correlation between the use of a conflict management system and the use of advanced human resource practices is not perfect, a growing number of managers have come to realize that delegating the responsibility for controlling work to teams is consistent with delegating authority for preventing or resolving conflict among the members of those teams (Lipsky, Seeber, and Fincher 2003).

Voos: Both HPWS and ADR systems have been instituted by employers who are seeking to reduce cost and improve productivity. ADR systems have been initiated in order to control litigation costs arising when dissatisfied employees seeking redress in the courts for perceived violations of employment law. Further, they may also address violations of the employer's established personnel policies.

HPWS often include assurances that employees will be treated fairly and will not be punished for exercising voice, that is, for criticizing existing practices and suggesting improved ones. Where employees are not union represented and lack grievance arbitration systems to protect "just cause," having an ADR system in place should make such assurances more credible. Hence, there is a positive correlation between the two.

Lewin: Is human resource management (HRM) being "crowded out" by organizational behavior (OB) in similar fashion to the earlier crowding out of industrial relations (IR) by HRM?

Kochan: There are both practice and research/teaching dimensions of the current state of HRM that are relevant here, and they are interrelated. In my view, the bloom is off the rose of "strategic HRM." Only in a subset of the largest U.S. firms do HR executives have a significant, influential role in firm strategy formulation; finance still rules the day, with HR far behind. Moreover, many of the operational tasks formerly carried out within the HR function are now being dispersed to contract firms, off-shore data management operations, line managers who do their own HR decision making, and subcontractors, temporary help, and consulting firms that provide workers and/or help in recruitment, training, and compensation research. The sooner that HR educators recognize these realities, the more they will have an opportunity to adjust their teaching of HR to managers and/or HR majors to match the nature of the jobs managers and HR professionals actually do. Until then, they will be educating and training people for the careers of yesterday and lose credibility with students and faculty peers.

Within universities, however, OB programs are doing no better in training the next generation of HR professors. Few OB graduates understand much about HR, even though they are increasingly asked to teach these courses. The opportunity therefore exists for modern IR or work and employment programs to fill this gap.

Eaton: I have no idea but I want to push back a bit on the idea of industrial relations—small "i," small "r"—research being crowded out by HRM. The teaching of IR and the institutionalization of IR have, without doubt, been crowded out by HR. However, there is reason to believe that there is a resurgence of research on topics that have traditionally been within the domain of IR. In particular, I would argue that with the continued decline of institutional approaches in the field of labor economics, sociology has slowly and steadily moved to fill this gap. Much of the best work on labor market outcomes is being done by economic sociologists, often using more or less the same research tools and methods that economists use. This has been most evident at Rutgers whenever we conduct a search for a new faculty member for my department (labor studies and employment relations): most, though not all, of the interesting research being done by young scholars in our areas of interest is being done by sociologists. It's interesting to note, too, that the labor and labor movements section of the American Sociological Association now claims 500 members! To put this in perspective, for 2005, the Labor and Employment Relations Association (LERA) reported only 940 academic members from all disciplines—and only 26 who identified themselves as sociologists. One question I have about this trend is whether sociologists in sociology departments will find ways to engage in policy debates with practitioners so that research informs practice and practice informs research.

Lipsky: My perspective on this question is shaped largely by my interactions with human resource management executives affiliated with the National Academy of Human Resources (NAHR) and the Cornell School of Industrial and Labor Relations's Center for Advanced Human Resource Studies (CAHRS). There is some overlap in membership between the two groups, but in total there are about 120 senior-level HR executives in the two organizations. I do not participate in all the programs and forums that the NAHR and CAHRS conduct, but to the best of my knowledge the question posed here has not yet been discussed by either organization. On the website maintained by the Society for

Human Resource Management—an organization that now has over 200,000 members—I checked recent conferences to see if this question arose in any of them, and I failed to find a single reference to it. What questions are these HR managers and practitioners currently discussing? There seems to be a blending of hardy perennials and seemingly new varietals. (I say "seemingly new" because to this veteran many of the so-called new topics seem to be old wine in new bottles.) For example, current and recent topics covered by CAHRS's executive education programs include "HR Strategy: Creating Competitive Advantage through People," "Managing for Impact: HR Metrics and Firm Performance," and "HR Transformation: Partnering to Achieve Functional Excellence." These topics might have appeared in the executive education curricula of any leading university 10 or even 20 years ago. Further, the same buzzwords appear over and over again in the programs sponsored by HR organizations: globalization, strategy, metrics, planning, culture, partnering, and so on. Other popular terms that have entered the lexicon of HR managers in recent years include agility, flexibility, talent, and alignment. Even more recently, I have noticed a growing infatuation with "engagement" and "branding." (Full disclosure requires me to acknowledge that I am currently developing a five-day executive education program that includes a full day on "engaging the workforce.")

Is HRM being crowded out by OB? Although there is no evidence in the current programs of major HR organizations suggesting that the answer is yes, perhaps those organizations are the last place one would find such evidence. Quite possibly, if I had a chance to interact regularly with CEOs and top-level managers in other functions, I might have a different impression. In the field research I have conducted in numerous corporations, I have definitely encountered individuals in other corporate functions who are disenchanted with the HR function. We do not have to conduct systematic research to know that many rank-and-file employees, first-line supervisors, and middle managers are not particularly fond of HR managers. The HR managers, many believe, are those picky bureaucrats who make us fill in multiple forms and get in the way of our doing the real work we need to do. And anyone who has spent any length of time in a corporate environment knows that turf wars are routine in many corporations. Innocently or not, HR has more than its share of such turf wars (see, for example, Lipsky, Seeber, and Fincher 2003, pp. 135–37). If OB is crowding out HRM, then I suspect a root cause is the ongoing tension between HR specialists and other constituencies in many organizations.

I would, however, like to say a word in defense of HR. To coin a phrase, some of my best friends are HR managers. The best HR managers are dedicated professionals who work hard not only on behalf of management and the company's shareholders, but also on behalf of the organization's employees. I do not know whether OB is crowding out HRM, but I do know that a first-class organization needs talented managers who are skilled at dealing with people. You can choose to call managers who specialize in dealing with employees "personnel managers," "employee relations managers," or "human resource managers," but at the end of the day someone has to perform this critical function in an organization. As the bard once wrote, "What's in a name? That which we call a rose . . . By any other name would smell as sweet."

Voos: This question seems to be largely about the internal politics of business schools, and I am not the best person to weigh in on that matter. Business school HR professors need to remember Marx when they think about this issue: It's not a matter of ideas dueling it out in the "superstructure," it's a matter of what is going in the economy, "the base."

The decline of the academic field of industrial relations in the United States has been due primarily to external factors. First, the integration of labor relations into "normal operating procedures" in unionized corporations meant that it was less interesting to academics—in the 1960s, for instance, labor relations were simply less of a pressing social problem than civil rights or other emerging social movements. Second, declining unionization took its toll. That is, industrial relations was not "pushed out" by HRM in any intellectual sense; rather, over time, there was a shift in academic jobs because of the need to train more HR professionals and fewer labor relations professionals, given declining unionization.

Currently, in some corporations, HR for lower-level employees is being outsourced, automated through online systems or call centers, and otherwise managed in ways to cut cost—as opposed to being used for strategic organizational purposes.[2] Insofar as there are fewer HR jobs, HR academics must be concerned. However, it seems to me that this contemporary tendency is inherently limited by the need for the HR function and by the fact that much of it cannot be satisfactorily outsourced for core employees. Of course, the key unanswered questions are "Who are the truly core employees in any corporation?" and "How many of them will be left as corporations restructure?"

Mitchell: HRM is a functional area of the firm. The area can be managed through an internal structure in the organization, and some aspects of it can be outsourced. But even in the outsourcing case, someone is performing the function. The U.S. Bureau of Labor Statistics (BLS) has estimated that in 2004 there were 820,000 "human resources, training, and labor relations managers and specialists." The BLS projects that this grouping will grow faster than average for the workforce as a whole through 2014. (The BLS's projections do not go beyond 2014, but that does not mean that the relative growth will stop as of that date.) Most of these workers are carrying out basic activities necessary for the functioning of their employers. While some of them have certainly been educated or trained in organizational behavior—or have at least been exposed to it—they are still carrying out the HRM function. And the job descriptions for these workers provided by the BLS do not suggest a substantial OB component.

As far as firms are concerned, therefore, the replacement of IR by HRM is not a precedent for the replacement of HRM by OB. IR was in practice linked to the union sector and to union–management relations. Therefore, IR declined as the union sector declined. There is no similar counterpart to this process when it comes to OB.

The answer is different when academia is the target of the question. OB can be viewed as a general management skill as opposed to HRM, which focuses on a particular function. The upper tier of MBA educational institutions, in particular, do not produce substantial numbers of graduates who plan to make their careers in HRM. Graduates of such programs are more likely to view themselves as management generalists. These tendencies suggest that within business schools, especially those in the upper tier of management education, HRM will in the future receive less emphasis and OB more.

Where, then, will the "human resources, training, and labor relations managers and specialists" come from, particularly since their ranks will be growing faster than average? Many will simply be college graduates or graduates of specialized master's programs that do focus on HRM. Others will receive their training on the job or through extension-type programs or at lower-tier institutions. A relatively small number will come from upper-tier business schools.

Lewin: What are the main benefits and limitations of government regulation of contemporary employment relationships?

Voos: U.S. industrial relations has a long tradition of emphasizing the limitations of government regulation—John Dunlop, for instance, often weighed in against the "one size fits all" nature of employment regulation, which inevitably is not appropriately sensitive to the tremendous variation in workplaces. More recently, Pfeffer (1994) argued that collective bargaining is preferable to government regulation because of its flexibility for the employer. Moreover, the government enforcement function is often underresourced and unable to effectively regulate the large number of employers in the United States. Further, much employment regulation relies on the desires of decent employers to abide by the law.

By contrast, the main benefit of government regulation is that it may be the best game in town. This is because when it is difficult to unionize or when unions have not organized the relevant market, government regulation may become the primary way to improve standards of work. Regulation has the benefit of "taking wages out of competition" in the broadest sense. Laws that are universal protect high-standard employers from low-standard competitors—or at least from those located in the same legal jurisdiction. Efforts to enact and enforce global labor standards might be understood in parallel fashion. In addition, laws are able to address the employment problems in those layers of the workforce, such as white-collar employees in private corporations, managers, and contingent employees, for whom unionism and collective bargaining are difficult to achieve. All of this makes me think that labor problems are increasingly likely to evoke public policy—that is, regulatory solutions— in the near future.

Lipsky: Although many people view government regulation as a partisan political issue, some reflection on the topic suggests that actually it is not. Similarly, some assume that Democrats favor government regulation and Republicans oppose it, but this generalization oversimplifies a complex issue. For example, many Democrats believe that corporations require more government regulation, while many Republicans disagree. At the same time, many Republicans believe that labor unions require more government regulation, while many Democrats disagree. When it comes to an interest group's view of government regulation, it depends on whose ox is being gored. It is worth remembering that the deregulation of American industry was begun by Jimmy Carter—a Democrat, of course—when my Cornell colleague, Alfred Kahn, then serving as chair of the Civil Aeronautics Board, persuaded the president that the deregulation of the airline industry was a good idea. (That deregulation very quickly resulted in decreased air service to and from Ithaca, New York, which made it much more difficult for all of us at Cornell—including Professor Kahn—to travel to Washington!)

My view of government regulation is substantially influenced by my training as an economist. Economists are generally skeptical of the utility of regulation and believe that markets are more effective than regulation in governing the employment relationship. All regulations should be subjected to rigorous cost-benefit analyses, economists believe, and there should be careful accounting in those analyses of the unintended consequences—externalities—of the regulations. My view of this matter, however, has been tempered by hard reality and personal experience. In recent years, my colleagues and I have conducted evaluations of a number of workplace dispute resolution programs, and I have been forcefully struck by the extraordinary difficulty of measuring the costs and benefits of these programs. In one case, our good-faith effort to do an honest evaluation produced a negative appraisal that offended the stakeholders who had established and supported the program we evaluated. In my (possibly biased) view, political interests trumped rational analysis in this instance.

I find it difficult to believe that an increasingly complex society does not require some optimal level of government regulation. The labor market is rife with imperfections—more than most economists are willing to acknowledge—and arguably government regulation can help counterbalance those imperfections. Even if labor markets conformed to conventional economic theory and produced efficient outcomes, there is no guarantee that such outcomes would be equitable. This truism constitutes the conventional case for labor market regulation. What is often missing from the conventional case, I believe, is adequate regard for the influence of politics and power on labor market outcomes. Political power can lead to regulations that tip the scales in favor of one or another interest group, and the remedy for that imbalance is not deregulation but a change in the power equation.

Certainly government regulation can significantly influence workplace employment relationships, and often the benefits of that regulation far outweigh the costs. But government regulation can also be a blunt instrument, ill suited for many types of employment problems. Historically, I believe, the most powerful force affecting employment relationships in the United States and most Western nations has been unionism. Arguably, a free and democratic labor movement has had a more dramatic influence on working conditions than government regulation, though I acknowledge that there have been exceptions to this generalization. For example, only strong government intervention could have undercut the racial segregation of jobs—a historic task that unions were ill equipped, and possibly disinclined, to perform. But the belief that government regulation is an adequate substitute for unionism and collective bargaining is, in my view, clearly wrongheaded. Over the last 30 years, worker wages have stagnated, job insecurity has increased, the cost of health care has skyrocketed and the number of workers without coverage has mushroomed, and our pension system has weakened, possibly to the point of collapse. Evidently, the relative decline in the union movement, the deregulation of American industry, and the contrasting growth of government regulation of the workplace over the last three decades has, on balance, turned out to be a bad deal for American workers.

Mitchell: It has traditionally been assumed by economists that "competitive" (i.e., nonunion) labor markets will provide an optimal matching of employer needs and employee preferences. In this view, only if information gaps exist—for example, workers don't know of the dangers entailed in certain job tasks but employers do—is there a need for government. In other words, with full information there is no problem. Those workers who are willing to take risks will become roofers while those who especially value job safety will become clerks. Employers will compete for workers by offering the mix of wages and benefits needed to attract whatever types of workers they need. If this model is taken as the default, then unions or government regulations that raise pay, alter the mix of pay to benefits, or impose safety or other standards, are inherently distortionary.

This view was not always prevalent. The early 20th-century institutional school of economists viewed the nonunion labor market as monopsonistic, a view also expressed in the preamble to the Wagner Act of 1935, which refers to an "inequality of bargaining power" tilted against employees. Economists of later decades acknowledged monopsony but viewed it as an unusual circumstance typically involving employer collusion. Thus, the perennial nursing shortage spawned a literature suggesting that hospital associations held down nurses' pay. Other examples include professional sports in which leagues restrained interteam competition, and isolated company towns dominated by single employers.

As Chris Erickson and I (Mitchell and Erickson 2005) have shown, monopsony is a useful way of interpreting a much larger segment of the nonunion labor market than just nursing, sports, and company towns. A simple search model produces an upward sloping supply curve of labor to an employer, and an upward sloping supply curve is all you need for monopsony. One symptom of such monopsony is employer complaints of labor shortage. Such shortages became commonplace in the late 1980s and again in the 1990s, when much of the labor market was not only nonunion but also not confronted with a threat of unionization. Another symptom is a constant refrain that immigrants are needed because Americans won't do the work. Yet, one might ask, "Who made the beds in hotels, washed the dishes in restaurants, and so on, in the 1950s, if not

ROUNDTABLE 303

Americans?" Or "If Americans won't do unpleasant jobs, who is mining coal nowadays in West Virginia?"

Monopsonistic labor markets will provide less-than-optimal working conditions, benefits, safety, and pay; thus, some form of regulation could improve efficiency. But all regulations are not justified by monopsony. There can be harmful regulations; the details matter. Moreover, as Erickson and I (2005) also show, there are some benefits to monopsony at the macro level. In essence, chronic labor shortages tend to moderate recessions because declining demand leads employers to "lay off" vacancies before terminating real employees. The puzzling stylized facts of the macroeconomy in the period beginning in the late 1980s can be explained by monopsony. These stylized facts include, among others, chronic labor shortages, shallow recessions, absorption of workers moved off welfare without a hike in unemployment, and growth in the relative share of company profits.

Kochan: We will definitely see a growing role for government regulation of employment relationships, continuing the trend that has been visible since the 1960s. The decline of unions and collective bargaining and the growing recognition that individual firms are not able or willing to protect worker rights or provide the benefits (health insurance, pensions, training, work-family leave, etc.) that workers expect and need will continue to put pressure on state and federal governments to respond.

The real question in my mind is whether we will develop more flexible enforcement tools to cope with increased regulations. These could include use of performance standards (i.e., holding firms accountable for meeting standards but leaving it to firms and their employees to decide how to meet them), some forms of ADR, and/or some forms of worker voice and representation in the design, monitoring, and enforcement processes. I continue to believe that we can develop a two-track enforcement strategy in which those firms that can demonstrate they have procedures and institutional arrangements in place to deliver and meet public policy standards are given the flexibility they want and need on how to meet them, while firms lacking these workplace institutions and procedures are regulated in more detailed, traditional ways. Incentives for moving from the latter to the former category would serve the economy, workforce, and society well.

Eaton: One of the chief limitations of government regulation is the globalization of the economy. As trade agreements begin to undermine national regulatory systems, not just of the labor market but of the environment, consumer–business relations, and so on, it is increasingly important to look at the potential but also the weaknesses of international forms of regulation. These may include trade and other agreements and treaties between or among nations, but they increasingly involve "voluntary" codes of conduct, sometimes negotiated between private parties (i.e., corporations and NGOs). It's interesting to note that at the same time that the United States is increasing its participation in what may be a nascent system of global regulation, many of the most interesting developments in government regulation of employment within the United States are taking place at the state level or on occasion at the local level, rather than at the national level. I'm thinking here of living wage ordinances or statutes, state minimum wage laws, state antidiscrimination laws that expand the list of protected classes or types of discrimination beyond those covered by federal law, and even attempts to push the boundaries of preemption in federal labor relations law.

Notes

[1] According to China's public security minister, Zhou Yonghang, 3.76 million Chinese took part in such "mass incidents" in 2005; he states that they were protests over specific economic issues, not efforts to bring down the one-party political system (Cody 2005).

[2] My colleague Jeff Keefe (2006) points out, "In the late 1990s with the labor market at full employment, there was a substantial boom in HR employment as rapidly growing firms searched for qualified employees. Some analysts misread a temporary phenomenon as a structural change in the strategic importance of the HR function within the corporation. Once the economy went into recession, taking costs out of organizations became imperative. One method for reducing cost selected by some organizations has been to outsource a range of HR functions."

References

Bingham, Lisa B., and Denise R. Chachere. 1999. "Dispute Resolution in Employment: The Need for Research," in A.E. Eaton and J.H. Keefe, eds., *Employment Dispute Resolution and Worker Rights in the Changing Workplace*. Champaign, IL: Industrial Relations Research Association, pp. 95–136.

Cody, Edward. 2005. "China Grows More Wary over Rash of Protests," *Washington Post*, August 10, p. A11.

Cobble, Dorothy Sue. 1991. "Organizing the Postindustrial Workforce: Lessons from the History of Waitress Unionism." *Industrial and Labor Relations Review*, Vol. 44, no. 3 (April), pp. 419–36.

Eaton, Adrienne E., and Paula B. Voos. 2004. "Managerial Unionism: Prospects and Forms." *Labor Studies Journal*, Vol. 29, no. 4 (Fall), pp. 25–56.

Fine, Janice. 2006. *Worker Centers: Organizing Communities at the Edge of the Dream*. Ithaca, NY: Cornell University Press.

Freeman, Richard B., and Joel Rogers. 1999. *What Workers Want*. Ithaca, NY: Cornell University Press.

Gosline, Ann, Lamont Stallworth, Myrna C. Adams, Notman Brand, Cynthia J. Hallberlin, Carole Schneider Houk, David B. Lipsky, Jennifer Lynch, Nancy E. Peace, Mary Rowe, and Anne Thomas. 2001. *Designing Integrated Conflict Management Systems: Guidelines for Practitioners and Decision Makers in Organizations.* Ithaca, NY: Cornell/PERC Institute on Conflict Resolution, Cornell University.

Heckscher, Charles. 2001. "Living With Flexibility," in L. Turner, H.C. Katz, and R.W. Hurd, eds., *Rekindling the Labor Movement: Labor's Quest for Relevance in the 21st Century.* Ithaca, NY: Cornell University Press.

Hurd, Richard W., and John Bunge. 2003. "Unionization of Professional and Technical Workers: The Labor Market and Institutional Transformation," in R. Freeman, J. Hersch, and L. Mishel, eds., *Labor Market Institutions for the 21st Century.* Chicago: University of Chicago Press.

Keefe, Jeff. 2006. Personal communication, January 27.

Lipsky, David B., and Ronald L. Seeber. 1998. *The Appropriate Resolution of Corporate Disputes: A Report on the Growing Use of ADR by U.S. Corporations.* Cornell/PERC Institute on Conflict Resolution, Cornell University.

———. 2003. "The Social Contract and Dispute Resolution: The Transformation of the Social Contract in the U.S. Workplace and the Emergence of New Strategies of Dispute Resolution." *International Employment Relations Review,* Vol. 9, no. 2 (June), pp. 87–109.

———. 2004. "Dispute Resolution in the Changing Workplace." *Proceedings of the Fifty-Sixth Annual Meeting* (Champaign, IL, Jan. 2004). Champaign, IL: Industrial Relations Research Association, pp. 30–40.

———. 2006. "Managing Organizational Conflicts," in John Oetzel and Stella Ting-Toomey, eds., *The Sage Handbook of Conflict Communication.* Thousand Oaks, CA: Sage Publications, pp. 359–90.

Lipsky, David B., Ronald L. Seeber, and Richard D. Fincher. 2003. *Emerging Systems for Managing Workplace Conflict: Lessons from American Corporations for Managers and Dispute Resolution Professionals.* San Francisco, CA: Jossey-Bass.

Mitchell, Daniel J.B., and Christopher L. Erickson. 2005. "De-Unionization and Macro-Performance: What Freeman and Medoff Didn't Do." *Journal of Labor Research,* Vol. 26, no. 2 (Spring), pp. 183–208.

Osterman, Paul, Thomas A. Kochan, Richard M. Locke, and Michael Piore. 2001. *Working in America: A Blueprint for the New Labor Market.* Cambridge, MA: MIT Press.

Pfeffer, Jeffrey. 1994. *Competitive Advantage through People: Unleashing the Power of the Work Force.* Boston: Harvard Business School Press.

Seeber, Ronald L., and David B. Lipsky. 2005. "The Ascendancy of Employment Arbitrators in U.S. Employment Relations." Paper presented at a symposium on "New Actors in Industrial Relations," sponsored by the *British Journal of Industrial Relations,* London, UK, September.

ABOUT THE CONTRIBUTORS

Alexander J.S. Colvin is an associate professor in the Department of Labor Studies and Employment Relations at The Pennsylvania State University. He received his J.D. in 1992 from the University of Toronto and his Ph.D. in 1999 from the Cornell University School of Industrial and Labor Relations. His research, which focuses on workplace dispute resolution, has been published in the *Industrial and Labor Relations Review, Industrial Relations,* and the *British Journal of Industrial Relations,* as well as other journals. Colvin received the 2000 Best Dissertation Award and the 2003 Outstanding Young Scholar Award from the Labor and Employment Relations Association.

Joel Cutcher-Gershenfeld is a professor and director of the Institute of Labor and Industrial Relations at the University of Illinois at Urbana-Champaign. Before joining Illinois in 2006, he served as a senior research scientist at MIT, with appointments in the Sloan School of Management and the Engineering Systems Division. He has authored or edited seven books and more than 80 articles, chapters, and technical reports. Cutcher-Gershenfeld has led many large-scale systems change initiatives with employers and unions in the United States, Japan, South Africa, Denmark, Australia, and other countries. He received his Ph.D. in 1988 from MIT and has served on the national executive board of the Labor and Employment Relations Association.

Adrienne E. Eaton received her Ph.D. in industrial relations from the University of Wisconsin. She is currently a professor and director of the Labor Extension Program at the School of Management and Labor Relations at Rutgers University. Her current research is focused around three long-term streams: union participation in management decision making and the relationship of unions to direct forms of worker participation; the negotiation, effectiveness, and outcomes of neutrality and card check agreements; and the unionization of managerial workers, in particular public sector supervisors. Eaton has been editor in chief of the Labor and Employment Relations Association since September 2002 and a member of the editorial board for the *Labor Studies Journal.*

Teresa Ghilarducci is a professor of economics and director of the Higgins Labor Research Center at the University of Notre Dame. Her book *The End of Retirement* (Princeton University Press) will appear in

2007. *Labor's Capital: The Economics and Politics of Employer Pensions* (MIT Press) won an Association of American Publishers award in 1992. Ghilarducci served on the Pension Benefit Guaranty Corporation's Advisory Board from 1995 to 2002 and on the Board of Trustees of the State of Indiana Public Employees' Retirement Fund from 1997 to 2002. She received her Ph.D. in economics from the University of California, Berkeley.

John S. Heywood is a professor of economics and director of the graduate program in human resources and labor relations at the University of Wisconsin-Milwaukee. An active researcher in personnel economics, he has published more than seven dozen articles and co-edited (with Michelle Brown) *Paying for Performance: An International Comparison*. He has held appointments in the United Kingdom, Germany, Australia, and Hong Kong.

Charles Jeszeck is currently assistant director for education, workforce, and income security issues at the U.S. Government Accountability Office. He has spent 20 years with GAO leading research on social insurance and labor policy issues, providing information to members of Congress and their staff on these matters. Before joining GAO, he taught economics at the University of Massachusetts, Amherst, and at Barnard College. Jeszeck has worked in the research departments of the Service Employees International Union (SEIU) and the California Labor Federation, AFL-CIO. He received a Ph.D. in economics from the University of California, Berkeley in 1982.

Uwe Jirjahn earned his Ph.D. in economics from the University of Hannover and currently teaches economics at the Faculty of Economics in Hannover, Germany. His research interests include labor economics and personnel economics. He published his research in the *Scandinavian Journal of Economics*, the *Journal of Economic Behavior and Organization*, the *Industrial and Labor Relations Review*, and *Industrial Relations*, among other journals.

Berndt K. Keller is professor of employment relations in the Faculty of Public Policy and Management at the University of Konstanz, Germany. His present interests include European integration, union mergers, public sector industrial relations, atypical employment/contingent work, flexibility, and social security. He is co-editor of *Industrielle Beziehungen, the German Journal of Industrial Relations* and member of the executive committee of the International Industrial Relations Association. His more recent books include *Einführung in die Arbeitspolitik. Arbeitsbeziehungen und Arbeitsmarkt in sozialwissenschaftlicher*

Perspektive (6th ed., Munich-Vienna, 1999), *Europäische Arbeits- und Sozialpolitik* (2nd ed., Munich-Vienna, 2001), and *Multibranchengewerkschaft als Erfolgsmodell? Zusammenschlüsse als organisatorisches Novum - das Beispiel ver.di* (Hamburg, 2004).

Brian Klaas is a professor of management and chair of the Management Department at the Moore School of Business, University of South Carolina, where he also serves as director of the Riegel and Emory Human Resource Center. He received his Ph.D. from the University of Wisconsin-Madison and works in such areas as compensation, workplace dispute resolution, and HR outsourcing. Klaas has published in such journals as *Personnel Psychology, Industrial Relations*, the *Academy of Management Journal*, the *Academy of Management Review*, the *Industrial and Labor Relations Review*, the *Journal of Management*, the *Journal of Labor Research*, and the *Journal of Applied Psychology*. His research has been funded by grants from the Upjohn Institute for Employment Research, the Society of Human Resource Management Foundation, and the Gevity Institute.

Thomas A. Kochan is the George Maverick Bunker Professor of Management at MIT's Sloan School of Management and co-director of both the MIT Workplace Center and the Institute for Work and Employment Research. He received his Ph.D. in industrial relations from the University of Wisconsin. He has done research on a variety of topics related to industrial relations and human resource management in the public and private sectors and is widely published. Kochan is a past president of both the International Industrial Relations Association and the LERA, formerly the Industrial Relations Research Association.

David I. Levine is a professor at the Haas School of Business at the University of California, Berkeley. He is also chair of Berkeley's Center for Health Research. Levine was an undergraduate at Berkeley and has taught at the Haas School since receiving a Ph.D. in economics from Harvard University in 1987. He has also visited the Sloan School of Management at MIT, the U.S. Department of Labor, and the Council of Economic Advisers.

David Lewin is the Neil Jacoby Professor of Management, Human Resources and Organizational Behavior in the UCLA Anderson School of Management. The author of 17 books and more than 150 journal articles, he serves on the editorial boards of the *Industrial and Labor Relations Review, Industrial Relations*, and the *California Management Review* and is co-editor of *Advances in Industrial and Labor Relations*. Lewin's research interests are in human resource management and business performance, conflict management, compensation systems and practices, performance management, and organizational governance and leadership. Lewin received both an M.B.A. and a Ph.D. from UCLA.

David B. Lipsky is the Anne Evans Estabrook Professor of Dispute Resolution in the School of Industrial and Labor Relations and director of the Institute on Conflict Resolution at Cornell University. He is currently president of the Labor and Employment Relations Association. In his research and teaching activities, he focuses primarily on negotiation, conflict resolution, and collective bargaining. Lipsky served as dean of the School of Industrial and Labor Relations at Cornell from 1988 until 1997 and has been a member of the Cornell faculty since 1969. He received a Ph.D. in economics from MIT.

Douglas Mahony is an assistant professor of management at the Moore School of Business, University of South Carolina. His research interests include alternative dispute resolution systems and the effects of participatory work practices on unions, organizations, and employees. He received a B.A. from the University of Toronto and an M.A. and a Ph.D. from the School of Management and Labor Relations, Rutgers University. Mahony's research has appeared in such journals as the *Industrial and Labor Relations Review*, *Industrial Relations*, and *Human Resource Management*.

Daniel J.B. Mitchell is Ho-Su Wu Professor at the Anderson Graduate School of Management and the School of Public Affairs, UCLA. He chaired the Department of Policy Studies in 1996 and 1997 and was formerly director of the UCLA Institute of Industrial Relations (1979 to 1990). Mitchell is a past president of the North American Economics and Finance Association and is currently co-editor of the journal *Industrial Relations*. His publications have generally been in the areas of wage determination, wage-price controls, concession bargaining, flexible pay plans, nonwage employee benefits, use of labor-market data, labor standards in international trade, and other aspects of labor market analysis.

Sophie Mitra, Ph.D., is an assistant professor in the Department of Economics at Fordham University, with research interests in labor economics and development economics. She received a doctorate in economics from the University of Paris I Panthéon-Sorbonne in 2001. Before doing her doctoral work, Mitra was a development practitioner and worked for the World Bank and the Overseas Development Institute, London. Her current research focuses on the welfare and labor market implications of disability benefit programs.

Frits K. Pil is an associate professor and research scientist at the University of Pittsburgh. He has published extensively on the dynamics of organizational innovation, organizational learning, and organizational change. His current work examines the tensions between imitation and innovation, the interplay between local and systemic performance improvement efforts, and the interaction between forms of capital across different levels of analysis. He received his Ph.D. from the Wharton School, University of Pennsylvania. He has been the recent recipient of an International Advances in Management Fellowship from the UK ESCR, the Labor and Employment Research Association's Outstanding Young Scholar Award, and an Excellence in Teaching Award from the Katz Business School.

Stephen R. Sleigh is currently with The Yucaipa Companies, a Los Angeles–based investment firm. From 1994 to 2006, he was director of strategic resources for the International Association of Machinists and Aerospace Workers. Prior to that, he was director of research for the Teamsters Union and deputy director of the Center for Labor-Management Policy Studies at the City University of New York. Sleigh has also served on the board of directors of the National Committee for Quality Assurance. He is past president of the Labor and Employment Relations Association and the author of two books and numerous articles and policy reports.

David Stapleton, Ph.D., is director of the Cornell University Institute for Policy Research in Washington, D.C. For the past 15 years, his work has focused on programs for people with disabilities and their impacts on employment and economic independence. He is research director for Cornell's Research Rehabilitation and Training Center on Employment Policy and co-principal investigator for Cornell's Research Rehabilitation and Training Center on Disability and Demographic Statistics. He recently co-edited, with Cornell colleague Richard Burkhauser, *The Decline in Employment of People with Disabilities: A Policy Puzzle* (The Upjohn Institute for Employment Research, 2003).

Paula B. Voos (Ph.D., Harvard University, economics) is professor and chair of the Labor Studies and Employment Relations Department, School of Management and Labor Relations, Rutgers University. She is the former editor in chief and past president of the Labor and Employment Relations Association and editor of the association's 1994 volume, *Contemporary Collective Bargaining in the United States.* Her recent research concerns the determinants of union bargaining power, the evolution over time in union bargaining power in the United States, and the implications for future union revitalization. She is also working on several projects related to employee benefits.

LERA CHAPTERS

For contact information on a chapter in your area, visit the LERA website at www.lera.uiuc.edu.

ALABAMA
  Alabama
ALASKA
  Alaska (Anchorage)
ARIZONA
  Arizona (Phoenix/Tuscon)
CALIFORNIA
  Gold Rush (Oakland/San Jose)
  Inland Empire (Riverside/
  San Bernardino)
  Northern (Sacramento)
  Orange County (Anaheim)
  San Diego
  San Francisco
  Southern (Los Angeles)
COLORADO
  Rocky Mountain (Denver)
CONNECTICUT
  Connecticut Valley (Hartford/New Britain)
DISTRICT OF COLUMBIA
  Washington D.C.
FLORIDA
  Central Florida (Orlando)
  West Central Florida (Tampa/Clearwater)
GEORGIA
  Atlanta
HAWAII
  Hawaii (Honolulu)
ILLINOIS
  Chicago
  LIRA (University of Illinois)
INDIANA
  Delaware County (Muncie)
IOWA
  Iowa
MARYLAND
  Maryland (Baltimore)
MASSACHUSETTS
  Boston
MICHIGAN
  Detroit
  Mid-Michigan (Lansing)
MISSOURI
  Gateway (St. Louis)
  Greater Kansas City

NEVADA
  Southern (Las Vegas)
NEW JERSEY
  New Jersey
NEW YORK
  Capital District (Albany)
  Central New York (Syracuse)
  Hudson Valley
  Long Island
  New York City
  Western (Buffalo)
OHIO
  Central (Columbus)
  Northeast (Cleveland)
  Southwestern (Dayton)
OREGON
  Oregon (Portland)
PENNSYLVANIA
  Central (Harrisburg)
  Northeast (Bethlehem)
  Philadelphia
RHODE ISLAND
  Greater Rhode Island
SOUTH CAROLINA / NORTH CAROLINA
  South Atlantic (Columbia/Charlotte)
TENNESSEE
  Tennessee Employment Relations Research
  Association (TERRA)
TEXAS
  Greater Houston
  North Texas (Dallas)
WASHINGTON
  Northwest (Seattle)
WISCONSIN
  Wisconsin (Milwaukee)

CANADA
  British Columbia (Vancouver)
  Hamilton District (Ontario)
FRANCE
  Paris

LERA Organizational Memberships

The LERA provides a unique forum where representatives of all stakeholders in the employment relationship and their views are welcome.

We invite your organization to become a member of our prestigious, vibrant association. The Labor and Employment Relations Association (LERA) is the professional membership association and learned society of persons interested in the field of industrial relations. Formed more than fifty years ago, the LERA brings together representatives of labor, management, government, academics, advocates, and neutrals to share ideas and learn about new developments, issues, and practices in the field. Members share their knowledge and insights through LERA publications, meetings, and LERA listservs. In addition, the LERA provides a network of 50 chapters where professionals meet locally to discuss issues and share information.

The purpose of the LERA is to encourage research and to foster discussion of issues affecting today's workplace and workers. To that end, the LERA publishes an array of information, including research papers and commentary presented at Association meetings; the acclaimed practitioner-oriented magazine, *Perspectives on Work*; a printed and online membership directory; quarterly newsletters; and an annual research volume. Recent research volumes include *The Ethics of Human Resources and Industrial Relations*, John Budd and James Scoville, editors: *Theoretical Perspectives on Work and the Employment Relationship*, Bruce E. Kaufman, editor; *Going Public: The Role of Labor-Management Relations in Delivering Quality Government Services*, Jonathan Brock and David Lipsky, editors; and *Collective Bargaining in the Private Sector*, Paul F. Clark, John T. Delaney, and Ann C. Frost, editors. Other member publications and services include online IR/HR degree programs listings, an online library, job announcements, calls and announcements, competitions and awards for students and practicing professionals, and much more.

LERA is a non-profit, 501(c)(3) organization governed by an elected Executive Board comprised of representatives of the various constituencies within the Association.

Organizational memberships are available on an annual or sustaining basis and include individual memberships for organization designees, a wealth of LERA research and information, and numerous professional opportunities. Organizational members receive all LERA publications and services. Your support and participation will help the Association continue its vital mission of shaping the workplace of the future. For more information, contact the LERA National Office, 504 East Armory Ave, Room 121, Champaign, IL 61820. Visit the LERA on the web at: www.LERA.uiuc.edu.

The LERA gratefully acknowledges the continuing support of its Sustaining and Annual Organizational Members

SUSTAINING MEMBERS
Sustaining Members provide a one-time contribution of $5,000 to $10,000.
AFL-CIO
General Electric
National Education Association

ANNUAL MEMBERS 2005-2006*
Albert Shanker Institute
American Federation of Teachers
Bechtel Nevada, Labor Relations Department
BlueCross & BlueShield Association
Business School - Korea University
Carlson School of Management - University of Minnesota
Centre for Industrial Relations - Univ of Toronto
Communications Workers of America
Communications Workers of America, Local 1034
Dept for Professional Employees, AFL-CIO
Dept of Industrial and Labor Relations - Indiana Univ of Pennsylvania
Dept of Labor Studies & Industrial Relations - Penn State Univ
Dept of Management - California State University-Fresno
Dept of Professional Studies - Chapman University
Erivan K. Haub School of Business - St. Joseph's Univ
Industrial Relations and Human Resource Management Program - LeMoyne College
Inst of Conflict Resolution - Cornell University
Inst of Human Resources and Industrial Relations - Loyola Univ of Chicago
Inst of Labor & Industrial Relations - Univ of Illinois at Urbana-Champaign
Integro Leadership Institute
Intl Association of Machinists and Aerospace Workers
Intl Brotherhood of Teamsters
Las Vegas City Employees Association
Las Vegas Metropolitan Police Department
Lucent Technologies
Master of Human Resources Program - Rollins College
Merrimack Films
Michelin North America
National Labor College
National Pilots Association
Orange County Transportation Authority
School of Industrial and Labor Relations - Cornell Univ
School of Labor and Industrial Relations - Michigan State Univ
School of Mgmt and Labor Relations - Rutgers Univ
Sloan School of Mgmt - Massachusetts Inst of Technology
Society for Human Resources Mgmt (SHERM)
United Food and Commercial Workers, Local 1776
United Steelworkers of America
Wilson Center for Public Research
Working for America Inst, AFL-CIO

Annual organizational memberships are available at the following levels:

Benefactor, $5,000 or more	6 employee members
Supporter, $1,000 to $4,999	6 employee members
Annual or Major University, $500	2 employee members
Educational or Non-Profit, $250	2 employee members